I0754614

Charles Butler

THE UNION THEOLOGICAL SEMINARY

IN THE CITY OF NEW YORK:

ITS DESIGN

AND

ANOTHER DECADE OF ITS HISTORY.

WITH A SKETCH OF THE LIFE AND PUBLIC SERVICES

OF

CHARLES BUTLER, LL.D.

BY

G. L. PRENTISS.

ASBURY PARK, N. J.:

M., W. & C. PENNYPACKER,

1899.

Dedicated

to

all true lovers of the divinely-given rights and liberties of Christian thought and scholarship.

Composition and Presswork by M., W. & C. Pennypacker,
Seaside Torch Press.

PREFACE.

THIS volume, although prepared at the request of the Board of Directors of the Union Theological Seminary in the city of New York, is published on my own responsibility alone. The subject was full of difficulty; and if the work is marred by mistakes and errors of judgment, or should seem to some readers too severe in its tone, the fault is mine, not that of the board. And yet from first to last I have tried to write without any unseemly passion and without prejudice. The book has cost me not a little hard work, as well as trouble of mind; it is anything but pleasant to criticise the unwise zeal, misunderstandings and wrong conduct of good men; and had not a foresight of the closing chapters of the volume relieved the pain of writing those that went before, I should have been tempted to abandon my task midway, as utterly distasteful if not hopeless. For much of the best material relating to the history, I am indebted to my dear friend, Dr. Hastings. It was found in eight large volumes of newspaper cuttings, pamphlets and letters bearing on the subject, which, with a sort of prophetic instinct, he had collected and carefully arranged during the long conflict between Union Seminary and the General Assembly. Without the help thus given me, joined to the constant aid and comfort of his wise counsel, this volume would have been simply impossible. To another old friend, Mr. D. Willis James, I am also greatly indebted for assistance, both in the way of encouragement and of judicious, timely suggestions. Unwittingly I have referred twice, somewhat at length and in the same language, to the so-called *spoils system* as illustrating the point, that a false doctrine or principle once clothed with power, is sure, sooner or later, to exert its baleful influence. (See pp. 64, 65 and pp. 238–240). The simple truth is, my hatred of that abominable system has been so active for half a century that, whenever there is a chance to denounce it I am always tempted to repeat myself.

The sketch of my revered friend, CHARLES BUTLER, needs, I trust, no apology. Much of it, to be sure, hardly belongs to the special subject of this volume, but the whole helps to show how Mr. Butler was fitted to render such inestimable service to Union Seminary. At all events it is my loving tribute to one of the best and most remarkable men I have been privileged to know at home or abroad. At his urgent entreaty, not without long delay and a certain dread, this history was undertaken; and I like to remember that one of his dying hours seemed to be cheered by the assurance that the work had been actually begun. The reader who never saw Mr. Butler's benignant countenance will see it truthfully pictured on the frontispiece as he looked in his ninety-third year.

G. L. P.

NEW YORK, *September 11, 1899.*

CONTENTS.

PART FIRST.

CHAPTER I.

CHAPTER II.

CHAPTER III.

CHAPTER IV.

CHAPTER V.

Part First.

THE

Union Theological Seminary

IN THE CITY OF NEW YORK:

ANOTHER DECADE OF ITS HISTORY.

(1888—1898.)

CHAPTER I.

THE THEOLOGICAL SEMINARIES OF THE OLD SCHOOL BRANCH OF THE PRESBYTERIAN CHURCH AND THEIR RELATIONS TO THE GENERAL ASSEMBLY.—ORIGIN AND DESIGN OF THE UNION THEOLOGICAL SEMINARY.—REUNION AND THE THEOLOGICAL SEMINARIES.—THE VETO POWER: HOW IT AROSE AND WHAT IT MEANT.

IT is not likely that at this time there would be any call for a second volume on the history of the Union Theological Seminary, had not its sixth decade been marked by a controversy with the General Assembly of the Presbyterian Church in the United States of America, which involved the autonomy and chartered rights of the institution. While writing THE UNION THEOLOGICAL SEMINARY IN THE CITY OF NEW YORK: HISTORICAL AND BIOGRAPHICAL SKETCHES OF ITS FIRST FIFTY YEARS, the thought of such a struggle did not cross my mind; nor, so far as I know, had it occurred to the directors, with perhaps one exception, or to the faculty.

The position asserted by Union Seminary cannot, therefore, be fully understood without a knowledge of facts not recorded or even referred to in the Semi-Centennial History. The only passage bearing directly upon the subject in the whole volume is as follows: "It [the seminary] was wholly independent, I repeat, of direct ecclesiastical control; and so it continued until 1870. At that time, in the interest of reunion and of larger freedom of other theological seminaries, whose professors had heretofore been chosen by the General Assembly, it generously relinquished a portion of its own autonomy."

The main design of the present volume is to give an account of the agreement of 1870 between the Union Theological Seminary and the General Assembly, and to explain the causes which led to the annulling of that agreement by the Board of Directors of the seminary. In order to do this most effectually it will be necessary to consider, first of all, the ecclesiastical status of the theological seminaries connected with the so-called Old School branch of the Presbyterian Church in the United States of America at the time of the reunion in 1869, as also the origin and design of the Union Seminary. Had not that seminary differed radically in its origin, charter and ecclesiastical position from the Old

School seminaries no such controversy as that which took place would have been possible. This will appear clearly as we proceed.

(*a*) *Relations of theological seminaries in the Old School branch of the Presbyterian Church to its General Assembly.*

These relations indicated the general plan and pattern and exhibited the characteristic features of the institution according to the Old School type. What then was the ecclesiastical status of Princeton, the Western, Northwestern, and Danville seminaries, all belonging to that branch, when the first Assembly of the reunited Church met at Philadelphia on May 19, 1870? It was that of unqualified subjection to and dependence upon the General Assembly. With one exception they derived their origin from the General Assembly, and the Assembly was their patron and the fountain of their powers. Such was the "plan," or constitution, upon which they had been organized and according to which they were governed and carried on. The General Assembly appointed their professors and directors. It held in its hand the initiative, as also the final decision, in all the principal matters of instruction, policy and discipline. After the disruption in 1838 the seminaries, then connected with the General Assembly, passed under the exclusive control of the Old School branch, which continued to adminster them in strict accordance with the original plan of 1812,—the plan upon which Princeton was founded. Its new seminaries were all fashioned after the same model. The Seminary of the Northwest, now McCormick, will serve as a good illustration. This institution, which had been started at New Albany, was later removed to Chicago, and there, through the munificent benefactions of Mr. McCormick, entered upon its present career of power and usefulness. In 1859, with an amended constitution, it came under the full control of the Old School General Assembly. What such control involved appears from Article II, Section 1, of this "amended constitution." It is as follows:

SEC. 1. The General Assembly shall have the general supervision and control of the said seminary, and of all its directors, professors, officers and agents; and shall have power to direct as to its management in all respects, and as to the disposition of its funds and property; to determine the number of its directors and professors, and to appoint the same, and to prescribe their term of office; to designate the branches of study to be pursued, and the titles and departments of the respective professors, and to suspend or remove from office any of the said professors at its discretion. And shall decide all questions and controversies arising between the Board of Directors and professors, or between the respective professors; and all questions referred to it by the Board of Directors; and shall have power of its own motion to review and to confirm, reverse or modify any decision of the Board of Directors, and generally have all other powers necessary for the accomplishment of the object for which the seminary was established.

This article was in force in 1870 at the time of my own call to the chair of Systematic Theology in the institution. And while in regard to certain details the ecclesiastical status of Princeton and the other Old School seminaries differed from that of the Seminary of the Northwest, all of them were alike in the matter of Assembly control and in the principles underlying that control.

(*b*) *Origin, design and ecclesiastical status of Union Theological Seminary.*

The Union Theological Seminary was intended not only to be a new school of divinity, but also, as such, to represent a distinct type of religious thought, sentiment and policy. It was largely the growth at once of the fervid evangelistic spirit of the time, and of that devotion to the cause of sacred science and a learned ministry, which marked all the churches of Puritan origin. In establishing it the founders, who were earnest, practical men, aimed to embody in a permanent form certain views of Christian piety and theological training, which they regarded as specially fitted to prepare young men for effective service in the ministry of the Gospel in their own age. And in carrying out these views, they took pains to organize the institution on a plan in harmony with them. While providing carefully for sound Scriptural teaching, and avowing also their adherence to Presbyterian doctrine and polity, they at the same time resolved to give the seminary perfect freedom and self-control in the management of its own affairs. Their noble temper of mind, their large outlook, and the sacredness they attached to their work, may be seen in the preamble to the constitution of the seminary. Here are portions of it:

That the design of the founders of this seminary may be publicly known, and be sacredly regarded by the directors, professors and students, it is judged proper to make the following preliminary statement:

A number of Christians, both clergymen and laymen, in the cities of New York and Brooklyn, deeply impressed with the claims of the world upon the Church of Christ, to furnish a competent supply of well-educated and pious ministers of the Gospel; impressed also with the inadequacy of all existing means for this purpose; and believing that large cities furnish many peculiar facilities and advantages for conducting theological education; having, after several meetings for consultation and prayer, again convened on the 18th of January, A. D., 1836, unanimously adopted the following resolutions and declarations:

1. *Resolved,* In humble dependence on the grace of God, to attempt the establishment of a theological seminary in the city of New York.

2. In this institution it is the design of the founders to furnish the means of a full and thorough education in all the subjects taught in the best theological seminaries in this or other countries.

3. Being fully persuaded that vital godliness, a thorough education, and practical training in the works of benevolence and pastoral labor are all essential to meet the wants and promote the best interests of the kingdom of Christ, the

founders of this seminary design that its students, remaining under pastoral influence, and performing the duties of church members in the several churches to which they belong, or with which they worship, in prayer-meetings, in the instruction of Sabbath-schools and Bible classes, and being conversant with all the benevolent efforts of the present day in this great community, shall have the opportunity of adding to solid learning and true piety the teachings of experience.

4. By the foregoing advantages, the founders hope and expect, with the blessing of God, to call forth and enlist in the service of Christ and in the work of the ministry, genius, talent, enlightened piety, and missionary zeal; and to qualify many for the labors and management of the various religious institutions, seminaries of learning, and enterprises of benevolence which characterize the present times.

The founders of Union Seminary were at the time mostly pastors or members of churches, nearly all of which sided later with the so-called New School branch. Of the clerical directors in the first board one only adhered after the rupture to the Old School, and he had recently come from a Congregational pastorate in New England. Of the first lay directors, also, nearly all belonged to the New School. The founders were in hearty sympathy with Albert Barnes, Lyman Beecher, and men of that stamp. They were enthusiastic believers in the new Christian evangelism at home and abroad. They believed also in the "voluntary principle," and were exceedingly jealous of all "high-toned" ecclesiasticism. They had no confidence in heresy trials as the way to defend orthodoxy. I doubt if a single one of them looked with favor upon the noted trials of Albert Barnes and Dr. Beecher; while the most of them regarded these trials with the strongest disapproval. They hated religious quarrels and bickerings. Their sentiments on these and similar points led to the establishment of the seminary, found expression in its constitution, and have shaped its policy from that day to this. Here is their own account of the matter:

It is the design of the founders to provide a theological seminary in the midst of the greatest and most growing community in America, around which all men of moderate views and feelings, who desire to live free from party strife, and to stand aloof from all extremes of doctrinal speculation, practical radicalism, and ecclesiastical domination, may cordially and affectionately rally.

In order to keep clear of all extremes of "ecclesiastical domination," they made the seminary independent alike of Presbytery, of Synod, and of General Assembly. Its autonomy was complete and unquestioned. As compared with Princeton and other seminaries of the earlier type, its establishment was essentially a new departure. In keeping clear of all direct ecclesiastical control it broke with the old traditions. This was in part the result of providential circumstances; but it was also, none the less, a result of deliberate purpose and conviction. The founders of Union Seminary held views respecting the best plan of a school of divinity, such as they proposed to establish, which differed materially from the views embodied in the "plan" of Princeton and other Old School seminaries. The very names of some of these founders indicate this to any one at all familiar with the Presbyterian Church of that day.

And then their design, as it will be seen, was not so much to train up ministers for the service of the Presbyterian Church in particular, as to train ministers and men for the great work of evangelization both at home and abroad. "Deeply impressed," to quote again their own words, "with the claims of the world upon the Church of Christ, to furnish a competent supply of well-educated and pious ministers of the Gospel; impressed also with the inadequacy of all existing means for this purpose; and believing that large cities furnish many peculiar facilities and advantages for conducting theological education," they resolved "in humble dependence on the grace of God, to establish a seminary in the city of New York, hoping and expecting thereby, with the divine blessing, to call forth and enlist in the service of Christ and in the work of the ministry, genius, talent, enlightened piety, and missionary zeal; and to qualify many for the labors and management of the various religious institutions, seminaries of learning and enterprises of benevolence which characterize the present times." Such was the catholic and world-wide scope of their design. It was in order more effectually to carry out this plan that they determined to make their seminary a free, self-governing institution, and thus to keep it clear of all extremes of "ecclesiastical domination." This design qualified and gave a peculiar cast to the whole movement. It contradistinguished Union from seminaries of the old type. In their generic character as Presbyterian, orthodox schools of divinity, with the Bible as their great charter, and the training of a learned and godly ministry as their practical aim, the old and the new were alike. But in respect of their origin, their patron, the fountain of their powers, and, as a consequence, in their government and administration, they were essentially unlike.

This radical difference was regarded by many, long wedded to the old plan of 1812, with strong disfavor. An illustration of this occurs in a letter of Dr. A. A. Hodge to Dr. Henry B. Smith, in which he characterizes Union Seminary as under an "*irresponsible* Board of Trustees." Of course Dr. Hodge meant no offence in using such a term, and yet from the point of view of a director, or professor of Union Seminary, the term was offensive in a high degree. Every director of Union Seminary held himself responsible to God, to conscience, and to public opinion; and every director solemnly bound himself to maintain the plan and constitution of the seminary as a Presbyterian, orthodox institution of Christian learning. But it was not under ecclesiastical control, and that was Dr. Hodge's complaint. In order to purge it of this "irresponsible" character, he urged Professor Smith to recommend to the New School branch of the Joint Committee on Reunion, that "*all* the seminaries of both parties be, as a *condition* of union, brought in on the same basis, so that there may be perfect equality." Here in a nutshell is the reason why Professor Smith considered Dr. Hodge's scheme inadmissible. It proposed in effect to "mediatize" Union Seminary; in other words, to make a radical change in the plan and constitution of the seminary by transferring the ultimate center of power and authority from the institution itself to one or more adjacent Synods.

All this was in entire accordance with the general theory and practice of the Old School branch, but it ran wholly counter to the ruling sentiment of the New School branch. The principle of local ecclesiastical control was indeed recognized in the case of Auburn—a seminary founded under the old system—and it is quite possible that there were some advocates of this principle among New School men in other parts of that branch. But I am not aware that any attempt was ever made, or any public desire ever expressed, to bring Union Seminary under Assembly control. The feeling on the subject was indicated in a resolution adopted by the New School General Assembly of 1857, a part of which is as follows:

The General Assembly would not claim any authority over the institutions where our ministry are educated; but it is hereby *requested* of the faculties of the Union and

Auburn Theological Seminaries in New York, of Lane Seminary near Cincinnati, and Maryville Seminary in Tennessee, and of any other similar institutions hereafter established, to furnish the General Assembly each year, through its Permanent Committee on Education for the Ministry, with a written statement of their condition, advantages and prospects, the names of their professors, the ordinary yearly expenses, and any other matters of general interest to the Church, to be read to the Assembly, and published as an appendix to the annual report of said committee; and the General Secretary is hereby charged with the duty of *presenting this request annually* to said faculties, in time to receive their written report before the meeting of the General Assembly.

The request of the Assembly was gladly complied with and had the happiest effect. The relations of the seminary to the Church became still more close and trustful. Union always considered itself as an institution of the New School Church. Its professors were sent as commissioners to the General Assembly. The names of William Adams, Thomas H. Skinner and Henry B. Smith are among the most honored on its roll of Moderators. After 1857 the seminary reported annually to the New School Assembly, precisely as it reported after 1870 to the Assembly of the united Church.

(*c.*) *Action of the Joint Committee on Reunion with regard to the theological seminaries.*

The question of the theological seminaries was one of the most difficult and perplexing with which the Joint Committee on Reunion, appointed in 1866, had to deal. This was owing partly to the nature of the subject, and in part to the great diversity of origin, constitution, environment and legal relations which marked these institutions. The ninth article of "the proposed terms of reunion between the two branches of the Presbyterian Church of the United States of America," reported by the chairmen, Drs. Beatty and Adams, to their respective Assemblies in May, 1867, was as follows:

If at any time, after the union has been effected, any of the theological seminaries under the care and control of the General Assembly, shall desire to put themselves under Synodical control, they shall be permitted to do so at the request of their Boards of Directors; and those seminaries which are independent in their organization shall have the privilege of putting themselves under ecclesiastical control, to the end that, if practicable, a system of ecclesiastical supervision of such institutions may ultimately prevail through the entire united Church.

The ninth article, as reported by the Joint Committee and adopted by the two General Assemblies in 1868, varied somewhat from this. It was as follows:

In order to a uniform system of ecclesiastical supervision those theological seminaries that are now under Assembly control may, if their Boards of Direction so elect, be transferred to the watch and care of one or more of the adjacent Synods, and the other seminaries are advised to introduce, as far as may be, into their constitutions, the principle of

Synodical or Assembly supervision; in which case they shall be entitled to an official recognition and approbation on the part of the General Assembly.

The changes in the article are highly significant, and indicate several points of objection made to it as reported in 1867. This amended article reappeared among the so-called "concurrent declarations" of the General Assemblies of 1869. In explaining it in their report of 1868, the chairmen said:

> A *recommendation* looking to some uniformity of ecclesiastical supervision, is all which the committee felt to be within their province or that of the Assembly, except that those seminaries, now belonging to either branch of the Church, should have every guarantee and protection for their chartered rights which they might desire.

This passage, both in its mild, even subdued tone, and in its explanation, throws a clear light back upon the devious path by which the committee had reached their conclusion. The discussion and criticism occasioned by their plan, as reported in 1867, had convinced them that the whole subject was beset with difficulties and perils, which required very delicate as well as skillful treatment. "*A recommendation*" [the italics are their own] looking to *some* uniformity of ecclesiastical supervision, is all which the committee felt to be within their province or *that of the Assembly*, except that the "*chartered rights*" of all the seminaries of either branch of the Church should be *carefully guaranteed* and *protected.* This was quite different language from that used in 1867: "Those seminaries which are independent in their organization shall have the privilege of putting themselves under ecclesiastical control."

The temper of mind, as also the way, in which the Joint Committee and the friends of reunion generally had come to regard the question of the theological seminaries, may be seen most distinctly, perhaps, in the speech of Rev. George W. Musgrave, D.D., LL.D., made on the occasion of the presentation of the report of the Joint Committee of Conference to the Old School General Assembly, sitting in the Brick Church in the city of New York, May 27, 1869. No one who heard it is likely ever to forget that speech or the remarkable old man who made it. A few extracts will indicate its spirit and its bearing on the question now under discussion. Its opening sentences were as follows:

It affords me great pleasure to be able to report a plan of union between what are known as the Old and New School bodies, and to be able to say that our report is *unanimous,* and is signed by every member of each committee. The Joint Committee report three papers to the Assembly. The first is a plan of union, containing the basis, which will be sent down to the Presbyteries for their acceptance or rejection. The second paper is a declaration, made that there may be a good understanding between the two branches. This paper is not a compact or covenant but it is a recommendation of certain arrangements as to seminaries, boards, etc. It is no part of the basis or terms of union. It only recommends certain arrangements as suitable to be adopted. The third paper is one recommending a day of prayer to Almighty God for His guidance and presence, that Presbyteries may be under divine influence when they come to vote upon this momentous question.

In the course of his speech Dr. Musgrave thus referred to the "concurrent declarations" on theological seminaries, boards, and other matters pertaining to the interests of the Church, when it should become united:

I have already stated to the Assembly that these articles don't form a part of the basis. They are not a compact or covenant, but they suggest to the Assembly what are suitable arrangements. I will not repeat what I have said, except to call your attention to that important distinction. They are not terms of the union. They may be amended or modified, as any future Assembly may deem proper. We told our brethren that we were unwilling to tie the future hands of the Church of God; and I, for one, was very decided on that point. And I will say to you that I would have risked the failure of this union at the present time, rather than concede that these articles should be unchangeable, though I cannot foresee that there will be any necessity in the future to change them. I am neither a prophet, nor the son of a prophet; but I think I have some little common sense, and I felt that it would be unsafe for us to imperil the future by trammeling the Church of God, preventing it from exercising its liberty, and from dealing with circumstances as they might arise in the providence of God.

Sir, we were very decided and determined that those articles should not form a part of the compact, but that they should be suggestions and recommendations, in order that the Presbyteries should get an understanding between the parties. But, sir, it is due to fairness that I should say, and I repeat it now publicly in order that it may have a response from this house, we did say to these brethren, "We will not consent to make these articles a covenant. We won't adopt them as a legal compact, binding upon the future; yet we are acting in good faith and as honorable men, and we say to you that we will not change them at any future time without obviously good and sufficient reasons."

It is enough to say, in proof of Dr. Musgrave's "common sense" and foresight, that had the "concurrent declarations" been made a term of reunion, the effect in the case of Princeton Seminary would have been to imperil all its endowments. Dr. Musgrave's expressions, "We told our brethren," "We did say to these brethren," refer to the New School brethren, and are explained by the following extract from a sketch of "The Assemblies of 1869," written by the Rev. Dr. M. W. Jacobus, Moderator of the Old School Assembly:

It may be mentioned, as part of the inside history of the negotiations, that when the Joint Sub-Committee met for the purpose of engrossing what had been passed upon by the Joint Committee of Conference, and to prepare the report to the Assembly, one of the members (N. S.) objected to the insertion of the words contained in the preamble to the concurrent declaration, viz: "Not as articles of compact or covenant, but as in their judgment proper and equitable arrangements." He admitted that the language fairly expressed what had been agreed upon, that the articles referred to were merely recommended, and if adopted by the united Church, might hereafter, for good and sufficient reasons, be modified or repealed. But he argued that the insertion of the words above referred to would make the impression that the articles are ephemeral, and would have a tendency to invite change. There was force in the objection. But to this it was well replied, that the words ought to be inserted. 1. Because they fairly express our mutual good understanding. 2. Because, if omitted, it might be hereafter argued that the articles were intended to be a compact between the two parties, which could not be honorably modified or repealed. 3. Because it was held to be in the highest degree important that the united Church should be left entirely free to adapt itself to any changes which, in the future developments of Providence, might be deemed necessary or expedient. This difference threatened to be a stumbling-block in the way, even within reach of the goal. At this very crisis, however, an eminent layman of the New School committee joined in this view of the case, with such cogent reasons as to prove the correctness of the position. Upon re-examination of the paragraph, the dissent was revoked, and the entire paper was then adopted by a unanimous vote. This meeting of the Joint Sub-Committee was held on the evening preceding the day of presenting the report to the General Assembly, and it was not until eleven o'clock at night that the decisive vote was reached in the committee room.

(*d*) *The veto in the election of its professors as conceded by Union Seminary to the General Assembly.*

We come now to a main object of this narrative, namely, the occasion, meaning and force of the veto power offered and given to the General Assembly in 1870, by Union Seminary. I have shown what was the action of the Joint Committee respecting the theological seminaries up to the time of the reunion. As the result of long and patient consideration aided by varied discussion throughout the two Churches, the ninth article, or "concurrent declaration," already given, had been reported to the General Assemblies and adopted by both bodies. This article is not a compact or covenant, but a "*recommendation*" and nothing more. So the case stood, when the first General Assembly of the reunited Church met at Philadelphia, in May, 1870. The work of this Assembly was principally one of readjustment and reconstruction. The articles approved by the two Assemblies at New York, in 1869, not as a part of the basis of union, or as a legal compact, but as "suitable arrangements" were now to be acted upon. The varying, not to say more or less conflicting, institutions, legal rights, customs, agencies, properties and activities of both branches, Old School and New, now no longer two but one, were all to be brought into harmonious relations, in accordance with the changed order of things and the new organic life. I was a member of the Assembly of 1870, and can testify as an eye witness, that its ruling spirit from beginning to end was the spirit, not of fear, or suspicion, or jealousy, or any such thing, but of power and of love, and of a sound mind. The presence of the sturdiest, foremost opponent of reunion, Dr. Charles Hodge, if not as a commissioner, yet as a most interested looker-on and even friendly adviser, along with the beautiful tribute of high regard and affection paid by New and Old School men alike to Albert Barnes, then about to pass to his great reward, happily symbolized this spirit.

As might have been anticipated, William Adams was placed at the head of the Standing Committee on Theological Seminaries. As chairman of the New School part of the Joint Committee on Reunion, he had won the confidence and admiration of the whole Church, alike by his wisdom, his Christian temper, his felicitous addresses and his masterly reports. But inasmuch as all the theological seminaries connected with the Assembly belonged to the Old School, Dr. Adams felt that delicacy forbade his acting as chairman of the committee on that subject. He, therefore, as a personal favor, asked permission to decline the appointment, suggesting Dr. John C. Backus in his place. But the Assembly insisted that he should serve.

"I think," said Dr. Musgrave, himself a director of Princeton, "the Moderator has shown his wisdom in appointing a man so entirely acceptable to all this house. We have no rivalship, no jealousies, no fear, but perfect confidence and love, and the Old School men would rather Dr. Adams should be in that position, because he was once a New School man. We have this additional evidence that we are one."*

And now, before proceeding further, let us return to Union Seminary, and the veto power offered by it to the General Assembly in the election of its professors.

(*e*) *Reasons and influences that induced Union Seminary in 1870, to give up a portion of its autonomy.*

1. First of all, it was done in the hope of furthering thereby the harmony and prosperity of the Presbyterian Church. Reunion had been already accomplished, and Union Seminary had from the first thrown the whole weight of its influence in favor of the movement. Henry B. Smith had struck its keynote, and later, in a contest of the pen, had met its ablest foe. He was indeed, as President Patton afterwards called him, "the Hero of Reunion." Dr. Shedd in the General Assembly at Albany, in 1868, had vindicated the cause of reunion, and at the same time the orthodoxy of the New School against the charges of Drs. Charles and A. A. Hodge, Dr. Breckinridge and other Princeton and Old School leaders. Their colleague, Thomas H. Skinner, a very eminent New School leader, was in heartiest sympathy with them; while William Adams, Jonathan F. Stearns and Edwin F. Hatfield, all direc-

* These two eminent leaders of the Assembly at Philadelphia early attracted the attention of spectators in the galleries, who by way of characterizing their peculiar traits, jokingly named Dr. Musgrave, "Old Unanimous," and Dr. Adams, "Old Magnanimous." See a letter of Rev. Dr. T. L. Cuyler, in "*The Evangelist*," written at the time, in which is a graphic pen-picture of the Assembly of 1870.

tors of Union, had been among the most active members of the Joint Committee. Such ardent friends of reunion as William E. Dodge, Charles Butler, Richard T. Haines, Norman White and other noted laymen also belonged to the Union board. It was altogether natural, therefore, that Union Seminary should have felt deeply interested in removing, as far as possible, all obstacles to the complete success of reunion out of the way. Dr. Adams was especially anxious that the wheels of the great Church organization, whose strength was now doubled, and which he believed to be fraught with vast power for good, should move right on without friction. He wielded at this time a greater influence than any other director of Union Seminary, greater perhaps than any other minister of the Presbyterian Church. He was the man of all others to appeal to in taking hold of the "plan" of 1870. These are some of the general considerations and motives that led him to propose and the directors of the Union Seminary to adopt that plan.

2. But the question here arises, why precisely such a plan, differing so materially from that recommended by the General Assemblies of 1869, should have been proposed? In the plan recommended by the General Assemblies, it will be noticed no mention was made of a veto in the election of professors. The Old School seminaries might, if their Boards of Direction desired it, be transferred from Assembly control to the watch

and care of one or more of the adjacent Synods; while the New School seminaries were "advised" to introduce, as far as might be, into their constitutions the principle of Synodical or Assembly supervision. Neither of these recommendations was followed. No Old School seminary was transferred from the control of the General Assembly to the watch and care of one or more of the adjacent Synods. Nor did Union Seminary introduce into its "constitution" the principle of Synodical or Assembly supervision. This shows what good reason Dr. Musgrave had for saying that the "concurrent declarations" lacked entirely the binding force or quality of a "legal compact," and it shows also that with all their uncommon ability and wisdom, and after years of deliberation, the Joint Committee had recommended what was altogether impracticable. Between the great ratification meeting at Pittsburgh, in November, 1869, and the meeting at Philadelphia, in May, 1870, it had become clear that Princeton, to say nothing of other Old School seminaries, could not be released from Assembly control, and put itself under the watch and care of one or more of the adjacent Synods without imperilling its endowments. In this dilemma Union Seminary was urged to come to the help of Princeton, nor did there then seem to be any other way of relief. The appeal was based largely upon a strong conviction, common to the wisest and best friends of both seminaries, that the election of professors by the General Assembly was open to serious objections, and would be open to graver objections in the future.

At the founding of Princeton in 1812 the Presbyterian Church was a small body, numerically and territorially, and the selection of theological teachers could very properly be entrusted to the knowledge and discretion of its General Assembly. The choice of the first professors of Princeton — those very admirable types of Presbyterian piety, wisdom and learning, Samuel Miller and Archibald Alexander — was doubtless the best possible. But in 1870 the Presbyterian Church had increased enormously both in numbers and extent; it covered the continent; and its branches reached to the uttermost parts of the earth. Even then in exceptional cases perhaps the General Assembly could judge as well as any Board of Directors, who was best qualified for this or that chair of instruction, but only in exceptional cases. As a rule, the General Assembly was every year becoming less fitted to exercise this difficult function.

The point is thus referred to in a letter of Dr. A. A. Hodge, written late in 1867:

> It is proper, it is almost a necessity, that each institution should be left in the management of those upon whose support it exclusively depends. The majority of any Assembly must be necessarily ignorant of the special wants and local conditions of any seminary, and of the qualifications of candidates proposed for its chairs of instruction. The best of these are generally young men, up to the time of their nom-

ination known only to a few. To vest the choice in the General Assembly will tend to put prominent ecclesiastics into such positions, rather than scholars, or men specially qualified with gifts for teaching. As the population of our country becomes larger and more heterogeneous, and the General Assembly increases proportionably, the difficulties above mentioned, and many others easily thought of, will increase.

Dr. Henry B. Smith, to whom this letter was addressed, thus expressed his own view in noticing some of the objections to the Joint Committee's report of 1867:

The plan allows those seminaries that are now under the Assembly to remain so, or if they choose, to put themselves instead under Synodical supervision; and it recommends the seminaries not under ecclesiastical supervision to attain unto that condition; *but does not insist on this, as of course, it could not.* . . . It is a fair and serious question whether a General Assembly, representing the Presbyterian Church throughout the whole United States, especially in view of the numbers in that Church, and the extent of the territory in twenty or thirty years, will be the best, or even a suitable body, to choose the professors and manage the concerns of all the Presbyterian seminaries scattered throughout the country. We very much doubt whether this would be a wise arrangement. It may work well in Scotland, but Scotland has its limits. It might bring into the Assembly local, personal and theological questions, which it would be better to settle in a narrower field.

The following strong expression of opinion, written by Dr. Adams, is from the memorial itself of the directors of Union Theological Seminary to the General Assembly:

> It has appeared to many, and especially to those who took an active part in founding the Union Theological Seminary, that there are many disadvantages, infelicities, not to say at times perils, in the election of professors of the theological seminaries directly and immediately by the General Assembly itself,—a body so large, in session for so short a time, and composed of members to so great an extent resident at a distance from the seminaries themselves, and therefore personally unacquainted with many things which pertain to their true interests and usefulness.

It is noteworthy that in the memorial of the directors of Union Seminary, offering a veto in the election of its professors, two reasons only are assigned, namely: first, a desire, as was said before, of doing all in their power to establish confidence and harmony throughout the whole Church; and, in the second place, a desire to secure to the Old School seminaries, in which those of the New School were henceforth to have a common interest, the privilege, so highly prized by themselves, of choosing professors in each institution by its own Board of Directors, instead of having them chosen in every case by the General Assembly. On these two grounds the memorial of the Board of Directors of Union Seminary was chiefly based. These two considerations the friends of Princeton appealed to with great force, when urging Dr. Adams to give them aid in their dilemma. For nothing is more certain than that the plan presented to the Union board on the 9th and 16th of May, 1870, was first suggested to Dr. Adams by his Princeton friends. Had that way of solving the problem of the theological seminaries originated with Dr. Adams, he would certainly have proposed it during the troublesome negotiations on this subject, which ran on for nearly three years prior to the reunion. There is no intimation that he ever did anything of the sort. And yet the point had been made again and again by Old School opponents of the terms of reunion, as proposed by the Joint Committee in their report to the Assembles in 1867, that the seminaries of both branches of the Church ought in fairness, to be placed on a footing of "perfect equality." Why, it was said, should the Old School institutions continue to be subject to the full control of the General Assembly, the New School coming in for an equal share in its exercise, while two at least of the New School institutions continued under what Dr. A. A. Hodge in a letter to Professor Smith, called "self-perpetuated and irresponsible Boards of Trustees." Such was the reasoning of opponents of the Joint Committee's report of 1867. Indeed so strong was the feeling and contention of not a few of them with regard to this point; so confident were they of the superior advantages of subjection to ecclesiastical control, more especially the control of the General Assembly, over any possible advantages of subjection to a Board of Directors or Trustees; and so persistent were they in asserting this view that their opponents could scarcely help being reminded of the fable, so dear to children, entitled "The Fox Without a Tail." The fox, it will be remembered, was caught in a trap by his tail, and in order to get away was forced to leave it behind; whereupon he resolved to try to induce his fellows to part with theirs; or, as Henry B. Smith expressed it, in his characteristic way, "to attain unto that condition."*

Had this mode of solving the question of the theological seminaries occurred to his own mind as the best, Dr. Adams, I repeat, would have brought it before the Joint Committee during the two or more years that committee was in existence. But there is no evidence that it was even mentioned. Neither the word "veto," nor the thing itself, appears in the report of the Joint Committee made in 1867, nor in that of 1868, nor in the report of the Committee of Conference in 1869. The veto first appears in the plan presented to the Board of Directors of Union Seminary at the meeting on May 9, 1870. That plan offered to the General Assembly a veto in the election of both directors and professors. At an adjourned meeting of the same board, held on May 16, it reappeared as a veto in the election of professors. Why this abandonment of

* So at the next assembly of foxes he made a speech on the unprofitableness of tails in general, and the inconvenience of a fox's tail in particular, adding that he had never felt so easy as since he had given up his own. When he sat down a sly old fellow arose, and waving his long brush with a graceful air, said with a sneer, that if, like the last speaker, he had lost his tail, nothing further would have been needed to convince him; but till such an accident should happen, he should certainly vote in favor of tails.—Ancient Fables.

the scheme recommended by article ninth of the report of the Joint Committee and by the General Assemblies of 1869? And why the sudden abandonment of the method proposed to the Board of Directors of Union Seminary on May 9th, and the substitution in its place, on May 16th, of still another method? The whole thing is curious and suggestive in a high degree. Consider that the adjourned meeting of the board occurred on Monday afternoon, May 16th, and that the General Assembly was to meet in Philadelphia on the ensuing Thursday, May 19th. No time, therefore, was to be lost. It was too late, however, to give to the public intimations of the plan of May 16th. *The Evangelist,* one of whose editors at that time was a prominent minister of the late Old School, contained a carefully written editorial, outlining the General Assembly's work. It was without doubt from his pen. In the course of this article is the following significant paragraph:

It is very desirable that the several theological seminaries connected with the Church be brought into the same or similar relations to the Assembly. The scheme proposed by the *Princeton Review,* April number, has met with much favor. Let it be understood that the boards of the respective seminaries shall be allowed to fill the vacancies in their own number, as that scheme contemplates; and to appoint the incumbents of the several chairs, *subject in each case to the approval* of the next General Assembly; and, it is thought, the seminaries of both branches will cheerfully come upon this platform. Princeton and Union are understood to be prepared for it and to desire it.

The article referred to in the *Princeton Review* for April, 1870, was doubtless written by Dr. Charles Hodge, the founder and then senior editor of the *Review*. The scheme was as follows:

Let the Assembly confide the supervision and control of the seminaries now under its control to their respective Boards of Direction, as now, with simply these alterations: 1. That these boards shall nominate persons to fill their own vacancies to the Assembly for confirmation. 2. That they shall arrange the professorships, and appoint the professors, subject to ratification by the Assembly. This would suffice for unification, so far as seminaries heretofore of the Old School branch are concerned.

It seems to us that it cannot be difficult for the seminaries of the other branch to reach substantially the same platform. They, of course, can report annually to the Assemblies [Assembly]. Without knowing all the details of their present charters, we presume there is no insuperable obstacle to their making the simple by-law that all their elections to fill vacancies in the board or boards of oversight and direction, also of professors, shall be submitted to the Assembly for approval before they are finally ratified. If the charters now forbid such an arrangement doubtless alterations could easily be obtained, which would admit of it, or something equivalent. [pp. 311, 312.]

On the 26th of April, 1870, at the annual meeting of the directors of Princeton Theological Seminary, the following paper was presented to the board:

In the negotiations leading to the union of the two branches of our Church it was unanimously agreed upon by the Joint Committee that as the theological seminaries connected with the New School were either independent or under Synodical control, any seminary under the General Assembly of the Old School might, at the discretion of its Board of Directors, be freed from the direct control of the Assembly of the united Church. This was regarded as due to fairness and courtesy.

As, however, the endowments of this seminary are held on condition that it shall be subject to the General Assembly of the Presbyterian Church, it can neither be rendered independent nor placed under the control of one or more Synods. The professors would, therefore, respectfully suggest to the Board of Directors, with a view of accomplishing the object contemplated by the Joint Committee, that the board should request the General Assembly so to alter the plan of the seminary that the directors shall hereafter have the right to appoint and to remove the professors, subject to the veto of the General Assembly; and also the right to supply their own vacancies, subject to a like veto. This would leave the institution subject to the control of the Assembly, as no man could have a place either in the faculty or in the board, of whom the Assembly did not approve.

The suggestion of the professors was adopted and their paper sent up to the General Assembly, unaltered, as a memorial from the Princeton directors.

On May 16th, 1870, the Board of Directors of the Union Theological Seminary adopted the following memorial to the General Assembly of the reunited Church, which was to meet in Philadelphia three days later.

WHEREAS, In the recent negotiations for reuniting the two branches of the Presbyterian Church, great importance was attached to some uniform system of ecclesiastical supervision over the several theological seminaries of the denomination; and,

WHEREAS, The directors of the Union Theological Seminary in New York, an institution founded before the disruption of the Presbyterian Church, belonging exclusively to neither of its branches, and administered upon its own independent charter, are desirous of doing all in their power to establish confidence and harmony throughout the whole Church, in respect to the education of its ministers; and,

WHEREAS, It has appeared to many, and especially to those who took an active part in founding the Union Theological Seminary, that there are many disadvantages, infelicities, not to say at times perils, in the election of professors of these seminaries directly and immediately by the General Assembly itself—a body so large, in session for so short a time, and composed of members to so great an extent resident at a distance from the seminaries themselves, and therefore personally unacquainted with many things which pertain to their true interest and usefulness; therefore be it

Resolved, That the Board of Directors of the Union Theological Seminary, in the city of New York, being all of them ministers or members of the Presbyterian Church, do hereby memorialize the General Assembly to the following effect, viz: That the General Assembly may be pleased to adopt it as a rule and plan, in the exercise of the proprietorship and control over the several theological seminaries, that so far as the election of professors is concerned the Assembly will commit the same to their respective Boards of Directors, on the following terms and conditions:

1. That the Boards of Directors of each theological

seminary shall be authorized to appoint all professors of the same.

2. That all such appointments shall be reported to the General Assembly, and no such appointment shall be considered as a complete election if disapproved by a majority vote of the Assembly.

And further be it *Resolved,* That the Board of Directors of the Union Theological Seminary, in the city of New York, persuaded that the plan proposed in the memorial will meet the cordial approval of the patrons, donors and friends of all these seminaries, and contribute to the peace and prosperity of the Church, do hereby agree, if the said plan shall be adopted by the General Assembly, that they will agree to conform to the same, the Union Seminary in New York being in this respect on the same ground with other theological seminaries of the Presbyterian Church.

At the opening, then, of the first General Assembly of the reunited Church, on May 19, 1870, the case stood thus: Princeton objected to the "recommendation" of the Assemblies of 1869 as unwise, and could not follow it without imperilling a portion of her endowments. Union, warned in time, refused to adopt the Princeton "scheme" with regard to directors, but accepted it in a greatly modified form with regard to professors, while both had memorialized the General Assembly. This posture of things was a logical, not to say necessary, outcome of the whole situation. It followed inevitably that Princeton should look forward with special solicitude to the possible action of the Assembly at Philadelphia, touching theological seminaries. Some of her dearest interests were, as she believed, involved in the issue. It would have been strange, indeed, had she not regarded with a certain misgiving the part which the new co-partners might take in shaping that issue. And then she was tempted to overestimate the importance of a "uniform system" in dealing with the theological seminaries, and to be too solicitous of having them all even as she herself was. The temptation of Union, on the other hand, was to yield too readily to the magnanimous impulses of the hour, and so allow her cooler judgment to be overpowered by the surging tide of reunion enthusiasm.

Pope Innocent XII wrote to the French prelates, who had procured the famous brief condemning Fenelon: "He erred by loving God too much." "*Peccavit excessu amoris divini;*" so one might say of Dr. Adams, that he erred, if at all, in too exclusive devotion to the peace and harmony of the reunited Church; and the same might be said of most of his associates in the directory of Union Seminary. But on one point Union and Princeton were in perfect accord. Both regarded it as exceedingly desirable that theological professors should no longer be elected by the General Assembly; Princeton primarily on her own account; Union, on account of Princeton, as also of the other Old School seminaries. It is fair to add that some of the strongest friends of Princeton were, no doubt, influenced by another reason for wishing to be liberated from further subjection to the General Assembly in the election of its professors, namely: distrust of the doctrinal soundness of the late New School Church. Dr. Charles Hodge led a whole company of eminent Old School men, who to the last protested and fought against reunion largely on this ground. To some of these, especially to Dr. Hodge himself, Dr. Beatty refers in a striking letter printed in *The Evangelist* of August 6, 1891: "Dr. Adams knew what great difficulties and conflicts of mind I had from the fact that my best friends were in opposition to my views; and I made the request of him that after my death he would state these things in some article in *The Evangelist.*" Did the simple fact of reunion at once change their honest convictions on this subject? Not at all. And, therefore, the sudden accession of the New School branch to equal power in the General Assembly, bringing what were regarded their "loose" notions of subscription and all their other objectionable views with them, intensified the desire to take the election of Princeton professors out of that body.

And it is only right to add further, that in voting, as they all did, in favor of remitting the election of professors in the Old School seminaries to their several Boards of Direction, the commissioners who belonged to the late New School branch were voting to dispossess themselves at once of a power in the control of those seminaries, which reunion had fairly put into their hands. It was the proper thing for them to do; but it was also a handsome thing to do so promptly and so heartily. On the basis then, of a common sentiment respecting the election of theological professors, both Union and Princeton memorialized the General Assembly; and through their joint influence, the plan first suggested by Princeton and proposed by Union, was unanimously adopted.

I have thus stated some of the principal reasons and influences that in 1870 induced Union Seminary to concede to the General Assembly a portion of its autonomy. Let us now go back and consider the matter a little more in detail.

(*f*) *Action and purpose of the Board of Directors in making this concession.*

The subject was first brought before the board by Dr. Adams at a meeting held on May 9, 1870. Among the directors present, were Edwin F. Hatfield and Jonathan F. Stearns, who with Dr. Adams had been members of the Joint Committee on Reunion; Joseph S. Gallagher, James Patriot Wilson, Charles Butler, Norman White, Fisher Howe, William A. Booth, D. Willis James and John Crosby Brown. These names speak for themselves and need no glossary. They represent moral strength, sound judgment, large and varied experience, world-wide influence, intelligent piety, and all the other qualities that go to make up solid weight of character. To most of the directors the plan proposed for their adoption was wholly new. They had never before heard of it unless as suggested in the April number of Dr. Hodge's *Review*. But as coming from Dr. Adams, as offered in the interest of the unity and harmony of the Presbyterian Church, and also in response to urgent persuasions from the old and honored seminary at Princeton, it won their consent, if not their entire approval. So far as its weak points were concerned, it took them at a serious disadvantage. They had no time for reflection. And so, while there was considerable discussion, with a single notable exception, none refused to support the scheme. Several of the professors were present, but they raised no objection. The record would probably be different had Henry B. Smith been among them. The plan of putting the institution under ecclesiastical control never pleased him. He considered the generous and self-governing liberty, which was its birthright, a blessing too great to be parted with at any price. He distrusted also a certain tendency and temper, or rather, as he viewed it, distemper, which again and again in the last century and in our own had troubled the peace and hampered the free development of American Presbyterianism. In 1837, at the age of twenty-one, he had been a watchful eye witness of the turbulent scenes at Philadelphia, when the four Synods were cut off and the great disruption was inaugurated. From that time he was a keen observer of all that went on in the two branches of the Presbyterian Church, and before coming to New York, thirteen years later, he had formed opinions on the subject which remained essentially unchanged to the day of his death. In a letter to me, dated Amherst, September 17, 1850, he wrote:

> I go to New York in full view of the uncertainties and difficulties of the position. . . . It [the seminary] stands somewhere between Andover and Princeton, just as New School Presbyterianism stands between Congregationalism and the consistent domineering Presbyterianism, and will be pressed on all sides. Whether it is to be resolved into these two, or to be consolidated on its own ground, is still a problem. . . . I am going to New York to work—to work, I trust, for my Master.

This "consistent domineering" element, so far as it prevailed in Presbyterianism, whether in the theological or the ecclesiastical sphere, he regarded with strong dislike. Had he been present, therefore, at the meeting of the board, on May 9, 1870, I believe he would have stood where D. Willis James so firmly stood with respect to the plan of conceding to the General Assembly so vital a part of the seminary's chartered rights and autonomy as the last decisive word in the election of its own directors and professors. And Henry B. Smith was probably the only man whose voice at that time, on any matter touching the theological seminaries, would have been equally potential with that of William Adams. But unfortunately, early in the previous year, just as reunion was about to triumph, Professor Smith, utterly broken down in the service of Union Seminary and of the Presbyterian Church, had fled for his life beyond the sea, and he was still abroad.

I have intimated that a single director only, D. Willis James, raised his voice against the plan proposed by Dr. Adams. Mr. James is a grandson of Anson G. Phelps, and thus is identified with the history of the seminary by his close kinship to three generations of its benefactors, as well as by his own long service and munificent gifts. At the memorable meeting of the Board of Directors of Union Seminary, held on June 5, 1891, Mr. James made the following highly important statement:

I feel it due to the Board of Directors to give to them a statement of what occurred at the meeting of the directors held on the 9th of May, 1870, when the matter of the connection of the seminary with the General Assembly of the Presbyterian Church was first considered. That meeting, from the circumstances of the case, and all that occurred there at that time, is most clearly and indelibly impressed upon my memory.

Dr. Adams proposed that the Union Theological Seminary should give to the General Assembly a veto power over the appointment of the directors and professors of the seminary, assigning as the reason, in much detail, that it would be a great aid to the other seminaries of the Church, whose professors were appointed by the action of the General Asssembly and not by the Board of Directors. He also stated that experience had shown that the professors thus appointed by the General Assembly were frequently not such as proved to be the best men for the several positions.

I strenuously objected to giving the veto power in the appointment of the directors to the General Assembly, on the ground that it was practically placing the control of the property and all the interests of the Union Theological Seminary in the hands of the General Assembly, and that such action was fraught with great danger.

A general discussion occurred, participated in by most of the directors, and I spoke a second time on the subject, calling attention most earnestly to the great danger, as it seemed to me, of any such action by which the large property of the seminary, and all its interests, would be practically turned over to the control of the General Assembly.

But when it seemed evident that a vote would be taken and that the resolution would be passed by the Board of Directors, I arose for the third time, feeling very strongly the importance of the matter under consideration, and said, in substance, that I should request, when the vote was taken, that it should be by ayes and nays, so that my vote could be recorded in the negative, and that I should also request that my most earnest and solemn protest be entered in full in the minutes, to the end that when the disaster came, as it certainly would from this action—perhaps after all those who were taking part in the discussion at that time had passed away—the seminary could then have the benefit of this protest and whatever legal advantages might come from such protest. I said that I did not desire to make factious opposition, but that I felt that the interests of the seminary were being jeopardized and that a great injury was being done to its future.

When I sat down Dr. Prentiss rose and said, substantially, that he would surprise the mover of the resolution by the action he was about to take, but that he had become impressed with the fact that it was wise to take further time for consideration, and would move a postponement of the matter for that purpose. This motion led to the postponement of the vote.

Prior to the adjourned meeting of May 16, 1870, I had an interview with Dr. Adams, and expressed to him my sincere regret that I had been compelled to differ with him and other members of the board, but he then tendered to me his thanks for my having taken the course I did, and said he felt that it was wiser not to have passed the resolution he first proposed.

He then suggested, in the interest of the other seminaries then controlled by the General Assembly, the motion which was presented and adopted on the 16th of May, 1870, viz: That the veto power in the appointment of the professors should be given to the General Assembly; and this solely in the interest of other seminaries which would be benefited by this action of the Union Theological Seminary. I expressed to him then the view that I held, that even this action, though much better than placing the control of the property in the hands of the General Assembly, was still a very serious mistake, and calculated to produce great and unfortunate mischief.

I said, however, that if he and other directors felt that this was the wisest course, and as they had yielded the matter of the veto power over the appointment of directors, while I would not vote in favor of the resolution, I would not go on record against it; and, as a result, the resolution was passed on the 16th of May, 1870, giving to the General Assembly only a veto over the appointment of professors and nothing more.

(*g*) *Did the directors of Union Seminary suppose that in their action on May 16, 1870, they were offering to enter into a legal compact with the General Assembly?*

When in 1891 the question first arose, it was assumed

by many, and strenuously argued by others, that this was their understanding of the matter; at all events, that such was the real quality and effect of their action. And on the ground of its possessing this character, the public was treated to somewhat elaborate definitions and expositions of the nature and binding force of a contract, the extent and limitations of *ultra vires*, and I know not how many other lessons in legal lore. And yet, according to the best of my own recollection, as a member of the board, and of my belief concerning all the other members present, not a single director supposed the board was entering into any such compact. Three directors who were present on May 9th and also on May 16th, had been members of the Joint Committee on Reunion, as I have said before: one of them, Jonathan F. Stearns, was also a member of the Joint Committee of Conference, which reported the final basis and plan of union to the two Assemblies in 1869. He aided in preparing that important report, voted for it, signed it, and gave it his hearty approval. And it was in this report made and explained to the Old School Assembly in the Brick Church, by Dr. Musgrave, that those emphatic sentences relating to the articles on seminaries, boards, and the like occur: "We will not consent to make these articles a covenant: we won't adopt them as a legal compact binding upon the future. This paper is not a compact or covenant: but it is a recommendation of certain arrangements as to seminaries," etc.

Dr. Stearns was the most trusted counsellor of Henry B. Smith, and not unlike him in sagacity and forethought, as also in devotion to Union Seminary and the Presbyterian Church. To Dr. Stearns more, in my opinion, than to any other man, did Union Seminary owe the coming of Henry B. Smith to New York. The New School branch of the Church especially never knew the full extent of her indebtedness to him, for he was as modest as he was wise, fearless and public-spirited. Is it likely that such a man would have sat quietly and given his vote for a settlement of the question of the theological seminaries in a way, and on a principle, and with an understanding contradicting so utterly the report which a few months before he had joined in framing and urging upon the acceptance of the General Assemblies? The thing is inconceivable.

But I have not stated this aspect of the case in its full strength. Dr. Adams himself was a member of the Joint Committee of Conference, and signed the report as its chairman. He also presented the report to the New School Assembly in the Church of the Covenant, as Dr. Musgrave did at the same time to the Old School Assembly in the Brick Church. He explained it in a careful speech, calling attention to the point that the articles of agreement or "concurrent declarations," were not a compact or contract, but recommendations only as to what might be suitable and expedient. Is it at all probable, is it really conceivable, that such a man as Dr. Adams, only a few months later, would have proposed to the Board of Directors of Union Seminary, a plan touching the whole future of that institution, which involved the very thing so distinctly repudiated by the unanimous vote of the Joint Committee of Conference, and repudiated too by both Assemblies.

The plan of 1870 was an expression of Christian confidence and good-will on the part of the directors of Union Seminary. In offering to give up so much of their autonomy as was involved in conceding to the General Assembly a veto in the election of its professors, they were not thinking of a legal compact, whereby the seminary would gain certain positive advantages in return, they were thinking simply of what seemed to them, on the whole, best fitted to promote the harmony and prosperity of the united Church, and the true interests of all the other theological seminaries. Their offer was in its very essence, as the General Assembly a few days after characterized it, an act of "generosity," or as Dr. Musgrave expressed it, in 1871, an act of "courtesy." "Courtesy" is one of the words used also by the Princeton professors in their memorial to the board and by the directors in their memorial to the General Assembly. But generosity and courtesy belong to a line of thought and action totally distinct from that of a legal compact with its definite obligations, considerations and advantages. Had the discussion in the Board of Directors of Union Seminary moved along the line of such a compact, nothing is more certain than that the plan of agreement would have failed utterly. No doubt there is an element of agreement in a legal compact. Every such compact is an agreement; but there are many sorts of agreement which are only differing forms of good understanding, friendly arrangements, acts of generosity or courtesy, which lose their most essential virtue and all their beauty the moment you invest them with the rigidity and binding force of a legal contract. The discussion on reunion, and especially the speech of Dr. Musgrave before the Old School Assembly — heard, probably, by most of the Union directors — had made the whole Presbyterian Church familiar with this distinction. "We will not consent," said Dr. Musgrave, referring to the recommendations about theological seminaries, boards, etc., "we will not consent to make these articles a covenant. We won't adopt them as a legal compact, binding upon the future: Yet we are acting in good faith and as honorable men, and we say to you that we will not change them at any future time without obviously good and sufficient reasons." Exactly so would the directors of Union Seminary have expressed themselves with regard to their generous arrangement with the General Assembly. Such words as "compact" "contract," "covenant," are carefully avoided in the memorial of Union Seminary and in the action of the General Assembly thereupon. Not one of them can be found in the historical record. "Plan," "rule," "agreement," "method," or the like, are the terms used. It was intended, just as the ninth article in the report of the Joint Committee was intended, "as a measure for the maintenance of confidence and harmony, and not as indicating the best method for all future time." (Moore's Digest, p. 384).

All that the article in the *Princeton Review* for April, 1870, written by Dr. Charles Hodge, or with his approval, ventured to suggest to the New School branch was "making the simple by-law that all the elections to fill vacancies in the board or boards of oversight and direction, also of professors, shall be submitted to the Assembly for approval before they are finally ratified." Who ever heard of a "simple by-law" that could not be suspended, changed, or repealed by the power that made it? The difference between the concessions asked, if not claimed, of the New School by the Old School opponents of the first plan of reunion, as reported by the Joint Committee in 1867, and the concessions hoped for just before the meeting of the Assembly in 1870, as stated in the above article of the *Princeton Review*, is very striking. It is the difference between a maximum and a minimum. Perhaps it cannot be better illustrated than by some extracts from a letter of Professor A. A. Hodge, of the Alleghany Seminary, to Dr. Henry B. Smith, written in December, 1867. The italics are his own:

Although I am in every sense unknown to you, my knowledge of and indebtedness to you through your writings, and especially our community of interest in the subject of this letter, emboldens me to intrude it upon you, and to urge your deliberate attention to it.

Undoubtedly one of the chief causes of uneasiness on the part of the Old School, in view of reunion upon the terms proposed by the Joint Committee, is the inequality between the positions of the two parties in respect to seminaries. This is evident from the fact that serious objection is made to the terms proposed in respect to this interest by a far larger number of Presbyteries than is necessary to defeat the whole matter. . . . Now, although I write without consultation with or the knowledge of a single person, I feel certain that a compromise to the following effect would be highly gratifying to the great majority of those most nearly interested in seminaries on our side, and further, that if proposed from your side it would be almost certainly accepted by our General Assembly as a condition of union.

Suppose then the matter be adjusted on the following principles:

1. *All* the seminaries of both parties to be, as a *condition* of union, brought in on the same basis, so that there may be perfect equality.

2. That you on your side admit the principle of direct ecclesiastical control, and put your seminaries each under the care of one or more contiguous Synods. The Synods to elect the Boards of Directors, the Boards of Directors to elect the professors. The General Assembly, for the sake of preserving uniformity of doctrine in the Church, to possess the right of peremptory veto in the case of the election of a professor.

3. That we on our side yield the principle of the immediate control of the seminaries by the General Assembly, and put each of our seminaries under one or more Synods in the manner specified above.

Such a plan might have some legitimate objections. It would certainly meet with decided opposition from some of the more distant portions of our branch, which would thereby be dispossessed of powers previously enjoyed. It would be *obviously unadvisable for such a proposition to be publicly offered* by any of our professors. Therefore, I shall do no more than make this suggestion to you. . . . If you agree with me as to the plan, and are willing to present it to the representatives of your branch in the Joint Committee, I have much hope that it will prevail.

Professor Smith, regarding the scheme so strongly urged in this letter as wholly impracticable, felt unwilling to recommend it to the New School representatives of the Joint Committee.

(*h*) *Scope and limitations of the veto in the election of its professors, offered to the General Assembly by the directors of Union Seminary in 1870.*

Passing from the question of the nature of this offer, let us consider its extent and its limitations. The language used is very exact and carefully chosen. It differs materially from that used in the plan presented to the board on May 9th. Before the meeting on May 16th legal counsel had unquestionably been taken. Nor have I any doubt that it was taken of one of Dr. Adams' closest friends and a member of his session, Theodore W. Dwight, LL.D., the eminent jurist and author. In nearly all, if not in all, the proposals and articles on the subject, prior to the meeting at Philadelphia, positive action by the General Assembly was contemplated as requisite to a complete election; in other words, every election or appointment, in order to be complete, must be directly approved, or else disapproved, by the General Assembly. This would be in accordance with the usual practice in the political sphere. Ordinarily the veto power goes along with the power of approval and confirmation. It is so with the Presidential veto. It is so generally with the veto power of governors and mayors. But it was not so here, and as a consequence, even the General Assembly itself, as we shall see, required twenty years fairly to learn the lesson of the extent of its power in the case. All that the Assembly could rightfully do, under the agreement of 1870, was either to disapprove or to do nothing.

This shows how sagaciously the whole matter was finally arranged. The plan bears on its very face marks of the utmost caution and forethought. Had it included the power of approval, as well as of disapproval, every election reported between 1870 and 1891 would then have come before the Assembly for confirmation, and might have led to any amount of a more or less excited discussion and conflict of opinion. An approval, if strenuously opposed by only a small minority, would be likely to prejudice even a good appointment; while an approval, if carried by a bare majority, could hardly fail to stir up bad feeling among the friends of the candidate, if not in his own breast. Whatever evils were incident to the election of theological teachers by the General Assembly, the plan of 1870 certainly reduced them to a minimum, as compared with a plan which should embrace the power of ratifying, as well as vetoing, every appointment. It is likely that between May 9th and May 16th Dr. Adams not only took legal counsel, but that he also sought the counsel of those two wise men and old friends, Dr. Stearns and Dr. Hatfield, with whom for nearly three years he had been in the habit of conferring on this very question of the theological seminaries in the Joint Committee on Reunion, or in the New School branch of it. That the General Assembly, under the rule of 1870 had no power of approval is admitted now on all hands.

But there is another point concerning which there was conflict of opinion; the point, namely, whether the transfer of a member of the faculty from one chair to another was an election in the same sense as an original appointment, and, therefore subject to the Assembly's veto. The General Assembly at Detroit, as we shall see, assumed that a transfer did not differ from an original election, and by a large majority voted to disapprove the transfer of Dr. Briggs from the chair of Hebrew and Cognate Languages to the new chair of Biblical Theology. The position of the Board of Directors on the other hand, was that the original election of Dr. Briggs, not having been disapproved by the General Assembly fixed his status, once for all, as a member of the teaching faculty of Union Seminary; and that his transfer to the chair of Biblical Theology could not therefore unsettle, suspend, or in any wise change that status; it was simply an assignment of new duties, belonged solely to the jurisdiction of the board, and lay wholly beyond the control or supervision of the General Assembly.

This view is enforced by several considerations: 1. It harmonizes with the exclusion from the plan, adopted by the directors on May 16th, of all direct power of approval. That exclusion indicates plainly the animus and latent, if not the deliberate, purpose of the board. I say "latent, if not deliberate purpose," because no evidence exists that in using the terms "election" and "appointment" there was any thought or suspicion in the mind of a single director present that the agreement included also a transfer from one chair to another. Not a word was lisped on this point.* Had it been raised then and there; had Dr. Adams, in explaining his revised plan, said to the board: "I feel bound to tell you frankly that this plan, faithfully carried out, will of necessity render the internal administration and housekeeping of Union

* Among the members of the faculty present was Dr. Philip Schaff. In a letter to me Dr. Schaff, referring to Dr. Adams' proposal "as a generous peace offering on the altar of the reunion of Old and New School," added:

My impression was that Dr. Adams had previously conferred with Dr. Charles Hodge, who in behalf of Princeton was anxious to get freedom from the control of the Assembly in the appointment of professors. Our loss was Princeton's gain. The distinction between the appointment of a new professor and the transfer of an old one to a new department was not mentioned and probably not even thought of at that time. I myself was transferred three times—to the Hebrew, to the Greek, and to Church History—and nothing was said about a veto.

Seminary, touching some of its vital interests, subject to the ultimate control of the General Assembly " Mr. James' protest of May 9th would have echoed throughout the room. The plan would have withered on the spot. Or, to state the case in another way, had the question been put to Dr. Adams: " Do you mean to include in the terms "election" and "appointment" a transfer also, such as we often make from one chair to another? In our relations to the General Assembly will the original status of one of our professors be lost by calling him to new duties in the institution, until it has been recovered by subjecting him again to the veto of the General Assembly?" the prompt answer, I am quite sure, would have been: " Most certainly not; that goes without saying. We are proposing to enter, not into a legal compact, but into a friendly and courteous arrangement by which the General Assembly shall have a voice in respect to the qualifications of every man who is to be a theological teacher in our seminary. But once admitted, unforbidden, into our faculty, the Assembly will have nothing further to do with him except indirectly, of course, as a Presbyterian minister. We are not trying to drive a bargain, but to do what seems to us a fair and wise, not to say very generous, thing in the interest of the peace and prosperity of the united Church."

2. And then it is certainly a strong incidental confirmation of the view taken by the directors of Union Seminary with regard to the scope of the agreement of

1870, that the official minutes of the board took for granted the correctness of that view. The board again and again assigned its professors to new duties and to new chairs. Three times it transferred Dr. Schaff from one chair to another. It created a new chair and selected Dr. Briggs to fill it, transferring Dr. Brown at the same time to the chair vacated by Dr. Briggs. The record of these and similar changes on the minutes of the board varied in language. The terms "elected," "chosen," "appointed," "transferred," were used more or less indiscriminately; and that for the simple reason that in the mind of the board there was no thought of any question touching its own proper authority in each case. *Transfer* was evidently the fitting term, expressing both the fact and the power; and this is the word which had been chiefly employed in the minutes of the Executive Committee and of the Board of Directors of Union Seminary. If all "appointments" in the literal sense were subjected to the veto of the General Assembly, temporary assignments of duty would have had to be reported to the Assembly; for nothing is more common than to "appoint" a professor to such special duties.

3. There is still another consideration which sustained the view that a transfer is wholly different from an original election; the fact, namely, that the strict rules and procedure in the original election were not observed in the case of a mere transfer. The disregard of these rules had in repeated instances been so positive

and varied as to invalidate the whole action of the board, if a transfer is the same thing as an original appointment. Alike in the open disregard of some of these rules and in inducting at once into the new or vacant chair without any respect to the General Assembly — as, for example, in the case of Dr. Briggs — we have a clear demonstration that in the view of the Board of Directors of Union Seminary, a transfer had always been regarded as simply an assignment of duties, and subject, therefore, neither to the veto of the General Assembly, nor to a strict observance of the usual forms prescribed by law and custom in first calling a man to the service of the seminary.

In the discussion of the extent of the Assembly's veto power, the singular point was made that we ought to distinguish between the different chairs and the subject matter taught in them. A Jew, for example—so I heard it argued by at least two eminent directors in a leading Presbyterian seminary — a Jew might make an excellent professor of Hebrew; but suppose, hiding behind the technicality of a transfer, you should put him into the chair of Systematic Theology, would not *that* have been a case for the intervention of the General Assembly's veto power? I reply, no; not if the Assembly had failed to disapprove of his taking the chair of Hebrew. I freely admit that there are devout, God-fearing Jews, abundantly qualified to be professors of Hebrew in any theological seminary. Isaac Nordheimer, my own beloved teacher, was such a man; but the best and most learned Jew in the world could not get into the chair of Hebrew in Union Seminary, to say nothing of his transfer to the chair of Systematic Theology. How could a Jew sincerely adopt the Westminster Confession of Faith as containing the system of doctrine taught in the Holy Scriptures? For that is the pledge.

(*i*) *Acceptance of the offer of Union Seminary made to the General Assembly in the memorial of 1870.*

Let us now go back to the meeting of the Assembly in Philadelphia. Dr. Adams, as we have seen, was appointed chairman of the Standing Committee on Theological Seminaries. He asked, as a personal favor, I repeat, to be excused from serving in that capacity, on the ground that all the seminaries under the care of the Assembly belonged to what had been the Old School branch, but his request was not granted. Before this committee came the memorial of Union Theological Seminary and also a memorial from Princeton of similar tenor; the difference between them being that Princeton asked what it deemed a great favor to itself, while Union asked what it believed would be a great favor to Princeton and other seminaries. The report of the committee led to no discussion, met with no opposition, and was unanimously adopted. I will give the larger part of this important report, italicizing a few passages:

That the relations of these several theological seminaries, differing in origin and administration to the reunited Church, should be regarded as a matter of no little delicacy and difficulty, was inevitable. On the one hand it is obvious that a matter so important as the education of its ministry should in some way be under the supervision and control of the Church, so as to secure the entire and cordial confidence of the Church. On the other hand, there is a liberty and flexibility in the matter which must be respected and allowed. If individuals or associations are disposed to found and endow seminaries of their own, there is no power in the Presbyterian Church to forbid it.

As to any project by which the entire control and administration of all our theological seminaries—for example, as to the election of trustees—can be transferred to the General Assembly on any principle of complete uniformity, your committee regard it as wholly impracticable, and the attempt to accomplish it altogether undesirable. To bring it about, should it be undertaken, would require an amount of legislation in six or seven different States, which would be portentious.

Besides, the intentions and wishes of benevolent men who have founded and endowed some of these seminaries, and aided others on their present footing, *should be honorably and zealously protected.*

Your committee, therefore, would recommend no change and no attempt at change in this direction, save such as may safely and wisely be effected under existing charters.

For example, the directors of the seminary at Princeton have memorialized this Assembly with the request that the Assembly would so far change its "plan" of control over that institution as to give the Board of Directors enlarged rights in several specified particulars, subject to the veto of the General Assembly.

Your committee are unanimously of the opinion that the changes asked for are eminently wise and proper. *If it were within the power of the General Assembly to remit the entire administration of this venerable institution to its Board of Directors without any of the restrictions* they have mentioned as to the supply of their own vacancies, *they would cordially recommend it.* But inasmuch as the endowments of this seminary are held on the condition that it should be the property and under the control of the General Assembly of the Presbyterian Church in the United States, that trust cannot be vacated nor transferred to any other body. The method desired and proposed by the directors themselves is open to no such objection, and is believed to be quite within the provisions of the law as now defined, being only a convenient and wise mode of executing by the General Assembly itself the trust which it now holds.

A memorial has been presented to this Assembly from the directors of Union Theological Seminary, in New York, bearing upon the point of uniformity as to a certain kind and amount of ecclesiastical supervision.

It had appeared to them—many of them having taken an active part in founding that seminary thirty-three years ago, in a time, as already noticed, of memorable excitement—that there were great disadvantages and perils in electing professors and teachers by the Assembly itself, without sufficient time or opportunity for acquaintance with the qualifications of men to be appointed to offices of such responsibility.

It is self-evident, as your committee are agreed, that a body so large as the General Assembly, and composed of men resident, most of them, at so great a distance from the several seminaries, is not so competent to arrange for their interests and usefulness as those having local and personal intimacy with them. Desirous of bringing about as much uniformity as was possible in the relation of the seminaries to the General Assembly of the Church, the directors of

Union Seminary have memorialized this Assembly to the effect that the Assembly would commit, so far as practicable, the general administration of all seminaries now under the control of the Assembly to their several Boards of Directors; proposing, if this be done, to give to the General Assembly what it does not now possess, the right of veto in the election of professors of Union. In this generous offer, looking solely to the peace and harmony of the Church, the memorialists did not include the same veto in regard to the election of their own directors, inasmuch as these directors hold the property of the seminary in trust. The trustees of Princeton Seminary being one of two boards, are a close corporation. The directors of Union Seminary in New York, being but one board, are the trustees.

Leaving all the diversities of method and administration in the several seminaries intact, save in the particulars hereafter provided for, your committee are happy to report that there is one mode of unifying all the seminaries of the Presbyterian Church as to ecclesiastical supervision so far as unification is in any way desirable. It is the mode suggested in the several memorials of the directors of Union and Princeton, and approved, or likely to be approved from information in our possession, by the directors of Auburn and Lane. This is to give to the General Assembly a *veto* power upon the appointment of professors in all these several institutions. This seems to your committee to secure all the uniformity, as to the relation of these seminaries to the Church, which can be necessary to ensure general confidence and satisfaction. Less than this might excite jealousy, more than this is cumbersome and undesirable. *

* The full report will be found in Moore's Digest of 1886, pp. 383-386. It is proper to say here, that two statements in the report are somewhat inaccurate, namely: that relating to the ecclesiastical connection in

I have said that the report of the Standing Committee on Theological Seminaries met with no opposition. The offer of Union Seminary, which was wholly unexpected to the great body of commissioners, whether of the Old or New School, made the happiest impression upon the Assembly and called forth strong words of satisfaction and thankfulness. And yet the committee appear to have been in some doubt whether all the seminaries, then belonging to the General Assembly, would be willing to pass from under its immediate control; for the report closes with this resolution:

> In case the Board of Directors of any theological seminary now under the control of the General Assembly should prefer to retain their present relation to this body, the plan of such seminary shall remain unaltered.

Whatever doubt, if any, led to this provision, it was solved in the acceptance of the Princeton plan by all the other seminaries hitherto belonging to the Old School; while Lane, that, like Union, was independent of ecclesiastical control, and Auburn, which was under the watch and care of adjacent Synods, fell in also with the new arrangement by conceding to the General Assembly a veto over the election of their professors. I do not find that, at the time, these changes involved any public discussion, or even attracted public notice. Such was the confiding and hopeful temper of the

1836 of the founders of Union Seminary, and that relating to "the design of its founders." Their own language touching this point, as also the facts with regard to their ecclesiastical connection, have been given in an earlier part of this volume.

reunited Church, that it seems to have accepted the action at Philadelphia almost as a matter of course.

I have thus endeavored to trace from stage to stage the course of discussion and of action with regard to theological seminaries in the Joint Committee on Reunion, in the Old and New School General Assemblies, in the Board of Directors of Union Seminary, and lastly in the Assembly of the reunited Church. It has been my aim to give as far as possible all the main facts, omitting nothing essential to a right understanding of the case. At the beginning of the investigation my mind was very much in the dark respecting a number of important points, but after patient research and inquiry, now and then not a little to my own surprise, the needed light appeared. I will now proceed to a sketch of the practical working and effects of the Assembly's veto power from 1870 to 1891.

(*j*) *Early and frequent misapprehension of the extent of this power on the part of the General Assembly. Its quiescence for twenty years.*

The facts bearing on this point are equally curious and instructive. They are curious as an illustration of the tendency in all popular bodies,—a tendency partly innate, and in part the effect of ignorance, prejudice or passion—to stretch their prerogative in the exercise of power. The facts are instructive as illustrating the old maxim that "the price of liberty is eternal vigilance," and also the painful truth that even a court of Jesus

Christ is not exempt from some of the unloveliest infirmities of human nature. Good men when, armed with authority, they meet together for the performance of important duties and the promotion of sacred objects, mean, of course, to do the thing that is right and, especially, to keep the whole law under which they act; but how strangely they often err, on the right hand and on the left!

Nothing would seem to be plainer than the power of disapproval as conceded to the General Assembly in 1870, and yet upon the very first opportunity to exercise this power, at Chicago in 1871, the Standing Committee on Theological Seminaries recommended the "approval" of certain elections reported to the Assembly; and had it not been for the presence of Henry B. Smith as commissioner from the Presbytery of New York, the recommendation would no doubt have been unanimously adopted. The "official journal" of the Assembly contained the following record:

UNION SEMINARY.

Prof. Henry B. Smith, D.D., LL.D., of Union Theological Seminary, New York city, moved an amendment to the report of the Standing Committee on Theological Seminaries, thus:

Resolved, That the clauses of the report of the committee be modified or stricken out which express in the name of the Assembly "approval" of the elections of directors or professors in the seminaries that have adopted the plan suggested by Union Seminary, and ratified by the Assembly in

1870 (see minutes, pp. 64, 65, 148); since according to said plan such elections are complete unless "vetoed" by the Assembly to which they are reported.

Dr. Musgrave hoped this amendment would be sustained. Union Seminary has courteously, and as he thought wisely, conceded this measure of control over it by the General Assembly, and it was only fair and honorable to accept this amendment. It was so ordered.

One would have supposed that this formal interpretation of the extent of its veto power contained in the resolution offered by Professor Smith, and seconded by Dr. Musgrave as "only fair and honorable," by a unanimous vote of the Assembly itself, would have settled the question for all time. It did no such thing. Only two years later at Baltimore the Standing Committee on Theological Seminaries, through the chairman, the Rev. Dr. R. R. Booth, then a director of Union, repeated the error of 1871, and was sustained in doing so by the unanimous vote of the General Assembly.* Nor was that the last of this remarkable misapprehension. Between 1870 and 1891 about sixty elections, appointments and transfers were reported to the General Assembly. Of these some twenty were "recognized," "approved," or their "confirmation" voted by the General Assembly; in other words, in a

*The committee would recommend that the Assembly approve the election of the Rev. Philip Schaff, D.D., to the Brown professorship of Hebrew, and of the Rev. George L. Prentiss, D. D., to the Skinner and McAlphin professorship of Pastoral Theology, Church Polity, and Missionary [Mission] Work, [See minutes of 1873, page 580].

third of the cases reported, the General Assembly did what, according to its own unanimous vote in 1871, it had no legal power to do.* These figures will be found nearly, if not altogether, accurate, and they show how easily the most intelligent and conscientious ecclesiastical bodies are led to exercise power that does not belong to them. The chronic misapprehension of which I am speaking cropped out at almost every turn in the newspaper discussions of the veto power which sprang out of the Briggs case.

For twenty years the veto power, conceded to the General Assembly in 1870 by Union Seminary, remained quiescent. During all this period it was never used. While many appointments were "confirmed," or "approved,"—illegally, to be sure—*not one was vetoed*; a striking proof, certainly, of the harmony and good-will that prevailed in the reunited Church, as also of the wise prudence of our theological seminaries in the choice of their teachers. It seemed, indeed, as if the fears of Henry B. Smith, D. Willis James and others, who regarded the agreement of 1870 with so much misgiving, were shown by the test of experience to have been groundless.

* Except in the case of Auburn Seminary. On entering into connection with the General Assembly this seminary in 1873 had adopted a by-law by which the appointments of its professors were "primarily made conditional upon the approval of the General Assembly." Why this change in the agreement of 1870 was made by the Board of Commissioners of Auburn Seminary, I do not know. But, of course, that seminary alone was bound by it.

The veto power, however, was not wholly forgotten. In the case of Rev. R. W. Patterson, D. D., in 1873, and perhaps a few other instances, a professor-elect and his friends were reminded, in a somewhat menacing way, that such a power, though dormant, was still in existence, and might of a sudden wake up.* Wherever real power exists, it is sure to make itself felt. Its turn always comes, sooner or later; nor is the opportunity apt to be neglected, when a much desired object, whether good or bad, can be secured by its exercise. What is called the "spoils system," for example—a system which has done so much to poison and vulgarize our political life—was largely the outgrowth of that simple power of removal, which the Congress of 1789 decided to belong exclusively to the President. At the time nobody seems to have dreamed that any special harm would come through an abuse of the power. Mr. Madison, whose influence was most potent in this decision of the first Congress, declared that if a President should exercise his power of removal from mere personal motives, or except in extreme cases, he would deserve to be impeached. And for more than a third of a century Executive patronage was used solely

*In 1873 my appointment to a professorship in the then Northwestern Theological Seminary was threatened with veto on the ground that I had lately in the Swing trial expressed the wish that the Confession of Faith might soon be revised. How would that sound now? But my orthodox opponents were quieted, as I was afterward informed, by the statement of the Committee on Seminaries, that in not vetoing the Assembly would not necessarily approve. Time changes both sentiment and logic. [Letter of Rev. Dr. Patterson, dated Evanston, Ill., Aug. 14, 1891].

as a public trust by Washington and the other great patriots who then ruled the country. Even after 1820, when the mischievous "Four Years" law was passed, during the second term of Monroe and the whole term of John Quincy Adams, very few removals were made, and those in every case for cause. Only here and there a far-seeing statesman surmised what, during the next third of a century, lay wrapped up in the unlimited power of removal, when, instead of being used as a public trust, it was going to be so largely prostituted to vulgar greed and the ruthless animosities of selfish partisanship. How different it is now! The "*spoils system*" has come to be regarded, not merely by a few far-seeing statesmen, but by tens of thousands of our most thoughtful and patriotic citizens, of both parties, as, on the whole, the greatest evil that, since the overthrow of slavery, has beset the moral life of the country. To this illustration from our political history how easy it would be to give still more impressive illustrations from the history of the Christian Church, of the way in which power long quiescent, may of a sudden, when the fitting opportunity occurs, spring into vigorous and baleful action.

CHAPTER II.

THE FIRST EXERCISE OF THE VETO POWER AND ITS CONSEQUENCES.—THE DETROIT ASSEMBLY.

We come now to a new and highly interesting chapter in the history of the veto given to the General Asssembly by Union Seminary in 1870. Months before the Assembly of 1891 met at Detroit, it became apparent to observing eyes that the transfer of the Rev. Charles A. Briggs, D.D., to the new chair of Biblical Theology in Union Seminary, was to be sharply contested, and, if possible, vetoed, The contest, of course, would rest upon the ground that a transfer was equivalent to an original election, and subject, therefore, to the disapproval of the General Assembly. There existed throughout the Presbyterian Church much dissatisfaction with some of Dr. Briggs' views as expressed in his writings; and had opportunity occurred sooner, it would doubtless have been seized to attempt his removal, by act of the General Assembly, from the faculty of Union Seminary.

The feeling against Dr. Briggs, already existing and wide-spread, was greatly intensified by the address he delivered on being inducted into his new chair, January 20, 1891. In response to this address, a large number of Presbyteries overtured the General Assembly on the subject. The address led also to the initiation of a judicial process in the Presbytery of New York When the General Assembly met on the 21st of May, the excitement about Dr. Briggs and his case had reached a very high pitch. The press, both religious and secular, discussed the matter with extraordinary interest. There had been nothing like it since the reunion; nothing, in truth, like or equal to it since the tempestuous days of 1837–38, when both the ecclesiastical and theological storm-centre swept down with such fury on the old "City of Brotherly Love." And the key to the whole situation was the veto power. Had it been admitted on all hands that a transfer differed essentially from an original election, and was not subject to the Assembly's disapproval, there still might have been a Dr. Briggs case, but it would not have been the case that in May, 1891, drew the attention of the whole country to Detroit.

(*a*) *The General Assembly at Detroit, and how to judge its course.*

Although my own opinion of the action of the General Assembly at Detroit, in the case of Dr. Briggs was anything but favorable, my impression of the Assembly itself was favorable, on the whole, in a high degree. The commissioners came from far and near, from city and country, from the Atlantic and the Pacific shores, and from the most distant parts of heathendom. They differed immensely in age, in training, in experience, in temperament, in social habits and tastes, in their way of looking at things, in the types of piety and religious thought which they represented; but they seemed to be very much alike in their love to Jesus Christ, in their faith in His blessed Gospel, in their reverence for the Holy Scriptures, in their God-fearing patriotism and philanthropy. Eye-witnesses told me that they never saw a body of good men who appeared more sincerely desirous to do right, and to do it in a Christian spirit. I was especially touched by what I heard about Judge Breckinridge, for it recalled pleasant boyish impressions of his distinguished and excellent father. He belonged to a historic family, and his own character added honor to the name. Only the evening before his sudden death he expressed to a friend of mine his keen anxiety respecting the case of Dr. Briggs, and his deep sense of responsibility in the vote he was about to give. His last words attest how sincerely he spoke.

It is quite possible to respect and even admire a man's character, and to take for granted the purity of his motives without always approving his conduct or assenting to his logic. And what is thus true with regard to individuals, may be no less true with regard to a body of men, to a party, to a community, and to a whole people. Were it not so, history instead of being one of the most interesting of studies, would be repulsive and demoralizing beyond expression. It will ever redound to the honor of the American people that when the stress and agony of their struggle for National life and union was once passed, the whirlwind of embittered passions it had aroused, began to subside, just as the waves of an angry sea dashing upon a rock-bound coast, die away after the storm is over. And these passions have been subsiding ever since. The magnanimous and patriotic sentiments of mutual confidence, love, patience and brotherhood, which are the crowning glory of our Christian civilization, have been taking their place, until the billows of sectional strife have at last

> Quite forgot to rave,
> While birds of calm sit brooding on the charmed wave.

What a striking illustration of the same thing our Presbyterian annals afford in the reunion of 1869! We retained, whoever cared to do so, our old differences of opinion respecting the causes and merits, or demerits, of the Exscinding Acts, the disruption of 1838, and the thirty years of alienation between Old School and New School; but for all that, led no doubt by a Divine hand, we came together again in the spirit of mutual trust and love, forgiving and forgetting, in order that we might the more effectually do the good works foreordained for us as a Church to walk in. And yet, even to this day, how far are we from thinking alike about the events of 1837–38, or about the wisdom of the men who taught and led the contending schools! But it now costs us probably no great effort to admit that they, at all events, were good men, fearing God, and honestly meaning, as well as trying, to keep His commandments.

For myself, I remember well the day when to my youthful fancy Albert Barnes was the very embodiment of pious good sense, meek wisdom, and uprightness, as well as freedom of mind in the interpretation of Holy Scripture; while Robert J. Breckinridge appeared to me as a pugnacious theological "fire-eater," a domineering ecclesiastic, and a persecutor of the saints. My impression of Albert Barnes was only confirmed when, years later, I learned to love and revere him as a personal friend. But time and memorable hours more than a third of a century ago, of most interesting talk with him, in the company of Henry B. Smith, Roswell D. Hitchcock, Howard Crosby, Taylor Lewis and Henry M. Field, and other congenial spirits, quite revolutionized my impression of Robert J. Breckinridge, and while not much changing my opinion of certain features of his course in 1837–38, his relentless hostility to reunion, or his way of doing things, I have ever since had no trouble whatever in thinking of him as a devoted servant of the Lord, as an able theologian, an humble Christian, a great-hearted patriot, and a brave, even if a somewhat rugged, type of old Kentucky manhood.*

*Here is an entry in my little diary under date of August 18, 1857: "Breakfasted at Mr. Field's, of '*The Evangelist,*' with Dr. Robert J. Breckinridge, the famous Exscinder, a very original and interesting man—a true Kentuckian."

While, then, I feel bound to criticise the Assembly's action in the case of Dr. Briggs as unfair, wrong, and unwise in the extreme, let no one suppose me to be imputing bad motives either to the Assembly or to all the men who, as I think, misled it. So far from imputing unworthy motives to most of the commissioners to the Assembly at Detroit, I can readily believe that they were actuated by the best of motives. By their votes in disapproval of Dr. Briggs' transfer to the chair of Biblical Theology, they meant to express no personal hostility to him, but a hostility to what they had read or been assured a hundred times over, and what they honestly supposed, were his opinions and teaching respecting the inspiration and authority of the Holy Scriptures. And had I been a member of the Assembly, viewed the subject as they did, and deemed it right to vote at all, my vote would probably have gone with theirs. From the bottom of my heart I sympathize with all pious and tender feelings toward the Bible, with jealousy of any rival to its authority, with pain and grief at seeing it assailed from without or lightly esteemed in the house of its friends, and with awe of the divine majesty and glory of its truths. Perhaps more or less of ignorance and prejudice may be mixed up with these sentiments. Be it so, but how much of prejudice and ignorance is apt to be mixed up with everybody's best sentiments! If I must choose between ignorant and prejudiced but sincere love to the Word of God on the one hand, and on the other a rationalistic, fault-finding, reckless temper of mind toward it, I infinitely prefer the former. The Word of God, which liveth and abideth forever, is the sure foundation and germinant principle of American piety. It was so in the beginning of our religious life as a people; it has been so ever since; and unless we prove recreant to our great trust, it will be so in all the years to come. So far as criticism of the Bible, whether literary or theological, aims or tends to subvert this foundation and put something else in place of this principle, I, for one, am opposed to it utterly. And had it not been my belief that Dr. Briggs could and would say amen to this sentiment, I should have been equally opposed to him also. Biblical criticism, whether of the higher or lower sort, is very far from being an exact science, and it mars its own best work just in the degree that it puts on the airs of an exact science, and shouts before it is out of the woods. That was the bane of rationalism, and if co-existing with it, is none the less a bane of the most orthodox Christian scholarship. *Seest thou a man wise in his own conceit? There is more hope of a fool than of him.* This senseful proverb applies not to persons alone. It applies also to every kind of knowledge relating to moral and religious truth, more especially to every branch of knowledge that deals with Holy Scripture. Scholarship may be never so able and learned, yet if puffed up with self-conceit, if not animated by the spirit of humility and reverence, it is certain to go astray. "Let no man," to use the words of Lord Bacon, "upon a weak conceit of sobriety or an ill-applied moderation, think or maintain that a man can search too far or be too well studied in the book of God's word or in the book of God's works, divinity and philosophy; but rather let men endeavor an endless progress and proficience in both; only let men beware that they apply both to charity and not to swelling; to use, and not to ostentation."

(*b*) *The case against Union Seminary as argued by John J. McCook.*

The case against Union Seminary had been set before the commissioners in a variety of ways, especially by the religious papers of the denomination, before they left home and on their way to Detroit. Probably its most plausible presentation after their arrival there was in an elaborate lawyer's brief, prepared by John J. McCook, a prominent member of the New York bar.* This brief, bristling with points, and fortified by an array of legal authority, was well fitted *prima facie* to impress the ordinary lay, or even clerical mind. And there is no doubt that both by its arguments and its statements it contributed not a little to confuse and mislead the General Assembly, as also the Christian

* One Hundred and Third General Assembly of the Presbyterian Church in the United States of America, Detroit, May, 1891. Memorandum of facts and the law controlling the relations of Union Theological Seminary in the city of New York to the General Assembly of the Presbyterian Church in the United States of America, by John J. McCook, commissioner from the Presbytery of New York.

public, in regard to the facts and law of the case. It contained charges, too, of a very grave character against the good faith of Union Seminary. For these reasons it requires special notice in this historical sketch.

It was noteworthy, first of all, that a lawyer's brief, prepared with such care and so confident in its tone, should have betrayed throughout utter misapprehension as to one of the most obvious features of the veto power, as conceded to the General Assembly, namely: that it was solely a power of *dis*-approval. Here are instances in point: "Thus all appointments of professors are, and the safety of the Church demands that they always should be, made by the directors conditionally first upon the *approval* of the General Assembly." (p. 18.) "It is intimated in a statement by the faculty of the seminary which appeared in the secular press of May 16, 1891, and in the opinion of Mr. Day, already referred to, . . . that Professor Briggs having been once appointed a professor in the seminary, with the *approval* of the General Assembly, his present appointment is merely a transfer." (p. 27.) "The only question before this Assembly is the exercise of the power granted to it by Union Seminary under the contract, viz., to *approve* or disapprove the appointment by transfer of Dr. Briggs to the new chair of Biblical Theology." (p. 31.) Here were three instances in which Mr. McCook stated as fact and law in the case what was in direct conflict with the unanimous decision of the General Assembly of 1871, a decision which at the time Dr. Musgrave declared to be "only fair and honorable"!

Mr. McCook opened his brief with a statement of what he regarded as the material facts bearing upon the case. He then proceeded to make this starting point: "*The memorial of the directors of Union Seminary of May 18, 1870, and the subsequent action of the General Assembly thereupon, constituted a contract upon valid considerations.*" As to the meaning of a contract he quoted Story's definition: "Whenever any injury to the one party or any benefit to the other party springs from a consideration, it is sufficient to support a contract." The contract between Union Seminary and the General Assembly, he said, contains considerations of both kinds mentioned by Story, "injury and benefit." "There was a substantial concession on the part of the General Assembly, in that it gave up rights of control which it had theretofore possessed over some of the seminaries [that was the *injury*]; and there was *benefit* to the Union Seminary in securing the influence and name of the General Assembly to reassure pupils and benefactors as to its orthodoxy." Of course Mr. McCook did not suppose he was jesting in the use of this language; he, no doubt, believed himself to be asserting a simple fact. But had William Adams, Henry B. Smith, Thomas H. Skinner, Roswell D. Hitchcock, Edwin F. Hatfield and Jonathan F. Stearns—not to mention others—

listened to such a statement they would have regarded its author as only jesting, and that in a very strange way. Not one of them, I am sure, ever heard a lisp of it from any responsible source, either before or after 1870. And although for nearly forty years connected with Union Seminary, as director or professor, I read it for the first time in Mr. McCook's Detroit brief. The statement implied that both pupils and benefactors, being in serious doubt respecting the orthodoxy of the institution, found relief in the agreement of 1870. What pupils? What benefactors? and where was the evidence that the seminary entered into the "contract" of 1870 in order to reassure its pupils and benefactors as to its own orthodoxy? There was no evidence. The whole statement was not only utterly without foundation but it involved a highly offensive imputation upon the General Assembly, upon Union Seminary, and upon all the parties concerned. Is it strange that when the directors, the faculty, and the friends of Union Seminary read it in Mr. McCook's brief, or as it was reported far and wide by the public press, they were filled with indignation?

No principle laid down in the basis of reunion in 1869 was more emphatically asserted than that of the perfect equality of both branches, Old School and New, in the matter of their orthodoxy. The whole movement hinged upon the distinct recognition of this principle. Had Dr. Musgrave, Dr. Beatty, and the other Old School leaders intimated that Union Seminary was not as sound in the faith as Princeton, and needed the influence of the General Assembly to "reassure pupils and benefactors as to its orthodoxy," that of itself would have broken up the negotiations for union.

The second "good and valuable consideration," received by the Union Seminary under this "contract," according to Mr. McCook, was "a large increase of its students," drawn from all parts of the reunited Church. This statement also lacked foundation. Reunion brought very few students to Union Seminary; while it tended, in several ways, to draw them elsewhere. It wrought a great change, for example, in the feeling of New School men toward Old School seminaries, as well as toward the Old School church; and thus led more or less of those studying for the ministry to enter these seminaries, who would never have thought of doing so before 1870. Prior to reunion few of the bright young men of the New School church cared to study theology in an Old School seminary. The following table furnished me by the Rev. Charles R. Gillett, D. D., librarian of Union Seminary, shows at a glance the number of students for twenty years before and twenty years after 1870, and will enable the reader to judge for himself as to the probable influence of the General Assembly upon the increase of its students by "reassuring pupils and benefactors of the orthodoxy" of the institution. This increase, it will be seen, was from the first somewhat irregular. Special causes from time to time depleted the seminary. The war for the Union had this effect in a marked degree. In the four years 1861–65, not a few Union students, or young men, who were intending to enter Union Seminary, were at the front, fighting the battles of their country. Then again special causes occasionally increased the number of students; as, for example, the expectation that the World's Fair would be held in New York. It is doubtful if the endorsement of its orthodoxy by the General Assembly during all the twenty years added a dozen names to the roll of students in Union Seminary.

STUDENTS IN UNION SEMINARY, BY YEARS AND CLASSES.
UNDERGRADUATES ONLY.

YEAR.	SENIORS.	MIDDLERS.	JUNIORS.	TOTALS.
1890–91 . . .	43	60	49	152
1889–90 . . .	43	49	66	158
1888–89 . . .	36	47	44	127
1887–88 . . .	35	39	51	125
1886–87 . . .	53	41	36	130
1885–86 . . .	37	49	33	119
1884–85 . . .	39	37	55	131
1883–84 . . .	33	37	41	111
1882–83 . . .	39	35	42	116
1881–82 . . .	37	40	43	120
1880–81 . . .	36	44	40	120
1879–80 . . .	38	42	50	130
1878–79 . . .	43	37	39	119
1877–78 . . .	45	50	47	142
1876–77 . . .	48	44	47	139
1875–76 . . .	36	49	51	136
1874–75 . . .	43	33	40	116
1873–74 . . .	37	40	34	111
1872–73 . . .	42	42	36	120
1871–72 . . .	36	40	38	114
Averages.	39.95	42.75	44.10	126.8

YEAR.	SENIORS.	MIDDLERS.	JUNIORS.	TOTALS.
1870–71 . . .	37	36	37	110
1869–70 . . .	39	37	37	113
1868–69 . . .	43	44	40	127
1867–68 . . .	44	42	47	133
1866–67 . . .	26	51	31	108
1865–66 . . .	35	38	50	123
1864–65 . . .	23	39	38	100
1863–64 . . .	26	27	32	85
1862–63 . . .	28	30	28	86
1861–62 . . .	38	32	39	109
1860–61 . . .	37	56	40	133
1859–60 . . .	33	49	59	141
1858–59 . . .	38	39	43	120
1857–58 . . .	25	40	43	108
1856–57 . . .	23	33	46	102
1855–56 . . .	19	31	40	90
1854–55 . . .	26	32	38	96
1853–54 . . .	27	31	40	98
1852–53 . . .	22	24	34	80
1851–52 . . .	23	21	30	74
Averages.	30.6	36.6	39.6	106.8

YEAR.	SENIORS.	MIDDLERS.	JUNIORS.	TOTALS.
1850–51 . . .	20	28	25	73
1849–50 . . .	31	20	41	92
1848–49 . . .	27	32	32	91
1847–48 . . .	30	37	36	103
1846–47 . . .	40	32	43	115
1845–46 . . .	25	45	30	100
1844–45 . . .	29	30	46	105
1843–44 . . .	22	40	31	93
1842–43 . . .	25	29	44	98
1841–42 . . .	32	31	39	102
1840–41 . . .	23	43	33	99
1839–40 . . .	24	41	55	120
1838–39 . . .	28	26	32	86
Averages.	27.4	33.4	37.4	98.2

The third "good and valuable consideration" received by Union Seminary under this "contract," according to Mr. McCook, consisted in the financial aid granted each year to its students from the Board of Education of the Presbyterian Church. But the students of Union Seminary had received financial aid every year from the New School Committee of Education. After 1870 they received similar aid from the Board of Education of the reunited Church. Was a dollar coming by way of Philadelphia a better dollar than used to come from the treasury of the New School Committee of Education in New York? Was there more silver or more gold in it? Was it stamped with a stronger assurance of orthodoxy?

The fourth and last "good and valuable consideration," binding Union Seminary fast to its "contract," consisted in "large additions to its endowments and funds such as those received from James Brown, Esq., Gov. Morgan, and others which have been asked for and received since 1870 upon the guarantee of its orthodoxy through its relation to the General Assembly under this contract and the provisions of its constitution." I do not pretend to say that none of the benefactors of the seminary were more or less influenced by their confidence in the orthodoxy of the institution, as guaranteed by its relations to the General Assembly. I do not know. Men are usually led by a variety of motives to give away their money, especially when they do it on a large scale. Of one of the benefactors named, Gov. Morgan, I feel entitled to speak with some confidence. In 1851 I preached a sermon to my people on the position, character, and claims of Union Theological Seminary, urging its immediate endowment. The sermon made no allusion to the General Assembly, or to what Mr. McCook seemed to understand by Presbyterian orthodoxy; but did set forth what I held, and still hold, to be the chief purpose and function of a great metropolitan institution of Christian theology and learning like Union Seminary. Thirty years later Gov. Morgan was kind enough to write to me respecting my sermon: "There is not an expression in it which I do not approve. I thank you from the bottom of my heart for presenting this vastly important subject in its true light." Here follow a few passages from the sermon which met his hearty approval:

The character of Union Seminary is eminently catholic in the true sense of the word; it is at once liberal and conservative. There is nothing that I am aware of in its history, nothing in its associations, nothing in its general policy, nothing in its temper, which would make this institution cleave inordinately to the past or to the future; which should render it unstable in the ways of old truth, or unwilling to greet new truth with a friendly welcome; nothing which commits it to any party or prevents its cordial relations with all parties that love the Gospel and Christian union. It stands in special connection with our own branch of the great Presbyterian family, but it numbers on its Board of Directors, and among its warmest friends, influential members of the other branch; while it seeks its professors and attracts its students as readily from the old Puritan body of New England, as if its predilections were all Congregational. If you will have an institution occupying as catholic a ground as the distracted state of the Church in our day seems to permit, I do not know how you can well come nearer to such a plan than have the founders of Union Seminary. Its main advantages are as accessible and useful to a Baptist, a Methodist, an Episcopalian, or a Congregationalist, as to a Presbyterian; and students of all these and of other denominations have availed themselves of them. Let it be understood that in what I have said, or may say, I cast no reflection upon any other seminary. All honor to Princeton, and Lane, and Auburn, and Andover, and Bangor, and New Haven, and others of whatever name, that are doing the Master's work!

As the seat, too, of a liberal and profound theological culture New York ought to stand foremost in the land. She ought for her own sake. There is perhaps no other power, after the Word preached, which would do more to preserve her Christian influence, wealth and enterprise from falling a prey to the show, self-aggrandizement, and other vices incident to the predominance of a commercial spirit. She ought for the sake of our country and the world. Let a wise, tolerant, Christian theology flourish here, and it would diffuse a beneficent radiance over the land, and even among pagan nations. The position, then, of the Union Seminary is unsurpassed, both for the training of ministers and for the cultivation of sacred learning. For this reason its founders planted it in the city of New York.

I have the clearest conviction that the Union Seminary is capable of doing a great work for Christ and the Church. It has already done much. Not a few of the most useful ministers in the land, not a few of our best missionaries to the heathen, are among its alumni. Already, too, has it made important contributions to the theological literature of the age. But I trust it is to have a still nobler career in the future. I look forward to the time when young men of piety and generous endowments shall flock to it in thousands from all quarters of the Republic; from California and Oregon, and from the islands of the sea, even; when its library shall be the resort of Christian scholars from neighboring towns and cities; when its professorships shall be multiplied so as to embrace one for each great branch of sacred lore; when it shall be the pride and glory of our churches and its treasury be continually enriched by the princely donations of the living and the dying; when, in a word, it shall be such a nursery of men of God, and such a citadel of holy faith as the voice of Providence commands us to build up in this emporium of the New World.

Gov. Morgan's letter to me closed thus:

I have always thought, and I still think, that New Yorkers, of all others, ought to do something for a good institution, like Union Seminary, *in their own city*, and not send all their money to Princeton. I am convinced now more than ever that my judgment in this respect has not been at fault.

In his letter to Dr. Adams offering to establish a fund of one hundred thousand dollars for the erection of a new library building and for the improvement, increase and support of the library, Gov. Morgan begins by saying: "I desire to show my appreciation of the usefulness of the Union Theological Seminary, and to *aid in the great work it is now doing for the country.*" No mention was made of Presbyterian orthodoxy as fixed by the "standard of the General Assembly." Nor do I believe any such thought passed through the mind of this strong man, either at that time, or later, when he added to his first gift two hundred thousand dollars more. Not long before his death, while busying himself with "Morgan Hall," his generous gift to Williams College, he said one day to a friend of mine: "I see now clearly that it has been the greatest mistake of my life that I have not engaged in this kind of thing before. It is one of the greatest pleasures I have ever experienced. And what a host of opportunities I have lost! If men of means could only realize what gratification is to be derived in this way, worthy and deserving objects would be fairly besieged with clamorous donors."

In a letter from the late Henry Day to Mr. John Crosby Brown there is still further testimony to the same effect:

Governor Morgan's interest in Union Seminary arose as follows: I was consulting with him about his will, and knew something of his views in regard to charities. I then advised Dr. Adams to call on Governor Morgan and lay before him the needs of the seminary. This he did. The Governor then consulted me with regard to the institution. I stated all the facts about it, but made no mention of the arrangement with the General Assembly, of which I myself was not then aware, and am sure he also had no knowledge. He finally concluded to give the seminary one hundred thouand dollars, and requested me to draft a letter expressing the terms on which the gift was bestowed. This I did.

The only wish he expressed in regard to it was that the principal should be used in erecting a library building, and the income, if any, should be applied to the improvement of the library. The views controlling him were that a seminary located in a great city, afforded the students better facilities for practical training for Christian work, than seminaries located in smaller towns, and that Union Seminary should have the finest site in New York.

Mr. McCook, some pages later, recurred almost pathetically to the distressing effect of a failure to veto Dr. Briggs: "It would work an irreparable wrong upon those donors, such as James Brown, Esq., Governor Morgan, Russell Sage, Esq., Daniel B. Fayerweather, Esq., and others, who have contributed so largely to the endowment of Union Seminary upon the faith of this arrangement with the General Assembly and the orthodoxy of the seminary, which was intended to be secured thereby." All the benefactors named but one long since have passed far beyond the reach of such "irreparable wrong," Russell Sage, Esq., alone surviving. Why Mr. McCook selected this gentleman in particular from among a score or more of five-thousand-dollar contributors to the fund of Union Seminary as a special object of his sympathy, I do not know.

Had I space it would be interesting to dwell a little upon some of the odd maxims of ecclesiastical wisdom scattered through Mr. McCook's extraordinary brief. They surpass anything I have ever found in books on

Presbyterian Church polity, after reading and lecturing on the subject for many years.

"The SOLE OBJECT of Union Theological Seminary is to uphold and teach the Presbyterian standards." (p. 15). "Upon questions of orthodoxy the directors, individually and as a Presbyterian body, are SUBJECT *to the General Assembly.*" (p. 16). "The Assembly merely *sets a standard of orthodoxy*, and the corporation, wishing to be orthodox, agree to appoint no agent of a certain class who does *not come up to it.*" (p. 18). "The standard of orthodoxy for the seminary, and for all Presbyterians and Presbyterian institutions, must be *set* by the General Assembly. What is more proper, therefore, than a CONTRACT providing that all appointees to the high and responsible office of a professor in such a seminary shall be measured by this standard?" (p. 17).

But let us pass to Mr. James Brown. Mr. Brown never expressed any doubt, nor is there any good reason for thinking he ever felt any doubt, with regard to the orthodoxy of Union Seminary, either before or after 1870. Years prior to the reunion he had been a generous friend of the institution. In 1865, by a gift of $15,000, in addition of another of $10,000 by his brother, John A. Brown, of Philadelphia—a man like-minded with himself—he endowed the chair of Hebrew and Cognate Languages. From this time on his interest in the seminary grew ever stronger and deeper. In January, 1870, months before the agreement with the General Assembly, he gave $30,000 toward the new endowment, being a part of the great five-million memorial fund. And then, in 1873, his various donations culminated in the splendid gift of $300,000, by which the endowment of every chair in the seminary was raised—some from $25,000, some from $50,000 or less—to $80,000. This was perhaps the most wise and considerate, as it was the largest, benefaction to the institution up to that time.

But while Mr. McCook failed to adduce any proper evidence, either documentary or oral, of his assertion respecting the supposed motives which prompted Mr. Brown's gifts to Union Seminary, it was not for lack of evidence, clear and unmistakable, as to the real motives of those noble benefactions. The story of what Mr. Brown did for Union Seminary forms one of the most striking and beautiful episodes in all its varied history. The institution owed to him several hundred thousand dollars, but it owed him something far more precious than money. I mean the inestimable blessing of having William Adams as its president and one of its teachers during the last seven years of his life. Dr. Hitchcock, in his address at the dedication of the new buildings on Park Avenue, thus referred to this auspicious event:

> The administration of Dr. Adams came upon us like a burst of sunshine. He had, of course, first of all, to take care of his own department of Sacred Rhetoric, which he handled with all the versatility and freshness of early man-

hood. To this he added the toils and cares of an office which had lain dormant for thirty years. The whole institution was toned up. Professors and students, equally and all, felt the magnetism of his courtly and stimulating presence. On all public occasions he was our ornament and pride. In all the dry details of our daily, weekly and monthly routine of work, he was a model of punctuality, precision and thoroughness. He possessed in an eminent degree what I will venture to call the institutional instinct and habit. He was a genuine University man, always promptly in his place, and always ready for his work. He also believed in new departures. At an early date our course of study was carefully revised in the interest of a severer discipline. During the first period of our history, and some way on into the second period, there had been only two lectures a day, and these were between the hours of four and six in the afternoon, partly for the convenience of such as were supporting themselves by outside work. Some time before the lectures had been pushed back an hour; and now we added a morning lecture at eleven o'clock, for the expressed purpose of bringing outside work within the narrowest limits possible. With Dr. Adams originated our two scholastic Fellowships, which have done so much for the higher grade of service in our colleges and seminaries. He secured for us in 1874, our present treasurer, Ezra Munson Kingsley, who seems now so indispensable, that we wonder how we ever got on without him. . . . In 1875, Dr. Adams procured the means of renovating our old buildings and erecting a new one, in the expectation of holding on indefinitely to the old location. It was Governor Morgan's gift on the 29th of March, 1880, of $100,000—partly for books and partly for a fire-proof building—which suddenly changed all that. Then our president began to look about for another site. Soon after, at his summer home on Orange Mountain, in New Jersey—looking off upon the sea, looking up into the sky—on the last day of August, 1880, the throbbing, busy pulse stood still. Of fifty years of signal service the last seven had been the golden autumn of his life.

To Mr. James Brown, I repeat, Union Seminary owed it that Dr. Adams spent the golden autumn of his eminently useful life in her service. And Mr. Brown fully comprehended the nature and extent of the blessing. Nor is the secret of his wise forecast far to seek. Mr. Brown (to borrow the words of Dr. Hitchcock concerning him) "was a man of rare qualities, in most symmetrical combination. With a judgment seldom at fault, strong of will, tender in his domestic relations, profoundly religious, no act of his life was ever challenged, and absolutely no shadow darkens his memory. In the year 1854 a terrible affliction befell him. A son, two daughters, a daughter-in-law, and two grandchildren, with two nurses—passengers on board the steamer *Arctic*, returning from Europe—perished by shipwreck. This, with other sorrows before and after, greatly enriched his religious life." It was in the soil of such deep experience that his interest in Union Seminary took root, grew to strong sympathy with the spirit and character of the institution, blossomed in various timely gifts, and at length ripened into the crowning benefaction of 1873. This great benefaction, it is asserted, had been "asked for and received" by Union Seminary upon the guarantee of its orthodoxy, through its relation to the General Assembly under the agreement of 1870. This assertion is based upon an entire misapprehension of the facts in the case. Mr. Brown's gift of $300,000 was never "asked for" at all. It was a purely spontaneous act on his part. When first announced his purpose was a complete surprise alike to his own family and to Dr. Adams, for whom he cherished a singularly tender and devoted friendship. But although a surprise when first announced, it soon became the subject of frequent talks and also of correspondence with his son, Mr. John Crosby Brown, now president of the Union Board of Directors, who entered with his whole heart into his father's plan, both with regard to the full endowment of all the professorships and the bringing of Dr. Adams into the faculty of the seminary. Most of the letters relating to this matter which passed between the father and the son, as also those which passed between Mr. James Brown and Mr. John Crosby Brown, on the one hand, and Dr. Adams on the other, are still in existence; and although replete with very interesting details, alike of plan and feeling, there is not in one of them the remotest allusion to the "orthodoxy" of Union Seminary as guaranteed by the agreement of 1870.

To return to Mr. Brown's motives. Here is the testimony of Mr. John Crosby Brown, the one man living specially entitled and best qualified to bear witness on the subject:

The motives which prompted my father's gifts to Union Seminary at this time, as I well know from frequent conversations with him, were mainly the following: (1) Sympathy with the principles upon which, and the objects for which, the seminary was founded. My father's preference was decided and often expressed for what he conceived to be the broader views and more liberal instruction enjoyed by the students of Union, in comparison with those afforded the students at certain well-known seminaries of the Church. (2) The conviction, also often expressed, that a great city offered superior advantages for the training of young men for the Christian ministry. His brother, Mr. John A. Brown, an old friend and parishioner of the Rev. Albert Barnes, shared his views on both these points.

The details connected with this gift of $300,000, formed the subject of many conversations between my father and myself. I thus became intimately acquainted with his views and the motives which prompted him, and am able to state with confidence, that he was in no way influenced by the agreement of 1870, as affording an additional guarantee of the orthodoxy of the seminary. In not one of our conversations was the agreement so much as mentioned; nor is there an allusion to it in the whole correspondence now in my possession between my father and the seminary, or between him and Dr. Adams, or in his letters to me, or in any other letters bearing upon the matter.

It can hardly excite surprise that the charges respecting Mr. James Brown's gifts to Union Seminary, made in Mr. McCook's "Memorandum" and speech at Detroit, should have greatly displeased Mr. Brown's family and friends. It is only right, therefore, to quote here a statement by Mr. McCook, made in 1892, just before the adjournment of the Portland Assembly, to which he was a commissioner.

Colonel John J. McCook made a frank statement, withdrawing any word which might have irritated or caused distress to the family of James Brown, one of the benefactors of the Union Seminary. He remarked that his object in referring to the matter, had been to express the view that, whether the benefactors of the seminary intended to do so or not, or whether they considered the legal propositions involved or not, their gifts having been once delivered to the seminary, they necessarily come under the trusts devolved by the charter, the constitution and the contract obligations of the seminary, including the compact of 1870.

(c) *Organization of the Detroit Assembly. The Standing Committee on Theological Seminaries. Its report. The speeches and the action of the Assembly.*

The One Hundred and Third General Assembly of the Presbyterian Church in the United States of America met at Detroit, Michigan, in the Fort Street Presbyterian Church, of which the Rev. Dr. Wallace Radcliffe was pastor, on May 21, 1891. The Rev. Dr. William Henry Green, the distinguished professor of Oriental and Old Testament Literature at Princeton, was chosen Moderator. Dr. Green was held in the highest esteem and affection, all over the land, as a veteran in the service of Christian scholarship. Nothing could have been more fitting than his unanimous election. The organization of the Assembly was thus described by the correspondent of the New York *Tribune*, under date of May 22:

This is pre-eminently a conservative Assembly; more, it is a Princeton Assembly. The Moderator is a Princeton man, the senior professor in that seminary; the Stated Clerk is a Princeton man, having been for a long time librarian of that institution; the chairman of the Standing Committee on Theological Seminaries, Dr. Patton, is president of Princeton College, and it is to this committee that the report of Union Seminary is to be submitted. Friends and opponents of Dr. Briggs are already forming their opinions as to what action this committee will report in regard to the New York professor.

Dr. Green announced the standing committees this morning. There is no special significance in the appointments, except in that of the Committee on Theological Seminaries. This is composed as follows: *Ministers*—Francis L. Patton, Princeton; William McKibbin, Cincinnati; John Lapsley, Danville; S. Bowden, Rochester; J. D. Hewitt, Emporia; J. K. Wright, Florida: T. R. Buber, Philadelphia; and M. A. Bronson, Detroit. *Elders*—S. M. Breckinridge, St. Louis; P. McDavitt, Chicago; E. W. C. Humphrey, Louisville; R. C. Totten, Pittsburg; P. Doremus, Montclair, N. J.; N. J. Frick, Fort Dodge; R. McConnaughy, Nebraska City. It was said by those professing to know that this was a decidedly anti-Briggs committee, but Dr. Patton, its chairman, assured the *Tribune* correspondent that he did not know how the members stood on any special question that might come before them. They had apparently been chosen by Dr. Green because he knew their fitness for the work before them.

Here are some passages from a letter of Dr. Parkhurst to *The Evangelist*, depicting the Assembly from his point of view, both as a director of Union Seminary and as a commissioner.

The General Assembly was made up for the most part of men that it did one good to look upon. It is a splendid thing for the country to have such people as an element of its population. They were Christian men with good heads and honest hearts. I am speaking of the body in its entirety, regardless of geographical relations or doctrinal affiliations. *Nine out of ten of that assemblage were anxious for nothing so much as to have the truth brought to the front, and the right prevail.* . . . I recognize the solid sense of the commissioners, but there are a great many questions in theology, as there are in every other science, that need something beside solid sense in order to handle them wisely. Take the matter of the higher criticism, which was repeatedly touched in the course of the debate. I doubt if one in twenty of the commissioners at Detroit would have dared to stand up in the presence of that company and attempt to state what the higher criticism is. Their one impression seemed to be that it was a frightful doctrinal disease of some kind, and that Dr. Briggs had it in its most malignant form. The General Assembly were frightened; I had better say panic-stricken. They had no desire to be rid of Union Seminary, but they were afraid of Dr. Briggs, and evidently supposed that in trying to exorcise him they were saving the seminary, and expelling the one evil spirit and foul demon by which it seemed to them to be possessed. I have thus far spoken about the nine out of every ten. I want now to pay my respects in the same frank way to the tenth man out of every ten. If ninety per cent. of the members were sheep waiting to be led, ten per cent. were bell-wether waiting to lead them, and Princeton was that bell-wether.

Before noticing the report of the Standing Committee on Theological Seminaries it will not be out of place to say a word of its chairman. The Moderator and his chief adviser knew very well what they did. Dr. Patton was by far the strongest man for that position in view of the object to be accomplished. No other commissioner could have filled his place. He was the ruling spirit at once of the Assembly and of the Committee. It is only fair, therefore, to quote a passage from Dr. McKibbin's speech, made in defence of the report. In view of his relation to Princeton, Dr. Patton was somewhat sharply criticised at the time for consenting to serve on the committee. I myself joined in this criticism. But I am bound to say, that for its recognition as a party in the case, with equal rights of its own over against the Assembly, Union Seminary was chiefly indebted to Dr. Patton. Here is the passage in Dr. McKibbin's speech:

Now I am going to tell you some secrets out of school. The chairman seemed to be hunting so hard for some way to peaceably settle this thing, that I began to find my own faith in him weakening. So far from shutting his eyes and ears—and I know you recognize his master-hand in that report—it seemed to me that he was bound to get through the inclosure if there was a hole anywhere in the fence big enough to let him through, before he would consent to say to this Assembly, as he has solemnly said, and we all say, there is no other way, because there is no other duty.

On May 27th Dr. Patton read the report of the committee, which was accepted and ordered to be printed. The report opened with an enumeration of sixty-three Presbyteries which had overtured the General Assembly respecting the recent utterances of Dr. Briggs. It also referred to the report of the directors of Union Theological Seminary respecting the transfer of Dr. Briggs to the chair of Biblical Theology. The report then proceeds thus :

On the 20th of January, 1891, Dr. Briggs delivered an inaugural address on the authority of the Holy Scriptures which has been the subject of some criticism, and which is the occasion of the recommendations which your committee feel constrained to make to the Assembly. In making these recommendations your committee feel that they are acting in the discharge of a delicate duty. The matter with which they have been called to deal bears in a very important way upon the purity and peace of our Church. The interest of the Union Theological Seminary should be most carefully considered, and great respect should be had for the judgment of those who, as directors and as members of its faculty, are administering its affairs. The committee feel, moreover, that while the Assembly has not been officially informed, the Presbytery of New York has taken steps that look toward a prosecution of Dr. Briggs on the charge of heresy; that well-known facts should be so far recognized as to secure from the Assembly the protection of the good name of Dr. Briggs in the discussion of the question that will come before the Assembly through this report, and also to prevent an expression of opinion on the part of this Assembly that could be justly regarded as prejudgment of the case that will soon, as it now appears, assume the form of a judicial process in the Presbytery of New York. It cannot be too carefully observed that the question before this Assembly is not whether Dr. Briggs, as a Presbyterian minister, has so far contravened the teaching of the Westminster Confession of Faith as to have made himself liable to a judicial censure, but whether, in view of the utterances contained in the inaugural address, already referred to, and the disturbing effect which they have produced throughout the Church, the election of Dr. Briggs to the chair of Biblical Theology in Union Theological Seminary should be disapproved. Your committee have examined the law of the Church regarding the relation of the General Assembly to the theological seminaries under its care. The relation of the Assembly to the Union Theological Seminary, so far as the appointment of professors is concerned, is embodied in the following statement taken from page 390 of the New Digest.

Having cited the statement referred to, the report continued as follows:

It appears, then, that according to the items of the compact quoted above, the directors of the Union Theological Seminary have conceded to the Assembly the right to veto the appointment of professors, and that an election is complete unless vetoed by the next Assembly following the election. Your committee would have been disposed to recommend that the report of the directors of Union Theological Seminary to this Assembly, so far as it referred to the transfer of Dr. Briggs to the chair of Biblical Theology, be referred to the next Assembly, if such a disposition of the matter had been possible; but the Assembly has clearly no power to postpone action. The control of the Church over the election of Dr. Briggs ceases with the dissolution of this present Assembly. Your committee are constrained, therefore, to say that in their judgment it is the duty of the Assembly to disapprove of the appointment of Dr. Briggs to the Edward Robinson chair of Biblical Theology in Union Theological Seminary.

Your committee desire to say, moreover, that while they are clear in their judgment that the Assembly has the right to veto the appointment of Dr. Briggs to the chair of Biblical Theology, it is possible to impose a meaning upon the apparently unambiguous phraseology of the compact between the General Assembly and the directors of the Union Theological Seminary, that would lead to a different conclusion. Fairness also requires us to say that the Assembly is one of the parties of the compact that it is called upon to construe. While your committee are of the opinion that the compact in question did not contemplate the distinction between the election of a person to be a professor and the appointment of one already a professor to the work of a certain department of instruction, it cannot be denied that such a distinction exists; the one act conferring status, the other only assigning duties. The seemingly irregular course of the directors of the Union Theological Seminary, whereby Dr. Briggs was inducted into office before the Assembly had been advised of his appointment, is doubtless to be attributed to their mode of construing their contract with the General Assembly. While your committee are sure that the Assembly will not, and should not, admit its right of disapproval is restricted to the original election of a person to a professorship of Biblical Theology in that seminary, and while they are of the opinion that, acting according to the light it now has, the Assembly cannot but disapprove of the appointment of Dr. Briggs to the professorship of Biblical Theology in that seminary, they are nevertheless of the opinion that, in the interest of the mutual relations of confidence and cordial respect subsisting between the Union Theological Seminary and the General Assembly, it would be eminently proper for the Assembly to appoint a committee to confer with the directors of the Union Theological Seminary in regard to the relations of said seminary to the General Assembly, and report to the next General Assembly. The committee, therefore, recommend the adoption of the following resolutions:

I. *Resolved,* That in the exercise of its right to veto the appointment of professors in Union Theological Seminary the General Assembly hereby disapproves of the appointment of the Rev. Charles A. Briggs, D. D., to the Edward Robinson professorship of Biblical Theology in that seminary, by transfer from another chair in said seminary.

II. *Resolved,* That a committee, consisting of eight ministers and seven ruling elders, be appointed by the General Assembly to confer with the directors of Union Theological Seminary in regard to the relations of said seminary to the General Assembly, and to report to the next General Assembly.

Before considering the report of the committee I wish to call attention to a statement of the chairman on reading it:

I would like to say that this committee have felt the responsibility that has been placed upon them; that they have not felt at liberty to divide this responsibility with any one; that they have studiously avoided consulting with any one who may have been supposed to have preconceived opinions on either side of the question; and having reached our conclusions, we present them to the Assembly for such action as the Assembly in its wisdom may see fit to take.

Was this not equivalent to saying that they deliberately refused to seek, or to receive, any light from anybody in reference to the momentous question which they were appointed to consider? Were these fifteen commissioners already omniscient when they shut themselves up in committee? Would their minds henceforth of necessity be biassed, or misled, by any addition to their knowledge touching the Union Seminary and Dr. Briggs? I say nothing about the other "side;" but so far as the Union Seminary was concerned, it had good right to be heard before that committee, if it desired or cared to do so. Three of its directors, Drs. Parkhurst, Dickey and White, were present in the Assembly, the first two as commissioners, Dr. White as Corresponding Member. Dr. Dickey stated that he offered, as a member of the Union Board of Directors, to give the committee any information in his power; not "preconceived opinions," but simple information. Dr. White made the same offer, both orally and in writing, and he was assured by Dr. Patton that the committee would be glad to hear him. He fully expected to be heard; but the committee "studiously avoided" consulting with him. In the letter to Dr. Field, already quoted, Dr. Parkhurst thus referred to the course of the committee:

> There were three of the directors of Union Seminary present in the Assembly, and we naturally supposed that the committee would like to have the light turned on, and that they would be pleased to confer with us before bringing in their verdict. Such simplicity on our part may be pitiable, but it is hardly censurable. Two out of these three even went so far as to volunteer their services, and to suggest to Dr. Patton's committee that we should be willing and glad to come before them, and state any facts that they might wish to question us upon. They met our overtures so far as to say that they should be glad to hear anything that we would communicate. One of us in particular was informed that such citation would be made. Nothing came of it. *Not one of us was sent for.* All of which means that that committee was constructed with the definite purpose of vetoing Dr. Briggs' transfer.

But this slight put upon the three directors of Union Seminary was only a prelude to a far greater slight put upon the seminary itself. It is true that the report of the committee distinctly recognized the fact that Union Seminary was a party in the case and had rights of its own as over against the Assembly. And yet the report recommended an *ex parte* decision of the vital question at issue without consulting in the least Union Seminary. The consultation was to come after the matter had been practically, and so far as that Assembly was concerned, irrevocably settled.

The exposition of the case in the report, more fully given in Dr. Patton's speeches and in those of other members of the committee, was remarkable for the manner in which it utterly ignored the deliberate action and testimony of the Board of Directors of Union Seminary, as also the carefully prepared statement of its faculty. These were not, it is true, officially made known to the Assembly, but neither was the action of the Presbytery of New York, looking to a judicial process in the case of Dr. Briggs; and yet the Standing Committee on Theological Seminaries kept that action constantly in mind in framing their report and *urged the Assembly to do so in considering it.* Why was not the Assembly also informed in this report of the exact position taken both by the Board of Directors and by the faculty of the seminary? Why was not the Assembly distinctly told that the board, by a unanimous vote and after careful investigation, had virtually pronounced the charges against Dr. Briggs unfounded, and that the faculty of the institution had done the same thing? Was this solemn testimony also "studiously avoided" on the ground that it consisted of "preconceived opinions"? *

Let me repeat the language of Dr. Patton's report: "The interest of the Union Theological Seminary should be most carefully considered, *and great respect*

* The action of the board in establishing the new chair and transferring Dr. Briggs to it, Dr. Frazer's charge, the resolutions of the Board of Directors sustaining and promising to stand by Dr. Briggs, and also the statement of the faculty will all be found in the Appendix.

should be had for the judgment of those who, as directors and as members of the faculty, are administering its affairs. The committee feel, moreover, that while the Assembly has *not been officially informed,* the Presbytery of New York has taken steps that look toward a prosecution of Dr. Briggs on the charge of heresy; that *well-known facts should be so far recognized as to secure from the Assembly the protection of the good name of Dr. Briggs* in the discussion of the question that will come before the Assembly through this report." Why, I repeat, was not the Assembly informed of "well-known facts" in the case of Union Seminary though not "officially reported"?

The debate upon the report of the Standing Committee on Theological Seminaries opened on May 28th and closed late on May 29th. Much of the discussion, while able and very earnest, was yet quite irrelevant. A good deal of it consisted in what is called beating about the bush. The first and fundamental point, namely, that of *jurisdiction,* was hardly touched upon except in the report of the committee.

With regard to this question the friends of the seminary were handicapped and tongue-tied from the outset. Their case was simply given away by the statement that the technical distinction, if any existed, between an original appointment and a transfer, *need not be discussed,* inasmuch as the directors of Union Seminary, at their meeting on May 12th, *had unanimously voted not to plead this distinction.* At that meeting the Executive Committe had presented to the board a report to the effect that it would be unwise to assume in advance that the General Asembly would misconceive the extent of its prerogative; and in any event it was better at this time not to raise an issue by the sending up of a resolution upon the distinction between an "appointment" and a "transfer." As the misstatement about the action of the board, strangely enough, met with no contradiction, the friends of the seminary had nothing to do but to oppose the adoption of Dr. Patton's report as best they could. Some of them did this directly; others by urging an amendment offered by Dr. Logan, to the effect that Dr. Briggs' transfer be disapproved "for the present;" and others still by advocating a substitute to Dr. Logan's amendment prepared by Dr. Worcester; both of which contemplated the postponement of final action to the next Assembly. But the distinction between the original election and a transfer, having been waived, the advocates of a veto had it all their own way. And their own way consisted in two things; first, to assert very positively that Dr. Briggs ought to be vetoed; and second, that he must be vetoed now or never.

The discussion, as I have said, was able and very earnest; and now that the excitement of the hour is all gone, much of it is full of interest and instruction. Some of the speeches have a historical value as photographs of the thoughts and impressions that ruled the

Assembly of 1891. I will quote from a few of them. The opening speech was made by Professor Henry Preserved Smith, of Lane Seminary. It discussed mainly Dr. Briggs' theological position and character, defending him with much scholarly ability and in an excellent spirit. Among the liveliest speeches was one by Dr. Bartlett, of Washington. Here are passages from it:

If there is any way in which all parties could be considered, and in which the unity and harmony of this great Presbyterian Church could be preserved, I am certain there are no two purposes about the advisability of doing just that thing. Now we are here as a company of Christian believers. I am in favor of the immediate action on this report, if action must be taken—and I don't say that we should veto this appointment "for the present." The imputation always is by men who argue for the higher criticism, that every Presbyterian minister is a fool, and that nobody ever read the Bible or had any private secret revelations but themselves. (Laughter.) I wish to say that over thirty years ago I was in the German universities, and I can take Dr. Briggs' books and do for them with absolute certainty what he guessed at with Moses, and can show him where he took every one of his positions from a rationalist German professor over thirty years ago; and I am prepared here to vindicate that statement. (Applause.) Now, gentlemen, there is scholarship and there is scholarship. No one ever doubted but what Strauss was a scholar. He is not a very learned man, and he began his career by tearing Moses to pieces, and he ended by stripping Christ of everything but being a plain Nazarene peasant. Yes, there is scholarship and scholarship. Why, Ignatius Donnelly is a scholar. He has marvellous secrets that nobody else has ever pried into. And right here I wish to say as to these intimations—in all these addresses that I have heard on the higher scholarship—about the marvellous teachings they are gabbing about, the wonderful things that they see which nobody else has ever explored—why, gentlemen, you could talk that a thousand years and back to peasants, but that is the charlatanism of scholarship to-day. I tell you, we know every fact that any man knows on higher criticism or anything else. There is water in the sea, there is water in the air and there is water in the rivers; but they are in communication with each other. Now, bring out your facts. The truth of it is that there are some peculiar minds in every age that look upon a class of facts that are perfectly familiar to Christian scholars, and they see in them the solution of great, doubtful and perplexed problems, which the great average level-headed scholarship of the day doesn't see. They have the same state of facts, but they differ in their interpretation. For instance, there are seven or eight hundred theories as to the origin of the Pentateuch. Now, I, the great level-headed scholar, look over them, and I state what I see, and I say it raises great doubt in my mind. And so the great scholar gives his students all the information he has upon it; brings it from the depths and puts it before them. Now, I say, state it, bring it before the students, keep nothing back, they are entitled to it. But they are entitled as well not to have a man with a peculiar tendency of mind and a peculiar mental sympathy fix the stamp of his authority on some one of those theories and say that, if he knows anything about Moses, Moses did not write the Pentateuch. Now, that is what I complain of. The higher criticism doubt has proved that Bacon wrote Shakespeare. In the Oxford investigations as to the origin of Homer they proved, I believe, that Homer did not write Homer, but that Homer was really written by another man of the same name. (Laughter.)

A member—"I rise to a question of order, Mr. Moderator."

Dr. Bartlett—Well, rise—and sit down again. You have had your time on this thing, and I propose to have mine. (Cries of "Order," "Order.")

A member—"I rise to a question of order."

Dr. Bartlett—Yes, this is the form of liberty accorded. In the name of liberty men often become bigots. They never dare to hear the truth.

A member—"I wish the chair would decide upon my question of order, whether the position of Homer and of Ignatius Donnelly has anything to do with the amendment before the house."

Dr. Bartlett—It is an illustration. (Laughter.) I was going to move a committee, consisting of Donnelly and Keely and Briggs and half a dozen others, to settle all questions of modern times. (Laughter.) I wish further to say a word about scholarship. The impression is always made that we don't want light. We say let the light in. The Presbyterian Church seeks scholars, but it does not on insufficient evidence ask men to draw inferences and shatter the very foundations of faith.

And now in regard to heresy. This is not an age of heresy-hunting. Why, there is no such thing in the air. The response that the Presbyterian Church officially has made to ten years of heresy-hunting is seen this morning in the report of this committee. The heretic has hunted the Church, and not the Church the heretic, if there is any heresy. For ten long years in book after book, periodical after periodical—culminating in the inaugural address—the

Presbyterian Church has been pursued. The man has rubbed against it with chips on his shoulder, defying it in every way. Now, I say that even a fire company has a right to have rules. Their rule is that their members shall wear red shirts. A fellow comes in with a blue shirt, and says he is going to wear it. Of course it is a small matter what color their shirts shall be, but their rule is that only red shirts shall be worn. Now, I say that any society has a right to have some defined rules, and after a Church has been pursued for more than ten years on this question, I say it is to be commended for long-suffering patience and for tender mercy and for quietness and peace. The implication has always been that there is heresy being sought; that this is an age of thumbscrews and all that species of humbug. In this case it does not apply. Every Church is free, but the Church must be free enough to decide the question independently and fairly. I like Professor Smith's dog story. It was a good one, and it reminded me of one that I will tell you. We had a bench show in Washington this winter and there were several $3,000 and $4,000 and I believe one $5,000 dog exhibited there. One day this $5,000 dog got out. He was a rather ferocious fellow, though very expensive, and running down the street he seized one of my fellow-citizens in a convenient place in the back (laughter,) and his owner, who was chasing him, cried out to the citizen who had been seized: "Don't injure that dog, you might spoil him, and he is a very valuable dog"—and all the while the dog was gnawing away, and the poor man had the impression that he was not in any great danger of injuring the dog, but that the dog was in great danger of injuring him. And so it is. We have been pursued and finally caught, and we wish for them to make the apology. Who has made this disturbance? Is it the

Presbyterian Church, through spies and queer and double construction chasing a man down to convict him of heresy? The Church is forced to regard it, and we simply say: Let go. Let us alone. And if the time has come when you must go out from the beautiful land of Egypt under the repression of this awful Pharaoh—the Presbyterian Church—we say, go, and take all your intimate friends with you. (Laughter and applause.) There is the end of the matter. We must face it fairly. There is no personal thing about it. We have talked of trying to save Professor Briggs. I know him, and I love him personally, as a man. But there is a question about saving the seminary and about saving the Church of God. The physician, when he came out from the sick chamber, said the mother was dead, and the child was dead, but he thought he might possibly save the husband. (Laughter.) I think it is about time for us to save the Church.

In kindness my heart responds to every kindly feeling. I was a Union Seminary man. I was there under that grand scholar whose fame is over the earth, Edward Robinson. I was under the scholarship and careful training of Henry B. Smith. I was under the superb rhetorician, Hitchcock, and I was there under that Chesterfield of a teacher, old Dr. Skinner, so sweet in his exterior and a St. John at his soul. In that elder day to be a Roman was greater than to be a king. I confess I have stood all my life in the advance line. I have been a radical of the radicals, but I drew the line when I have known the quality of this criticism for over thirty years—and I got it fresh from Germany, too—I know its tendency, and I know where it leads. Give us the learning, give us the study of the books, give us professors that know how to handle it. The implication always is that it is never studied in any other seminary but New York; but I believe it is studied in every theological seminary of the earth, and I believe that in them all to-day these things are current facts. Bring them to their natural result, and then let the students find that the subordinate things are relegated to the rear, that we are not ordained to discover whether Moses wrote the Pentateuch or not, but to preach Christ.

Dr. Israel W. Hathaway, of Jersey City, opened the discussion on the 29th of May. Here follow some passages from his strong speech in favor of Dr. Logan's amendment:

It is one of the glories of our Presbyterian Church that every minister, elder and brother is to do his own thinking. Notwithstanding my regard for these brethren in high places, yet I must in duty to my own conscience and to the Presbytery which I represent here, do my own thinking. We have seen here the master-strokes of the great giants of debate; but nevertheless I in my humble place have the temerity to controvert their conclusions. This beautiful argument, so finely drawn by Dr. Patton, is builded upon the supposition that it is impossible for us to postpone this action. Dr. Patton said here yesterday in our hearing that he wished it were possible, that we all would love to postpone this action if it were possible. Now, I claim that it is not in the precedents of the ecclesiastical courts of our Church, in interpreting the law, to give that construction to the technical interpretation of the law as it is given in the civil courts. It has never been the custom of the Presbyterian Church so to do. I will admit that technically they are right, but that is the letter that killeth, while the spirit giveth life. And it will be a sad day for the Presbyterian Church when we allow the technicalities of the law to defeat justice. It is that justice may prevail, and not that we may use technicality in order to defeat justice, that our ecclesiastical courts are constituted.

It is upon this point now that I make my argument that it is in the precedents of the Presbyterian Church to interpret this in the spirit and not in the letter. And I say that on that supposition and upon that fact all the argument of Dr. Patton topples to the ground. He admits it himself if we can maintain this point. And now, brethren, I ask you to note for a moment the form of that report. There is no reason given. Dr. Patton tells us that the reason why there are no reasons given is that it would be unjust, that it would be unfair, that it would prejudice the case before the New York Presbytery. Well, now, I ask you in all candor—for I have the utmost confidence in the judgment and the scholarship of all the members of this body, and in their ability to think for themselves—I ask you, brethren, whether you have carefully noted what the ultimate effect of this position is? Why, sir, who ever heard of a man being condemned without a reason given? And this report is thus drawn without reason. It seems to me, whether in the intent of the committee or not, it is a fact that its effect will be to catch all possible votes, that you may read into it all the reasons that you choose. The very widest opportunity is given for every member to have his own reason. Some of our brethren who will vote to sustain this report will so vote because they feel that Dr. Briggs is heretical. Others of you will vote to sustain this report because you feel that the infelicities of his manner and his idiosyncrasies incapacitate him for his position. One will vote upon one ground and another will vote upon another, because there are no reasons given.

And now one word as to the unfairness of all that. Why, I had rather meet a thousand foes with square reasons given than an inference. If there be any unfairness in putting the reasons in, there is an hundredfold more unfairness in leaving the reasons out, because then it is open to all manner of construction.

And then Dr. Patton, in your hearing, after saying it would be unfair and unjust, proceeded to give us the reasons in part, and said that there were many others lying back, opening the field for our imagination to play in its largest scope. Now I ask you furthermore, what will be lost by postponing this for a year? Where is the danger? Why, it is said here that the Church is being run down. Our brother from Washington yesterday drew his illustration of the dog, you remember. Why, if the great Presbyterian Church of America is likely to be destroyed by this man, then how much is it worth? The danger, dear friends, is on the other side. How long has this beloved brother been a professor in this seminary? He has been teaching the same things that he will teach to-day, and has the Church been ruined thereby? Can we not afford to wait one more year? And I am sure, brethren, that our brother, by reason of the warning and by feeling the pulse of the Church will adjust himself to the conditions, if time be given.

Dr. Patton says, "Have we not the right?" I concede the right. Shylock had the right to have the pound of flesh. So has this Assembly the right to veto and destroy the usefulness forever of that brother, and perhaps lose the Union Seminary to our beloved Church. Dr. Patton himself intimated that it might go into the civil courts, that it might take its course through all the courts and vex our Church for years. And this action that it is proposed to take is the very thing that will precipitate that result. But let us not claim the pound of flesh. Let us not draw the blood that shall make much of the inheritance of our Church confiscate. Now, dear brethren, I plead not for Dr. Briggs, for I am a loyal Princetonian. God has given me a son who has chosen the ministry, who graduated with high honors under Dr. Patton last June, and who has already made his arrangements with our beloved Moderator to enter the seminary next September, while he might attend Union and board at home; but with my advice and approval he goes to Princeton, and thus I prove my loyalty to that institution. I plead not for Dr. Briggs; I plead for charity, I plead for peace, I plead for the broadest liberty of investigation in the scholarship of our Church. And if it be possible for Dr. Briggs, or those whom he represents, to destroy our Bible, then I want it destroyed. I do not give a farthing for a Bible that is conserved by the deliverance of a General Assembly. Let us not be afraid of dangers that I think have been magnified in our mind. I think a sort of wave of enthusiasm for the old orthodoxy has taken possession of us, so that we know not of what spirit we are. I plead that you will halt; I plead that you will for a moment wait and think of that which is before you. We are making history to-day, brethren. Let us be careful that we do not make a history that our children will have to apologize for, as the Presbyterian Church has ever been apologizing for Calvin when he consented to the burning of Servetus in Geneva. Let us not make history so that our children will have to apologize for our position as some have in their position toward Albert Barnes. Let us halt until the waters shall quiet down. I plead not for Briggs, I plead not for heresy. I plead simply for the broadest charity and the broadest investigation, the most liberal investigation in our Church. I do not believe that the Presbyterian Church can afford to take any other position than this. Some of my brethren have said to me: "We care not what the world says; we must not be influenced by the world." But, dear brethren, we are dealing with a world lost in sin. We are here to bring them to grace, to bring them to a knowledge of the saving love of God in Jesus Christ our Lord. We have to deal with the world, and the world may misinterpret us if we take this action to-day. They will not even give you the credit of honesty of purpose, some of them; and so I plead that you will in the magnanimity of your hearts consent to the adoption of this amendment in the interest of the peace and harmony of our Church.

Suppose that it was one of you. Suppose it was you, my brother, that had made some mistake; that had said things that you ought not to have said, and the eye of the Church was focussed upon you, and that this General Assembly was discussing your case. Would you consider it a great thing if they held off their hands for a little until this matter could be investigated in the judicial manner provided in the form of government in our Church, through the Presbytery of New York? I think not. I think you would think it was a very hasty action to do otherwise. It makes a vast difference, brethren, whose ox is being gored. So it is for this that I plead. Let us turn to the great thoughts and objects of our Church. This is not the greatest subject. This sinks into insignificance beside the great commission, "Go ye into all the world and preach the Gospel to every creature." Why, if the position taken by Dr. Briggs be false it will come to nothing. If it be true, what are we that we shall stand against it? lest with Paul we be found fighting against God.

In explaining his amendment—"for the present"—Dr. Logan said:

It is not a very gracious task to undertake to attack such an ecclesiastical lawyer as Dr. Patton, or such civil lawyers as have spoken from the platform on this subject. But it is a queer kind of law that these brethren have given us, as it strikes an old Presbyterian. I am amazed at the report of this committee. . . . I say it is not wise as a work of administration to take this judgment as announced by the committee which impeaches the act of the Board of Directors of Union Seminary, which impeaches the character of Dr. Briggs as a professor—and all this without having the parties before us, and without having a full understanding of the case, and in the face of those categorical answers to direct questions, which the Board of Directors have issued as a vindication of their acts—I say it is not wise. It will lead to bickerings and misunderstandings; it will lead to controversy, and it will have a bad effect. But, on the other hand, if we go slowly, if we go to these men kindly, they may see the wrong; the things that need mending may be mended, and, if not, the evil will develop itself distinctly so that the Church of God shall be able wisely to destroy it. That is my reason for this amendment. I beg you to walk slowly and reach a decision, on which you may be able to present a united Church before the living God for the glory of our one Lord. (Applause).

Dr. Ramsey, of New York, followed Dr. Logan in a vigorous protest against the report of the committee. Here is an extract from his speech:

I venture to doubt the constitutionality of any Presbytery passing over its right of original jurisdiction to the court of final appeal. I believe, sir, that whatever we do in this case, however we may disguise it, it will be a virtual trial of the case.

This leads me, therefore, to the second point, that I do not think it constitutional. This proposed action infringes on the right of the individual. Dr. Briggs is not here. He has no case in court. The directors of the Union Theological Seminary in their plight, in their anxiety, asked that Dr. Briggs and—mark now, I am not a Briggs man in the sense that that term is used—solemnly to state what he believed, and he wrote that short catechism, with its yeas and nays, and which, if it had been handed in by any other man than Professor Briggs, would have been received as the correct interpretation of previous utterances. Instead of that, sir, as you all know, it has met with a destructive analysis, and this catechism has been finally interpreted back by the inaugural. Brethren, if there is one thing I do, I stand for the rights of a man, whether he be my friend or my foe. I do not believe that this glorious Presbyterian Church can ever let the semblance of a trial pass without the due forms had been taken; and yet we are drifting toward a virtual verdict before the Presbytery has even framed its indictment.

Now, that is the case of this man as he stands before us. His last utterance, solemn utterance, satisfactory to the directors of Union Seminary, has been utterly ignored here; and, sir, if it means anything, it means that we doubted its sincerity. Perhaps you say, "we have the right." But God Almighty grant that the day be far distant when we may impeach an uncondemned brother's veracity or receive his words as if they came from a Delphic oracle, or assume that his writings may be read between the lines. If the evidence is convincing, I shall follow up this case and be found voting against Dr. Briggs. Yet, sir, he shall have any guard thrown around him that I can possibly aid in giving him in any stage of his trial. . . . I think this action is an infringement on the constitutional rights of the Presbytery of New York. It is an advanced shadow of a decision, at least in a higher court. . . . If this goes through the whole matter of a trial may secure a weak force. I protest as a New York Presbyterian against any action by this Assembly that anticipates final action.

Here are a few passages from Dr. Worcester's forcible and manly speech:

When I heard that this matter had been intrusted to some of the clearest brains in the Church I felt reassured, and it was with profound disappointment that I listened to their report when they presented it to this Assembly. The course proposed in that report is an extreme course. Dr. Patton told us yesterday that this was the very least that this Assembly could do. What more could this Assembly do? You cannot hang Dr. Briggs; you cannot imprison him; you cannot cast him out of the Church; you cannot depose him from the ministry; you cannot impeach his orthodoxy or touch his moral character. The one thing that you can do is to veto, bluntly, absolutely, without a reason given, his appointment. Even upon your power to do that the committee admit there rests the shadow of a doubt, sufficient to make them think it necessary to appoint fifteen wise men before another year to clear it away. But in the meantime—and I wonder if I am the only commissioner to whom the relation of the two resolutions in the report was a surprise—while we admit that there may be some question about our authority to do this, we will behead the man and then we will confer with the directors as to whether we had the right to do it.

Then I object to this report because it is an arbitrary report. It says that we disapprove this appointment, and gives no reason. Judge Breckinridge said yesterday, and we all recognize its force, that a judge might often give a wise decision founded on bad reasons, and therefore, it was better never to give reasons if you could help it. But in a matter which touches the standing, the reputation of a man, in a matter which may produce an ecclesiastical trial already initiated, you cannot help it; you have no right to help it. Why, if I remember rightly, it is not so many years since there was a great controversy over the question whether the President of the United States had the right even to behead a postmaster without giving a reason for it. Now we propose to behead officially a theological professor without stating any reason for it. We were told by President Patton that a great many reasons might be given. Why don't the committee give a reason? Mr. Moderator, I fear it was because the committee knew that no one reason would carry a majority of this Assembly with it. Dr. Patton admitted that it would not do to say that it was on account of the idiosyncracries of the Professor. He said the theological reasons, not amounting to a charge of heresy, might have been given; but he admitted that, with all his power of lucid statement, in which he has not a peer in this Assembly, those reasons would be so intricate and obscure that a very few would be able to distinguish them from a charge of heresy. He admitted that it would not do to charge him on the ground that he is not sound in faith, because that would be anticipating the decision of the Presbytery of New York. And the only reason that I could discover that he would urge as a practical reason that might have been given was that Dr. Briggs is under suspicion. Sir, shall we disapprove of this appointment because Dr.

Briggs is under suspicion, when we know that steps have already been initiated to sift this suspicion and ascertain whether it is right or wrong. Is it not one of the principles of our Church to stand by a man who is under suspicion until this suspicion has been sifted to the bottom? At all events I protest against a bare disapproval of this election without any reason being given. I protest against it because it will inevitably, as Mr. Ramsey has so well said, have an influence upon the judicial proceedings of the Presbytery of New York. The world will believe, and the New York Presbytery will believe, that if this Assembly has not suspected Dr. Briggs of serious departure from the faith it would never have taken this action, and the only way in which you can prevent that impression from being made on the mind of the Church and on the mind of the country is to give some other reason with your resolution.

Dr. Erskine opposed the second resolution of the report, and also Dr. Worcester's substitute, but was heard by the Assembly with not a little impatience. This part of his speech, at least, seemed to show that he understood the subject far better than some of his more eloquent brethren. Here is what he said as to the second recommendation of the committee:

It is proposed that we appoint a committee and go and hold a conference with the Union Seminary directors in regard to Dr. Briggs' relation to that seminary, and to give them some advice. Mr. Moderator, what authority have we for that? Where have we any authority in regard to Union Seminary, excepting that which is embraced in the compact between that seminary and us in the articles of agreement which were adopted in the year 1870 in the General Assembly at Philadelphia? And where have we any authority to go to them and advise with them, to do anything outside of the compact? None whatever. This proposition is a misleading proposition. It would have us surrender the only authority we have in regard to the instructions which are given to our candidates for the ministry in Union Seminary, and to assume an authority that does not belong to us. If we do so, we just allow ourselves to be misled and outwitted. The only control as an Assembly that we have over the theological seminary—I mean directly, except through the Synod and the Presbytery where we may reach ministers and elders—is embraced in that compact which has been entered into between the General Assembly and our theological seminaries, and the power that we have is the power of disapproval in regard to a professor that has been elected; and if you surrender that power, you surrender all the controlling power that you have in regard to the instructions that are given in these seminaries. Suppose you adopt this substitute; suppose you appoint your most prominent, most influential and wisest representatives. You go there and make your propositions. Why, they will receive you very cordially and politely, and say: "Gentlemen, we will take this into consideration; we will take time to consider this. We are obliged to you; we shall treat it with great respect and great courtesy." And they will take it into consideration, and what will be the result? You can all anticipate it. The majority of the directors in that theological seminary have sat upon this question again and again. There is a minority in that board with whom you might deal if you had the power, and they had the power; but the majority of that Board of Directors have acted upon this, and they have expressed their approval and their confidence in the views held by the person in question. And so if we were to go into this arrangement it would be vetoing the great issue. It would be surrendering the power that we have, and it would be putting you in a position just to be treated with simple courtesy by that board. You have no authority over them, and I don't know that they have any authority to carry out the proposition that is made.

This common sense view of the relations of the Assembly to the directors of the Union Seminary may very well be compared with that expressed, or implied, by Dr. Patton, for example, in the following passages of his speech :

We have recognized that as a judge we are bound to construe, and we have recognized that as a party Union Seminary claim that their rights have been infringed by our construction, and if they see fit they can take us into the civil courts for a judicial and authoritative interpretation of this compact. . . . Now we understand that you intend to take us in the courts.* Well, brethren, is that the best course to pursue? Can't we talk the matter over? It is possible, you know, that you may be wrong. Is it not possible, therefore, that they may come around? You might elect a man as professor of Elocution, and then transfer him to the chair of Theology. Isn't it possible that the directors will feel that the Assembly was right, after all? Why, certainly. On the other hand, isn't it possible that your committee would change their view, and that they would recommend the next Assembly to reverse the judgment of this Assembly? Isn't that possible? Why, of course it is possible; all things are possible. (Laughter and applause.)

* This was an idle rumor. The board never thought of taking the Assembly into court. How could it have done so?

That would be a representative committee—eight ministers and seven elders, composed of the best men, the wisest lawyers, and to such a committee would we intrust this duty. Isn't it possible that both parties, in their inability to change their views, may say: "Well, we do not want to go to the courts. We remember what Paul said about prosecuting these matters before the heathen court." But cannot the General Assembly on the report of this committee and the Board of Directors of Union Seminary agree to refer the constitutional interpretation of this old compact, which is liable to come up and be a source of disturbance in years to come—refer it, not to this committee, not to the Board of Directors of Union Seminary, but to some Christian men outside, known for their wisdom, praised for their fairness, and saying on our part as a General Assembly, while they say on their part as a Board of Directors, "Dear brethren, we are perfectly willing to let any fair-minded set of men arbitrate this question?" These are the possibilities in the case.*

The vote was taken late in the afternoon of May 29th. It resulted in the adoption of the resolutions of the committee by the overwhelming majority of 447 to 60. On the afternoon of May 28th Judge Breckinridge, a commissioner from St. Louis, at the moment of closing a speech in favor of the report, dropped dead in the presence of the whole Assembly. This startling incident, following so quickly upon the almost equally sudden death of the Rev. Henry J. VanDyke, D.D., professor-elect to the chair of Systematic Theology in

*These quotations, as all others, from the speeches made in the Assembly, are taken from the revised reports of the New York *Tribune*, printed in pamphlet form under the title, The Presbyterian Faith.

Union Seminary—a noble man and one of the foremost leaders in the Presbyterian Church—tended naturally to deepen the serious feeling which already pervaded the Assembly.

I have said that the advocates of a veto had it all their own way, which consisted in asserting very positively that Dr. Briggs ought to be vetoed, and that he must be vetoed "now or never." The latter point was urged with great solemnity and most impressive reiteration. "We are under obligation," said Mr. McCook, "as honest men, as Christian men, to carry out in its exact terms all the provisions of that compact, and we cannot, we dare not, postpone action. We must act now and before the adjournment of this Assembly, or the right to disapprove is lost FOREVER." Dr. Patton was equally emphatic as to the "now or never," giving as a reason how *he* should feel if threatened with a veto in the indefinite future. Here is what he said:

The question is whether we have the right to veto. I think we have. . . . Very well, suppose we have that right, how long does that right last? One General Assembly has said that it can last only during the Assembly immediately following the election of the professor. Very well, I think that is a good rule. It may seem a singular thing for me to play the role of an advocate of freedom; (laughter) but I am. I am a professor. I have the prejudices of my class, and I tell you that, in the name of that class, I will protest against the right of an Assembly to hold the threat of a veto over me for a dozen years in succession. They have their chance once, and if they don't veto my appointment then, they ought not to have the chance four or five years hence. Suppose you admit that you can postpone this veto. By and by some other professor will be saying something that is not right, as we think, and we shall say, "Let us go and veto him. We did not veto him then, but we will do it now." Who is safe? I tell you it is in the interest of freedom; it is in the interest of a proper freedom that you should not allow that it is possible to postpone the veto. You have to do it now, or not at all. Very well. Now, then, you have the right to veto, and if you veto, you must veto now.

A veto, after all, was a terrible thing to be threatened with! It seems to have made the chairman of the Standing Committee on Theological Seminaries himself squirm to think of being the possible subject of it. Theological freedom, too, might be at stake; and theological freedom, the proper liberty of a Christian scholar and teacher, in the last decade of the nineteenth century, was a very serious matter. If it must be done, let it be done quickly and put the man out of his misery. Precisely so; but who would have guessed it from other parts of this speech?

But even admitting, for the moment, that the Assembly had a right to veto Dr. Briggs' transfer, was it true that *now* or *never* was the absolute condition of its exercise? Nothing could be further from the truth. The rule adopted by the Assembly, that the veto power must be used, if at all, by the Assembly to which the election is reported, formed no part of the agreement of 1870, but was suggested and adopted a year later. The

Board of Directors of Union Seminary had nothing to do with it. Although a very sensible rule, it was yet in the nature of a mere by-law, belonging to the administrative functions of the Assembly, and in such an exigency might have been suspended without the slightest impropriety. But the leaders of the Assembly—not to speak with any disrespect—seem to have had "compact," as well as the veto of Dr. Briggs, "on the brain," as the phrase is, and so a simple rule of fairness and prudence, with which, however, Union Seminary had nothing to do, took on, in their reasoning, the color and rigidity of a law of the Medes and Persians which changeth not! A good deal in the whole matter impelled one to say with Faust,

—der casus macht mich lachen,

but nothing, I think, like this "now or never" plea.

The Assembly then, it is plain, was fatally misled by the "now or never" plea. That plea was based upon a sheer mistake. But it served its purpose quite as well as if it had been based upon an opinion of Chief Justice Marshall, or upon the latest decision of the United States Supreme Court. It deluded the Assembly into just the right state of mind for the stern work in hand—vetoing Dr. Briggs. See how skillfully Dr. Patton put the case:

We are here; the Presbyteries have sent us here, and the report of the Union Theological Seminary has brought this question right up to the bar of every man's conscience, and you cannot avoid it, and you dare not avoid it. I do not use the word "dare" in an unkind sense at all, I simply use it in the moral sense. There we are. Now for us not to express technical disapproval is for us to express technical approval. And it is not a matter of reflection upon Union Seminary, or a matter of sentiment or regard for their feelings, or a matter of how much disturbance this is going to occasion the Church, but it is a question as to the discharge of a solemn duty at the bar of your conscience and of mine, here and now. Then I think that every man of us will agree that the question is here. It is here. We must say, seeing that we have a right to veto, and seeing that we can never veto, if we do not do it now, we must say whether or no there is occasion for the veto. Now is there an occasion for veto?

Could he have got his hearers just where he wanted them more adroitly? They were in exactly the "solemnized" mood and posture of thought to hear most attentively his answer to the question, "Now is there occasion for veto?" No wonder, as the Detroit reporter said, they listened "spell-bound." This solemn, reiterated plea, "now or never," coupled with the "compact" plea, carried all before it. The only wonder is how sixty commissioners kept cool enough to vote against vetoing Dr. Briggs. I am really afraid I myself should have vetoed Dr. Briggs, had I been a commissioner. As to the skillful way in which the "compact" plea was handled, who can fail to admire it? The chairman of the Committee on Theological Seminaries took the "compact" under his special care and guardianship. He was very jealous of the slightest interference with it, even by so honored and learned an ecclesiastic as Dr. Moore. Hear him:

If we are going to veto under the terms of the compact, we must veto in the terms of the compact.

Dr. Moore (the Permanent Clerk)—"Excuse me, Doctor, a moment. I want to call attention to the fact that while the first of that is the compact, the second is simply the decision of the General Assembly."

Dr. Patton—That is not relevant to my remarks. . . . And so I go back to my statement, in spite of the *instruction* that I have received, and I say that if you intend to veto under the terms of the compact, you must veto in the terms of the compact. Now, what are the terms of the compact? . . . Now, when you talk of disapproving "for the present" you depart from your compact, and you have simply expressed your oral dislike and put the stigma of your moral disapproval upon the case, but you have done nothing.

I tried to count up the number of times in which "compact" occurred in this speech, but my memory failed me. How extremely interested, not to say entertained, Williams Adams, George W. Musgrave, Henry B. Smith, Jonathan F. Stearns and Edwin F. Hatfield would have been in listening to this exposition of "the compact of 1870," and *now* or *never*, by so adroit an ecclesiastic as the president of Princeton College!

The most striking point in the chairman's discussion of the question, whether there was occasion for veto, is "kindness" to Dr. Briggs. Can the records of American Presbyterianism furnish another instance of such peculiar kindness? It was "kindness" to Dr. Briggs that forced him to turn a deaf ear to all entreaties for "reasons." "Well, but," it is said, "couldn't you state some reasons without involving the question of heresy?" "Yes," I said, "I could." "Well," said some one, "you have been working in theology; couldn't you draft such a report?" "Yes," I said, "I might." But "kindness" to Dr. Briggs forbade it. Here are some passages about Dr. Briggs:

When your feelings cool down, brethren, you will see that this is a much kinder thing than you think, and it is not so cold, either; we made it cold, but it is not so cold. . . . So far as Dr. Briggs is concerned, I will yield to none of his friends, not even the best, in my recognition of his learning, in my admiration of his industry, in my conviction concerning his piety. He is my friend. It is my privilege to call him so. I venture to hope that in spite of my relations to this debate he will not be unwilling to reciprocate my expression of the relationship between us. . . . I wish to say that we have done this in the interest of kindness to Dr. Briggs. I would be unwilling for the Assembly to pass a resolution, in the full body of which there should be the stigma of a constitutional kind, that would affirm that Dr. Briggs' idiosyncrasies are such that he should not be a professor in a seminary. Why, a man's idiosyncrasies go with him through life, and I don't know but they go into the middle state, (laughter) and I am not willing to say that Dr. Briggs is not fit to be a professor in any seminary. I am not willing to say that he is not fit to be a professor in Union Seminary. Not at all. . .

I said, "Brethren, it is not kind, it is not right for the Assembly, in its explicit utterance on the adoption of a report, to say a word that can be construed, even remotely, to the detriment of Dr. Briggs." That is why we did not give reasons, but it was not because we had no reasons. We had reasons.

Dr. Patton and his committee, then, had reasons. The reasons appear to have been as plentiful as blackberries. But nobody was the wiser for them. Nobody is the wiser for them to this day. I have been unable to find any authentic record of them; otherwise they would have appeared in these pages. Every now and then at Detroit they seemed, to be sure, on the very point of leaking out, both in the speeches of the chairman and in those of several members of his committee. In other speeches they not only leaked out, they came gushing out, explicit and unmistakable. I said that a good deal of the discussion at Detroit consisted in beating about the bush. In this the chairman surpassed all his brethren. The logical agility and deftness with which he beat, and beat about, this particular bush of "no reasons" was something remarkable. He kept saying, as it were:

Fain would I, but I dare not; I dare, and yet I may not.

It appears, then, that while the Standing Committee on Theological Seminaries had plenty of reasons—good, valid reasons, as they believed—for recommending the veto of Dr. Briggs' transfer, they purposely concealed these reasons, alike from the Assembly and from the

Christian public. Nobody, I repeat, knew then, or knows to this day, unless privately informed by some member of the committee, what was the real ground of the decision for which they were responsible to Christian scholarship, to history, and to God. They themselves acted, as they said, in the light of their own reason and conscience. They left the Assembly to act in the dark and adopt their decision on trust. If the President of the United States disapprove a bill passed by Congress, he is required to return the bill with his objections. If the Governor of New York disapprove of a bill passed by the Legislature, he sends it back with his reasons for vetoing it. And this is according to the true genius of republican liberty. Our American idea of free government abhors arbitrary, reasonless exercise of power. If the agreement of 1870 had given the General Assembly "the right of *peremptory* veto," as proposed in the letter of Dr. A. A. Hodge to Henry B. Smith, then, indeed, the recommendation of Dr. Patton's committee would have been in order. A *peremptory* veto is a veto that requires no explanation. It is like an edict of the Sultan—an arbitrary act, pure and simple. The American Presbyterianism, in which Union Seminary was born and nurtured, was never fond of such acts. It likes to give a good reason for what it does, as well as for what it believes. The power of intelligible, rational, Christian disapproval, not a *peremptory* veto, was the power conceded by Union Seminary in 1870.

Before passing from this topic I desire to add still another word respecting the course of the Standing Committee on Theological Seminaries. When I wrote the article in *The Evangelist* of May 21, 1891, on the veto power, I purposely restrained myself, and carefully omitted to say what would be, in my judgment, the inevitable effects of a veto of Dr. Briggs' transfer. In this perhaps I erred; if so, it was in the interest of the peace of the Church. The crisis seemed to me serious enough to demand the utmost caution, not to say reticence, on the part of every friend of Union Seminary. Having expressed the opinion that the question about the veto power touched in *principle* all the other theological seminaries in the Presbyterian Church, I closed my article as follows:

> The General Assembly is shortly to convene and show its judgment upon the matter. Nor, for myself, have I any fear of the result. Many of the ablest, wisest, and best men in the Presbyterian Church, both of the ministry and eldership, will sit in that Assembly, and they will not be likely to countenance any hasty or unjust action.

This was my honest feeling and expectation. When, therefore, the result came, my disappointment was all the keener, especially with regard to Dr. Patton. Although my acquaintance with him was slight, I had for many years admired, as I admire still, his varied gifts and his remarkable power of swaying a popular assembly. His oft-expressed reverence for the character and memory of my bosom friend, Henry B. Smith, touched me in a very tender spot. There were few men in the Presbyterian Church, perhaps there was not another one, of whom I could have honestly said just what in my letter to Dr. Field, in *The Evangelist* of June 11, I wrote of him. And what was there written of him expresses so truly my feeling and opinion still, that I can only repeat it here:

> He had an opportunity to speak a word and strike a blow for justice, for sacred scholarship, for reasonable liberty, both of thought and teaching, for the suppression of clamor, as an ecclesiastical and theological force, and for the highest interests of Christian truth, which, like the shot fired by the "embattled farmers" at Lexington, would have been "heard round the world." Acting, I do not question, from a strong sense of duty to the Presbyterian Church, he failed to seize it; and he will be a fortunate man indeed, if Providence ever again entrusts to him such an opportunity.*

The wrong done to Union Seminary by the General Assembly at Detroit, especially in the composition and action of its Standing Committee on Theological Seminaries, met with severe censure in one of the strongest and most conservative religious newspapers of the

*Since writing the above criticism of the action of the Standing Committee on Theological Seminaries, the stenographic report of the meetings of the Board of Directors and the Committee of Conference has been put into my hands. In this report is a very frank statement by Dr. Patton himself of the reasons why Dr. White and Dr. Dickey were not invited to come before his committee at Detroit. It is due to him that this statement should be published. It will be found in the Appendix.

denomination. Here is the judgment of Dr. Gray, the plain-spoken, fearless editor of *The Interior*, pronounced a year later, in a review of the course of Dr. Young, Moderator of the Assembly at Portland, Oregon, in appointing the Judicial Committee and that on Theological Seminaries :

His selections showed that he was not only fair but magnanimous to the minority. He gave them representations on both committees, not only equal to, but larger than their proportion as shown in the votes. This was in the widest contrast to the scandalous proceeding of last year; in that the minority not only had no representation in the Committee on Theological Seminaries, but were denied a hearing before the committee, though they urgently requested it. That was, in our opinion, partly the cause of the defiant attitude taken by Union Seminary. No one can have any doubt in regard to Dr. Young's convictions on the present issues, nor is there doubt of the side he would have taken had he been on the floor of the Assembly. But he is large enough as a man to be what he is, an American Presbyterian.

The principle is that the majority have the right of a majority on the committee, — no one would think of questioning that right—and that the minority have a right to proportionate representation on, and a full hearing before, a committee. This has never been denied in any reputable deliberative body, civil or ecclesiastical, with the single exception which occurred in Detroit, last year. We did not dwell upon it at that time, not wishing to add to the general excitement, but now that it has been fully rectified and the Assembly's dignity restored, we express the hope that no such wrong may ever again mar her fair escutcheon.

(*g*) *The action of the General Assembly in the case of Dr. Briggs as an eye-opener.*

Before closing this chapter I will add a few words about the action at Detroit as an eye-opener. The effect of the veto of Dr. Briggs was instantaneous and far-reaching. In a moment, as by a flash of lightning, the agreement of 1870 was seen, as it had never been seen before. It was seen to involve alarming possibilities of harm to the Presbyterian Church, to free Christian scholarship, and to the cause of theological truth and progress. It was, probably, at once the cause and the subject of more anxious thought in one week after the vote at Detroit, than during all the previous twenty years. That vote revealed it as an arrangement full of explosive mischief. Instead of contributing to the "peace and prosperity of the Church," by promoting mutual confidence and love, it showed itself, of a sudden, as a stirrer up of strife and bitterness. It proved that the many disadvantages, infelicities and perils, which, to those who took an active part in founding the Union Theological Seminary, appeared so serious in the election of professors by the General Assembly itself, were no less incident to the veto power in the election of professors, when exercised by the General Assembly. In other words, the action at Detroit demonstrated that the two principal grounds upon which the veto power had been conceded to the General Assembly by Union Seminary in 1870, were deceptive and untenable. The evils specially deprecated and to be guarded against by the concession of that power were sprung upon the Church in its very first exercise. With the best intentions in the world, both the Board of Directors of the Union Seminary and the General Assembly greatly erred as to the effects which, sooner or later, would be caused by arming the Assembly with authority to forbid, year in and year out, at its absolute discretion, every election of a professor in every Presbyterian theological seminary in the United States.

For a time it may have served, as the ninth "concurrent declaration" of 1869 had been intended, "to allay the apprehensions of any who might imagine that the sudden accession and intermingling of great numbers [that is, the coming in of the New School branch] might overbear those who had hitherto administered these seminaries which had been under the control of one branch of the Church. It was intended as a measure for the maintenance of confidence and harmony, and not as indicating the best method for all future time." As a measure for the maintenance of confidence and harmony during that critical period of transition from a divided to a reunited Church, it was, perhaps, of use. But time had long since allayed any apprehensions, which the Old School might have felt, of being overborne in the administration of their seminaries by a sudden accession of the New School to equal power in the General Assembly. Old School and New School were fast becoming obsolete terms. And yet who can wonder that, in 1870, some "apprehensions," if not "jealousy," with regard to this matter still existed on the Old School side, especially at Princeton?

The General Assembly of the Presbyterian Church in the United States, to return to my point, is a grand and powerful religious body. In its own proper sphere it is a mighty agency for building up and extending the kingdom of God on earth. But it is singularly unfitted to make the best possible choice, or to ascertain and forbid the unwise choice, of a theological professor. The chances seem to me as ten to one that, in all ordinary cases, the choice of a professor in Princeton, or Auburn, or McCormick, or Union, or San Francisco, or any other seminary, will be far more wisely made by its own Board of Directors than by a popular Assembly composed of some five hundred men, living thousands of miles apart, coming together for ten days, subject to numberless misleading influences through ignorance of the candidate, and restrained perhaps by only a feeble sense of direct personal responsibility in the case. Twenty votes in a Board of Directors, composed, as the boards of our theological seminaries usually are, of judicious, experienced, high-minded Christian men, stand for more, and are worth more, than five hundred votes in General Assembly. Of course, the best boards are liable also to commit mistakes. No device or method of election can insure against possible errors and imperfections of human judgment, whether it be the judgment of eight and twenty directors or of five hundred commissioners.

Personally, no man has better reason than I have to speak well of the General Assembly in this regard. I myself bear its *imprimatur* as "the standard of Presbyterian orthodoxy." Under the lead of that apostolic servant of Christ, Dr. Charles C. Beatty, the first General Assembly of the reunited Church, by a unanimous and rising vote, elected me to the chair of Systematic Theology in one of its most important seminaries; and upon my declining the call, re-elected me with similar unanimity in 1871. Never can I cease to feel grateful in remembrance of such uncommon kindness and honor; grateful also in memory of the special tokens of personal interest and good-will which I received from the layman so distinguished at once for his stanch Presbyterianism and his generosity, whose name the Seminary of the Northwest now bears.

I will now proceed to note some of the ways in which the action at Detroit, in the case of Dr. Briggs, proved to be an eye-opener.

(1) In disclosing the doubts and scruples respecting the agreement of 1870 which existed at the time, but had never, so far as I am aware, been made public. I refer more especially to Lane Seminary, which, like Union, was entirely independent of ecclesiastical control. An extract from a letter of the Rev. Henry A. Nelson, D.D., addressed to Hon. James B. Cox, of

Auburn, and published in *The Evangelist* of June 25th, shows what was done at Lane and why it was done. Dr. Nelson was a member of the Joint Committee on Reunion, as well as a professor at Lane, and is known far and wide as an eminently wise and true man. Here is the extract:

Our Lane Seminary charter made its Board of Trustees a close corporation, empowered to fill vacancies in its own membership, and to appoint all professors and instructors, who should hold their chairs *at the pleasure of the board.* Hon. Stanley Matthews, afterward a justice of the United States Supreme Court, was consulted on the legal questions involved. He stated clearly and positively that the Board of Trustees, a corporate body, could not legally delegate any of its powers to the General Assembly or to any other body. . . . Our Board of Trustees adopted the by-law (as its charter empowered it to do) in words like the following, as nearly as I can remember: * "Every election of a professor in this institution shall be reported to the next General Assembly, and if the said Assembly shall by vote express its disapprobation at the election, the professorship in question shall be *ipso facto* vacant from and after such veto of the General Assembly; it being understood that in such case *it is not the pleasure of this board that such professor shall continue in office.*" Judge Matthews said that this by-law, being adopted by the Board of Trustees, could at any time be repealed by the board. The board could not divest itself of this power. But as long as it should keep that rule on its own book and govern itself by it, it would no doubt have

* I give the resolution of the Lane Seminary board exactly as it was passed.—*Moore's Digest*, p. 384.

all the moral effect which was sought for. No one of us imagined that it could have any further legal force or effect than was thus defined by that competent legal adviser.

Dr. E. D. Morris, later professor of Systematic Theology at Lane, occupied in 1870 the chair of Church History in that institution. Dr. Morris has long ranked among the ablest and most judicious writers in this country on questions of ecclesiastical law and polity. *The Evangelist* of July 23, 1891, contained a striking article from his pen, entitled "The Compact of 1870." The following are extracts from this article:

The writer does not hesitate to say at this point, that having occasion in 1871 to look into the matter of *legality*, so far as Lane was concerned, he was led to the conclusion that, in the eye of the civil law, this compact, excellent as it was in intention, was wholly unwarranted. Indeed it was questionable in his judgment whether it lay within the constitutional prerogative of the General Assembly to accept such a function if proffered to it, and the recent experience has appeared to him to give some degree of reasonableness to that doubt. But on the civil side of the matter, it must be ordinarily clear to any student of the charter of that institution, that its trustees are the sole and only party having, or that can have, or gain, any authority whatsoever in the appointment of those who, in whatever capacity, give instruction in it. These trustees are limited by but one condition, that such instructors shall be in good standing in the Presbyterian Church. But they have no right to go to the Assembly to inquire whether such or such a teacher is in good standing, nor has the Assembly any power, by mere resolution, to declare the standing of any such person to be either good or bad. They might go to the records of some Presbytery having jurisdiction, and inquire whether the person involved was *rectus in curia* there; but they could not commit to such a body the matter of approving or disapproving their choice of him as a teacher. In that choice they are absolutely and forever sovereign, with no chartered right to delegate their responsibility to, or even share it in any particular with any other body whatever. If the question were one of financial administration, no court in the land would justify these trustees in calling on the General Assembly to guide or to control them in the care of the funds and properties of that institution, and the same legal principle holds no less truly in the exercise of any other part of their corporate trust. The board of Lane Seminary is in every particular, and at all times, the official authority, and there can be no other.

Such was the view which the writer was compelled to take twenty years ago, so far as one of these three seminaries was concerned, and the recent discussions have served to make it evident that the trustees of Auburn and Union are by the charters of those institutions in a very similar position. Looking at the matter as one of legal principle simply, to be determined judicially, is it not clear that these boards of trust could not hand over to a General Assembly a right of ultimate control over any of the endowments committed to their keeping? And is it not just as clear that they could not ask a General Assembly to create any new department, or prescribe any change in the methods of instruction, or to choose or even nominate a professor for any work within these institutions? All such matters are committed by law to these several boards, and to them alone, in the exercise of their corporate sovereignty, and there is ground for the query whether their failure to exercise such prerogative in the way prescribed by their respective charters would not ultimately work a forfeiture of the funds intrusted to their keeping. No such board could, for example, discharge their corps of instructors and close the institution indefinitely, without becoming subject to civil suit, even though it should resolve to commit its endowments meanwhile to the care and keeping of the General Assembly. And the same principle must apply to all their acts.

Turning from the question of legality to that of *expediency* and *desirableness,* we enter a field more difficult of discussion, yet one where a dispassionate examination will be likely to lead thoughtful men into substantial agreement. The compact is a good one so long as there is no occasion to apply it. As a simple expression of good will and cordial confidence between the parties it is admirable. But the moment a case arises, in which the judgment of any of these boards of trust goes in one direction, and that of an Assembly goes in another, and the Assembly overrules such board by vetoing its action and displacing a teacher, whom, in the exercise of its chartered prerogatives and its corporate wisdom, it has chosen, there will always be trouble; *it cannot be otherwise.* If the Assembly acts without giving any reasons, simply interposing its final negative in the case, it exposes itself at once to the charge of arbitrariness, and to those immediately affected by its action, that action inevitably savors of a tyranny to which any born Presbyterian will find it hard to submit. On the other hand, if an Assembly attempts to give reasons for its veto, all such reasons must resolve themselves into two—the lack of fitness to teach, and the lack of orthodoxy. How difficult it is for an Assembly to adduce either of these reasons in support of its decision without precipitating serious trouble, will be evident on very slight reflection.

Suppose the reason to be the *lack of fitness to teach*, whatever may be the special nature of that lack. At once a series of questions spring up, such as the following: What constitutes fitness to teach in a theological seminary? What are the special requisites to success in this or that particular department of the theological study? Is the Assembly as well qualified as the particular board of trust to ascertain whether the person appointed possesses such fitness, and in what degree? It it right for a board, after it has chosen a teacher as the result of the most minute investigation it can make, to let its deliberate judgment be set aside by the veto of a body every way less prepared to decide the matter wisely? Would it be just to the man himself, if, after he and the board had settled the matter, and a call had been presented and accepted, the Assembly should step in, and with only such knowledge as a body so constituted would possess, should hold him up before the whole Church and before the world as a person incompetent to teach, and unfit for the place to which he had been chosen?

So serious are such questions that it is doubtful whether any General Assembly could be induced to take such a step on this ground. The case must be an exceptional one indeed; and the veto of the Assembly would become not merely a remarkable and destructive condemnation of the man, but also a verdict of gross incompetency against the board who had appointed him. And the case would be more exceptional still if the chosen instructor had already been before the Church for many years in some similar capacity, perchance in the same institution, and the board that chose him had acted on the basis of an experimental acquaintance with his abilities as a teacher.

But the second ground, *the lack of orthodoxy*, is a hundred fold more perplexing. Suppose an Assembly should openly say, in any given case: We put our veto on this appointment, because in our judgment the chosen instructor is not orthodox, or is heretical, according to our standards. Suppose it should vary the statement, and say in a more guarded form: We do not condemn this man as a minister, but we do pronounce his teachings doubtful and dangerous in quality, and even heretical, and on this ground declare him unfit as a teacher. The Assembly of 1836 has established a precedent against any declaration of the latter sort, before which it would be very difficult to set up valid opposition. The distinction between the minister and professor, between the man and his teachings, vanishes the moment it is touched. It is simply impossible to pronounce the teaching heretical without condemning the man also; and it is simply impossible to condemn the teacher without pronouncing judgment on the minister also. But this is clearly inadmissible under our form of government. The obvious principle in the case, as the precedent of 1836 affirms, is that the Assembly cannot do by indirection what it cannot do directly and under constitutional warrant, and for such a declaration and distinction as this there can be no constitutional warrant whatever.

The declaration of the first sort is still more obviously inadmissible so long as the Presbytery to which such a teacher is amenable, regards and treats him as orthodox. At this point the Assembly is powerless. The experience of the Southern Church in the case of Professor Woodrow ought to be a sufficient guide and warning here. It is not needful that the person implicated be already undergoing judicial examination before the only body on earth competent of pronouncing upon him ecclesiastically. The simple fact that he stands unimpeached before that body, is enough to forbid the Assembly from assuming any judicial prerogatives in his case. No difference of this sort can be recognized in our form of government, between one minister and another, between a teacher in a seminary and a pastor in his pulpit, and any attempt to set up such a distinction can only end in trouble. In a word, the Assembly is absolutely precluded by our constitution from pronouncing an opinion by mere resolution upon the good standing of even the humblest minister in our Church.

The compact of 1870 thus betrays its weakness in whatever aspect it may be regarded. To say the best that can be said, the only two grounds on which the Assembly can possibly act under it are doubtful and dangerous grounds. It loads the Church with a responsibility which is pleasant enough so long as there is no occasion to wield it, but which is as certain as fate to bring in trouble wherever there is fair room for doubt as to either the capacity or the orthodoxy of any candidate for professional service. The experience of the current year will inevitably be repeated in every like case as long as the compact lasts. Differences of interpretation as to its intent and scope will always arise, as they have unhappily sprung up in this instance. Diversities of judgment and more or less dissatisfaction with the result will always make their appearance, and whatever may be the effect upon the seminary involved, the Church is sure to suffer much more than it gains.

Add to this calm statement that the "compact" of 1870 was no legal compact at all, but simply a friendly agreement, and Dr. Morris' argument becomes irresistible.

Let us now turn to Auburn. This seminary, unlike Lane and Union, was already under ecclesiastical control, namely, that of adjacent Synods. Here also there was doubt and scruple respecting the legal aspect of the agreement of 1870. It was not until 1873 that Auburn consented to enter into the arrangement. The following was its official action in the case:

The committee to whom has been referred the question as to whether the proposal of the General Assembly to submit the election of professors in the seminary to the control of that body can be complied with without a change of the charter of this institution, would respectfully report, that they have carefully examined said charter, and sought legal counsel on the subject. They find that the board of commissioners is invested with the sole and ultimate authority to appoint its professors, and *they cannot legally delegate this power to any other body.* They are, however, convinced of the fact that they may in their primary action make a conditional appointment, subject to the approval of the General Assembly, and that the right of such approval may be accorded to and recognized from that body without necessarily interfering with their ultimate authority. The committee regard the seminary as standing in an organic relation to the General Assembly *through its commissioners, who are themselves ecclesiastically amenable to the action of that body*, and that, therefore, there is a generic propriety in submitting their appointments conditionally to its advisory action.

They further find that it comes within the sphere of power accorded to the board by the charter that they make whatever by-laws and regulations they may regard as essential for the prosperity of the seminary; and, therefore, deeming it desirable that this institution be classed on an equal basis with others of a like character as under the patronage and supervision of the General Assembly, the committee would hereby present and commend for adoption by the board the following by-law, viz: "That hereafter the appointments of professors in this seminary be primarily made conditional upon the approval of the General Assembly, and that such appointments be complete and authoritative only upon securing such approval."—[Minutes of the Board of Commissioners of Auburn Seminary, meeting May 8, 1873.]

(2) But while at Lane, and, later, at Auburn also, the agreement of 1870 between Union Seminary and the General Assembly excited at the time serious doubt, and was adopted only in a modified form upon the advice of able legal counsel, the agreement yet met with general acquiescence as a "suitable arrangement." For twenty years it remained, as we have seen, quiescent and undisputed. Nobody challenged either its legality or its expediency, and this for the simple reason that the power with which it clothed the Assembly was never used. For several months before the meeting of the Assembly in 1891, it is true, the veto power was widely discussed in the religious papers, but chiefly as to its direct bearing upon the case of Dr. Briggs, not as to its legality or its wisdom. Only after the action of the General Assembly were men's eyes opened to discern its real character. That action, as is apt to be the case with all unfair and arbitrary exercise of power, aroused thoughtful public opinion in a high de-

gree, and precipitated, so to say, conclusions and a judgment touching the whole matter which years of ordinary discussion could not have reached.

The public reason and conscience, under certain conditions, give their verdict very quickly, and in a way not to be gainsaid. It was so in the present instance. No arguments could shut again the eyes which were opened so wide by the action at Detroit. Not alone Union Seminary and its oldest and best friends, but thousands of the best and most discerning friends of Christian scholarship and reasonable liberty of theological inquiry and teaching throughout the country, felt that a hard blow had been struck at a great interest common and equally dear to them all. It would be easy to illustrate the intensity and strength of this feeling by numberless testimonies, given in private letters and coming from all parts of the Union. I myself read scores of such letters, some of them written by men noted for their fine culture, their piety, their zeal for the truth as it is in Jesus, and their unusual weight of character. Of the public testimonies and protests called forth by the action at Detroit, time would fail me to speak at length. Two or three only must suffice; and I give them just as they appeared, without, of course, holding myself responsible for all they contain. The first was from the pen of the Rev. C. H. Haydn, D.D., LL.D., pastor of the First Presbyterian Church of Cleveland, Ohio, a man whose name stands for whole-souled devotion to the kingdom of

Christ. Dr. Haydn was a member of the Assembly at Detroit, and chairman of its Standing Committee on Foreign Missions. Of the veto of Dr. Briggs he said, addressing his own people:

> Had the Union Seminary acquiesced in this veto, *I question whether a twelvemonth would have gone by before men in at least three other seminaries would have been called to account in one way or another, and liberty within the lines of Holy Scripture would have had a set-back from which it would not have recovered in a quarter of a century.* Princeton would have triumphed all along the line, and nothing could well be worse than to have Princeton dominate the thinking of the Presbyterian Church. Already, to my view, it begins to dawn that Princeton's ecclesiastical lawyer has overreached himself, and unwittingly aided the very cause that he thought to put under the ban of the Church.

My next extract is from a letter of the Rev. Robert W. Patterson, D.D., of Chicago, then past his seven and seventieth year. Dr. Patterson was a venerated patriarch, as he had been for more than a generation the New School leader, of the Presbyterian Church in the great Northwest. He was Moderator of the General Assembly in 1859, and was also a member of the New School branch of the Joint Committee on Reunion. If there was another man in the whole Interior who stood higher in the estimate of his ministerial brethren, or whose judgment in matters relating to the order and prosperity of the Presbyterian Church, was entitled to greater weight, I do not know his name. Here is what Dr. Patterson said:

I am distressed about our seminaries. The plan of allowing the General Assembly a veto on appointments is, I am persuaded, unwise. I question with many as to the fitness of Dr. Briggs for the place to which he was elected by the Union directors, but I think it very unsafe for the Assembly to veto the action of such a board, especially when a trial of the professor-elect is pending. It must necessarily be in a great measure a prejudgment of the judicial case. And in most instances of veto, a judicial case will be likely to follow or to be actually pending.

Besides, it is not clear that in ordinary cases the Assembly is as competent a judge as a well-selected board. Moreover, if the Assembly were the more competent body, it could not fail to awaken dangerous antagonism for it to exercise such authority. It is not like a veto of a *nomination;* it is a veto of an *appointment,* so far as the board can make one, and it is, therefore, an injurious judgment against the professor-elect and also against the board electing.

And, still further, it is likely to create a wide sympathy for the injured parties, and give currency to the very errors which it was designed to prevent. This is evidently so in the present case, in which grossly partsian action has been taken. The proper check upon unwise appointments is the *discipline* of the Church, if serious errors are taught by the appointee. The New School Church never lodged any veto power in the Assembly. Such power ought not now to be continued; it is virtually the trial of a man without process and without forms of law. Not one quotation from Dr. Briggs was made in the debate at Detroit, so far as I heard, and no reasons were given in the final judgment. *This was monstrous.*

Along with this emphatic expression of opinion I

will quote some passages in the same strain from a private letter of Dr. Patterson:

I have not liked Dr. Briggs' utterances, especially the tone of them. But I regard the action of Princeton in the matter as a startling illustration of the grievous injustice that will always be liable to be done to a professor-elect and to a seminary, so long as the power of veto remains with the Assembly. It is a sort of lynch-law condemnation on technicality, without trial and with no reasons responsibly alleged, but with utterly untrue reasons implied or assumed. . . . I see no escape from a like injustice in any case where a veto can be plausibly demanded. First, get up a clamor, and then have a one-sided committee appointed to report that something must be done at once, or the Assembly will be held as approving, and give no reasons, leaving every man to sustain the report for his own reasons, or on the ground of his prepossessions. This is a receipt for crushing out any and every appointee that happens to incur popular displeasure on a question about which the Church is sensitive. How easy to apply the guillotine in every such case! and if the candidate for decapitation cannot be easily answered on the main points, the motive is greater to dispatch him by *votes*. . . I have written simply because I feel like it. I do not agree with Dr. Briggs on some important questions, but I would not, if I could, overrule the directors in regard to any such question, and no more would I concede this right to the Assembly. We cannot afford to have our able men brushed aside by popular clamor, even if on some points they may have gone too far. If they become heretics, let their heresy be *judicially proved.* But let not the Assembly prejudge indirectly its future disciplinary action. The day has passed for *settling* critical questions by votes of councils or assemblies. But it is possible to distress and distract a whole denomination for a generation by attempting this impossibility. The numbers will increase of those who will say with Dr. Van Dyke: "If we cannot have orthodoxy and liberty both, let us have liberty."

I will give one more testimony and protest. It is from a letter of the Rev. S. M. Hamilton, D.D., addressed to Dr. Field, editor of *The Evangelist*, and dated Louisville, Ky., June 5, 1891. Dr. Hamilton for more than half a generation was pastor of the old Scotch Church in Fourteenth Street, New York, where he won the confidence, respect and love of his ministerial brethren and of all the churches by his charming personal qualities, by his fine scholarship, and by his solid Christian character and services:

The outside public have received a very definite impression that our highest ecclesiastical court has acted unfairly and unjustly towards one of our foremost Biblical scholars. The issue will not increase the respect of the world for the Presbyterian Church. She has suffered immensely more than Dr. Briggs. Thoughtful men are saying—I have heard them—that our Church will not allow her scholars to make a thorough study of the Bible by the modern scientific methods unless they first bind themselves to come to no conclusions, save such as are acceptable to a certain theological school in the Church. Such an impression— and it exists and is spreading—is calamitous, not to the Church only, but to religion itself. Add to this the feeling which is abroad, that the Assembly has condemned an eminent professor without assigning any reason therefor, and on the report of a committee, not a member of which was a friend of the professor or of Union Seminary, and the injury to the reputation of our Church cannot be calculated.

I have been on terms of intimate friendship with Dr. Briggs for years. I have lived with him, I have walked the mountains with him, I have talked with him for hours together, and I say deliberately that he has done more to make the Bible a real living book to me, the true Word of God, than all other ministers and teachers I have known in the whole course of my life. His friendship is one of the things for which I shall always have reason to be thankful. In my judgment Dr. Briggs is the most *inspiring* teacher of the Bible our Church possesses. No vote of any Assembly can impair his reputation among the Biblical scholars of Christendom.

(3) The action at Detroit was an eye-opener with regard to the un-wisdom of trying to regulate theological opinion and teaching by popular vote. The instant the attempt is actually made, its futility is demonstrated. I doubt if the vote at Detroit really moved theological opinion a hair's breadth. Nor was it at all more effective in the matter of theological instruction. Unless further enlightened respecting divine truth by deeper study and fresh inspirations of the Eternal Spirit, Princeton, and Union, and Lane, and all the rest, continued to teach in 1892 what they taught in 1890. As aforetime, they took counsel of Holy Scripture and of the venerable standards of the Presbyterian Church, as also of the old creeds of Christendom. They still read diligently the writings

of the great masters of divinity, whether of ancient, or medieval, or later ages; they tried to discern the signs of the times; and they exercised themselves in working out more fully their own honest thought. But they took very little note of what was said, or voted, on the subject at Detroit. When in 1845, at Cincinnati, the Old School General Assembly, led by some of the strongest men in that branch of the Presbyterian Church, decided by a vote of 173 to 8—a majority not of 7 to 1, as at Detroit, but of more than 20 to 1—that what was called "Romish Baptism" is spurious and unchristian, Dr. Charles Hodge of Princeton, in spite of the brilliant Dr. Thornwell, and of Dr. L. N. Rice, and of Dr. Junkin, and of nearly the whole Assembly, not only went right on teaching his students the old Protestant view, but he attacked the decision of the Assembly as wrong in fact and false in doctrine, demonstrating, with most cogent reasoning, that, notwithstanding her errors, the Church of Rome is still a branch of the Christian Church, and that baptism duly administered by her, is Christian baptism. Dr. Hodge knew very well that if such questions were to be decided by a majority vote in a popular Assembly, instead of being decided according to the truth of history and the voice of Scripture, the occupation of the theological professor is well-nigh clean gone forever. This veto power is like one of those terrible pieces of new ordnance of which we have read lately so much. It is not only a most formidable instrument for destroying an enemy, but of self-destruction as well, unless handled with consummate skill. Setting five hundred men, mostly untrained for the task, to firing it off all together, even under the direction of an ecclesiastical boss or expert, is extremely dangerous and against all the lessons of even worldly prudence.

Do I mean, then, that it is no function of the Presbyterian Church to bear faithful witness against prevalent errors in doctrine and practice, or, if necessary, in the way of godly discipline, to put upon them the stamp of her censure and condemnation? No, that is not my meaning. It seems to me one of the highest functions of a church of Jesus Christ to bear constant, earnest witness for Him and His truth, and to put the mark of her disapproval upon all errors contrary thereto. This is one great end for which the Church exists in the world. When she ceases to be a witness-bearer and the enemy alike of false doctrine and evil practice, her glory is departed. The question is: How shall she best fulfil this duty? And here there is need of the wisest discrimination, of large experience, of the amplest knowledge, of much self-restraint, and of Christian justice, candor, and magnanimity in their finest expression.

It is far from my meaning, I repeat, that the Presbyterian Church, or any other church of Christ, is not bound to hold fast to the faith once delivered to the saints; to stand up for soundness both of doctrine and morals; to bear witness against error; and to be very jealous for the honor of God and His inspired oracles. No church can here exceed the measure of her duty. Nor do I in the least question that the Presbyterian Church, in the performance of this solemn duty, may often speak and act most effectually through the voice and votes of the representative Assembly. The popular voice and vote, thus expressed, is a ruling principle in our American system of republican government; and it is a ruling principle no less in American Presbyterianism—the source in large measure of its elasticity, freedom, and working power. Nobody shall surpass me in admiring it and its splendid achievements.

But alike in the civil sphere and in that of religion there are some things, which in their very nature, belong to the domain and jurisdiction, not of the many, but rather of the select few. There are questions in the civil order which the judges of the land, not the legislators, alone are authorized and competent to decide. And so in the religious sphere there are matters which only learned divines and scholars—specially trained, chosen, and set apart for the purpose—are qualified to pass judgment upon. Such, for example, are many of the questions raised by what is called the higher or literary criticism of the Bible. No popular vote, however honest and intelligent, can decide them; nor are ordinary scholars, however learned, competent to decide them. They must be decided, if at all, by the ablest sort of trained minds, just as there are questions in law, in finance, in every department of science, which only experts of the highest class are qualified to settle for us.

I have thus endeavored to consider the action at Detroit in the case of Dr. Briggs in its bearing upon Union Seminary and upon the Presbyterian Church. It has been my aim to tell the truth, so far as possible, and nothing but the truth. And it has been my aim, also, to do this in a frank and Christian way. Certainly, it would have been much easier to write in a freer style. If now and then I have used language savoring of severity, or even ridicule, it is because the truth seems to me to demand such language. No reasonable man could have supposed that the friends of Union Seminary were going to keep silent, or that when they did speak they would speak with bated breath. If trained in no special awe of a General Assembly, they did stand in awe of God and His truth, of Christian justice, and of that glorious liberty wherewith their divine Master had made them free.

Whatever hostile feeling prevailed at Detroit and in the struggle that followed against Union Seminary, was, as I believe, largely the effect of simple ignorance or misapprehension. Union Seminary stood firm on her original foundations as an institution of Christian theology in the service of the Presbyterian Church and of the Church Universal. Taking the inspired Word of God as her rule of faith and practice, she was striving in all things for the faith and furtherance of the

Gospel; first in our own land, and then over all the earth. These were her ambitions and she has no other. With every other school of divinity, of whatever name, she desired to keep step to the music of the whole Church militant in fighting the battles of truth and righteousness, here and everywhere. Especially did she desire to march and fight in fellowship with all other seminaries of the Presbyterian Church. She was ready, as she is still ready, to say to them, in the words of Henry B. Smith,—words penned before the reunion, but still fresh and true as ever:

> Let us advance with open brow to meet the greater questions which are fast advancing to meet us. Let us not make so much account of Old School and New School; and even if we believe the substance of the Old is better, let us not deny that the earnestness, the philosophic spirit, the advancing movement, the wider aims of the New, are of inestimable good. Who can so afford to be patient as the orthodox, who know that the right faith will in the end surely triumph. Let us eschew the arts of intrigue, of defamation, and innuendo. These are easily learned. They are the offspring of fear or of hate. They show a timorous or a dogmatic spirit. Let us not deny until we understand, or insult feelings before we know their reason, for it is easier to be extreme than to be candid, to denounce than to examine. In the spirit of love and wisdom let us maintain cogency of argument, energy of faith, and urgency of zeal.

CHAPTER III.

THE PARTING OF THE WAYS.—SKETCH OF THE CONFLICT BETWEEN UNION SEMINARY AND THE GENERAL ASSEMBLY.—THE ECCLESIASTICAL VETO.—POSITION OF THE ASSEMBLY'S COMMITTEE OF CONFERENCE.—ANTAGONISTIC POSITION OF THE SEMINARY.—IMMEDIATE ISSUE OF THE STRUGGLE.—A TRUCE.

We come now to the parting of the ways. The action of the Assembly at Detroit was regarded by the Board of Directors and faculty of Union Seminary, and by the friends of the institution generally, as most unwise and unjust. Those who understood the case saw at a glance, that the seminary was in imminent peril of falling a prey to what Henry B. Smith in his letter to me, already quoted, called the "consistent domineering Presbyterianism." But how to extricate it from this peril was not yet so plain. The best solution of the problem, however, soon began to appear; and at the close of the final meeting of the Board of Directors with the Assembly's Committee of Conference, it was in full process of evolution.

(*a*) *The interpretation of the agreement of 1870 by the Board of Directors of Union Seminary.*

The Assembly at Detroit, as we have seen, regarded the agreement of 1870 not only as in the strictest sense a legal compact, or contract, but also as involving the right to veto a transfer no less than an original election. And just here arose the trouble. Had Dr. Briggs been called to the new chair of Biblical Theology from the pastorate, or from another institution, and had his appointment been disapproved by the General Assembly, no question of its jurisdiction in the case would have been raised by the directors of Union Seminary. Whatever their disappointment, and however unfair or unwise they might have felt it to be, the board would have bowed at once to the Assembly's decision. In other words, while the agreement lasted it would have been regarded by them as morally binding. But it so happened that for some seventeen years Dr. Briggs had been a professor in the Union Theological Seminary. He was simply transferred to another chair. And this transfer, as the Board of Directors held, was merely an exercise of the authority given them by the constitution of the seminary not only to "appoint" all professors and teachers, but also to "determine their duties;" and was not, therefore, subject to the Assembly's disapproval. Hence the conflict, which so disturbed the peace of the Presbyterian Church.

As I have said already, the agreement of 1870 for twenty years required no interpretation. It had excited no controversy and no hostility. Hardly anybody, particularly among the younger generation, knew aught about it. Thousands of our ministers, ruling elders and private members had, probably, never heard its name. So far as it gave to the seminaries, hitherto under Assembly control, the privilege of electing their own professors its operation had been quiet, normal and highly satisfactory. So far as it contained in the veto power possibilities of harm, either to the Church or to the seminaries, the evil lay dormant and unsuspected. The action at Detroit first revealed its real character.

This point seems to me especially noteworthy. A negative by the General Assembly on the election of both professors and trustees had, indeed, existed in the case of the Union Theological Seminary in Virginia as early as 1826. And the term "veto" itself was familiar as an ecclesiastical term to all readers of the Life of Dr. Chalmers and of the story of the Free Church of Scotland. The "Veto Law" passed by the General Assembly in 1834 under the lead of Dr. Chalmers, played an important part in the struggle, which issued in the great disruption of 1843. I am not sure, however, that the term "veto" was employed even in the case of the Union Theological Seminary in Virginia; nor can I find that the negative of the General Assembly on all appointments of professors or trustees in that institution, was ever actually used. If used, it could hardly have attracted public notice, or involved any conflict of theological opinion. Still, the connection of Union Seminary in Virginia with Princeton was close and almost personal. It was a sort of family connection; very likely, therefore, the Assembly's negative on the election of its professors and trustees may, in 1870, have suggested to the professors at Princeton a similar negative in the case of their own institution. It is to be carefully noted that in the report of the Joint Committee on Reunion made in 1867, in that of 1868, and in that of the Joint Committee of Conference in 1869, the word "veto" never occurs. The only instance of its use between 1866 and 1870, that I have been able to discover, is in the letter of Dr. A. A. Hodge to Henry B. Smith, dated December 29, 1867, in which he proposed as a "*condition* of union" that "the right of peremptory *veto*" on the election of professors in all the seminaries should be given to the General Assembly, and urged Professor Smith to recommend this "compromise" to the New School branch of the Joint Committee on Reunion. But it should be remembered that this letter, as Dr. Hodge said, was written "without consultation with or the knowledge of a single person," and that probably no eye save Dr. Smith's ever saw it until after his death.*

To the Presbyterian Church of that period, whether of the Old or of the New School branch, the ecclesiastical veto was certainly a novel thing, and the power,

*I have examined carefully the correspondence which Dr. Adams and Dr. Beatty carried on with each other between 1866 and 1870,—a correspondence full of details and suggestions touching the reunion negotiations —but the word "veto" does not occur in it from beginning to end.

expressed and now understood by it, was quite as unfamiliar as the term. I will venture to refer to my own experience in illustration. Although a director of Union Seminary in 1870, and, as such, in close confidential relations with my associates in the board, Drs. Adams, Stearns and Hatfield,—all members of the Joint Committee; and though myself taking an active part in the memorable action on May 9 and 16 of that year, it never crossed my mind that instead of promoting mutual confidence and harmony, which was its "sole object," the veto power on the election of professors would, in actual exercise, have just the contrary effect. I say the veto upon the election of professors, for Mr. D. Willis James' earnest protest against conceding it to the Assembly in the election of directors, did startle me, and led to my motion for an adjournment from May 9 to May 16, when that feature of the plan was dropped. Let me add further, that not till after the 20th of January, 1891, when Dr. Briggs' utterances, on being inducted into the chair of Biblical Theology, began to call forth such sharp censure throughout the Presbyterian Church, did it distinctly occur to me that his transfer to that chair, on being reported to the General Assembly, might possibly be regarded as equivalent to an original election, and as such encounter the Assembly's veto.

My own state of mind with regard to the Agreement of 1870, was, I believe, substantially that of the Board of Directors of Union Seminary, as late as the beginning of 1891. That it was also the only view taken in the Presbyterian Church, so far at least as any distinct view prevailed, I am not prepared to assert. On the contrary, I incline now to think that a different view existed though mostly latent and unexpressed. Otherwise, it is not so easy to account for the very decided opinion on the subject which declared itself far and wide after the publication of Dr. Briggs' address, and then suddenly crystallized at Detroit into such a determined and overwhelming vote of disapproval. Whatever may have been the influence of misunderstanding, of theological alarm, of misrepresentation in bringing about that result, it is fair to assume that the result was brought about also in part by honest belief and conviction. Or, to express it in another way, different ecclesiastical theories and habits of thought, whether inherited or acquired, largely shaped the result; and in order to do justice to both sides this point must be kept in mind.

The position of the Board of Directors in regard to the transfer of Dr. Briggs to the new chair of Biblical Theology, is most clearly shown in its successive conferences with the committee of the General Assembly. That committee consisted of eight ministers and seven ruling elders, namely:

Ministers:	*Ruling Elders:*
Francis L. Patton, D.D., LL.D.,	George Junkin,
John H. Worcester, Jr., D. D.,	John J. McCook,
William E. Moore, D.D.,	Russell Murdock, M.D.,

Ministers:	*Ruling Elders:*
William H. Roberts, D.D.,	George H. Ely,
Samuel J. Niccolls, D.D., LL.D.,	Samuel J. Wardell,
Herrick Johnson, D.D., LL.D.,	Edward P. Durant,
John S. Macintosh, D.D.,	George U. Ketcham,
George Alexander, D.D.	

All the members of the committee, excepting Dr. Worcester, were present at the first meeting, which was held at the seminary, in New York, on the 28th and 29th of October, 1891. The time was taken up partly in direct conference; partly in separate discussion in the board and in the committee. President Hastings acted as the leading spoksman on the side of the directors; President Patton on the side of the committee. One of the first points made respected, very naturally, the attitude of the board touching the present validity of the agreement of 1870. Did the board still hold itself bound by that agreement? The board replied in the affirmative. This answer opened the way for further inquiry and discussion. At the close of the meeting of the board and the Committee of Conference on the 29th of October, an adjournment was agreed to until another meeting should be called by the board. Thus far little had been accomplished by the two parties beyond friendly greetings and a better understanding of each other's views and temper. The following papers passed between the board and the Committee of Conference at the meeting in October, 1891.

I.

PAPER READ BY DOCTOR HASTINGS AT THE CONFERENCE, ON BEHALF OF THE BOARD OF DIRECTORS, OCTOBER 28th, 1891.

This board will consider carefully what the Assembly's committee has said to us. In courtesy to this committee, we have postponed the consideration of some questions which have been pressed upon our attention. We have felt that it is due to the Assembly that we should first hear what its appointed representatives might have to say. We shall in due time forward to this committee through our chairman, our reply to what you have said to us.

Meanwhile, I am requested to explain to this Committee of Conference, the views of our board with reference to the transfer of Dr. Briggs, by reading a carefully prepared statement upon that subject, which was presented to our board on the 12th of May last, before the late meeting of the Assembly at Detroit. This paper is a part of the report of the Executive Committee to the board.

MEANING OF THE ACTION OF 1870.

Your committee have considered the question of the relation of this seminary to the General Assembly, in regard to which there has lately been much discussion in the public prints. The report that a large number of Presbyterians have memorialized the approaching General Assembly to disapprove authoritatively of the recent transfer of one of our professors to the new department of Biblical Theology, indicates, as your committee believe, a misunderstanding in regard to the authority of the Assembly in this matter. It is not to be assumed in advance, that the Assembly itself will misconceive the extent of its prerogative, and your committee do not deem it either necessary or expedient that any resolution in regard to it should be transmitted to that body.

Nor in their judgement would it be advisable, even though the Assembly should proceed to take formal action, for the board to raise at this time an issue in regard to which there might possibly be discussion and grave differences of opinion; but inasmuch as the recollection of those who were members of this board in 1870, when this seminary voluntarily divested itself of a measure of its independence, is distinct as to the limits of its concession then made, and inasmuch as the board has always clearly distinguished in its mode of procedure between the election of a new professor and the transference of a member of its faculty from one department of instruction to another, your committee recommend that in order to prevent future misconception of the understanding of the board in this matter, the following minute be entered upon its records, viz.:

Inasmuch as there appears to be in some quarters a misconception of the meaning and intent of the action taken by this board in 1870, whereby all appointments of professors were to be reported to the General Assembly; and further providing that no such appointment should be considered as a complete election if disapproved by a majority vote of the Assembly; this board would hereby record its conviction that the said action of 1870 was then understood and has been ever since understood by this board, to refer to the election of additional members of the faculty, and not to the assignment to new departments of instruction, of professors already in office or to their transfer from one chair to another, as may appear expedient to the board.

To this may be added the simple statement that before the late meeting of the Assembly, this board had carefully investigated the charges which the Presbyteries were bringing against Dr. Briggs, and received from him a clear and positive denial of each charge on the ground of which denials the board resolved to sustain him, saying that "we will stand by him heartily on the ground of this report," (i. e. the report of his denials received from the Committee of Investigation).

After the adjournment of the Assembly, a special meeting of the board was called on the 5th of June, to arrange for the filling the vacancy in the faculty, occasioned by the sudden death of Dr. Henry J. Van Dyke, our professor-elect of Systematic Theology. After this important business, for which the meeting was called, had been arranged, the board considered the action of the Assembly at Detroit, and decided that it was due to our students to know what to count upon for the coming year's instruction; and that it was due to ourselves and to Dr. Briggs that we should be true to the promise we had made to "stand by him." Accordingly the following resolution was adopted:

> *Resolved*, That this Board of Directors, after having taken legal advice, and after due consideration, see no reason to change their views on the subject of the transfer of Dr. Briggs, and feel bound in the discharge of their duties under the charter and constitution, to adhere to the same.*

This action was taken in the conviction that the transfer of Dr. Briggs, as already stated, did not in our judgment come under the jurisdiction of the General Assembly according to the arrangement adopted in 1870. In view of a statement made in the Assembly, that transfer "did not make any change in status, but only in duties," we would further say that the transfer did not even make any real change in duties; for Dr. Briggs had been teaching Bible Theology for ten years. The only change was that he gave up two lectures a week in Hebrew exegesis to his colleague, Dr. Brown.

*The opinion of the board's legal adviser, Mr. William Allen Butler, will be found in Appendix C.

No disrespect to the Assembly was intended in our action; for it did not enter our minds that the Assembly could have any jurisdiction in the case.

II.

CONFERENCE COMMITTEE'S FIRST PAPER.

Resolution of the General Assembly's Committee on Conference with the directors of the Union Theological Seminary, October 28, 1891:

Whereas, it appears by the written communication of the directors of Union Seminary received this day at the conference between this committee and the directors, that the directors adopted the following minute on June 5, 1891, to wit:

Resolved, That this Board of Directors, after having taken legal advice, and after due consideration, see no reason to change their views on the subject of the transfer of Dr. Briggs, and feel bound in the discharge of their duties, under the charter and constitution, to adhere to the same, and

Whereas, it appears that this action was based upon the opinion of their legal adviser, and

Whereas, in that opinion submitted to us by the directors for our information, they were advised that the agreement or arrangement made by the General Assembly and the directors in 1870, was not binding upon the directors, and

Whereas, President Hastings, representing the directors, communicated to this committee orally, that the directors reserved the right to determine this question hereafter, and at the same time expressed the readiness of the directors to hear the views of the committee upon this subject;

Therefore, this committee states that the General Assembly has always regarded the same agreement or arrangement as binding legally and morally upon both parties to the same; and it desires to know the views of the directors upon this fundamental point, for if the agreement is not legally and morally binding upon both parties, it is of no practical use to discuss what is the true construction of the said agreement or arrangement.

III.

CONFERENCE COMMITTEE'S SECOND PAPER.

The General Assembly's Committee of Conference submit for the consideration of the Board of Directors of the Union Theological Seminary in the City of New York, the following paper:

DEAR BRETHREN: We have considered the written statements, as well as those made orally to you, with reference to the transfer of Professor Briggs. It is manifest you hold an interpretation of the terms of the agreement between the General Assembly and the seminaries under their care, widely different from that held by the Assembly under whose authority this committee is now acting. We are sincerely desirious, as we believe you are, to find some way of reconciliation both for the present and for the future, which will lead to a harmonious execution of the agreement between the Assembly and the seminaries. We can not, even were we so disposed, change the action of the body we represent with reference to Professor Briggs.

Again, we are embarrassed by the action of your board, taken in seeming disregard of the authority of the Assembly, and thus debarring us from making any recommendations which do not involve a denial of the right of the Assembly to do what it did. Some concessions, not of principle, but with reference to modes of action, must be made, in order to place the matter of interpretation at issue, between the General Assembly and the Board of Directors in the future, for an amicable settlement.

We would, therefore, ask you most respectfully, if you would not so far modify the action you have taken, as to submit to the action of the General Assembly, for the present, under protest, if your conscientious judgment so demand, and to regard the election of Professor Briggs as incomplete, until the matter shall again be brought before the Assembly in such form as your wisdom may suggest. If this was done, the way would be opened for us to recommend to the General Assembly the advisability of taking such action in conference with all the seminaries as would leave the transfer of professors in cases not involving an essentially different and new department of instruction, (such as the division of the instruction of a particular chair), to the entire control of the directors of the seminaries.

In making this suggestion we do not ask you to surrender or deny any of your real or supposed rights under your interpretation of the agreement of 1870. We recognize also the fact that you had no desire or purpose in the transfer of Professor Briggs, to act contrary to the agreement. We also find from your statements that you did not elect Professor Briggs to the chair of Biblical Theology, under the conditions prescribed by your laws and observed in all other cases of election, and that you intended to limit his duties to a department of instruction in which he had already been, as you supposed, properly engaged. In view of all this we hope that you will unite with us in an effort to procure from the General Assembly, such legislation as will define for the future, the questions raised in the present issue.

William H. Roberts,
Secretary of the committee.

[A true copy.]

IV.

ACTION OF THE BOARD OF DIRECTORS IN VIEW OF THE FIRST PAPER OF THE GENERAL ASSEMBLY'S COMMITTEE OF CONFERENCE, OCTOBER 29, 1891.

Whereas the question has been raised by the committee of the General Assembly now in conference with this board, as to the attitude of this board toward the arrangement of 1870:

Resolved, That this board, without surrendering its interpretation of said arrangement, fully recognizes its binding force until it shall be proved to be illegal, or shall be properly abrogated.

V.

ACTION OF THE BOARD OF DIRECTORS IN VIEW OF THE SECOND PAPER OF THE GENERAL ASSEMBLY'S COMMITTEE OF CONFERENCE, OCTOBER 29, 1891.

Resolved, That this board desire more time to consider the second paper which has been laid before us by the committee of the General Assembly; that they will take it up at an early day and report their action to the said committee and will then ask for another conference with the said committee.

Resolved, That the said papers be referred to the Executive Committee for examination and to report their views to this board.

The adjourned meeting took place on Wednesday, January 20, 1892, and closed on the afternoon of January 22. There was earnest debate in the Board of Directors, in the Assembly's committee, and in joint sittings of both. The discussion in the board turned chiefly upon two points: first, arbitration in regard to the question whether a transfer was equivalent to an original election; and second, the report to be made to the next General Assembly as to what the seminary would consent to do in reference to the future. For reasons, which will be given later, the Committee of Conference withdrew the proposal of arbitration. As to several other points the views of the board were expressed in the following paper, addressed to the Committee of Conference:

THE BOARD OF DIRECTORS OF THE UNION THEOLOGICAL SEMINARY TO THE GENERAL ASSEMBLY'S COMMITTEE OF CONFERENCE:

DEAR BRETHREN: Having answered your proposition in the second paper submitted to us, we desire in addition to present to you the following considerations.

I. You have said to us,—"We recognize the fact that you had no desire or purpose in the transfer of Professor Briggs to act contrary to the agreement." On our part we would reciprocate fully the courtesy of this acknowledgement and say that we believe the General Assembly did not mean to violate the agreement of 1870, or to transcend the power then conceded. We do not question that the Assembly acted conscientiously in its interpretation of that agreement. We are willing also to believe that the Assembly had no intention to dishonor or to wrong this institution. And yet the action taken at Detroit was virtually a verdict against either the character, or the competency of the Board of Directors; a verdict without reasons given, and without a hearing. With a full knowledge of all the facts, and after long consideration, the board had endeavored to do its whole duty in the case at issue. Dr. Briggs was carefully questioned upon all the points in which he had been assailed, and the questions, and his direct and satisfactory answers to the same, had been published and widely circulated, together with the unanimous action of his colleagues in the faculty. But our judgment and decision, and the opinion of the faculty, apparently received no recognition whatever. The wrong thus caused or occasioned to this board and to this seminary, it would be hard, perhaps, to parallel in the history of Christrian institutions in our time. Certain Presbyteries hastened to do what they could to prevent students from coming to us. The Synod of Baltimore has virtually asked the Assembly to disown us, and that in language of an extraordinary character. We have seen little evidence of respectful waiting for the results of your appointed conference with us. But while we shall not ask the General Assembly to reconsider its action, we do ask that our inability to concur in the Assembly's interpretation of the agreement of 1870 be so fully and justly recognized that the past shall be left to tell its own story. In our judgment the mutual understanding of the two parties to that agreement should rest in this conclusion,—we cannot agree in our views of the rights involved, and neither party can undo what has been done.

II. But we have a strong conviction that something more than this is requisite to protect the peace of the Church in the future, and you will allow us frankly to express that conviction.

As chairman of the Standing Committee on Theological Seminaries, Dr. William Adams said to the Assembly in 1870 that our directors in their memorial were "looking solely to the peace and harmony of the Church." (Minutes of 1870, p. 63). In that memorial our directors expressed themselves as "desirous of doing all in their power to establish confidence and harmony throughout the whole Church in respect to the education of its ministers." Doubtless, in those early days of reunion, the agreement did serve temporarily a beneficent purpose in promoting confidence and harmony. The possibilities and the perils of this agreement lay dormant until at last the time came for their revelation by a practical test. The true nature and effect of a law may remain unknown for years, unless that law is applied to an actual case. Months before the late Assembly met a sudden agitation spread through the Church, a general alarm was sounded and many Presbyteries took part in the movement by overturing the General Assembly. When, therefore, the Assembly met at Detroit the veto of Dr. Briggs' transfer seemed to be a foregone conclusion. So for the first time in twenty years the agreement of 1870 was really tested as a working power; and in the light of recent events, as we need hardly say, it was found to be a dangerous element in the life of the Church not calculated to promote general peace and harmony, but full of the possibilities of evil.

In 1869, in presenting the report of the Committee of Conference on reunion, Dr. George W. Musgrave said to the Old School Assembly, referring to the articles contained, not in the "plan of union," but in the "declarations,"—that "they are not a compact or covenant, but they suggest to the Assembly what are suitable arrangements. They are not terms of the union. They may be annulled or modified as any future Assembly may deem proper. We told our brethren that we were unwilling to tie the hands of the future Church of God." (The Presbyterian Reunion Memorial volume, p. 546.) If the General Assembly, as one party to the agreement of 1870, could "annul or modify" that agreement, then as the other party, the seminary must of necessity have the same right and power.

In the general Assembly of 1870, as chairman of the Standing Committee on Theological Seminaries, Dr. William Adams said, referring to the ninth Article of the "declaration:" "It was intended as a measure for the maintenance of confidence and harmony, and not as indicating the best method for all future time." Such was the understanding of those leaders of the Church, as on the height of reunion feeling they looked off into the future. They did not presume that they had determined "the best method for all future time." They had seen or felt, as it is expressed in the memorial of this board to the Assembly of 1870, (Minutes, p. 148) "that there were many disadvantages, infelicities, not to say, at times, perils in the election of professors of the seminaries directly and immediately by the General Assembly itself,—a body so large, in session for so short a time, and composed of members to so great an extent resident at a distance from the seminaries themselves, and therefore personally unacquainted with many things which pertain to their true interest and usefulness."

In a similar vein wrote Dr. A. A. Hodge to Dr. Henry B. Smith in December, 1867, and we venture to quote his wise and significant words:

It is proper, it is almost a necessity, that each institution should be left in the management of those upon whose support it exclusively depends. The majority of any Assembly must be necessarily ignorant of the special wants and local conditions of any seminary, and of the qualifications of candidates proposed for the chairs of instruction. The best of these are generally young men, up to the time of their nomination, known only to a few. To vest the choice in the General Assembly will tend to put prominent ecclesiastics into such positions, rather than scholars, or men specially qualified with gifts for teaching. As the population of our country becomes larger and more heterogeneous, and the General Assembly increases proportionately, the difficulties above mentioned, and many others easily thought of, will increase.

Dr. Henry B. Smith stated his own views in the following language:

It is a fair and serious question whether a General Assembly, representing the Presbyterian Church throughout the whole United States, especially in view of the numbers in Church, and the extent of the territory in twenty or thirty years, will be the best or even a suitable body to choose the professors and manage the concerns of all the Presbyterian seminaries scattered throughout the country. We very much doubt whether this will be a wise arrangement. It may work well in Scotland, but Scotland has its limits. It might bring into the Assembly local, personal and theological questions which it would be better to settle in a narrower field.

Such are the views which led the Assembly to surrender the right, which it had possessed before the reunion, of electing the professors in those seminaries which were and are distinctively its own, either because founded by the Assembly, or because entirely under its control. But these same considerations apply at least equally to the exercise of the "veto power" by the Assembly, only with this important difference. The veto is virtually a verdict, not to say a stigma, both against the professor appointed and against the Board of Directors which appointed him; and as such it is much more harmful to the individual and to the institution concerned, than could be the failure by the General Assembly to elect as professor one who had been merely nominated. The veto is positive, the failure to elect is only negative in its influence. We claim in the light of recent events that the objections so successfully urged in 1870, against continuing to the Assembly the electing power, have still greater force against continuing to that body the veto power. The first exercise of that power, instead of promoting, has greatly disturbed the peace and harmony of the Church; it has wronged the institution, and the individual whose good name has been branded with a disapproval based upon no trial and accompanied and justified by no reasons. The judgment of those who had close and long experimental knowledge of the effects of Dr. Briggs' teachings was ignored and overridden by the decision of a multitude who had looked on from a distance, and were not guided in their judgment by intimate personal knowledge.

III. But it will be said that the Church should be able to protect herself against erroneous teaching. This we do not question, and here our admirable Presbyterian policy provides, as it seems to us, for all the necessities involved.

The right of "original jurisdiction" in the case of a minister, whether he teaches from the pulpit or from the professor's chair, inheres in the Presbytery to which he belongs, and not in the General Assembly. It is as unjust as it is un-Presbyterian to discriminate between a pastor and a professor to the detriment or the peril of either. The Church needs no other protection against heresy in the pulpit or in the seminary, than that which our polity affords. In an extreme case, such as is conceivable, the Assembly, through the Synod, can even require the Presbytery to which a professor belongs to arraign for trial. At Detroit, the Assembly was involved in an inextricable tangle by the simple fact that the veto power, as they interpreted it, impelled them to express their disapproval of a man who at that very time was under charges by his Presbytery, and whose case might later be brought before the Assembly as a court of appeal. The action thus taken could not fail to embarrass the Presbytery of New York in undertaking judicial proceedings. Hence, as it seems to us, the agreement of 1870 has proved itself by the test of experience dangerously inconsistent with a fundamental principle of the polity of our Church as also with the true spirit of American Presbyterianism.

IV. In the conclusion of your second paper, to which we have replied, you said:

We hope that you will unite with us in an effort to procure from the General Assembly such legislation as will define for the future the questions raised in the present issue.

With all due respect to that body we would say that in this matter the General Assembly, in our opinion, has no right whatever to legislate. In the agreement the Assembly is simply one party and this seminary is the other.

In view then of the considerations we have presented concerning the practical and the ecclesiastical aspects of the agreement of 1870, and in view of the fact that the recent exercise of the veto power by the Assembly must make it seriously difficult in the future to induce scholars to accept appointments in our seminary faculties, we sincerely believe that both parties to the agreement of 1870 should equally desire its abrogation, alike for the sake of the Church, and for the sake of the seminaries.

But this board is certainly bound to regard the safety and welfare of the institution under its direction, and must act according to its own best judgment. Since we stand alone in our solemn responsibility and obligations as the appointed guardians of this great institution of Christian learning, so we must reserve the right, if need be, to act alone according to the light and grace we have. We yield to none in heartfelt loyalty to our beloved Church, and we have pledged ourselves also to be loyal to the history, constitution and chartered rights of Union Seminary. Conscience forbids us in any way to surrender or to imperil this sacred providential trust.

We shall be thankful and glad, honored brethren, if you can see these things as we do, and can so represent them to the General Assembly that they shall be convinced that it is better for the Church as well as for us, that such relations as this seminary sustained to the Church before 1870, which for more than a third of a century, were so harmonious and fruitful of good, should now be restored.

Such was the immediate issue of the conflict between the Board of Directors and the Assembly's committee. It was a sort of truce until the meeting of the next General Assembly. A few days after the adjournment the following statement was addressed to the public:

The adjourned conference, which began on Wednesday last, between the Assembly's committee and the directors of the Union Theological Seminary, was concluded on Friday evening. A full, free and calm discussion was held of all the points at issue. There was throughout an obvious and earnest desire to reach harmoniously some conclusion.

The committee did not and could not yield as to the General Assembly's interpretation of the agreement of 1870. On the other hand, the seminary directors did not yield their position with regard to the transfer of Dr. Briggs. The fact is accepted on both sides that there is an honest difference of opinion between the two parties to the agreement of 1870, which difference will be reported to the General Assembly as for the present irreconcilable. The committee recommend that the *status quo* be recognized, in the hope that some action may be taken which will lead to a harmonious settlement of the questions involved.

The members of the committee and the directors of the seminary have reached a better understanding of one another by the free and courteous interchange of views, and on both sides there has been an honorable disposition to seek those things which make for peace.

In the conclusion of the conference the venerable Dr. Butler addressed the committee in a few kindly and impressive words, to which Dr. Patton responded in like spirit, and then, with the doxology and the benediction, the conference was adjourned.

FRANCIS L. PATTON,
Chairman of the General Assembly's Committee.

THOMAS S. HASTINGS,
For the Directors of Union Theological Seminary.

The following letter from Dr. Hastings will explain itself:

NEW YORK, May, 1898.

MY DEAR DR. PRENTISS:

You ask me for my impressions regarding the several meetings of the Board of Directors with the General Assembly's Committee on Conference, October 28, 1891, and January 20, 1892. At this distance it is possible to write calmly of things which at the time profoundly moved us all. Of course the interviews of the board and the committee were characterized by the utmost courtesy on both sides. There was no apparent heat in the protracted and repeated discussions. But it was evident from the first to the last that the committee assumed that the General Assembly must be right and therefore the seminary must be wrong. No concession was made to the seminary; but it was evidently expected that we would make to them concessions which we felt, and tried to show them, we could not in honor make. The only propositions which the committee made to us required that we should ignore the deliberate and conscientious action which we had taken, and to which we were bound by every principle of Christian honor and integrity to adhere. Our papers carefully prepared and submitted to the committee showed very clearly wherein the Assembly had mistaken our position, and had transcended the right conceded to them in the agreement of 1870. But the committee would concede nothing, while Dr. Patton crowned and practically concluded the conference by deliberately saying that if he had it all to do over again he would do exactly what he did at Detroit. This made upon the board and upon me a very unpleasant impression. It was evident that further conference was useless.

Referring to the cry of "now or never," which was heard so often at Detroit, I asked Dr. Patton if he thought that if either Dr. Butler or I had been telegraphed from Detroit, asking if we would be willing to waive the limitation of time in the agreement there would have been the slightest hesitation on our part in sending an affirmative reply? But to this question there was no satisfactory answer.

The committee yielded nothing, though they wanted us to yield everything, and at the conclusion of the conference they asked that the several papers which we had presented as containing our case, should not be given to the public. Mr. George Junkin said, in urging their suppression:

> I do not like the idea of having copies made of these two papers, because they are really a very powerful argument setting forth the directors' view. I think it would be perilous to the peace of the Church if these papers should get out.

We parted in a kindly and fraternal way, but with the feeling that nothing had been gained or lost on either side.

These in general are my impressions which you desired me to give of the memorable conferences between the Assembly's committee and our Board of Directors.

With sincere regard, yours truly,

THOMAS S. HASTINGS.

(*b*) *Discussion of the agreement of 1870 in the secular and religious press, especially that of the Presbyterian denomination.*

The public interest aroused by Dr. Briggs' address and the Detroit veto was very lively and widespread. There had been nothing quite like it since 1837–38. Both subjects touched the popular mind at many points and in various ways. Nor can there be any doubt that, whatever else may be said of them, they served an excellent purpose as object-lessons in ecclesiastical ethics, opinion and manners. A good deal of what was written against Union Seminary, especially in the religious papers, was very bitter and rasping; but much on the other hand, while decided and even severe, was marked by such evident sincerity and strong conviction as to disarm angry feeling. The leading secular journals of New York watched the case with the greatest interest and furnished the public with a vast amount of information on all its successive phases. In preparing this volume I have been constantly indebted to the records of their energetic and persistent labor. For the most part they were impartial and eager to get at and to tell the truth, the whole truth and, as far as the infirmities of human nature in the matter of news would permit, nothing but the truth. One of them, however, "the Leading Evening Paper," was an exception. Its proprietor at that time, who was said to be also the author of some of its sharpest editorials on the subject, was one of the most estimable men in New York; kind-hearted, generous, and full of varied Christian activity; but his zeal for Presbyterian orthodoxy was not at all according to knowledge; Dr. Briggs was to him a *bête noire*, and "higher criticism" only another name for downright infidelity. The editorials on these subjects were laden with the wildest sort of personal abuse and denunciation. They were just what for the honor of fair and truthful journalism they should not have been. Dr. Briggs, his colleagues and friends, Union Seminary and its Board of Directors, day after day, and month after month, were stigmatized in frenzied assaults of blind passion and calumny. And yet this paper was sent far and wide to ministers and elders of the Presbyterian Church in countless numbers, renewing old theological prejudices and sowing the seeds of new ones. As a faithful historian of Union Seminary I have felt bound to refer to this painful instance and illustration of the kind of warfare which it had to endure.

Besides innumerable articles, editorial or contributed, in the newspapers, several pamphlets appeared in exposition and defence of the Assembly's action.

They also were widely circulated and did much to fortify and increase the hostility to Union Seminary as in rebellion against the General Assembly. One of these entitled *The Ecclesiastical Status of the Theological Seminaries,* was written by the Rev. Dr. William H. Roberts, then professor at Lane. It was first published in *The Herald and Presbyter* of December 2, 1891. As an exposition of the most stringent theory of Assembly control it matched perfectly with the actual embodiment of the principle in the first section, Article II, of the "Amended Constitution" of the Seminary of the Northwest, already cited. The points were made with no little force and ingenuity, as also with an assurance not unbecoming a Chief Justice of the United States Supreme Court in announcing a unanimous opinion of that great tribunal. Dr. Roberts contended that the agreement of 1870 brought Union Seminary under the control of the General Assembly in a sense essentially the same as that in which all the Old School seminaries were, and had ever been, under Assembly control; in other words, wrought a radical change in the plan and constitution of Union Seminary, annulled its most characteristic principle, and so put an end to its independent existence. He took ground in direct conflict with that of the Standing Committee on Theological Seminaries at Detroit, as also with the opinion of the Detroit Assembly itself. Dr. Patton said in his report that the seminary was "one of the parties of the compact;" and, later, in his speech he said, "We have recognized that as a party Union Seminary may claim that their rights have been infringed by our construction, and if they see fit they can take us into the civil courts for a judicial and authoritative interpretation of this compact." He said still later: "We concede that we are parties in equal interest. Neither can compel the other to accept its construction." Dr. Roberts denied that the seminary had any right whatever as a party over against the Assembly. But I will let his article speak for itself, simply underscoring a few words. Here is his own recapitulation and summing up of the argument:

CONCLUSIONS.

From the considerations, facts, laws and precedents presented, the following conclusions are drawn as pertinent to the present ecclesiastical status of the theological seminaries:

1. That concurrent declaration No. 9, as agreed to and enacted at reunion by both the Old and New School General Assemblies, *established*, as a principle of action for the reunited Church, a uniform method of ecclesiastical *control* of all the theological seminaries.

2. That the General Assembly in 1870 and 1871 passed acts which put into effective operation said concurrent declaration No. 9; certain features of the act having been suggested in a memorial presented to the Assembly by the directors of the Union Theological Seminary.

3. That the Church now *exercises control* over all theological seminaries through the supreme *legislative and executive body*, the General Assembly.

4. That the power to modify and *interpret* said acts of 1870–71 rests *solely* in the General Assembly. While, how-

ever, the Assembly would appear at present to be obligated to maintain the act of 1870–71, in its several features, it is clear that under the agreement *made at reunion,* should circumstances arise requiring action, the Church gathered in *General Assembly may place the seminaries under* ANOTHER *method of control.*

5. That the several theological seminaries are so *obligated* by the *agreements* connected with *reunion,* by the Assembly's acts of 1870–71, and by the acts of their own directors, that they can neither except to the authority of the General Assembly, nor withdraw on their own motion from the control of the Presbyterian Church in the United States of America.

6. That the General Assembly, by virtue of the constitution, of the agreements made at reunion, and by the acts of the directors of the several theological seminaries, is invested with power to disapprove or veto appointments of professors of the seminaries, whether said appointments are original elections or transfers.

Without stopping to criticise Dr. Roberts' pamphlet in detail and leaving his "conclusions" to speak for themselves, it is only needful to call attention to two or three errors of fact that vitiated all his reasoning. On page 6 of the pamphlet Dr. Roberts said:

There was unanimous assent at reunion to the principle that the Church should exercise, in some definite form, control of her theological institutions. And it is held that the effect of reunion, and of the joint unanimous adoption of the concurrent declaration, by the Old and New School Assemblies, was to make the principle contained in declaration No. 9 binding upon all parties to the reunion until said declaration should have been modified or rescinded by the General Assembly of the united Church. Whatever may be thought of details in the method of its administration, the principle stands, and the law containing it is subject to change only by action of the General Assembly.

But the declaration No. 9 was expressly stated by the chairmen of the Joint Committee, Drs. Adams and Beatty, in their report to the two Assemblies which adopted it, to be only a "*recommendation*" (the italics are their own). How, then, could it be treated as an "established principle" and "law" of the Church? Did the mere recommendation of a constitutional amendment make it a part of the organic law? Again, on page 8 of his pamphlet, Dr. Roberts used this singular language:

As a result of the new status created by reunion, the directors of the Union Theological Seminary appeared as petitioners at the bar of the General Assembly. They were not there, it is to be noted, to perform any act involving the assertion of their independence as over against the Church. They were simply petitioners, requesting from the supreme legislative authority of the Church the performance of an act, which the General Assembly alone was empowered by the constitution and the reunion to perform. The directors ask "that the Assembly may be pleased." The memorial, therefore, as a petition to the General Assembly, by its directors, is the full proof that the Union Theological Seminary *was prepared to accept ecclesiastical control.*

The ecclesiastical control of all the theological seminaries was *vested by reunion* in the reunited Church, and could best be exercised through the General Assembly. The Union memorial definitely asked "that the General Assembly may be pleased to adopt it as a plan and rule in the exercise of its proprietorship and control over the several theological seminaries," etc. The directors of Union Theological Seminary recognized distinctly that reunion had wrought a change in the relations of that institution. Nowhere in the memorial does there appear any objection to the control by the Church, or any assertion of independence as over against the Church.

In these passages Dr. Roberts applied to Union Seminary language of the memorial respecting the Assembly's "proprietorship and control" of the theological seminaries, which referred *exclusively to the Old School seminaries;* and this is the simple and sole explanation of the directors of Union Seminary coming to the Assembly as petitioners and asking that body to "be pleased to adopt it as a plan and rule," etc. Union Seminary sought a favor not for itself, but for the Old School seminaries which belonged to the Assembly,—a favor which the General Assembly alone could grant,—and it naturally used the language of deference and solicitation, but in the very act of doing so it evinced its own freedom and independence by *offering* the Assembly a veto on the election of its own professors, in case the favor sought, viz.: the transfer of the election of professors in the Assembly's institutions to their Boards of Directors, were granted.

Had Dr. Roberts aimed in his *Ecclesiastical Status of the Theological Seminaries* to exemplify the type of

Presbyterianism most repugnant to the convictions and practice of the whole New School Church, from 1838 to 1870, he could not have done so more effectually. Its tone and its arguments were alike utterly alien to the Presbyterianism which founded and had always inspired the Union Theological Seminary.

The contention of Dr. Roberts in regard to the meaning of the "concurrent declaration" No. 9; namely, that it pledged both branches of the Church to the principle of ecclesiastical control over the theological seminaries as a term of reunion, met with wide acceptance in those sections of the Church which had been Old School. It soon became a common belief among them that the concession of the veto power *preceded* reunion as one of its conditions; and, furthermore, that this concession was made in fulfilment of a "pledge" embodied in the "concurrent declaration," No. 9. *The Presbyterian and Reformed Review* for July, 1892, contained an article on the 104th General Assembly, written by its able and scholarly editor, Dr. Warfield, in which this belief is expressed in the strongest manner. Here are passages from the article (pp. 532–33) bearing on this point:

As to the request itself—that is, to concur with the seminary in annulling the arrangement of 1870—the Assembly could not, of course, yield to it. Such a procedure would introduce that inequality in the relations of the seminaries to the Church which was recognized as intolerable when the negotiations for the reunion of the Old and New School

Churches were in progress, and without adequate pledges for the removal of which that reunion was fully understood to be impossible. The generosity of Union's concession of the existing measure of control by the Assembly of her appointments, consisted just in this—that by engaging to concede this control, or by withholding it, it was in the power of the seminary to enable or to prevent the consummation of reunion; and it chose the generous path of concession and thereby rendered reunion possible. It ought to be generally understood.

1. That it was held to be intolerable that the Assembly of the reunited Church should have direct control of the elections to the professorships in the Old School seminaries and no control over them in the New School seminaries.

2. That reunion could not, therefore, have been consummated without sufficient pledges that all the seminaries should be placed under something like equal ecclesiastical control.

3. That these pledges were given in the "concurrent declarations," and carried out immediately, the concession of the veto power by Union being the act by which, on its part, they were carried out. That the requirements as to theological seminaries were not made part of the reunion contract itself, but only a debt of honor (if we can say "only" in such a case), did not lead the fathers of the reunion period to feel them any the less binding.

4. That the ecclesiastical control actually conceded by Union Seminary in the proposition of 1870, was less, not more, in amount than had been contemplated in any plan that had been in discussion before reunion had been consummated—the reunited Church meeting the generosity of the seminary by generously yielding to its representations as to the legal difficulties in the way of the concession of a veto upon the election of directors.

5. That to annul this arrangement of 1870, as regards Union Seminary, would introduce the same inequality in the ecclesiastical relations of the seminaries, pledges of the removal of which were a prerequisite of reunion; and that such an inequality would be as intolerable now as it was then. Above and behind all this there stands also the manifest duty of the Church, as guardian of the doctrinal purity of its ministry, to retain some efficient direct control of the institutions in which its candidates are trained, a duty safeguarded by the requirement of the form of government that candidates shall be placed under the direction of "approved" teachers. In these circumstances the action of the Assembly could not be doubtful. But the generosity of the form in which it was taken passes all precedent; as, indeed, in all the discussions and in all the rulings of the Moderator, generous kindness toward a great institution which (however mistakenly) felt itself aggrieved, was allowed the fullest play.

So far as the concession of the veto by Union Seminary is concerned, all this must be ascribed to entire misapprehension of the facts in the case. No doubt the leading opponents of reunion regarded "inequality" in the relations of the seminaries to the Church as an "intolerable" feature of the situation. This is plainly indicated by Dr. A. A. Hodge's noted letter to Henry B. Smith, written in December, 1867. But the "concurrent declaration" contains no "pledges," simply a "*recommendation*" and that underscored. Dr. Warfield may, I think, be safely challenged to produce any evidence that Dr. Beatty, the wise and great-hearted chairman of the Old School Committee on Reunion, ever uttered a word in favor of requiring "pledges" touching New School theological seminaries as a term of reunion. But, allowing for the moment that Dr. Warfield's version of the matter is correct, how came it to pass that, in spite of the solemn "pledges," which, he says, made reunion possible, its ablest opponents, Dr. Charles Hodge, Dr. A. A. Hodge and Dr. Robert J. Breckinridge—not to mention others—still fought against it to the bitter end. Why were they not satisfied with the "pledges"?

Another paper, entitled *Union Seminary and the Assembly*, was published by the Rev. William McKibbin, D.D., of Cincinnati, in reply to a pamphlet of my own. It is interesting as showing what strange illusions on the whole subject got possession of men noted for their intelligence and Christian character. Dr. McKibbin was a leading member of the Standing Committee on Theological Seminaries at Detroit, and made one of the ablest speeches in favor of disapproving Dr. Briggs' transfer. A few sentences from the opening part of this speech will show how he regarded the question at issue:

> I believe that we are taking part in the greatest crisis through which the Presbyterian Church has ever passed. I believe that the issue or the issues which were involved in the Old and New School difficulties were mere bagatelles compared with the issue which is now at stake.

It is not surprising that, looking at the subject in

this way, Dr. McKibbin should have taken very strong ground against Professor Briggs. His speech was in an excellent spirit, and contained more or less with which I, for one, was in hearty sympathy; as, for example, its closing sentences: "I want that Book handled reverently; and I don't care whether it be in the name of higher criticism or of an angel from heaven, if he preaches any other Gospel than that of reverence for the Word of God, I say reject him." One of the most remarkable things in Dr. McKibbin's reply to my pamphlet, was his contention that Union Seminary is "the property of the Presbyterian Church in the United States of America." In order to show this, following Dr. Roberts, he applied the language of the Union memorial of 1870 in regard to the Old School seminaries, which were all under the proprietorship and control of the General Assembly, to Union Seminary. This seems almost incredible; but here are the passages, and they show, as hardly anything else could, what the friends of Union Seminary had to contend with in the way of argument.

Union Seminary had belonged to the New School body, and the Assembly of the reunited Church had inherited all the rights and privileges which this relation involved. As the debate turned upon the Assembly's rights *under the compact,* there may have been a failure to recognize and sufficiently emphasize this other and primary connection. But that such relation exists is unquestionable, and it throws great light upon the meaning to be attached, in Union's memorial of 1870, to the words, "That the General Assembly may be pleased to adopt it as a rule and plan, in the exercise of the proprietorship and control over the several theological seminaries." (p. 23).

Can there be any doubt that Union Seminary did belong to the New School Church and does now belong to the reunited Church, which inherited all the rights of both branches of the Church, or, to use the language of the plan of reunion, which possesses "all the legal and corporate rights and powers pertaining to the Church previous to the division of 1838, and all the legal and corporate rights which the separate Churches now possess"? Can Union, after having been aided and endorsed and commended as and because a New School seminary, and after securing its support under such a representation of itself for over thirty years, now deny the fact? And if they cannot deny this, can they deny that this relation has been transferred to the united Church? And must we not conclude that the memorial of the Union board of 1870 expressed the exact truth when it stated this relationship to be one of *proprietorship and control*? (pp. 27–8).

Again, if the New School body did convey its "proprietorship and control" to the united Church, are not its members who are now living bound to protest against a course which implies that they conveyed powers they did not hold, and transferred rights they did not possess? If the United States Government has a right to demand that the Russian Government in the Behring Sea matter shall sustain it in the assertion of all the rights which Russia claimed to have possessed and transferred to it, against England's counterclaim, has not the united Church a right to demand that all members of the New School body now living shall sustain it in asserting rights transferred to it by the New School body? (pp. 28–9).

This analogy between the case of the General Assembly against Union Seminary and that of the United States Government against England in the Behring Sea matter, recalls Fluellen's account of the resemblance between Harry of Monmouth and Alexander the Great: "There is a river in Macedon; and there is also, moreover, a river at Monmouth; . . . and there is salmons in both." If the question were whether before 1870, Union was a New School seminary and belonged, to all intents and purposes, to the New School Church, though in no wise under the proprietorship and control of its General Assembly, the answer would be plain and simple. Dr. McKibbin's quotations from the New School minutes to prove this are all so many mares' nests. But his contention went far beyond this. "The idea," he said, "that the New School body had any different mode of connection with its seminaries from the Old School body, or the Church before the division, is a pure fiction. Both New School and Old School claimed all the powers of the Church before the division, but were only able partially to enforce their claim. The New School claimed Princeton, and Western, and the Old School claimed Union, Auburn, and Lane." Really, had Dr. McKibbin contended that the Old School "claimed" Yale and Hartford and Andover and Bangor, it would not have been a bit more preposterous. When, where, and in what manner did the Old School ever "claim" Union Seminary?

The closing part of Dr. McKibbin's reply is so curious and suggestive that I quote almost the whole of it. Nothing could indicate more clearly the ecclesiastical animus which marked his paper. The italics are his own :

THE POWER OF THE ASSEMBLY TO ENFORCE THE FULFILLMENT OF THE COMPACT.

The question has been raised as to what the General Assembly is "going to do about it" in case Union Seminary continues to resist its authority, or severs its connection with the Presbyterian Church. This question is squarely raised by Dr. Prentiss with reference to Union's relation to the Assembly when he says : "The single tie which in 1870 of its own free will, connected it with the General Assembly, by its own free act it can sever at any moment for good and sufficient reasons." Of course we are to infer that Union claims to be the sole judge of what are good and sufficient reasons. This sounds like a menace. Coming from one who is not "a man of war" it cannot be attributed to abnormal belligerency, or an easily excited temperament. *The Presbyterian Church in the United States of America must face this question.* Here is the cry of seminary sovereignty raised as against the federal supremacy of the whole Church. It sounds like a cry heard in 1861 with reference to State sovereignty. And there is ten times more said in the constitution of the Presbyterian Church with reference to its federal supremacy than there was in the constitution of the United States of America with reference to the supremacy of the general government. Let Union, before this cry becomes more distinct and threatening, remember that a majority of the Presbyterian Church were either participants in or sympathizing witnesses of the struggle in which that question was settled, and that they will not be unequal to the vindication in the ecclesiastical sphere of a principle as fundamental to the existence and integrity of the Presbyterian Church as it was to the existence and integrity of the nation. Let us then see what answer can be framed as to what the General Assembly could do.

1. The Assembly, so long as Union defies its authority, may, without surrendering any of its own rights, decline to give to Union "official recognition and approbation" and call the attention of the Presbyteries to the form of government, chapter xiv, section 5, in which, "it is recommended that no candidate, except in extraordinary cases, be licensed unless he shall have studied divinity at least two years, under some approved divine or professor of theology."

2. It can arraign Union's directors before the bar of the Church, if, after heresy is proven against one of its professors, they continue to retain him as an instructor in the institution, as faithless to their ordination vows, viz: "To study the peace, purity and unity of the Church," for they would then aid and abet the propagation of such heresy. *Facit per alium, facit per se.*

3. It can have recourse to the civil courts. What the civil rights of the Assembly are, and the rights of donors and directors in sympathy with the Assembly, and what the mode or modes of enforcing them, I will not discuss. It is to be hoped that no such discussion will be necessary in the settlement of the questions at issue.

Two other pamphlets against Union Seminary ought to be noticed, for they were scattered broadcast throughout the Presbyterian Church and did much to mystify and mislead even fair-minded, good men. Their author appeared upon the scene a year or so later than Dr. William H. Roberts and Dr. McKibbin; but he soon made up for lost time and was widely regarded as far surpassing them in the lawyer-like acuteness and vigor of his attacks. One of his papers was first published in the New York *Sun* of October 17, 1892, a few days after the Board of Directors of Union Seminary had voted to annul the agreement of 1870. It soon appeared in a pamphlet form under the title, *Union Theological Seminary vs. the General Assembly of the Presbyterian Church. The Case to Date,* by Thomas McDougal, Cincinnati. In reading this pamphlet I was inclined to apply to it an expression my brother once used in depicting the report of the United States Secretary of the Treasury on the notorious defalcations of Swartwout and others. He called it "a fragment of chaos." It were hard to say whether ignorance of the law and facts in the case, or sweeping, not to say truculent, charges against the moral character and conduct of the directors of Union Seminary contributed the largest share to this chaotic mixture. A few extracts will enable the reader to judge for himself:

> Between 1870 and 1892 Union Seminary has received from the membership of the Presbyterian Church over one million and a half dollars, on the faith of its contract relation with the Assembly, and on its express representation made in circulars, constitution, by-laws, personal appeals and otherwise, that the seminary was distinctively Presbyterian, and was, by the compact of 1870, in ecclesiastical connection

with the Presbyterian Church, on the same footing with the other seminaries of that Church.

The Assembly having refused to surrender its contract rights, and to annul the contract, the seminary, of its own motion, now declares that the contract is illegal and void, because, as it alleges, of the lack of corporate power on its part to make the same, refuses to obey its terms, and, without the consent of the Assembly, the party to the contract, attempts to annul the same. It constitutes itself a judicial forum to try the question of the validity of the contract which it had made, without a hearing from the other party, and acting as the judge in its own case, a thing which no civil court in Christendom could, or would, attempt to do, annuls its own contract, and that without a return to the other party of what it had received on the faith of the contract and the relation as represented by it. In order to justify its action in refusing to carry out its contract—which it concedes is binding if it had the power to make it—it obtains from a learned lawyer, whom it employs, an opinion that it had no power under the charter to make the contract, and that therefore no contract in fact exists.

Here is Mr. McDougall's view of the very eminent lawyer whose opinion the seminary had ventured to solicit:

We are advised that the learned counsel who gave the opinion to the seminary is not a member of the Presbyterian Church, nor a believer in the Christian faith, and assume that he was selected for the purpose, because of his ability, and of being wholly disinterested and without bias so far as the Christian faith could bias him in his opinion. He knew, and the board knew that neither he nor the board was competent authority to determine the question between the parties, of the validity of the contract. Both knew that a competent forum existed in which that question could be authoritatively decided, and both knew the only party interested in the contract that can now legitimately question its validity on the ground of charter power, is the State of New York, and that that State has never questioned the exercise of the power by the seminary, but has knowingly permitted its exercise for a period of more than twenty years, without question.

It is a novel experience in jurisprudence to find a party to the contract, and one who has received the benefits of the contract on its part calling in its own lawyer to sit in judgment upon the validity of the contract thus made, and deciding to annul it and declare it illegal and void, on the ground of a want of authority on its part to make it, and refusing to perform its terms, and that without returning the consideration it has received on the faith of the contract and the relation created by it, and at the same time placing itself on high moral grounds, and averring that if it had the power to make the contract, it would willingly obey it.

Here is Mr. McDougall's way of looking at the position and office of such professors of Christian theology and learning as Archibald Alexander, Charles Hodge, Addison Alexander, Edward Robinson, Thomas H. Skinner, Henry B. Smith, W. G. T. Shedd, William Adams, Roswell D. Hitchcock and Philip Schaff:

The professors and teachers are merely employees of the corporation. They are not named in the charter, perform no essential corporate function, and are in no sense necessary to corporate existence. How then can their employment, however or by whoever made, be held to be a delegation or surrender of corporate power.

Why could not Union Seminary create the office of a general manager and refuse to appoint any professor he disapproved of? or contract with another seminary to supply it with teaching, or to appoint only such teachers as it would approve? If it may do this for one professor for one year, why not for all and for an indefinite number of years? Does the validity of the exercise of the power as to being within the charter or in excess of it depend on the number of the professors to be approved of, or the length of time the right of approval is exercised?

The professors hold the same corporate relation to the seminary, as the janitor, or the book-keeper, or the errand boy; and are on the same plane as the foreman, superintendent or manager of a manufacturing company.

We are unable to find an adjudicated case by any court sustaining the proposition as laid down by counsel for the seminary, that a corporation created for the purpose of carrying on a business of any kind can not contract with the purchaser of its product, whether that product be houses, engines or ministers, to turn out that product on a model satisfactory to the purchaser; and in order to that end, shall have the employment of the architect, mechanic or teacher, who is to make the product which he is to take, conditioned on his approval. That is all that underlies the contract between the Assembly and the seminary, and yet, as we have already seen, the seminary as a party to that contract hires its own attorney, constitutes itself its own judge in the case, and jealous of the interests of the corporation, and zealous for good faith and good morals, determines that such a contract is not within the scope of its corporate powers, is therefore illegal and void, and refuses to perform it, while retaining the consideration it has received by reason of it.

And here is the manner in which Mr. Thomas McDougall expressed his mind about the venerable Charles Butler, William A. Booth, D. Willis James, John Crosby Brown, William E. Dodge, Morris K. Jesup and others like them, in executing their solemn trust as directors of Union Seminary:

We submit that if such an attitude had been assumed by a corporation whose directors were Mohammedans or Hindoos, its conduct might have been assailed as dishonest, immoral, and a deliberate breach of faith. Does it alter the case that the conduct is that of a Board of Directors, whose members are members of the Presbyterian Church, and who take their code of morals on this important question from their attorney, who has given them the opinion he has, on high moral grounds, without even suggesting to his clients the moral obligations of such a contract and the duty of returning the million and a half dollars which they have received on the faith of the contract, and the relation created by it with the Presbyterian Church.

And here is the conclusion of the whole matter according to "The Case to Date":

The action of the board in annulling the compact of 1870 and refusing to discharge the moral obligations of that contract, evidences conclusively—all protestation to the contrary—that no moral obligations will be permitted to interfere with her separation from the Presbyterian Church. Her constitution, by-laws and oaths of allegiance to the Presbyterian Church are her own voluntary acts, which she can at any moment annul or abandon. She may require her faculty to teach Unitarianism or Popery, and no legal power can prevent her action and the application of her funds to that end.

In the absence of any legal relation to the Presbyterian Church by charter or contract, she is in no sense and can never be in any sense a Presbyterian seminary.

We assume it is safe to affirm that every dollar of her endowment and property received prior to 1892 was given to her on the belief whether expressed or not, that she was and would continue to be a Presbyterian seminary. Many of the donors who were Presbyterians have passed away. In the absence of any expressions to the contrary in making their gifts, in view of the compact of 1870, the fact that the directors were Presbyterians, the representations in constitution and by-laws, the history of the seminary and otherwise the conclusive presumption is that all gifts made by Presbyterians were made to what they believed to be a Presbyterian seminary. What an object lesson to the Church and the world, we have in the conduct of her directors. Over two millions of dollars thus contributed, free to be used for all time to come in teaching any kind of theology other than that which donors intended it should be used to teach, and no power to prevent the misapplication of the funds.

How perfectly idle to talk of moral obligations being sufficient to insure the fulfillment of trust obligations. The compact of 1870 is the test of the strength of the sense of moral obligations possessed by the present directors of Union Seminary.

This compact repudiated and the money retained, it is worse than idle to talk of moral obligations being any safeguard for the protection of funds contributed for the purposes named, or for the fulfillment of either legal or moral contract obligations.

The question is not one of sentiment; it is not one of the honesty or the sincerity of the belief of the Board of Directors. The question is above all such considerations, and is not to be beclouded or lost sight of by fireworks or sentiment without reason as to the high character or disinterestedness of the directors. Is there any reason, in law or morals, that will justify them in refusing to carry out their contract, while retaining the million and a half of dollars received from the Presbyterian Church on the faith of the seminary being Presbyterian by reason of the relation created by the contract?

Not very long after "The Case to Date" appeared, Mr. McDougall published a second pamphlet, in which he took me to task with no little severity.*

It was another "fragment of chaos," and even surpassed the first as a legal, ethical and ecclesiastical curiosity. Nothing quite like it, as far as I know, had before seen the light. Its author evidently had not the slightest knowledge of me. He called me an "ecclesiastical lawyer" and said I was one of the directors of Union Seminary. All he seemed to know about me was that I had written a pamphlet defending Union Seminary against the charges of Mr. J. J. McCook at Detroit, in regard to ex-Governor Morgan's and Mr.

*The Moral Qualtity of the Conduct of the Directors of Union Seminary—An open letter to the Rev. George L. Prentiss, D.D.—A Lesson in Ecclesiastical Morals, Construction of Ecclesiastical Control, etc., by Thomas McDougall, Cincinnati.—Robert Clarke & Co., Printers, 1893.

James Brown's munificent gifts to the institution. As in the case of Dr. W. H. Roberts and of Dr. McKibbin, I will give a few characteristic passages from this pamphlet and leave every candid reader to decide for himself whether they are marked by such an impartial, humble and truth-loving spirit as fairly entitled their author to sit in judgment upon "the moral conduct of the directors of Union Seminary."

One of Mr. McDougall's points was that the plan and constitution of Union Seminary of themselves afforded no proper safeguard against the misappropriation of its funds, or the abandonment of its Presbyterian principles: in other words, the directors of Union Seminary at any moment, if they chose to do it, could perjure themselves, violate their solemn pledge and turn the institution over to the support of any kind of religious error or unbelief! He refers to this point again and again: "By the agreement of 1870 the institution had put itself under the control of the General Assembly and was henceforth legally bound to use Mr. Brown's and Governor Morgan's and other gifts exclusively for Presbyterian purposes." As to what is Presbyterian, and what is not, the General Assembly is the supreme judicatory, and its decisions are final and binding on all parties in the denomination. Addressing me, he says:

It would be interesting to have you discuss how Union Seminary is in any sense a Presbyterian seminary, if the compact of 1870 is annulled. How is it Presbyterian in the sense that any gift made to it on the faith that it was a Presbyterian seminary whose orthodoxy was guaranteed can be secured beyond peradventure for the purposes for which it was given. . . . If you could only realize that a professor, in the eyes of the law, is nothing more than an employee, and occupies no higher legal relation than the janitor or the bookkeeper, and is no more essential to the corporate vitality than these servants are, you might change your conclusions as to what is and what is not a delegation of corporate power. One of the troubles with this whole question grows out of what appears to be a sacred, mysterious, indefinable, inexplicable relation which professors sustain to the seminaries of the Church. They are mere servants, who seem to be treated, however, as if they were greater than their masters, creatures greater than their Creator. Their appointment, by whomsoever made, and however made, is no more a delegation of corporate power than is the appointment of the janitor or the engineer, and it is an extraordinary assumption to place them on an equality, so far as corporate functions are concerned, with the directors of the corporation, as you have done.

The present directors, in annulling the compact of 1870, and asserting what they choose to call the "independence of the seminary, as provided by its charter," have placed themselves in the attitude of saying: "We are a Presbyterian seminary only by our voluntary act. So long as we choose to be a loyal Presbyterian seminary, we will be loyal as a matter of choice, but not of obligation. When it is our interest or pleasure to be disloyal, we propose to be in a position to carry out our interest or pleasure. Under no circumstances do we intend the Presbyterian Church, either through the General Assembly or any of its members, to interfere with us, or compel us to be Presbyterian, or to compel us to use our funds for the purpose of teaching any theology that we do not desire to have taught. We will be Presbyterian when it suits us, otherwise when we choose to be. Whatever trust attaches to the funds given to us, moral or otherwise, will not be permitted by us to stand in the way of our complete independence of Presbyterian control." Such is the position assumed by the present directors of Union Seminary, and such is their complete ignoring of the moral obligations resting upon them by the compact of 1870, and the trust relation they sustain to the donors of the money given to them to be used for the purpose of a Presbyterian seminary.

UNION'S PURPOSE IN MAKING THE COMPACT OF 1870.

Union Seminary sought, by the compact of 1870, to place itself in such relation to the Presbyterian Church as would give it the confidence, indorsement and patronage of the denomination, in order that it might obtain funds from the membership of that Church. Whatever may be said touching the legal quality of the relation thus created, the moral obligation is of as high a quality as the ordination vow of a minister, and the moral trust attaching to the gifts thus received, is of as binding a character in the forum of conscience as any trust, whether legally enforceable or otherwise. Fidelity to its obligations, and the relations thus created, cannot be affected by the fireworks of liberality, broad views and liberal instruction.

True liberty is implicit obedience to law, and fidelity to obligation. True orthodoxy is true liberty. True charity is as just as it is generous, and above all things, seeketh not her own, but is loyal even unto death to the obligations it has assumed toward others.

The modern chatter that "liberty is preferable to orthodoxy," and the gush of charity that deliberately violates moral obligations, are destructive of that righteousness which is the crowning glory of the Christian religion, and of which loyal Presbyterians should be the highest exponents.

This "open letter" closes with the following literary suggestion to me:

It might be interesting, instructive and profitable to have you write a treatise on the quality of moral and contract obligations, and fidelity to trust relations, taking the high grounds on these subjects which men of business honor occupy. Such a treatise might prove in this controversy a moral tonic, a breath of fresh air in a foggy atmosphere, and do more to aid clear thinking and right acting than all the special pleas heretofore made by you for the directors of Union Seminary—of which you are one—in attempting to cancel the compact of 1870, and ignoring the moral obligations and trust relations they occupy to the Presbyterian Church, and the donors of the funds to the seminary.

Yours respectfully,

THOMAS MCDOUGALL.

CINCINNATI, January 9, 1893.

I will give a single extract from the supplementary "Lesson in Ecclesiastical Morals"—a lesson intended, perhaps, to show me how and in what temper my "treatise" should be written.

Dr. Prentiss was one of the directors of Union Seminary when the agreement was made. It is remarkable that he did not present a copy of his ecclesiastical lexicon to the General Assembly, and draw attention to his construction of this contract, before the Assembly entered into it, and the other seminaries of the Church became parties to it.

If such is the teaching on the subject of contracts in ecclesiastical circles, what is to be thought of the students who are moulded by such teachers? What kind of a product will we receive at the hands of such instructors? What appreciation of the obligation of ordination vows and fidelity to the faith and creed of the Church can be expected from the students who are taught "that agreements are not legal compacts, but only expressions of confidence and good will, acts of generosity and courtesy," and that ordination vows and loyalty to the faith, purity, peace and discipline of the Church may lose their most essential virtue and all their beauty, the moment they are invested with the rigidity and binding force of a legal contract?

In view of such teaching is it remarkable that the directors of Union Seminary, after declaring in 1891, in answer to the Assembly's Conference Committee, that they "fully recognized the binding force of the agreement of 1870, until it shall be proved to be illegal or shall be properly abrogated," have attempted to annul the agreement, and have refused to discharge its legal, moral and trust obligations before it has been proven illegal, or has been properly abrogated? To call in their own lawyer, ask for his own opinion—and that without notice or consent of the other party—and upon that opinion such as it is, as if it were a judicial fiat in a proper case, declare the contract illegal, is without a parallel in history.

The money received from Presbyterians for Presbyterian uses while the compact of 1870 and the relations and obligations it created existed, and while the directors were loudly proclaiming their loyalty to the Presbyterian Church, and which amounts to one and a half million dollars, is coolly retained, no tender is made to those from whom it was thus obtained, and the Church is politely invited to attend to its own business.

Before passing from this most disagreeable subject I desire once more to show how utterly gratuitous and without foundation were the charges, each and all, which Mr. McDougall and so many other enemies of Union Seminary brought, year after year, against the good faith, integrity and Christian honor of the directors of that institution. I will give two papers bearing upon the subject; one a summary statement in regard to the endowments of the seminary, prepared at my request by Mr. Kingsley, its recorder and treasurer; the other, entitled *Union and the General Assembly*, being a letter to the editor of the New York *Tribune* by John T. Terry, an eminent merchant of New York. Here is Mr. Kingsley's paper:

The Board of Directors of Union Theological Seminary in the autumn of 1869, with the purpose of removal, purchased a site in the upper part of the city, and their plans for such removal made necessary a largely increased endowment, estimated at $500,000. The work of procuring the required amount was undertaken with great energy. The first effort was limited to $300,000, and at the regular January (1870) meeting, a public appeal was agreed upon which was issued over the several signatures of the entire directorate.

Rev. Edwin F. Hatfield, D.D., was appointed financial agent, and he entered promptly upon his official duty. A portion of the compensation for Dr. Hatfield's service was conditioned upon the obtaining the full amount of this undertaking, and as the records of January, 1871, show the payment of the additional sum, no better evidence of the complete success of the effort could be desired.

The public appeal under which this endowment was obtained, made no reference to any relations with the General

Assembly, for the excellent reason that no such relations existed, and none were then contemplated. In the beginning of the year 1871, encouraged by the succcss of the year preceding, jubilant over the accomplished reunion, and hopeful in view of the "agreement" with the General Assembly which had been perfected in May, 1870, the board undertook to raise the remaining $200,000. The agency of Dr. Hatfield was continued and an appeal to the benevolent public was issued, in which the new relations with the General Assembly were mentioned with emphasis. The result of this effort and this appeal was disappointing. From a careful examination of the seminary's financial records it appears that beyond the $300,000 subscribed under the first appeal, which was payable at the option of the subscribers in one, two and three years, not one-half of the desired amount was realized. A memorandum book containing in Dr. Hatfield's own handwriting, dated in 1872, what is evidently a complete list of subscriptions to the fund gives an aggregate of something less than $350,000 which accords substantially with the treasurer's accounts, and marks the second effort as a signal failure.

The permanent endowments of the seminary began in 1853, with the Davenport professorship, which was in the sum of $20,000, and was followed in 1855 by the Roosevelt and the Washburn professorships each in the sum of $25,000.

Scholarship endowments began in 1860, and have increased in number to about thirty. Library, Elocution, Lectureship and Fellowship with other professorship endowments have since been established, until the number of individuals who have thus expressed their interest and confidence in the institution, is about sixty. It is remarkable that in no single instance, have the founders accompanied their gifts with the faintest allusion to the General Assembly.

The present financial condition and credit of the seminary is in striking contrast with the straitened circumstances of its early history. At a meeting of the board held May 6, 1840, the following resolution was adopted: "*Resolved*, That in the judgment of the board a sufficient sum has been raised by subscription to justify the board in continuing the seminary in operation for the ensuing year." Twelve years later, in August, 1852, a Mr. Barclay was found willing to loan $10,000 on the seminary property for three years, at seven per cent. per annum, payable semi-annually, "prompt payment of principal and interest to be guaranteed by Caleb O. Halsted, Richard T. Haines, Anson G. Phelps, Charles Butler and David Hoadley jointly and severally," which terms were accepted.

E. M. KINGSLEY,
Treasurer and Recorder.

NEW YORK, April, 1898.

Here is the noble letter of Mr. Terry to the New York *Tribune:*

SIR:—Since the death of Governor E. D. Morgan I have occasionally seen intimations of what he would or would not have done if he could have foreseen the state of affairs now existing in the Presbyterian Church. It is a very easy matter to speculate upon what can neither be proved nor disproved, but some assertions have been made with a directness and assurance that are not warranted by any known facts, specially those with reference to Governor Morgan's benefactions to the Union Theological Seminary.

Governor Morgan was educated in his early life in a Congregational church, his father for a long series of years filling the office of deacon in the church at Windsor, Connecticut. When he removed to Hartford there were four prominent Congregational churches in that city, three of which were of a pronounced conservative type; the other one was under the pastorate of Dr. Horace Bushnell, and it was to this church that he gave his allegiance, and it was here that I first knew of him in the years 1835 and 1836. He came to Brooklyn to reside in 1837, and, finding no Congregational church there he connected himself with the New School Presbyterian church under the pastorate of Rev. Dr. Samuel H. Cox. If Dr. Storrs' church had been established in Brooklyn when he came there to reside, I am sure that you would never have heard of Governor Morgan as a Presbyterian in that city. He, like many others, became a Presbyterian by force of circumstances, not by choice. He removed to New York about 1844, and continued his connection with the Presbyterian Church. Governor Morgan was, during his long and useful life, engaged in mercantile business and affairs of State, and I do not think he ever considered himself a theologian. He certainly was not what may be designated as a crank either in matters of business, politics or religion. He was a man of liberal tendencies, and I can hardly conceive of anyone supposing that he would approve of the "rule or ruin" policy advocated by those who are at present in power in the Presbyterian Church.

I became connected with Governor Morgan in 1841, and until 1883, the period of his death, I was in almost daily intercourse with him when he was not absent from the city. When he stated to me that he was making his will and that he found it a difficult matter to determine exactly what to do, I suggested that we all owed something to New York, to which he assented, and I found upon reading his will that he had adopted some suggestions which I then made. He told me of some of his intentions with regard to Union Seminary, and I inferred that his benefactions were made there because it was an institution for the education of young men for the ministry and of liberal tendencies, and in the city of New York, and, further, that it afforded him much gratification to make the bequest, owing to his great regard and affection for Dr. Roswell D. Hitchcock.

To undertake to belittle his character by assuming that he would regret having given his money to the Union Theological Seminary upon the ground that it is not conducted absolutely upon the lines that would be approved by the majority at present in control of the General Assembly is to do his memory a great injustice.

JOHN T. TERRY.

NEW YORK, May 23, 1895.

If Mr. McDougall is not satisfied with these papers, or detects flaws in them, he can, no doubt, obtain further light by applying to the gentlemen themselves. They are two of the best and most highly esteemed citizens of New York, and are both, I believe, ruling elders in good and regular standing. Their only weak point, so far as I know, is that they get their orthodoxy from the Bible and not from a General Assembly.

(c) *High-Church theory about the powers of the General Assembly. Reunion Presbyterianism. Dr. Beatty and Dr. Adams.*

There are two very different theories of American Presbyterianism; and they have, every now and then, come into sharp conflict with each other. One of them may be called a rigid High-Church theory; while the other, varying in name or form, shuns domineering ways and has ever shown a special affinity for evangelical tolerance, moderation and liberty. Both have contended for orthodoxy and the faith once delivered to the saints; but not exactly in the same spirit or by the same methods. It seems to me that in the papers of Dr. Roberts, Dr. McKibbin and Thomas McDougall we have marked specimens of the High-Church type. The tone of these papers is a tone of rigid ecclesiastical authority and rule, not to say menace, whenever the power of the General Assembly is referred to. I have had occasion of late to familiarize myself somewhat with the tone which characterized the leaders and friends of reunion in 1869–70; and it struck me as an almost ideal expression of the true spirit of American Presbyterianism. The papers of Dr. Roberts and Dr. McKibbin and Thomas McDougall make a different impression. They uphold a theory of Assembly power and rule which I cannot but regard as in conflict with vital principles of American Presbyterianism. The whole New School branch of the Church always set its face, like a flint, against such a theory; and so did many of the weightiest men in the Old School branch. As for Union Seminary, it was born and nurtured, and has always moved and had its being, in another ecclesiastical atmosphere. Its difference of tone and theory from Dr. Roberts' and Mr. McDougall's reactionary Presbyterianism is like the difference in theory and spirit between American liberty and the autocratic despotism of the Russian Czar.

Let me show just what I mean by the rigid "High-Church theory of the powers of the General Assembly." I will do so by giving an extract bearing on the subject, from the life of George Junkin, D. D., LL.D., written by his brother, the Rev. Dr. David X. Junkin. No one can read this life of that champion of Old School orthodoxy without learning to esteem him as an eminently good man; nor did his renowned son-in-law, Stonewall Jackson, excel him in strong qualities of character. Here is his opinion on the subject in question:

He deplored the assumption by the General Assembly of powers not granted to that body in the constitution, powers which he verily believed were dangerous to the liberties of God's people, and destructive of the beautiful and well-balanced Presbyterianism which our fathers had deduced from the Bible. He felt that the assumption by the General Assembly of the powers of a court of original jurisdiction in cases of discipline was unconstitutional, and tended to the utter destruction of our system of appeals from a lower to a higher court. He abhorred the doctrine of the "omnipotence of the General Assembly," and in a series of vigorous articles published in the *Northwestern Presbyterian*, a paper ably edited at Chicago, by the Rev. E. Erskine, D. D., and the Rev. D. McKinney, D.D., he showed the unconstitutionality and the dangerous tendencies of this dogma, and besought his brethren to beware lest in their excited zeal for a good end they should adopt doctrines and measures which were revolutionary and destructive. . . . It is believed that his views of this matter are the views which prevail with the great mass of Presbyterians, especially since the reunion. The Old School branch before the reunion had substantially receded from and repudiated positions taken in 1865 and 1866, and the New School branch stand committed by all their deliverances in all their separate history against the High-Church doctrine of the "omnipotence of the General Assembly," the right of the Assembly to assume original jurisdiction in cases of discipline, and the possession by the highest court of all the powers of the inferior judiciaries. This would be a consolidation of power more puissant than the Popedom, and more dangerous to the liberties of God's people. Against it Dr. Junkin left his latest, almost his dying testimony, for in some of the last letters traced by his pen he charges his brother to *resist it everywhere and at all times.* *

But far better to me than the best written statement on the subject were two types of American Presbyterianism exemplified in the men who, as chairmen of the Old and New School Committee on Reunion, led that great movement with so much skill and such far-sighted wisdom. I refer to Charles C. Beatty and William Adams.

In preparing this volume I have had the privilege of reading many of the letters which passed between Dr. Adams and Dr. Beatty while they were acting as chairmen of the Joint Committee on Reunion. I say the privilege,—for while the letters relate largely to points and difficulties no longer of any special interest, the spirit pervading them all is so admirable, so full of zeal for the unity and peace of the Church, so full, too, of mutual confidence and love, that their perusal has been to me a real edification. It was this spirit which contributed more than aught else to bring about reunion. Without this spirit that happy consummation would have been impossible.

* The position of the New School Church is clearly and forcibly set forth by the committee appointed by its General Assembly in 1855, "to report to the next Assembly on the constitutional power of the Assembly over the subject of slave-holding in our Churches." The committee consisted of Albert Barnes, Asa D. Smith, afterwards president of Dartmouth College, Hon. William Jessup, Augustus P. Hascall and A. H. H. Boyd, of Virginia. The report will be found in the New School Minutes of 1856, pp. 197-201.

Charles C. Beatty and William Adams were men of the highest qualities of personal character, greatly beloved and admired by all who knew them. Dr. Beatty, who was seven years older than Dr. Adams, represented the Old School in its most solid and attractive characteristics. Son of an officer of the Revolutionary army, grandson of an eminent Presbyterian minister, an alumnus of both the college and seminary at Princeton, he had passed his life in the West, chiefly in Ohio, where he was universally honored and revered, especially as a devoted and munificent friend of education. In face of the strongest opposition he led the Old School in the reunion movement with consummate good sense and judgment as also with the very meekness of wisdom. Probably no other man was so well fitted to serve as chairman of the Joint Committee on the part of the Old School. Dr. Adams was not less signally fitted to serve the New School in the same capacity. He was the son of one of the foremost American educators of the early half of the century. On the mother's side he traced his lineage back to Governor Bradford of the Mayflower. A graduate of Yale College and of Andover Theological Seminary, and first settled as pastor over a Congregational church near Boston, he was seasoned, through and through, with Puritan and New England ideas — those vitalizing ideas of religion, freedom and social progress which had so largely ruled the spirit and shaped the growth and policy of the New School churches. At the same time his soundness in the faith was unquestioned, and he wielded an influence not in the New School branch alone, but in the other branch and in the whole Christian community, which in its peculiar elements of strength and persuasiveness was hardly equalled by that of any other minister in the Presbyterian Church. When the reunion was at length accomplished, everybody felt that he had been one of its chief instruments. Dr. Shaw, of Rochester, a man whose own praise was in all the land, wrote to him: "The Church owes you a debt so large that no one but God is rich enough to pay it."

These two eminent servants of the Lord deserve to be held in lasting remembrance as rare examples at once of Christian character and of the far-reaching power of genuine Christian influence. Their relations to each other while chairmen of the Joint Committee were very beautiful, as may be seen by the following extract from a letter of Dr. Beatty to Mr. John Crosby Brown, written after Dr. Adams' death:

My previous personal knowledge of Dr. Adams had been very slight; but upon our first interview he met me with such cordiality, as well as courtesy, and in all our conferences showed so kind, frank and confiding a manner as at once won my heart to love as well as respect him; and this feeling on my part was retained to the close of his life. I think it was reciprocated. We did not so much correspond as we had personal intercourse at his home in New York. The two reports to the General Assembly were, at my request, principally prepared by him. Some parts, chiefly the historical, were written out by me, but the general form and style was his; all was submitted to the members, and sometimes modifications were made at their suggestion, and finally I had the review; but in anything material the reports were from the pen of Dr. Adams.

We talked over the subject very freely and unreservedly, and prayed over it earnestly, for we both felt that there was a great responsibility resting upon us to God and the Church. He knew what great difficulties and conflicts of mind I had from the fact that my best friends were in opposition to my views; and I made the request of him that after my death he would state these things in some article in *The Evangelist*, which he promised to do—for we then had little thought that I could survive him. On one occasion, after the reunion, both of us expressed our conviction that the position we had held had been a means of grace to us, in drawing us nearer to God, and enabling us to feel more fully our entire dependence on Him for light and aid in our work. I consider it a great privilege and blessing to me to have been thus associated with him in this matter.

I shall not forget his kind manner towards me at the close of the Council at Edinburgh. He said to me, "I have been requested to make the closing address at the Council, and I have asked that you officiate in the religious exercises." He introduced me to the Assembly as his dear friend, making some beautiful remarks about my age and sacrifice in coming in despite of my blindness.

I have spoken of the two chairmen of the Joint Committee and of the correspondence between them. Among the other members of the committee on both sides were ministers and elders of wide influence, who also rendered invaluable service to the cause of reunion. And they did it because they, too, like Charles C. Beatty and William Adams, were such faithful patterns of the American Presbyterianism which has its root and life in the Gospel of Christ.

CHAPTER IV.

REASONS IN FAVOR OF ANNULLING THE AGREEMENT OF 1870.—THE GENERAL ASSEMBLY REQUESTED BY THE BOARD OF DIRECTORS OF UNION SEMINARY TO CONCUR WITH THEM IN THIS SOLUTION OF THE PROBLEM.

The action at Detroit left the friends of Union Seminary only the slightest hope of a peaceful settlement of the veto question except by unconditional submission to the claims of the Assembly. And few of them cherished even this slight hope after the adjourned meeting of the Board and the Assembly's Committee of Conference, January 20–22, 1892. Their chief concern was now to sever the tie that for twenty years had bound the institution to the General Assembly, with the least possible disturbance of the peace of the Presbyterian Church. At the special request of my old and revered friend, CHARLES BUTLER, the president and only surviving founder of the seminary, I prepared a paper on the subject, in which was set forth the conclusion my own mind had reached with regard to the relations of the seminary to the General Assembly, as also the reasons leading to such conclusion. The paper, entitled THE PROBLEM OF THE VETO POWER, AND HOW TO SOLVE IT, was published in March, 1892, on my own responsibility, but with the approval of Mr. Butler and other friends of Union Seminary. My conclusion and reasons coincided in all essential points with their own. I venture, therefore, to embody a part of the paper in this historical record substantially as it was written early in 1892.

THE PROBLEM TO BE SOLVED AND THE BEST WAY TO SOLVE IT.

I propose to give some reasons why the agreement of 1870 between Union Seminary and the General Assembly should be annulled. I shall state these reasons frankly as they present themselves to my own mind, fully conscious of the grave issue involved, and sincerely desirous to avoid a single word that could justly be charged with unfairness or prejudice. After long reflection I have slowly reached the conviction that, in the interest of all the parties concerned, the best and only safe way out of the present trouble is to annul the agreement of 1870. Several distinct lines of thought have led me to this conclusion. And the first line of thought relates to the legal bearing of that agreement.

(*a*) *The agreement of 1870, conceding to the General Assembly a veto on the election of professors in Union Seminary, should be annulled because inconsistent with the chartered obligations of the Board of Directors.*

Great stress was laid upon the point of legality by the Joint Committee on Reunion, by the first united Assembly at Philadelphia in 1870, and by most, if not all, of the theological seminaries themselves. In explaining the ninth article of their report of 1868 the chairman of the Joint Committee said that a "*recommendation,*" looking to some uniformity of ecclesiastical supervision, was all which the committee felt to be within their province or that of the Assembly, except that those seminaries, now belonging to either branch of the Church, "should have every guarantee and protection for their *chartered rights* which they might desire."

The Standing Committee on Theological Seminaries at Philadelphia, in 1870, said in their report, which was unanimously adopted by the Assembly:

> Your committee would recommend no change, and no attempt at change, in this direction, save such as may *safely and wisely be effected under existing charters.* For example, the directors of the seminary at Princeton have memorialized this Assembly, with the request that the Assembly would so far change its "plan" of control over the institution as to give the Board of Directors enlarged rights in several specified particulars, subject to the veto of the General Assembly. Your committee are unanimously of the opinion that the changes asked for are eminently wise and proper. If it were within the power of the General Assembly to remit the entire administration of this venerable institution to its Board of Directors, without any of the restrictions they have mentioned as to the supply of their own vacancies, they would cordially recommend it. But, inasmuch as the endowments of this seminary are held on the condition that it should be the property and under the control of the General Assembly of the Presbyterian Church in the United States, that trust *cannot be vacated nor transferred to any other body.*

In 1871 the Board of Directors of Danville Seminary reported to the General Assembly that they had appointed a committee to investigate the whole subject of entering into an arrangement with the Assembly and to report to the directors, whether "they can *legally* adopt the plan of the Assembly." In the same year the Board of Directors of the Northwestern Theological Seminary report: "In regard to the relation of the seminary to the General Assembly, the board, finding that there are *legal points* involved in this question which require careful investigation, referred the whole matter to a committee with instructions to report to the directors at their next annual meeting in April, 1872." Similar difficulties arose in the case of Lane and Auburn Seminaries. It is plain, then, that the question of legality was considered of vital importance in reference to adopting the Assembly plan.

This brings us back to the case of Union. And here it becomes me to speak with much diffidence, seeing I am no lawyer. But the interpretation of a simple charter, like the Act of Incorporation of Union Seminary, is, in part at least, a function of common sense as well as of legal skill and learning. Every director is presumed to understand it. What is the charter of Union Seminary? So far as concerns the present discussion it is compressed into a single section, which is as follows:

The government of the seminary shall at all times be vested in a Board of Directors, which shall consist of not less than twenty-eight members; one-half of whom shall be clergymen and the other half laymen.

Voila tout! One word expresses it all, but that word, in the domain of law and authority, is one of the most comprehensive, as well as of the most potential, in the English language. It means sovereign power. "The government shall be upon His shoulders." Government has all things under its feet. The government of the United States bears sway over the President and his Cabinet; over Congress; over the Judiciary; over the army and navy; over all the people; over the whole land. In saying, then, that "the government of the seminary shall at all times be vested in a Board of Directors," the people of the State of New York, represented in Senate and Assembly, enacted that the Board of Directors should themselves, individually and as a body, exercise and fulfil this trust.

How could they delegate such a trust to several hundred men assembled at Detroit, or at Portland, or at any other place—men coming together for ten or twelve days and then scattering far and wide over the land? And how could such a fugitive, unincorporate collection of men carry on the "government" or execute the trust, "at all times vested in a Board of Directors"? How can this Board of Directors "*appoint* all professors"—and yet its appointment of every professor be so imperfect that a majority vote of the General Assembly can utterly nullify it? No act of "the government of the seminary" is so high, or so vital and characteristic, as the appointment of its professors; and to let a General Assembly or any other body step in at the last moment and forbid this act, deliberately performed by the Board of Directors, in whom it is "at all times vested," does seem to me to involve a distinct violation of chartered rights and duties.

Such was the opinion of the eminent legal counsel, Mr. Stanley Matthews, consulted by Lane Seminary in 1871. Mr. Matthews, afterwards a Justice of the United States Supreme Court, stated clearly and positively that "the Board of Trustees, a corporate body, could not legally delegate any of its powers to the General Assembly or to any other body." Two years later the legal counsel of Auburn Seminary gave a similar opinion. Both seminaries followed this opinion and entered into their several arrangements with the General Assembly in pursuance of it. They guarded against the violation of their chartered obligations, as they believed, by a special provision or by-law. Here it is in the case of Lane:

> Every election of a professor in this institution shall be reported to the next General Assembly, and if the said Assembly shall by vote express its disapprobation of the election, the professorship in question shall *ipso facto* be vacant from and after such veto of the General Assembly: it being understood that in such cases *it is not the pleasure of this board that such professor shall continue in office.*—[New Digest, p. 389.]

The action of Auburn was to the same effect. The committee appointed to consider the subject said in their report:

> They have carefully examined said charter and sought legal counsel on the subject. They find that the Board of Commissioners is invested with the sole and ultimate authority to appoint its professors, and they *cannot legally delegate this power to any other body.*

Thereupon the board adopted the following by-laws:

That hereafter the appointments of professors in this seminary be primarily made conditional upon the approval of the General Assembly, and that such appointments be complete and authoritative only upon securing such approval. *

No such provision or by-law was ever adopted by Union. It is very plain, therefore, that if Lane and Auburn were right, Union Seminary was wrong. In delegating the ultimate decision in the election of its professors to the General Assembly it undertook to do what exceeded its chartered power.

The question may here be asked, why this legal point was not considered by Union Seminary before offering to the General Assembly a veto on the election of its professors? And why it was not considered, also, by the General Assembly before accepting that offer? For the General Assembly was as much bound not to

*This action of Auburn, conditioning its appointment of a professor upon "the *approval* of the General Assembly" was one cause, perhaps, of the solicitude which Dr. Adams expressed about this time and subsequently concerning the veto power. The following letter from Mr. Kingsley will explain what I mean:

MY DEAR DR. PRENTISS: In May, 1874, just before I started on my journey as commissioner to General Assembly, Rev. Dr. William Adams called upon me, and, with an earnestness of manner which I could not then understand or explain, charged me to see that the Assembly, in any action touching theological seminaries, should not attempt, or allow, any control over Union Seminary beyond the one point of "*disapproval*" of professorial appointments. He appeared to me alarmed unreasonably, and as he expressed a similar anxiety on two or three subsequent occasions, the matter impressed itself distinctly upon my memory.

I have learned more recently that in 1873 the Assembly at Baltimore assumed and exercised the power of "*approval*" of the transfer of Dr. Schaff; and that action perhaps accounts for the extreme concern manifested by Dr. Adams. Yours truly,

E. M. KINGSLEY.

accept the offer without being first assured of its legality, as the Board of Directors was bound not to *make* the offer without being first assured that the charter of the institution would not thereby be violated. The question may be answered in several ways. The necessity of being aided by legal counsel was distinctly recognized by the Joint Committee, as appears in the thirteenth article of their report of 1867, recommending the appointment by the General Assemblies of a committee of six distinguished lawyers "to investigate all questions of property and of vested rights, as they may stand related to the matter of reunion." Such a legal committee was designated; but owing to the death of Mr. Daniel Lord, one of its members, and the inability of several other members to act, the Joint Committee on Reunion informed the General Assemblies of 1868 that they had as yet received from this committee no report in regard to "questions of property and vested rights." After 1868, the whole subject of the theological seminaries retired into the background, the question of a Presbytery's right to examine ministers applying for admission from other Presbyteries having largely taken its place.

Another answer to the question why both Union Seminary and the General Assembly did not carefully investigate all the legal points involved before entering into the agreement of 1870, is the haste which of necessity marked the whole matter. It was all compressed into two or three weeks. Between the meeting of the Board of Directors of Union Seminary on May 9th, and that held on May 16, 1870, legal counsel was sought with regard to the veto which had been proposed on the election of directors. Less than three weeks later, in the report of the Standing Committee on Theological Seminaries at Philadelphia occurs the following significant passage:

In this generous offer [viz., Union's offer of a veto on the election of its professors] looking solely to the peace and harmony of the Church, the memorialists did not include the same veto in regard to the election of their own directors, *inasmuch as these directors hold the property of the seminary* IN TRUST.—[Minutes of 1870, p. 63.]

I cannot find that with this exception any distinct question of legality was raised either by the Union board or by the General Assembly. Both seem to have taken for granted that what they were doing was all right. How often has the same thing been true of important acts of Congress and of State Legislatures, afterward declared illegal, or unconstitutional, by the judgment of the United States Supreme Court!

(*b*) *The agreement of 1870, conceding to the General Assembly a veto on the election of professors in Union Seminary, should be annulled because inconsistent with the plan and constitution, as well as with the charter, of the institution.*

And here we come at once to very close quarters with the ethical side of the problem before us. It is a question of conscience and personal duty, and not merely nor mainly a question of opinion, or of ecclesiastical order. Every director of Union Seminary made the following declaration in the presence of the board:

Approving of the plan and constitution of the Union Theological Seminary in the city of New York, and of the

Westminster Confession of Faith, and of the Presbyterian Form of Church Government, I do *solemnly promise* to maintain the same, so long as I shall continue to be a member of the Board of Directors.

What is the meaning of this declaration? It means that every director binds himself to maintain the plan and constitution of Union Seminary in the same sense that he binds himself to maintain the Westminster Confession of Faith as the doctrinal standard of the institution, or the Presbyterian Form of Church Government. When no longer able to do this in good conscience he virtually pledges himself to resign his directorship.

Now what is the "plan" of Union Seminary, which every director declared his approval of and solemnly promised to maintain? One of its most distinctive and vital features is the autonomy and self-governing freedom of the institution. If anything enters into the essence of its plan, as conceived and carried out by its founders, it is independence of ecclesiastical control. This plan was guaranteed by its charter. "The government of the seminary shall at all times be vested in a Board of Directors." Whether a good or a bad plan, such was the actual plan of the institution.

Every director next makes a solemn promise to maintain the constitution of the seminary. At Detroit this "constitution *so-called*" was held up before the Assembly as a very small affair,—a mere "corporation's constitution." But is it really so small an affair that every director solemnly promises to maintain? Let us consider the question for a moment. What makes Union Seminary a Presbyterian institution?

Certainly not the charter.* Its charter makes Auburn a distinctively Presbyterian seminary. But the charter of Union would serve equally well for an Episcopal, a Methodist, a Roman Catholic, or a Unitarian institution. What declares it to be a Presbyterian seminary is its constitution. And so, also, with its orthodoxy. The constitution, prepared by men of wisdom, skill and experience, as well as piety, sets forth the design, character and limits of its corporate powers. The first section of Article I, reads:

> No person shall be eligible to the office of director unless he be a minister or member in good standing of some evangelical Church accepting the Westminster Confession of Faith, as adopted by the Presbyterian Churches of this country.

And now wherein was the agreement of 1870 inconsistent with the constitution of Union Seminary? In this, that it conceded to the General Assembly the exercise of a right and duty, which the constitution, as well as the charter, entrusted to the Board of Directors alone. The third section of Article I, reads as follows:

> In order to carry out the powers vested in them by the Act of Incorporation, the Board of Directors shall have authority to make their own by-laws; hold, manage, and disburse the funds of the seminary; *appoint all officers, professors, and teachers;* fix their salaries; *determine their duties;* make laws for the government of the institution; and, in general,

* In the report on theological seminaries at Philadelphia in 1870, it is said that Lane and Union "by their *charters*, most cautiously prepared, are made Presbyterian institutions." (New Digest, p. 384.) This is a mistake in the case of Union. Its charter makes no allusion to Presbyterianism.

to adopt all such measures, *not inconsistent with the provisions of said act and of this constitution,* as the interests of the seminary may require.

Here is section first of Article II:

> The faculty shall consist of a president and professors, all of whom shall be ordained ministers of the Gospel, and all of *whom shall be appointed by the Board of Directors.*

These clauses are mandatory, explicit, and leave no place for any rival or superior authority. If the Board of Directors can lawfully delegate to the General Assembly the power of vetoing the appointment of a professor, it can just as lawfully delegate to the General Assembly the power of vetoing the appointment of president, directors, treasurer, and all other officers of the institution. Will any one say that it can lawfully do this? Nothing short of an amendment to the constitution of the seminary could have empowered the Board of Directors in 1870 to give to the General Assembly a veto upon the appointment of its professors. Even this, as I think, would have been insufficient; for the charter would still have barred the way. Without such amendment their way was doubly barred. And this necessity of a change of the constitution in order to bring the seminary under ecclesiastical supervision was distinctly recognized as early as 1868. The ninth article of the plan of union reported by the Joint Committee of that year, reported again in 1869 and adopted by both Assemblies, was as follows:

> In order to a uniform system of ecclesiastical supervision those theological seminaries that are now under Assembly control may, if their Boards of Directors so elect, be trans-

ferred to the watch and care of one or more of the adjacent Synods; and the other seminaries are *advised to introduce*, as far as may be, *into their constitutions, the principle* of Synodical or Assembly supervision; in which case they shall be entitled to an official recognition and approbation on the part of the General Assembly.

It thus appears that, according to the deliberate judgment of the Joint Committee on Reunion in 1868, of the Joint Committee of Conference in 1869, and of both General Assemblies in 1869—the Assemblies that adopted and carried out the final plan of union—the only way by which Union Seminary could place itself under Synodical or Assembly supervision was to amend the constitution of the seminary by introducing into it the principle of ecclesiastical supervision. This, therefore, is what they all, one after the other and in perfect concert, "advised" Union Seminary to do. But Union Seminary did not see fit to follow this advice. It never introduced into its constitution "the principle of Synodical or Assembly supervision;" and this not having been done, any such measure as the agreement of 1870 was and is "inconsistent with the constitution" which every director solemnly promises to maintain. Why the "*recommendation*" of the Joint Committees and of the two Assemblies was not acted upon by the Union board, I cannot say. I was a member of the board and can only testify that the subject never came before it. Mr. D. Willis James' opposition to conceding to the General Assembly a veto on the election of Union directors and professors was based, not specifically upon illegality or unconstitutionality, but upon its un-wisdom and inherent perils.

And here let me add that when Princeton was freed from the direct control of the General Assembly of the united Church, the "plan," or constitution, of the seminary was at the same time amended in order to allow of the new arrangemnnt. The Assembly was asked by Princeton "so to *alter the plan* of the seminary that the directors shall hereafter have the *right* to appoint and to remove professors, subject to the veto of the General Assembly." And the Princeton professors in their paper say that if their suggestion is adopted "it would *require* the following changes in the plan"—that is, in the constitution. (See "Plan as Amended by the Assembly of 1870," New Digest, pp. 381–383.) Similar constitutional changes were made by the Western, Northwestern and Danville Seminaries.

At first thought it does seem hard to believe that such men as the directors of Union Seminary and such a body as the General Assembly of the Presbyterian Church could have agreed upon a method of settling the question of the theological seminaries, that was inconsistent both with the charter of Union Seminary and with its constitution framed in order to carry out the powers vested in it by that charter. But we must consider that wise men sometimes do hasty and unwise things, especially when acting under the pressure of circumstances and of unselfish, generous sentiment. At the best the world is largely ruled by mistaken views; and if a stronger, more far-seeing power than man's was not at the helm, the mistakes of even good and right-minded men would be sure to wreck human progress.

In this very matter of reunion we have elsewhere a striking illustration of error of judgment on the part of the Joint Committee and of both Assemblies. Is it not natural to assume that in dealing with so important a question as the theological seminaries and after years of discussion any scheme of settlement, unanimously agreed upon by both parties, would have been, if not actually the best—a point which experience alone could determine—yet at least feasible and not illegal? This, however, was confessedly not the case in the present instance. The plan recommended by the Joint Committee on Reunion and adopted without objection by both Assemblies in 1868, proposed again by the Joint Committee of Conference in 1869, and once more adopted without objection by both Assemblies, was vitiated by a fatal error. The error was discovered only at the last moment. "As the endowments of this seminary are held on condition that it should be subject to the General Assembly of the Presbyterian Church, it can neither be rendered independent [like Union and Lane] nor placed under the control of one or more Synods" [like Auburn]. Such was the language of Dr. Hodge and the other Princeton professors, addressed to the Board of Directors of that seminary on the 25th of April, 1870. And yet, as I have shown, a learned committee had been appointed to look particularly at all the legal points involved, while the whole subject had been under discussion for nearly three years!

In view of this simple fact I submit to every candid mind whether the memorial of the directors of Union Seminary, adopted on May 16, 1870, in which they ask the General Assembly to remit the election of professors in the seminaries under its "proprietorship and control" to their several Boards of Direction, and offer in that case to concede to the Assembly a veto on the election of Union's professors, was after all so very strange, even though such concession would be in direct conflict with the "plan and constitution" of this seminary? To the best of my own recollection and belief no definite question of either chartered, or constitutional, right was raised at this meeting. The discussion turned upon quite other points. But this is no more an impeachment of the perfect honesty, intelligence and right feeling of the Board of Directors of Union Seminary or of the General Assembly in the action of 1870, than it is an impeachment of the honesty, capacity and patriotic sentiment of Congress or of any legislative body, that its deliberate action is later decided by the Supreme Court to have been wrong. How much easier it often is to be wise afterward than to be wise at the critical, eventful moment. In offering to the General Assembly a veto on the election of its professors the Board of Directors of Union Seminary acted under a misapprehension of its corporate and constitutional powers; and the Assembly erred no less in accepting the offer. But for all that the whole transaction, even though unwarranted, was inspired by the best motives and did honor to the spirit of peace and harmony that governed alike both of the parties to it.

(*c*) *The agreement of 1870 should be annulled because the veto on the election of professors has proved highly injurious to the very object which that agreement aimed to secure.*

In conceding the veto power the directors of Union Seminary, as they said, were "looking *solely* to the peace and harmony of the Church." But as a matter of fact nothing, in the twenty years since reunion, has so disturbed the peace and harmony of the Church as the very first exercise of this power. And there is every reason to believe that its exercise in the future would be fraught with similar effects. In 1870 the ecclesiastical veto was, to all intents and purposes, an unknown power. It was in the nature of an experiment. Nobody could tell how it would work. We know now by the sure test of trial and experience just how it works. As I have said before, real power, wherever it exists, is sure to make itself felt. Its turn always comes, sooner or later; nor is the opportunity apt to be neglected, when a much desired object, whether good or bad, can be secured by its exercise. What is called the *spoils system*, for example—a system which has done so much to poison and vulgarize our political life—is largely the outgrowth of that simple power of removal, which the Congress of 1789 decided to belong exclusively to the President. Who dreamed at the time what immense harm would come to the nation through an abuse of the power? Mr. Madison, whose influence was most potent in this decision of the first Congress, declared that if a President should exercise his power of removal from mere personal motives, or except in extreme cases, he would deserve to be impeached. And for more than a third of a century Executive patronage was used solely as a public trust by Washington and the other great patriots who then ruled the country. Even after 1820, when the mischievous Four Years' law was passed, during the second term of Monroe and the whole term of John Quincy Adams, very few removals were made, and those in every case for cause. Only here and there a far-seeing statesman surmised what, during the next third of a century, lay wrapped up in the unlimited power of removal, when, instead of being used as a public trust, it was going to be so largely prostituted to vulgar greed and the ruthless animosities of selfish partisanship. How different it is now! The "spoils system" has come to be regarded, not merely by a few far-seeing statesmen, but by tens of thousands of our most thoughtful and patriotic citizens, of both parties, as, on the whole, the greatest evil that, since the overthrow of slavery, has beset the moral life of the country. While I am writing this paper in a lovely mountain valley of Vermont one of the most distinguished of her sons is depicting her heroic services in the Revolutionary war and the civic virtues which rendered her so meet, in advance of all others, to join the Old Thirteen by admission to the Union. It is a romantic and inspiring story, told with an eloquence not unworthy of Daniel Webster or of Edward Everett. And I find in it this golden passage: "We have lived to see the prohibition of slavery in the earliest constitution of Vermont become a part of the fundamental law of this nation. May the time be not far off when its declaration against that other and more widespread curse which corrupts and degrades free government, [the 'spoils system'] shall be likewise put in force by the body of the American people."*

Illustrations still more impressive of the way in which power long quiescent may of a sudden, when the fitting opportunity occurs, spring into vigorous

* Oration at the dedication of the Bennington Battle Monument, etc., by E. J. Phelps.

and baleful action, might be drawn from the history of the Christian Church. Alike in the civil and in the ecclesiastical sphere unlimited power will always act, sooner or later, according to its quality, its opportunities, and the passions or weaknesses of human nature. When all these are combined they produce the appropriate results according to an inexorable law of cause and effect.

Let it once appear that the mind of the Church is especially sensitive respecting a certain questionable opinion relating to theology or to Biblical criticism, for example, and nothing is easier than to arouse suspicion, distrust, or hostile feeling toward any man who is supposed to entertain that opinion. And if he chance to be a professor-elect in a theological seminary and subject to the disapproval of the General Assembly, nothing will be easier than to facilitate such disapproval by idle rumor, false charges, misunderstanding, and all the varied methods of ecclesiastical influence and manipulation. Had the New School General Assembly possessed in 1850 a veto on the appointment of professors in Union Seminary, and had the theological atmosphere then been as susceptible of sudden, violent changes as it is to-day, I have great doubt whether Henry B. Smith could have taken the chair of Church History without a sharp struggle. He was charged with being too ardent an admirer of "German Theology;" and his splendid eulogy of Schleiermacher in the famous address at Andover on the Relations of Faith and Philosophy, in 1849, which seemed to afford some countenance to the charge, excited anxiety and misgiving, not to say positive hostility, in the minds of not a few excellent men, who at the time represented the old orthodoxy. Upon his nomination in the Union Board of Directors in 1850 questions relating to this subject were asked, to which, fortunately, such men as Dr. Adams and Dr. Stearns were able on the spot to give satisfactory answers. But had these questions got into the religious newspapers, been scattered broadcast over the Church, and so aroused public notice and controversy, the result would probably have been a peremptory withdrawal of his name by Professor Smith, or else a disapproval of his appointment by the General Assembly.

And so, a few years later, had the New School General Assembly possessed the veto power, and had the theological atmosphere been as strongly charged with anxiety, suspicion, or hostile feeling, as it is in the Presbyterian Church to-day, I believe the nomination of Roswell D. Hitchcock to the chair of Church History would almost certainly have resulted in the ultimate defeat of his election. As it was, and in spite of the earnest support of such directors as Dr. Adams and Dr. Stearns and of Professor Henry B. Smith in the faculty, misrepresentation did its work so effectually that, by the advice of his friends and of friends of the seminary he withdrew his name as a candidate. Not until a year later, when unreasonable suspicions and whisperings had spent their force, was he renominated and unanimously elected. And those, I may add, who had most strenuously opposed his appointment, were soon numbered among his warmest friends. The case forcibly illustrated the wisdom of Professor Smith's objection to the election of professors by vote of the General Assembly. "It might bring into the Assembly local, personal, and theological questions, which it would be better to settle in a narrower field."

Had the General Assembly of 1837 possessed a veto upon the election of professors in the new seminary, just founded in the city of New York, it is highly probable that the appointment of Edward Robinson, too, would have met with strong opposition, if not actual disapproval, on the part of the Assembly. "German Rationalism" or "Neology," was at that time regarded with the utmost apprehension, and no one suspected of sympathy with it, still more of following its exegetical and theological methods, would have been allowed to pass, unchallenged, into the chair of Biblical Literature. Moses Stuart, to whom Biblical learning in this country owes such a lasting debt of gratitude, was widely viewed as a dangerous man, if not a heretic; and Dr. Robinson had for years been intimately associated with Moses Stuart at Andover, in cultivating and naturalizing German scholarship on this side of the Atlantic. It is well-known that on this account leading ministers in the Presbyterian Church felt in doubt about him. Had his election as a Union professor been subject to the veto of the General Assembly, which passed the Exscinding Acts—and that was the Assembly to which the appointment would have been reported—no one can say, I repeat, that it would not have been sharply contested, if not positively disapproved.

The simple truth in the case is, that those best qualified to fill the most important chairs in our theological institutions, are apt to be comparatively young men, and young men, too, of so much originality, intellectual force, and independence of thought and utterance, as easily to expose themselves to be misunderstood and distrusted by old-fashioned conservatives, with whom they are yet at bottom in genuine sympathy. It was so with Henry B. Smith, Roswell D. Hitchcock, Lewis F. Stearns, and others I might name. How true is what Dr. A. A. Hodge wrote in his letter to Professor Smith:

> The majority of any Assembly must be necessarily ignorant of the special wants and local conditions of any seminary, and of the qualifications of candidates proposed for its chairs of instruction. The best of these are generally young men, up to the time of their nomination known only to a few. To vest the choice in the General Assembly will tend to put prominent ecclesiastics into such positions, rather than scholars, or men especially qualified with gifts of teaching. As the population of our country becomes larger and more heterogeneous, and the General Assembly increases proportionately, the difficulties above mentioned, and many others easily thought of, will increase.

When these objections to the election of professors by the General Assembly are added to those already mentioned, how very strong they are! And yet the objections to the exercise of the veto power by the General Assembly seem to me to involve nearly all the evils, infelicities, and perils of the electing power, with still others and even greater ones peculiar to itself. These objections, should the veto power be continued, are likely to increase very much the difficulty of obtaining the best men to fill chairs of instruction in our Presbyterian seminaries. The Assembly's veto will repel them, especially if they belong to other communions. I can speak here from personal knowledge. One of the first points raised by my nephew, the lamented Professor Stearns, of Bangor, against accepting the call to

Union Seminary, given him in the summer of 1890, was the possibility that, even should he accept, be received without objection into the Presbytery of New York and enter upon the duties of his chair, the General Assembly might, five or six months later, undo all that had been done, veto his appointment, mark him as not competent or not sound, and thus set him adrift in the world. I thought at the time that such fears were chimerical. I cannot think so now. The action at Detroit forbids it. Lewis F. Stearns is now recognized as a theologian of the very best type, and his sudden death is universally deplored as a heavy loss to the American Church. In 1890, he was comparatively unknown; his inaugural address at Bangor had not escaped severe criticism; although a conservative, he was also a liberal, independent, and fearless thinker; and I can readily understand now, as I could not in 1890, what a plausible case in favor of disapproving his appointment might readily have been made out before the General Assembly. At all events, the veto power helped to deter him from accepting the call to Union Seminary. And if continued, it will tend strongly to deter others like him from accepting a similar call.

It is argued, I know, that the Presbyterian Church ought surely to have some voice in the education of her own ministers and teachers. I do not deny it. Much that is said on this point seems to me just and reasonable. I assent to it heartily. The trouble is not in the principle, but in its application. By what method can the Church, in the actual condition of things, make its influence felt most wisely and effectually in training up her own pastors and teachers? That is the question. And what I now maintain is, that the veto power on the election of professors in her theological seminaries is not the right method. It does not meet the real difficulties. It does not at all meet the difficulty, for example, in the case of that large number of future Presbyterian ministers who are receiving their education in the academies, colleges, and theological seminaries of other denominations. Nor does it meet the difficulty, or solve the problem, when they are in training in our own institutions. A great deal may be done and is done in the academy, in the college, and in the seminary, through the kindly and wise supervision of the local church and its pastor, of the Presbytery and of the Board of Education. And then as to the choice of the best theological instructors,—best in learning, in character, in gifts of teaching, in soundness of doctrine, in zeal for the cause and kingdom of Christ,—such Boards of Directors as those of Union, Princeton, Auburn, McCormick, and the rest, are far better qualified to make it than any General Assembly. A Board of Directors can take weeks or months, if needful, to investigate and make inquiries. It is perfectly familiar with "the special wants and local conditions" of the institution under its care. Every director acts under the pressure of a "solemn promise," and of a feeling of direct, personal, as well as official, responsibility hardly possible in the case of a great popular Assembly. The best Board of Directors, it is true, is an imperfect body and may commit mistakes. But mistakes are inevitable under any method. Imperfection and possible errors cling to every system.

(*d*) *Would an ecclesiastical veto on the appointment of religious editors be a good thing?*

How would this veto power work in other spheres? Look, for example, at the denominational religious newspaper by which opinion and character in the Presbyterian Church are so largely influenced. It is one of the most powerful of all agencies in the training alike of her ministers, her elders and private members, and, above all, in the training of her children. How many of her homes it enters every week! And in every one of these homes it is read with avidity; it wins confidence and affection; becomes a trusted friend and counsellor; shapes in no small degree all the family thinking about Christian truth, about the kingdom of God, about the ways of Providence and whatever is going on in the world. It is, in a word, a ruling power in the Presbyterian Church, alike in the domain of thought and action. As an instrument of immediate, all-pervading influence, whether over private or public opinion, it far surpasses the theological seminary. At what a disadvantage a professor speaks compared with the editor who has the ear of thousands and tens of thousands every Sabbath day, and, more or less, all the other days of the week! Should not the Presbyterian Church have some kind of supervision of an agency so closely connected with her duty to the families under her care and with her dearest interests? Ought she not to have some voice in selecting the men who, directly or through their contributors, speak to her people so often and with such immense effect? It seems to me that, in answer to these questions, an argument in favor of subjecting the denominational religious paper to ecclesiastical control by giving the Assembly a veto upon the appointment of its editor, might be made out quite as strong, to say the least, as that for the veto on the election of theological professors. And yet the argument would never convince American Presbyterians—and it is of them I am now speaking—that the great religious papers of the denomination, *The Evangelist, The Observer, The Presbyterian, The Presbyterian Journal, The Presbyterian Banner, The Herald and Presbyter, The Interior, The Northern Presbyterian, The Occident,* and all the rest, would, on the whole, be as effectively, or as wisely and safely, conducted by editors appointed, directly or indirectly, by the General Assembly, as under the existing independent system they are conducted by the veterans, who with so much toil and skill have made them what they are. My patience has, now and then, been sorely tried by the "course" of some of these veterans; but it would, probably, have been tried far more severely had their places been filled by a majority vote of the General Assembly. And if some of them have seemed to me at times very unfair and harsh toward Union Seminary in the present "unpleasantness," I can never forget what invaluable service they rendered to the cause of reunion, while that great event in our Presbyterian annals was passing into history.

The religious press has its faults and imperfections, like everything human; but it is an agency of vast power and reach in furtherance of the kingdom of Christ on earth. And as it advances nearer to its ideal and becomes more completely guided and inspired by the Sermon on the Mount, this will more and more appear. One of the wisest men I ever knew and one of my best friends was Asa Cummings, the biographer of Dr. Payson, and for many years editor of the old *Christian Mirror.* I owe him no small debt of gratitude for the influence of that paper, while under his care, upon my early religious life and opinions. And it left its beneficent impress upon all the Congregational churches of Maine. But to return to the point: my contention is, that the argument in favor of an Assembly veto on the election of professors in our theological seminaries, on the ground that the Church ought to have some direct supervision of the education of her ministers, is quite as strong in favor of an ecclesiastical veto on the appointment of the editors of our religious family papers; and yet that it is equally undesirable in either case. Is it not very strange, then, that among the many wise men who concurred in vesting in the General Assembly a veto power on the election of professors, no one seems to have forseen this? Not more strange, I reply, than that among the many wise men who took part in planning and founding Princeton Seminary, for example, no one seems to have foreseen that, sooner or later, the election of its professors by the General Assembly would have to be abandoned for a simpler and better method. Time and experience taught the friends of Princeton and other seminaries this better method; nor would anything now tempt them to return to the old system. And, as I have said before, if the veto power were freely given up by a unanimous vote of the General Assembly, just as the electing power in 1870 and later was freely given up, the result, I for one do not doubt, would be equally satisfactory.

(*e*) *Objection to annulling the agreement between Union Seminary and the General Assembly on account of the other seminaries.*

It has been argued, I know, that the agreement of 1870 was not only a strict legal compact between Union Seminary and the General Assembly, but between Union and the other seminaries; and that its abrogation would at once remand the other seminaries to their state anterior to the reunion. But the argument seems to me to be based upon an entire misapprehension of the facts in the case. Why should this follow? The General Assembly of 1870, of its own free will, by a unanimous vote, offered to remit the election of professors in the seminaries under its proprietorship and control to their own Boards of Direction, and actually did remit it in the case of Princeton. And this was done expressly on the "self-evident" ground "that there were great disadvantages and perils in electing professors and teachers by the Assembly itself, without sufficient time or opportunity for acquaintance with the qualifications of men to be appointed to offices of such responsibility." Is not the ground as "self-evident" now as it was in 1870? And surely no one will question the perfect authority of the Assembly, then or now, to let the seminaries under its "proprietorship and control" elect their own professors. And as to Lane and Auburn, if they desire to go back to their state in 1870, the repeal of a mere by-law will enable them to do so; or, better still, a simple expression of such desire to the General Assembly would, probably, secure the object, and that without controversy or friction.

The special reason for investing the Assembly with the veto,—namely, to allay "jealousy,"—having ceased, what harm could come of giving up the veto power itself? No seminary would cease thereby to be just as truly a Presbyterian institution as it was in the beginning, and is now. It is not in any sense the veto power that makes Union, for example, a Presbyterian seminary. Its history, its plan and constitution give it this character. Its connection with the great Presbyterian Church does not depend in the least upon its being under the proprietorship and control of the General Assembly. Every one of its professors will still have to be an "ordained minister of the Gospel" and to "approve of the Presbyterian doctrine and Form of Government." Every one of its professors will be under the supervision and control of a Board of Directors representing the intelligence, wisdom, public spirit, and Christian character of the whole adjacent Presbyterian community. "The board shall watch over the fidelity of all who may be employed in giving instruction; *shall judge of their competency, doctrine and morals;* and shall have power to remove any officer, professor or teacher from office." (Article I, Section 4.) And then committees from Synod and Presbytery are cordially invited to attend the annual examinations and freely report concerning the same to their several bodies. In the way of supervision what more than all this can reasonably be asked for? And when I look over the catalogues of Princeton, Auburn, McCormick, Lane and other seminaries, and read the names of their directors, I repeat the question: In the way of supervision what more can reasonably be asked for than the watch and care of such weighty bodies of select Christian ministers and laymen?

Let us keep in mind that no method or amount of formal supervision can insure against more or less practical shortcoming and mistakes in the training of our ministers. When the Church has done the best she can do, she will have to confess that the whole matter is beset with difficulties beyond the control of mere human wisdom. And in any case no small proportion of the ministers and theological teachers of the Presbyterian Church will continue to be trained in other than Presbyterian schools of divinity. Our Churches will continue to call pastors and our theological seminaries will continue to call professors in view of their qualifications, rather than with reference to the places where they were educated. William Adams, Edward Robinson, Henry B. Smith, Roswell D. Hitchcock, were trained in Congregationalism; and how many more of the leading New School ministers and scholars came from other denominations? How many of the most learned, useful, and honored Presbyterian pastors and teachers of to-day were called from other branches of the Church of Christ?

(*f*) *The issues wider than Presbyterianism.*

And this leads me to say, that the problem to be solved involves issues of far wider scope than the bounds of Presbyterianism. It concerns vital interests of the whole Christian scholarship of the country. Such, at all events, is the conviction of many of the foremost—and, I may add, most conservative—representatives of that scholarship in New England, in the Middle States, and throughout the Great West. I wish it were proper to make public the letters bearing upon this point, which have come to me, as also to Union directors, from far and near; for the fair and catholic temper in which the writers express the conviction would carry hardly less weight than their distinguished names—names honored alike in Church and State. "I do not believe," writes one of them, a theologian held in universal respect for his learning and impartial judgment, "I do not believe that in the times in which we are now living there can be a due amount of freedom in a school of theology which is dependent, in the appointment of its professors, on the will of a great ecclesiastical body like the General Assembly of the Presbyterian Church." "I confess," writes another, a pastor of eminent gifts and wide influence, "I confess that to my mind nothing could be more disastrous than ecclesiastical management of our theological seminaries. If the Presbyterian Church should establish such a supervision and rigidly carry it out, its institutions would soon cease to have any part in Christian leadership." Another, ranking among the first men in the nation, both as a jurist and a diplomatist, closes a letter thus: "There is no doubt, in my mind, that the general intelligence of the country is on the side of the seminary."

It is, in a word, the common interest of American Christianity and of sound scholarship that the claims of a reasonable liberty in theological and Biblical inquiry and study should be carefully guarded to the end that the truth may have free course and be glorified. I advocate no license to rash and destructive criticism or teaching. Nor, to quote the words of the founders of Union Seminary in the preamble to the constitution, have I sympathy with the "extremes of theological speculation" any more than with those of "ecclesiastical domination." I have no wish to silence the rightful voice of the Church in the assertion and defense of those great doctrines of

Revealed Truth, which are the very substance of her faith, or in bearing witness against the errorists who deny them. I believe most profoundly in the inspiration and ruling authority of the Holy Scriptures. And no Church in the land can more safely or better trust its theological seminaries than the Presbyterian. It is a Church of deep and strong convictions. It is a Church, committed, through and through, to the principle that God alone is Lord of the conscience, to the infallible authority of His word, and to the "inalienable rights of private judgment" in the intepretation of that word. It is a Church that loves and knows how to work for the Divine Master, and is full of the genuine enthusiasm of humanity. It has its faults, to be sure, but its virtues outweigh them a hundred fold. Howard Crosby's memorable words, which amidst great applause rang through the Church of the Covenant on the 27th of May, 1869, shortly before the whole vast audience rose to give its unanimous vote for reunion, are yet, I trust, to be fulfilled to the letter: "I hope when the conservators of orthodoxy and the conservators of liberty come together, as Dr. Adams has said, *there will be an orthodox liberty and a free orthodoxy such as the world has never seen.*"

The solution of the veto problem by annulling the agreement of 1870 commended itself to a large majority of the directors of Union Seminary as the only one now feasible; and accordingly, in a memorial to the General Assembly which met at Portland, Oregon, on May 19, 1892, the board requested the Assembly to join with it in such a settlement. The friends of the seminary were much encouraged to hope for a favorable issue of this request by the emphatic language of *The Presbyterian*, of Philadelphia, one of the ablest and most influential, as well as conservative weekly papers of the denomination: "We have no doubt that if this is the wish of the authorities of the seminary, and they made known their desire to the Assembly, it would be ready to give the seminary a full release."—Their hope, unhappily, proved, as we shall see, altogether fallacious.

CHAPTER V.

THE MEMORIAL OF THE BOARD OF DIRECTORS OF UNION SEMINARY, ASKING THE ASSEMBLY TO JOIN WITH IT IN ANNULLING THE AGREEMENT OF 1870.—THE ASSEMBLY REFUSING TO COMPLY WITH THIS REQUEST, PROPOSES ARBITRATION.—THE SEMINARY THEREUPON SEVERS ALL CONNECTION WITH THE ASSEMBLY CAUSED BY THE AGREEMENT OF 1870, AND RESUMES ITS ORIGINAL FREEDOM AND INDEPENDENCE OF ECCLESIASTICAL CONTROL.—A GENEROUS GIFT.—SEQUEL TO THE ASSEMBLY'S ACTION IN REGARD TO UNION SEMINARY.

We come now to the closing scene and incidents of the conflict between the seminary and the General Assembly. The scene opens with an appeal to the Assembly, which met at Portland, Oregon, on May 19, 1892, to join with Union Seminary in annulling the agreement of 1870.

(*a*) *Memorial of the Board of Directors to the Assembly at Portland.*

This memorial and other documents which, it was thought desirable to lay before the Assembly, were carried across the continent to Oregon by a special messenger, Mr. E. M. Kingsley, the recorder and an honored member of the board. This was done in token of high respect for the Assembly as well as to give it important information bearing upon the action and feeling of the directors. Mr. Kingsley was himself invited to read the memorial; and received, both on the platform and on the floor of the Assembly, the friendliest treatment. "At 2 P. M., to-day [so he wrote on May 23d to President Hastings] I was allowed the honor of the platform and read our two papers as impressively as my somewhat husky voice would permit. The full house listened attentively and at one or two points applauded vigorously. Dr. Briggs and wife arrived this morning. This is to be an interesting week, for Revision, Heresy and Rebellion are exciting topics." Indeed, so far as concerned the seminary, my impression is that at this time, and throughout the whole painful controversy, the institution itself was still regarded with general pride and affection. Such names as Edward Robinson, Thomas H. Skinner, Henry B. Smith, William Adams and Roswell D. Hitchcock had still kept for it a tender spot in the heart of the Presbyterian Church. The memorial of the Board of Directors was as follows:

TO THE GENERAL ASSEMBLY OF THE PRESBYTERIAN CHURCH IN THE UNITED STATES OF AMERICA.

REVEREND AND DEAR BRETHREN:

There are certain points which we could not properly embody in the report of our conference with the committee sent to us by the last General Assembly. These points we desire to present in the following memorial, as they have an important bearing upon our case in this Assembly.

1. We desire first of all to say that, while we do not question that the Assembly believed they had the right to do as they did at Detroit, yet we claim that, as one of the parties to the agreement of 1870, our understanding of that agreement must of necessity govern our action. We claim that the Assembly at Detroit transcended its power under the agreement in such a way as to inflict a serious wrong upon this institution. We are far from thinking that the General Assembly intended to violate the agreement of 1870 in any way, and your committee has conceded that this board had no such intention.

2. For more than twenty years the agreement has remained unquestioned, simply because untested. The possibilities and the perils of such an agreement must, in the nature of the case, lie dormant until revealed by a practical application. The one and sole aim of the concession of the veto power made by Union Seminary was "the peace and harmony of the Church." But the very first exercise of the power has greatly disturbed "the peace and harmony of the Church," and compelled us to realize that it is a power fraught with peril alike for the seminaries and for the Church. In 1869, in presenting the report of the Committee of Conference on reunion, Dr. George W. Musgrave said to the Old School Assembly that the articles in the "declaration" "are not a compact or covenant, but they suggest to the Assembly what are suitable arrangements. . . . They are not terms of the union. They may be annulled or modified as any future Assembly may deem proper. We told our brethren," he said, "that we were unwilling to tie the hands of the future Church of God." (The Presbyterian Reunion Memorial Volume, p. 546.) In the same spirit with Dr. Musgrave, referring to the ninth article of the "declaration" which dealt with the question of the seminaries, the Assembly of the

united Church in 1870 said: "It was intended as a measure for the maintenance of confidence and harmony, and not as indicating the best method for all future time. It had been discovered by years of experiment in the Old School branch that the election of professors in the seminaries directly by the General Assembly involved many 'disadvantages, infelicities, not to say, at times, perils.'" (Minutes, 1870, p. 148.) In December, 1867, Dr. A. A. Hodge wrote to Dr. Henry B. Smith: "It is proper, it is almost a necessity, that each institution should be left in the management of those upon whose support it exclusively depends. The majority of any Assembly must be necessarily ignorant of the special wants and local conditions of any seminary, and of the qualifications of candidates proposed for its chairs of instruction. The best of these are generally young men, up to the time of their nomination known only to a few. To vest the choice in the General Assembly will tend to put prominent ecclesiastics into such positions, rather than scholars, or men especially qualified with gifts for teaching. As the population of our country becomes larger and more heterogeneous, and the General Assembly increases proportionably, the difficulties above mentioned and many others easily thought of, will increase."

Dr. Henry B. Smith, expressed his own views in the following language: "It is a fair and serious question whether a General Assembly, representing the Presbyterian Church throughout the whole United States, especially in view of the numbers in that Church, will be the best or even a suitable body to choose the professors and manage the concerns of all the Presbyterian seminaries scattered throughout the country. We very much doubt whether this will be a wise arrangement. It may work well in Scotland but Scotland has its limits. It might bring into the

Assembly local, personal and theological questions which it would be better to settle in a narrower field."

These views were generally accepted by the united Church, and led the Assembly at the time of the reunion, to offer to surrender the power of electing the professors in those seminaries which had been under the control of the Old School branch of the Church.

3. But it is our conviction that there are more and stronger objections to the possession of the veto power than of the electing power of the Assembly. The failure to elect a professor nominated by a seminary is comparatively a negative thing. The veto is a positive verdict, both against the professor appointed and against the Board of Directors which appointed him; and, as we have seen, it may be a verdict without a trial, without a hearing, and without reasons given. The injustice and the peril of such an exercise of ecclesiastical power in our judgment, can hardly be overestimated. The multitude, who had looked on from a distance, who had heard only one side of the case, and who had no close personal knowledge of the interests involved, could disregard and override the matured judgment of those who had the fullest personal knowledge, and who had at stake rights commensurate with their obligations. The veto power may be hasty, arbitrary, unjust and even cruel. The electing power may be unwise and hasty, but it cannot begin to do such injury as may be done by the veto power. We are persuaded, therefore, that it would be far better for the Church, as well as for the seminaries, that the veto power should no longer reside in the General Assembly.

4. But it is claimed by some that, in order to protect the Church against heretical teaching in the seminaries, the Assembly must have and maintain the veto power. Does that really protect her? If a professor, one year after his ap-

pointment, or at any later time, depart from the faith, the temporary veto power cannot reach him. Has the Church then no other and better resource for her defense? Evidently the power of disapproval is insufficient; it can reach only exceptional cases, and can afford no general or permanent protection. Our admirable Presbyterian polity is far better than the artificial device of 1870 for protecting the Church against unsafe teaching in the seminaries. A Presbyterian minister, whether he teach from the pulpit or from the professor's chair, has the inalienable right to insist that, if his teaching be called in question, he shall first of all have refuge and defense in his Presbytery, to which alone belongs "original jurisdiction." In this regard the professor and the pastor have equal rights; but under the arrangement of 1870, there is a special discrimination against the professor. The Assembly has no veto power over the appointment of a pastor. To us this seems an abnormal and unjust discrimination, not consistent with our polity. If either professor or pastor teach heresy, the one resort alike for each is, in the first instance, the Presbytery. If in any case a Presbytery fail to do its duty, the General Assembly can, directly or through the Synod, reach and rebuke that Presbytery, and require that the unsound teacher be brought to trial. Besides this, another normal method of protection is in the right of the Presbyteries to examine carefully the graduates of the seminaries who apply for licensure, and to reject such as have imbibed false teaching and are not sound in the faith. This twofold protection by the Presbytery, it seems to us, is as ample as it is constitutional. In our judgment, therefore, those who insist that the veto power is necessary for the protection of the Church, show a radical lack of confidence in our Presbyterian polity, which lack of confidence we cannot share.

5. As the appointed directors and guardians of this school of Christian learning, we deeply realize our solemn obligation to act faithfully for its interests according to our own conscientious convictions, under our charter and constitution. We are charged with a sacred trust handed down to us from the past by noble men whom the Presbyterian Church has long delighted to honor. We must keep that trust inviolate. There can be no conflict between real obligations. Our loyalty alike to the Church and to Union Seminary constrains us to believe that it would be far better, for both Church and seminary, that the relations which existed so harmoniously between the two, far more than a third of a century before 1870, should now be restored.

6. It is claimed, however, by some that if the agreement of 1870 should be abrogated, Union Seminary would cease to be Presbyterian. Can that be? Does its Presbyterianism date from 1870? What was this seminary before that time? No charge of heresy was ever brought against it. Can those who remember such honored names among our founders and directors as Erskine Mason. Albert Barnes, Samuel Hanson Cox, William Adams, Edwin F. Hatfield, Jonathan F. Stearns and J. Few Smith, besides such laymen as Richard T. Haines, William E. Dodge, Anson G. Phelps and Norman White, not to mention others no less distinguished,—can those who remember these names say that before the reunion this seminary was not Presbyterian? We submit that if it be only the concession of the veto power to the Assembly which made this institution Presbyterian, then its Presbyterianism is something which we cannot understand. Our Presbyterianism is in our whole history, and in the personnel of our directors and of our faculty.

In conclusion, permit us to say, that through all this painful misunderstanding it has been to us a marvel inexplicable that any of our brethren could possibly suppose that men, so well known to the Church as are our directors and our professors, could or can tolerate anything that will undermine the divine authority of the inspired Word, to which we cling with all our hearts as the only infallible rule of faith and practice, and to whose maintenance all our lives are consecrated.

There are other and weighty considerations which we have preferred not to urge. While there exists the undoubted right of either party to the agreement of 1870 to act alone in its abrogation, yet this memorial is submitted with the earnest hope that your reverend body may cordially concur with us in annulling the arrangement of 1870, thus restoring Union Seminary to its former relations to the General Assembly.

With great respect on behalf of the Board of Directors,

[*Signed*] CHARLES BUTLER, *President.*

[*Signed*] E. M. KINGSLEY, *Secretary.*

May 5, 1892.

(*b*) *Report of the Detroit Committee of Conference with Union Seminary. Report of the Standing Committee on Theological Seminaries as adopted by the Assembly at Portland. Arbitration again proposed.*

The Rev. S. A. Mutchmore, D. D., chairman of the Standing Committee on Theological Seminaries, was one of the publishers and editors of *The Presbyterian*, of Philadelphia; and the confident opinion, expressed by a weighty editorial in the paper that, if Union Seminary so desired, the Assembly would be ready to give it "a full release," naturally led the friends of the seminary to hope that, as chairman of the Committee on Theological Seminaries, he might be able to bring about the fulfillment of *The Presbyterian's* assurance. But a very different result followed. Here is Dr. Mutchmore's report:

Having due regard to the overtures and all the other papers in the case of Union Theological Seminary, etc., referred to the committee, the Assembly takes the following action:

1. That the Assembly endorses the interpretation of the compact of 1870 as expressed by the action of the Assembly of 1891.

2. That the Assembly declines to be a party in the breaking of the compact with Union Theological Seminary.

3. That the Assembly is persuaded that the Church should have direct connection with and control over its theological seminaries.

4. That the Assembly appoint a committee of fifteen, eight ministers and seven ruling elders, to take into consideration the whole subject of the relation of the Assembly to its theological seminaries, confer with the directors of those seminaries, and report to the next General Assembly such action as in their judgment will result in a still closer relation between the Assembly and its seminaries than that which at present exists.

5. That the Assembly dismiss the Committee of Conference appointed last year, with the heartiest thanks for its faithfulness and highest appreciation of the service rendered the Church.

An additional paper, on the Arbitration of the Theological Seminary Compact of 1870, in the matter of the transfer of a professor from one chair to another in the same seminary, was adopted, and is as follows:

Resolved, 1. That this General Assembly recognize the *status quo* as to the difference of interpretation given by the directors of Union Seminary to the Theological Seminary Compact of 1870, from that given by the Assembly's Committee of Conference, and in accordance with the proposition suggested by the six members of the Committee of Conference in their supplementary report, this Assembly agrees to refer the difference of interpretation of the said compact of 1870 as to transfer, to a Committee of Arbitration.

Resolved, 2. That a committee of five members, representing this Assembly, shall be appointed by the Moderator, which shall select five persons as arbitrators, to meet a like number selected by the directors of Union Seminary; and these ten shall select five others; and by the fifteen thus chosen shall the interpretation of the compact, (viz: as to the transfer of a professor,) be decided.

The proposal of arbitration, with which this report closed, at once astonished and shocked the friends of Union Seminary. The question of arbitration had been raised at the meeting of the board with the Assembly's Committee of Conference, held in January, 1892; and both parties agreed that the case was not, under the circumstances, a proper subject for arbitration. This decision gave great relief to the Board of Directors, for reasons which can easily be imagined. But there is no occasion for imagining what the reasons were. The following memorandum can leave no doubt respecting their character or their conclusive, unabated force:

NEW YORK, January 25, 1892.

While my recollections of the closing scenes with the General Assembly's Conference Committee (22d inst.) are yet fresh and vivid, I desire to record them for future reference.

Two papers were presented to the board; the first that which was finally adopted, and the second a proposal for the arbitration of the questions at issue. We saw at once that the first paper was a modification of one which had been presented informally upon his own responsibility, at a previous meeting, by Mr. Edward S. Durant. We missed the word "parity" as applied by Mr. Durant to the two parties to the agreement of 1870. Some other changes also were noted. After discussion it was decided by the board to send Mr. William A. Booth and myself as a committee to make the three following inquiries of the Conference Committee:

1. Why was the word "parity," as applied in Mr. Durant's paper to the two parties to the agreement of 1870, omitted in the paper now presented to us?

2. Would the adoption of this paper which your committee has presented to us, in your judgment involve in any way the surrender of our reserved rights with reference to the agreement of 1870 as those rights have been set forth in the supplementary paper presented to you for your consideration.

3. The arbitration proposed in your second paper, would it be decisive of Dr. Briggs' case, or would it decide only the abstract question as to the future?

The answer to the first question was that the word "parity," was omitted because it was regarded as "inexpedient;" it might be misunderstood. The answer to the second question was addressed to Mr. George Junkin because he is a lawyer and which he pleasantly referred to Dr. Patton, saying "he is as good a lawyer as I am." I said to Mr. Junkin, I do not think Dr. Patton is as good a lawyer as you are; I want your opinion. If we accept this paper, do you consider that we shall sacrifice or surrender any of those points in our case which are presented in our supplementary paper with reference to the agreement of 1870? He answered "No." Mr. McCook, said, "Of course not," and Dr. Patton assented to this opinion. I remarked, we are *intensely* desirious to be entirely frank with you. We do not want you to go away and afterwards say that we had not dealt plainly with you. If we should see fit, under painful necessity at any time, to assert that we must withdraw from the agreement of 1870, and on the grounds stated in that supplementary paper, would you feel that our right to do this had been compromised by our acceptance of your paper? They assured me that they understood that we would be at liberty to act according to our judgment. As to the third question, they said that arbitration would involve the concrete case of Dr. Briggs and not merely the abstract question for the future, of the difference between an appointment and a transfer. Thereupon I appealed to them on the ground of personal considerations. If we accept arbitration, Dr. Briggs will instantly resign. *That I know.* Probably Dr. Brown will resign. That I believe; and probably there would be a general breaking up of our faculty. But more than all this. Arbitration would call in question the crowning act of Dr. Butler's life. We all revere and love him and could never consent to involve him in arbitration. Would you as Christian gentlemen, be willing to put us to such a disadvantage before the Church and the world as our refusal to accept arbitration would certainly involve? With real magnanimity and kindness, they answered "No. We would by no means take such advantage of you." Dr. Johnson said, "I proposed arbitration in your interest and should be glad to withdraw the proposition." This was an immense relief to me. Hardly had we returned to the board, before Dr. Patton and Dr. Johnson appeared and requested permission to withdraw the second paper which proposed arbitration. It was accordingly withdrawn and evidently the board was greatly relieved by this generous and kindly action. Thereupon the first paper with the condition on record that it should be understood in the light of our supplementary paper was adopted by a rising vote, four members of the board declining to vote. Then the Conference Committee was called in and the result was announced to them. I insisted that my report of the Conference Committee's answers to the three questions as given above, should be repeated in their presence and in the presence of the board, so that there should be no mistake in our record of the condition on which we had accepted the final paper. Accordingly, I repeated the answers to the three questions as given above, and the answers were taken down by the "sworn stenographer." Only one correction was made and that by Dr. William H. Roberts. I had omitted the word "inexpedient" in the answer to the first question. That word was at once inserted, and then the record was accepted as complete and accurate.

It was directed that only such notice should be given to the press as Dr. Patton and I could agree upon. It was also agreed that, under the terms of the paper just adopted, the report of the board to the General Assembly should first be submitted to Dr. Patton, and that his report to the General Assembly should be submitted to me.

Then after the singing of the doxology, the benediction was pronounced, and the conference adjourned *sine die*.

[*Signed*] THOMAS S. HASTINGS.

My recollections accord with the above.

[*Signed*] WILLIAM A. BOOTH.

Owing to Dr. Patton's illness, his report to the General Assembly was not submitted to Dr. Hastings until the Assembly had actually met at Portland. In acknowledging the report, Dr. Hastings wrote:

> If this were *all* that your committee had presented to the General Assembly, every one in our board would be en-entirely satisfied; but, if it be true, as the papers represent, that Roberts and McCook have added thereto the recommendation to appoint a committee of arbitration *that* will be regarded by us as a breach of faith.

The memorandum signed by Dr. Hastings and Mr. Booth speaks for itself and needs no interpreter. Certainly, the renewed proposal of arbitration could not have been the result of ignorance or misapprehension; for not only were six members of the Detroit Committee of Conference commissioners to the Assembly at Portland, but they themselves suggested the proposal of arbitration. It was a part of their supplementary report. Dr. Wm. H. Roberts, the secretary of that committee and Stated Clerk of the General Assembly, was one of the six, and offered the resolution. During the discussion on the report of the Committee on Theological Seminaries he said: "I rise to a question of privilege as a member of the Assembly's Committee of Conference. I desire to remove a false impression in many minds that the committee was unanimous in the action reached by it in conference with the directors of Union Seminary. For the information of the house, I simply read two lines from the minutes of the committee:

'On the vote to adopt the paper as a whole, both Dr. Roberts and Mr. McCook gave notice that they reserved the right to act independently upon such portions of the paper as were not satisfactory to them.'"

The paper referred to seems to have been Mr. Durant's as modified by the committee. Dr. Roberts, in the Assembly at Washington, a year later, justified his resolution on the ground that it proposed a different sort of arbitration from that proposed in New York; viz., the abstract question respecting the transfer, not the concrete case of Dr. Briggs. But the speech of Mr. George Junkin made no such distinction, and he was one of the six members of the Detroit Committee of Conference, who drew up the Portland report and proposed arbitration. Mr. Junkin advocated arbitration as the best way of settling not only the abstract question about a transfer, but the concrete case of Dr. Briggs. He made no allusion to the proposal of arbitration in New York. That proposal, indeed, seems to have been carefully concealed from the public. Here is what Mr. Junkin said:

MR. MODERATOR AND BRETHREN:—We have nothing to do with any statements of what took place in the Conference Committee, and all allusions to stenographic reports and all reflections on Dr. Patton and the last Assembly are out of order. We have simply to do with reports made to us by our committee and by the memorial from Union Seminary. We have kept our mouths closed as to what took place in that conference, because it was so understood, and those who have not done so, in my opinion, have done wrong. Now, what is the condition of things? They reported to us that we were in *status quo.* That meant, we recognized that Union has a right to consider that agreement, and it has construed it conscientiously and believes it has a right to keep Dr. Briggs in his chair. We say they did wrong. Now, on the other hand, the seminary recognized that we acted conscientiously. There we were face to face. How are we to settle it? Are we to stand in that position year after year? Six of us came to this Assembly having no meeting of our Conference Committee, owing to Dr. Patton's illness. The report presented by Dr. Patton is not the report of the Conference Committee. It is all right, however. We six presented a report in the interests of peace. We had no desire to do what I have heard politicians do, try to put anybody in a hole. I would like to have a man come to me and tell me that I was capable of trying to put Union Seminary "in a hole"! It has been said that we can go to law. No, we said we would arbitrate. If the arbitrators say that Union is wrong, then let Union have the grace of God to acknowledge it. If, on the other hand, the arbitrators say the General Assembly is wrong, then I hope the grace of God will give the Assembly the impulse to say to Union, "You were right, and you had a right to keep Dr. Briggs there." Is not that the Christian way in which honest men ought to settle their differences? I am a lawyer, but I always advise my clients not to go to law if they can help it, because the law, while perfect, has to act through human instrumentality, which is wonderfully imperfect. And why can't we settle this matter so that Union won't go out like Ishmael from the tent of Abraham among the heathen, possibly. (Laughter.) Well, I did not mean what you are laughing at, but sometimes a man builds wiser then he knew. (Renewed laughter.) But I take it all back, because it is not in my heart to throw any slur upon Union. I want to keep her in the Presbyterian fold; and I do not believe that Union Seminary directors are going to lay down this compact after twenty years, in the face of our Christian effort to effect a settlement by arbitration. (Applause.)

In Dr. Hastings' memorandum, allusion is made to answers taken down by the "sworn stenographer." There are two large volumes of notes taken by this "sworn stenographer" during the discussion in the board and also in conference with the Assembly's committee. A few extracts from this stenographic report will serve to throw additional light, backward and forward, upon the attitude and temper of both the parties concerned. Here is a copy of Mr. Durant's paper as first presented to the board:

Recognizing the parity of the two parties to the agreement of 1870 and agreeing substantially to all the facts relative to the present conflict of opinion between the parties, something like the following might be done if the Board of Directors and the committee should concur therein: each party may fully respect the opinion of the other, and conclude that the difference, for the present, is irreconcilable. The seminary might report to the next General Assembly, substantially, that their understanding of the compact differed from that of the General Assembly, as applied to transfers, and that although the Assembly had disapproved of the appointment of Dr. Briggs, they had not seen their way clear, in view of their own obligations, to do other than continue him in the active duties of his office.

It would seem that they might with propriety do this, because the language of the Assembly's action is that the Assembly disapproves of the appointment of Dr. Briggs to the chair of Biblical Theology by transfer from another chair. It is not defined as to what the effect of disapproval shall be, and the seminary would naturally have some range in treating of the matter and in construing their own action. The committee, on the other hand, might report the facts to the Assembly, and in view of the parity of the parties, and in recognition of and in respect for the integrity of the parties and their honest difference, recommend that the *status quo* be recognized and no action taken.

Then it would seem desirable that the committee recommend to the Assembly the careful appointment of a suitable committee to confer with representatives of the several seminaries, and recommend to the Assembly, with the concurrence of the seminaries, such changes in their mutual ecclesiastical and legal relations as may be deemed wise and best.

Here is Mr. Durant's paper as revised and presented to the Board of Directors by the Committee of Conference:

Recognizing the fact that the General Assembly and the Union Theological Seminary are parties to the agreement or compact of 1870, as contained in the memorial of the directors to the Assembly of 1870, and also the fact that there is a wide difference of opinion in the matter of the interpretation of said agreement or compact, something like the following might be done:

First. Each party may fully respect the opinion of the other and conclude for the present that the difference is irreconcilable. *Second.* The seminary might report to the next

General Assembly, substantially, that their understanding of the compact differed from that of the General Assembly as applied to transfers, and that although the Assembly has disapproved of the appointment of Dr. Briggs, the directors had not seen their way clear in view of their own obligations to do other than to continue him in the active duties of his office. *Third.* The committee on the other hand might report the facts to the Assembly, and in view of the relations of the parties, and in recognition of their honest difference, recommend that the *status quo* be recognized in the hope that some action may be taken which may lead to a harmonious adjustment of all the matters at issue.

Second paper. The General Assembly's committee would also express its willingness to join with the board in asking the General Assembly to agree to refer the difference of interpretation of the compact of 1870 as to transfers, to a Committee of Arbitration.

Mr. Durant's paper, as thus modified by the Committee of Conference, elicited while under discussion in the board some very striking expressions of feeling and opinion. I will give a few of them. Here is Henry Day's comment upon it:

MR. PRESIDENT:—There is to my mind a very studied intention in that third section to bind this seminary hand and foot in regard to the legal connection between it and the General Assembly. In the first place, Mr. Durant's opinion as to whether we are equal parties or not has been cut out. I had a long talk of two hours with Dr. Roberts and Mr. Durant together yesterday morning, and Mr. Durant insisted that we ought to be recognized as equal parties here and he meant to bring that in in his paper, and if you recollect, he put it in. Dr. Roberts said he doubted very much whether we were equal parties; he thought that when we were handed over by the New School to the General Assembly, the General Assembly had acquired right over us; that they controlled us legally, and that they had a perfect right to legislate for us exactly as they do for Princeton. Now, gentlemen, that is the view of the other side—of Mr. Junkin and of Dr. Roberts—and that is the view of a certain class of men in the Presbyterian Church that mean to hold and take and control forever this seminary. Mr. Junkin is one of the sharpest and shrewdest men I know.

What they want is this, that we shall let this issue slide along and say nothing about it, so that within a year or two years they can say: "Gentlemen, this whole question was up when we, representing the General Assembly, were conferring with you; you never saw fit to take action in regard to this vital point, then; you have let it slip, and now you have assented to it." They will say, and say properly that that was the time—then or never—with us to say to them, "We feel that there is essential trouble at the bottom of this very contract, we feel that it is illegal" and that when we had a committee of the General Assembly here, we ought to have taken steps to reform it and make it legal.

You see that this question may come up again, it may come up any day. They may except to any one of our professors that we may nominate within a year or two, and then you will have this question again upon you, was it legal or not? Now, gentlemen, is the time to settle this question of legality, and if it is not settled now, you can never open your mouth again, and you ought not to. You never can say that the rights that you have properly transferred to them they did not properly exercise, and for one I say distinctly and frankly, I do not wish to sit on this board and have that construction put upon it and carried to the General Assembly for them to act upon it. I think you will destroy this seminary if you do. You will never get another dollar of money, in my opinion, to help build it up, and I believe its usefulness will be ended.

I do not sympathize at all with some of my brethren who say: "The Church is against us; this is an awful row that they are getting up." I do not say I don't care for the Church. I do care for the Church, but I say when we are right, when we are on the line of right, I do not care what may be said; we can bide our time. Five years will tell whether this seminary, which stands in the grandest part of the grandest city in the country, will or will not stand right before the Church; and it will stand right if we assert our independence, as our charter obliges us to do, as the preamble to all our proceedings. That preamble asserted that we were to be an independent seminary, and if we fail to so maintain it, we fail to uphold the plan of its founders.

Now, brethren, I do not say that if this action is not taken, I will have lost my interest in this seminary. I would not under any circumstances accept the paper presented, unless I put a rider to it, and I should not vote for it in any event as it is put now; but if it is to be accepted, I would put such a rider to it as this "without hereby assenting to the construction by the General Assembly of the agreement of 1870, and reserving our right to act hereafter, according to our views of the obligations imposed upon us, we hereby accept the proposition of the General Assembly's committee as a measure for the readjustment of said agreement." But recollect, they will not have it readjusted except as to the matter of transfer; that is all this controversy is about between us—merely about this transfer of Dr. Briggs—and we have had this trouble and will have settled but this single case. We ought to settle forever our rights and connection with the General Assembly; if we do not settle them now, we never can—we have bound ourselves and given ourselves over. Now, in this rider I say that we accept the proposition of the General Assembly's committee as a measure intended for the readjustment of the said agreement—the whole agreement. If we are to talk about it by a committee, we want it all readjusted, and this is the theory we talked about the other day; namely, that when we had a committee of the General Assembly here we would readjust our entire relations. Now they readjust nothing. What do they readjust? Nothing but this matter of transfer, whether when you transfer a man that is an election, that is all; whereas the readjustment of the said agreement should be in a manner which shall be consistent with the views of this board as to their rights and duties.

Other directors preceded and followed Mr. Day along similar lines. All seemed to regard the situation as perilous in the extreme. Dr. Ludlow said:

We have come to the critical moment in the history of our institution. We have come to a chasm and are in danger of dropping into it. . . . We have come to the very edge of the chasm—where self-respect and the life of the institution are at stake. That is the reason I offer the resolution that no further action be taken by us until the Committee of Conference shall have responded to our papers submitted for their consideration. They are good papers and we do not want them shelved or pigeon-holed, while this movement for arbitration comes up.

Drs. Parkhurst, C. Cuthbert Hall, and Frazer followed in favor of the resolution. Mr. D. Willis James said:

I agree that this is a crisis in the seminary. We are not dealing here with men alone; for within a few years all of us will have passed away. We are dealing with the life of this institution. If we are not faithful to the great trust imposed upon us, if we act in a way to jeopardize that trust, woe be to us. I beg that no vote be taken in a hurry. I beg you will stand on the papers, vigorous, courteous and strong, that we presented to the Conference Committee; await their answer in writing, and then let us see whether we cannot come to some just and wise conclusion. But let us take no hasty vote which we may regret as long as we live, and which may cause this seminary to descend from the heights to which it has been brought by the labors of men who have gone before.

Dr. Merle Smith said it was a pleasant thing to read in Mr. Durant's paper the frank admission that the Assembly and the seminary are on grounds of perfect parity. He then proceeded to argue earnestly against a continuance of the arrangement of 1870. That arrangement, in the first place, does not protect the Church against heresy, as it cannot touch professors in a seminary; and, second, it interferes with the right of the Presbytery; and third, whenever the veto is exercised it is sure to plunge the Church into confusion.

Mr. William E. Dodge said:

I was greatly interested in the paper of Mr. Durant. The board feel that our present relation to the General Assembly is dangerous and cannot continue without menacing the Church with trouble. It is painful to hear some of the remarks of Dr. Patton. He states that if the same matter came up again, he should feel bound to act in the same way. It seems to me that the way in which the matter was treated in the General Assembly at Detroit, was so unkind, so un-Presbyterian, so unfair, that it should not be done again. Here was a case which brought up virtually the reputation of a man. There was an utter refusal on the part of the committee to hear a single word on the other side. No evidence of any kind was allowed. The whole thing was decided entirely *ex parte*. It is simply impossible in this country in the 19th century to have the character, the reputation and usefulness of any man imperilled by that sort of "star chamber" examination. That is just the trouble we have had.

Drs. Dickey, Dana, Holmes, Booth, Clark, White, McIlvaine, Frazer, and Messrs. Jesup, Kingsley, Hoppin and William A. Booth, also at various points took part in the discussion. At length the opinion was expressed that if certain questions bearing upon the subject were to be answered by the Committee of Conference, it might be very helpful to the board in reaching a right conclusion. Mr. McAlpin, therefore, suggested whether it might not be well for Dr. Hastings and Mr. William A. Booth to go to the Committee of Conference and ask just those questions. That would not commit the board at all. The questions are of vital importance to this board. If President Hastings and Mr. Booth go and ask these simple questions, it will aid us very much. Let us get an explanation from the committee on these points. Mr. McAlpin's suggestion was adopted; three distinct questions were formulated and carried to the committee by Dr. Hastings and Mr. Booth, with the result given already in their paper written at the time. During the conference between the Detroit committee and the board, a letter of Judge Noah Davis, of New York, in regard to the legality of the agreement of 1870, which had recently appeared in print and excited much attention, was repeatedly alluded to. "The opinion of Judge Davis," said Dr. Hastings, "is not in the hands of this board, and has not been, and was not published at our suggestion, or with our knowledge." The opinion will be found in the Appendix.

What came of the proposal of arbitration, made by the Portland Assembly, appeared later in the report of the Standing Committee on Theological Seminaries at the Washington Assembly in 1893. In the course of the discussion on that report a very noteworthy statement was made by a member of the Detroit Committee of Conference, one who was not present at Portland. I refer to Dr. Herrick Johnson. His statement was as follows:

I think it due to the Union Theological Seminary that a word should be said with reference to certain matters occurring year before last in the interview with the Board of Directors by the committee appointed by the Assembly at Detroit, in order that this refusal to arbitrate may not seem to be so rude as it now seems on the surface. The question of arbitration was submitted by that committee. I remember this very distinctly, for I was the author of the motion in the committee to ask the Board of Directors to unite in requesting the Assembly to appoint a Committee of Arbitration. This was before the Assembly met at Portland, and after the meeting of the Assembly at Detroit, the committee having been appointed by the Assembly at Detroit to confer with the Board of Directors to see if some adjustment of the situation might be made. This question of arbitration was submitted to the board, and the board respectfully requested that we withdraw that proposition, as it would seriously interfere with the efficiency of the Union Seminary. It was accordingly withdrawn, *with the express understanding that it should not be brought before the next Assembly.* I think this modifies somewhat the attitude of the seminary.

A member—"Will you *repeat* that?"

Dr. Johnson—I say that the question of arbitration was moved in the committee appointed by the Assembly at Detroit—the Committee of Conference with the Board of Directors. I made the motion myself. We submitted that matter to the Board of Directors in our interview, and asked that they unite with us in appointing a committee that should go to the Assembly and request a Committee of Arbitration. The board very respectfully asked us to withdraw that suggestion, for reasons which were indicated, and on that account it was withdrawn *with the understanding that the proposition should not be made to the Assembly.*

We now approach the conclusion of the whole matter.

(*c*) *Final action of the Board of Directors annulling the agreement of 1870. The vote.*

At a special meeting held October 13, 1892, the board was notified of the General Assembly's action in regard to Union Seminary by a letter from Dr. William H. Roberts, its Stated Clerk. Thereupon, after leading directors had given utterance to their strong convictions of right and duty in the case, the following paper was adopted:

The Board of Directors of the Union Theological Seminary in the city of New York, addressed a memorial to the General Assembly of the Presbyterian Church in the United States of America, which met at Portland, May 19, 1892. In that paper we stated, with the utmost courtesy, some of the practical reasons which render it necessary, in our judgment, that the veto power, conceded to the General Assembly in 1870, should no longer reside in that body. The memorial concluded with this language: "There are other and weighty considerations which we have preferred not to urge. While there exists the undoubted right of either party to the agreement of 1870 to act alone in its abrogation, yet this memorial is submitted with the earnest hope that your reverend body may cordially concur with us in annulling the arrangement of 1870, thus restoring Union Seminary to its former relations to the General Assembly." The hope thus expressed was disappointed. With no official notice whatever of the reasons assigned by us, the answer to our memorial was: That the Assembly declines to be a party to the breaking of the compact with Union Theological Seminary. In view of this action of the late General Assembly, we are constrained now to urge those considerations which we had preferred to reserve. They are constitutional and legal.

1. *The Constitutional Considerations.*

There is no provision whatever in our charter and constitution for "the principle of Synodical or Assembly supervision." The Committees on Reunion and both Assemblies in 1869 recognized this important fact, and advised the introduction of that principle into the constitution. Upon this advice no action was taken. The constitution was not changed. Therefore the seminary could not rightfully give, and the Assembly could not rightfully receive or exercise the veto power under our existing charter and constitution.

2. *The Legal Consideration.*

Since the action of the General Assembly at Portland, the Executive Committee of our board has sought and obtained the best legal advice as to the point at issue between the seminary and the Assembly.* This advice leaves us no room to doubt that, under the laws of the State of New York, the agreement of 1870 is illegal. We "cannot abdicate any of our official duties in whole or in part."

THEREFORE, As the sole directors of Union Seminary, we are compelled by the practical considerations, presented in our memorial, and by constitutional and legal considerations, to maintain our rights and to fulfil our chartered obligations, which can neither be surrendered nor shared. In this action we regret deeply that we have been refused that concurrence of the Assembly, which we respectfully asked, and which would have done much toward softening the past and relieving the present. Obliged to act alone for the protection of the institution committed to our care, and actuated by sincere regard for the highest interests both of Union Seminary and of the Church we love, we do now

Resolve, 1. That the resolution passed by the board, May 16, 1870, adopting the memorial to the General Assembly of the Presbyterian Church in the United States of America, which provided that all appointments of professors "shall be reported to the General Assembly, and no such

*See the Opinion of James C. Carter in Appendix D.

appointment of professor shall be considered as a complete election, if disapproved by a majority vote of the Assembly," be and the same is hereby reconsidered and rescinded;

Resolve, 2. That the said arrangement between the Union Theological Seminary in the city of New York, and the General Assembly of the Presbyterian Church in the United States of America be and the same is hereby terminated; thus reinstating the relations between the seminary and the General Assembly as they existed prior to May, 1870.

Resolve, 3. That official notice of this action be duly given to the General Assembly, and also to the public, with the assurance of the undiminished loyalty of Union Seminary to the doctrine and government of the Presbyterian Church in the United States of America, to which the directors and faculty are personally bound by their official vow, and of our earnest desire for the restoration of our former relations to the General Assembly.

The vote stood 19 yeas and 1 no. Twenty directors were present; viz., Charles Butler, LL.D., President; Rev. Drs. T. S. Hastings, R. R. Booth, Charles H. Parkhurst, S. W. Dana, Edward L. Clark, C. Cuthbert Hall, D. R. Frazer, John McC. Holmes, J. H. McIlvaine, J. M. Ludlow, W. M. Smith; Messrs. William A. Booth, John Crosby Brown, D. Willis James, Henry Day, William E. Dodge, Morris K. Jesup, D. H. McAlpin, E. M. Kingsley. The only negative vote was cast by Dr. R. R. Booth.

The feeling of satisfaction and gratitude caused by the action of the board was very profound, both in the seminary and among its friends throughout the country. Those especially, who had taken an active part in the struggle, had borne the heavy cares and responsibility attending it, and had now won the victory, were scarcely able to give utterance to their sense of relief or their joy. I cannot help quoting the following letter by way of illustration:

NEW YORK, October 17, 1892.

MY DEAR DR. HASTINGS:

I have been so happy since the last meeting of the board that I have hardly known how to express my thanks. It was a wonderful triumph and I feel the greatest respect for such men as Dr. Holmes and Dr. Dana, who were governed solely by their judgment and what they deemed to be right.

But the one man who deserves the heartiest thanks of all interested, is our honored president. Had it not been for your marvellous tact, good temper and great ability, the results which have been accomplished could never have been reached. I sincerely congratulate you and thank you with all my heart.

I trust now you will rest and gain strength. The victory is won and we have nothing more to say. I have read with great interest the reports in the papers this morning and think them admirable.

Very sincerely your friend,

D. WILLIS JAMES.

TO REV. THOMAS S. HASTINGS, D. D.

(*d*) *A gift explaining and crowning the vote.*

At the next meeting of the board, on November 8, 1892, the following letter was received:

TO CHARLES BUTLER, ESQ., PRESIDENT OF THE BOARD OF DIRECTORS OF THE UNION THEOLOGICAL SEMINARY IN THE CITY OF NEW YORK.

DEAR SIR:—Inasmuch as the Union Theological Seminary has resumed the position intended by its founders, its charter, and its constitution, we desire to express our hearty approval of the principle of its management by its own Board of Directors, and also our confidence that its affairs will be so administered as best to promote the spiritual life and growth of its students and of the Presbyterian Church, of which we are members. Therefore, in order that the seminary may be placed on a sound financial basis by a substantial addition to its general fund, and by the completion of the endowments of its professorship funds, we take great pleasure in presenting to you, without conditions, the sum of $175,000. We remain,

JOHN CROSBY BROWN, W. E. DODGE,
D. WILLIS JAMES, MORRIS K. JESUP.

The following extract from a leading article of the New York *Sun*, November 17, 1892, will show how the signers of this letter are regarded in the community at large:

Four of the members of the Board of Directors of the Union Theological Seminary have made an unconditional gift of $175,000 to the general fund of the institution. They are Mr. D. Willis James, Mr. William E. Dodge, Mr. John Crosby Brown and Mr. Morris K. Jesup, and the purpose of their benefaction is, to express emphatically their sympathy with the course of the seminary in separating itself from the Presbyterian General Assembly, in order that it may be undisturbed in its theological teachings. All these four gentlemen are Presbyterians of such distinction that they are known to their own communion and to the public generally throughout the United States. They are Presbyterians by inheritance, and a few years ago if we had been called upon to select four laymen in New York more especially representative of the conservative character of that denomination, theirs are the names which would have occurred to us first. All of them, too, are men of great wealth and of high standing in business and financial circles and in the society of New York. For many years they have been liberal promoters of the religious and charitable institutions of the Presbyterian Church, and their loyalty to its faith and doctrine has never been questioned until recently. Coming from strict Presbyterian families, it is probable that all of them were carefully instructed in the Westminster Catechism in their youth, and all of them have remained devout and influential members of leading Presbyterian churches of the city since that time.

(*e*) *Sequel to the annulling of the agreement of 1870. Action of the General Assembly of 1893 relating to the Union Theological Seminary.*

Although the annulling of the agreement of 1870 closed all further controversy on the part of the Board of Directors, it by no means ended discussion of the subject, both in the religious papers unfriendly to Union Seminary, and also in the General Assembly. Nor did it end vigorous effort on the part of the Assembly, through two of its committees, to bring about a settlement of the trouble. This appears most clearly in the proceedings of the General Assembly, which met at Washington, D. C., on May 18, 1893. The report of the Committee on Theological Seminaries, along with the speeches accompanying it, show very distinctly the final attitude and temper of the General Assembly toward Union Seminary. The Rev. Dr. John Dixon, chairman of the committee, on June 1st, presented the report. The part bearing upon Union Seminary was as follows:

From Union Seminary has been received the usual report. The Board of Directors have also sent a special communication which is as follows:

[This special communication, announcing the action of the Board of Directors of Union Seminary, annulling the agreement of 1870, has been given already and need not here be repeated.]

COMMITTEE ON ARBITRATION.

To your committee was also referred the report of the committee appointed by the last General Assembly as arbitrators with Union Seminary.

TO THE GENERAL ASSEMBLY AT WASHINGTON, D. C.

The committee consisting of five members, appointed by the General Assembly at Portland, in 1892, "as arbitrators, to meet a like number selected by the directors of Union Seminary," with power to select five others, to which was referred for settlement the difference of interpretation of the theological compact of 1870, as to the question whether the transfer of a professor from one chair to another in the same seminary is an appointment, and therefore subject to veto by the General Assembly, respectfully submits the following report:

On July 10, 1892, the Stated Clerk of the General Assembly notified the Board of Directors of Union Seminary of the appointment of arbitrators who were to confer with said board, and on August 4, 1892, the chairman of this committee communicated the action of the General Assembly in regard to the appointment of arbitrators and the duties assigned them, to Mr. E. M. Kingsley, the secretary or recorder of the Board of Directors of Union Seminary, and received from him a reply dated August 6, 1892, in which he stated in substance that it would be impracticable for the Board of Directors to meet and take any action on the subject before the middle of October.

In view of this statement the chairman of the Assembly's committee called a meeting of the committee to be held in

New York City, November 2, 1892, and all the members were present at a meeting held in New York at that time. A communication was sent by the committee to the Board of Directors of Union Seminary, informing them of the committee's presence in New York City, and saying, "It will be pleased to receive such communication as you may see fit to send it; or to meet your board or a sub-committee from it, in personal interview at such time and place as you may indicate."

The receipt of this communication was acknowledged by the president of the board, and on the 8th of November, 1892, your committee received a communication from the Board of Directors of Union Seminary, in which they say: "Since the meeting of the General Assembly at Portland, by an almost unanimous vote—a vote of 19 to 1—this board has rescinded the resolution of 1870, adopting the memorial to the General Assembly, in which a veto on the election of professors was offered to that body, thus terminating the special relation then constituted between the General Assembly and Union Seminary. By this action the question whether a transfer is an election and subject therefore to the Assembly's veto, is no longer to us an open question. Therefore no further action in this matter is called for."

As your committee was appointed to arbitrate a single question at issue between the General Assembly and the Board of Directors of Union Seminary, and the foregoing action of the Board of Directors, taken as we understand on the 13th of October, 1892, without waiting for a conference with the Assembly's committee, shows that the board has declined to have the question at issue arbitrated, your committee asks to be discharged.

The chairman of the committee, Rev. T. Ralston Smith, D.D., and George Junkin, Esq., LL.D., are both absent from the country.—Dr. Smith as a delegate from the General Assembly to the Free Church of Scotland and Mr. Junkin for the benefit of his health,—and therefore their names are not subscribed to this report.

B. L. Agnew,
Logan C. Murray,
E. W. C. Humphrey.

To the special communication from the directors of Union Seminary your committee have given careful and prolonged consideration. While they would recommend the Assembly to recognize the fact, that the directors of Union Seminary have declared upon their own motion and authority that the compact of 1870 is void and of unbinding effect; and while insisting that such action is wholly without warrant, yet they advise the Assembly for the present simply to place on record, by way of protest, its views of the situation.

For twenty-one years the most cordial relations existed between Union Theological Seminary and the General Assembly. In the discharge of what seemed its plain but most painful duty, the General Assembly at Detroit declared its disapproval of the appointment of Professor Briggs to the chair of Biblical Theology. The Board of Directors, instead of removing Dr. Briggs, or at least requiring him to desist from teaching in the seminary, until the question at issue between the Assembly and the seminary as to the full and proper compact had been decided, resolved to continue Dr. Briggs in the chair which the Assembly had declared he ought not to occupy. This action was the more questionable because the Assembly appointed a committee of fifteen to confer with the directors of the Union Theological Seminary in regard to the relation of the said seminary to the General Assembly. This conference resulted in practical failure to remove the misunderstanding, and it was so reported to the Assembly of 1892, meeting in Portland. That Assembly appointed five arbitrators to meet a like number selected by the directors of Union Seminary, with power to select five others to determine the interpretation of the compact, viz. as to the transfer of a professor. The Stated Clerk of the Assembly notified the directors of the seminary on July 16, 1892, that the Assembly had appointed such a Committee of Arbitration. On the 11th of August Dr. T. Ralston Smith, chairman of the committee, addressed a similar communication to the directors. To this the recorder of the board responded that the board could not take any action before the middle of October. On the 15th of October the Board of Directors met and resolved to terminate the compact. This action was taken nearly three months after the board had been officially informed of the appointment of a Committee of Arbitration, and before any opportunity was given to the committee of the General Assembly to present their case. This extraordinary action of the Board of Directors is inexplicable to the Assembly. The high character of the gentlemen composing the board, fully warranted the expectation that so fair a proposition as that of arbitration would not be treated in such a way.

While there remained to the Assembly the hope that by a conference of arbitration the difficulty that had arisen would be removed, the Assembly did not think it best to discuss the points raised by the directors of the Union Seminary, in attempted justification of their action. But now the Assembly takes issue with the statement made in the memorial presented to the Portland Assembly, that "there existed the undoubted right of either party to the agreement of 1870 to act alone in its abrogation." No such right is expressed in the agreement, and in the nature of things no agreement where valuable interests are involved, not to say valuable considerations are given and received, can in good morals be abrogated by one party to the agreement, without the consent and against the expressed desire of the other party.

The claim that the words of Dr. Musgrave, spoken in the Old School Assembly of 1869, and quoted by the directors in their memorial to the Portland Assembly give warrant to either party to abrogate the agreement, is not in accordance with a proper understanding of those words. The "declaration" referred to by Dr. Musgrave, was not a compact or covenant as one of the terms of reunion. The relation of the seminaries to the Assembly was a different problem. The arrangement in the "declaration" he was discussing, proved to be unacceptable to Union Seminary and was not adopted. The following year, Union Seminary came to the Assembly with a memorial, setting forth an arrangement which was accepted by the Assembly and agreed to by all the seminaries. This is the compact or arrangement not discussed by Dr. Musgrave in 1869, which Union Seminary has declared on its own motion that it has abrogated. Whatever force the constitutional and legal objections may have to the making and continuance of such a compact by the directors, there was an easy and simple way to remove them if the directors so desired. The Legislature of the State of New York would doubtless have amended the charter if the members had requested it.

Because, then, of the strange and unwarranted action of the directors in retaining Dr. Briggs after his appointment had been disapproved by the Assembly; and because of the refusal by the directors to arbitrate the single point in dispute between the Assembly and the board; and because of the attempt of the board on its own motion and against the expressed desire of the Assembly to abrogate the compact of 1870, the Assembly disavows all responsibility for the teaching of Union Seminary, and declines to receive any report from its board until satisfactory relations are established. The Assembly, however, cherishes the hope, and will cordially welcome any effort to bring Union Seminary into such a relationship with itself as will enable the Assembly to commend the institution again to students for the ministry.

Your committee would further recommend that the Board of Education be enjoined to give aid to such students only as may be in attendance upon seminaries approved by the Assembly.

Your committee would also recommend that the re-election of the Rev. Charles A. Briggs, D.D., by the Presbytery of New York as a director of the German Theological Seminary at Bloomfield, N. J., be disapproved by this Assembly.

The reasons assigned in this report why the Assembly disavowed all responsibility for the teaching of Union Seminary, and declined to receive any report from its board, along with the recommendation that the Board of Education be enjoined to give no aid to its students—in other words, to "boycott" it—were regarded by the venerable president and the other directors, by the entire faculty, and by friends of the seminary through the world, as a very great wrong, not only to the institution itself but to fundamental principles of American Presbyterianism, to the cause of a reasonable theological liberty, and to the entire Christian scholarship of the country.

In concluding the account of this unhappy conflict between the General Assembly and the Union Theological Seminary it is only fair to say further, that in all the official records of the action of the directors in the case I have not found a single word, or expression, unbecoming their sacred trust or the character of Christian gentlemen.

CHAPTER VI.

BEARING OF THE CONFLICT WITH THE GENARAL ASSEMBLY UPON THE QUESTION OF ECCLESIASTICAL CONTROL OF THEOLOGICAL SEMINARIES.—LESSONS TAUGHT BY THIS CONFLICT RESPECTING THE DESIGN OF UNION SEMINARY AND THE MOTIVES OF ITS FOUNDERS.—HOW THE CHARTER FITS INTO AND SERVES THE DESIGN.

Before concluding it may not be amiss to add a few words about the bearing of the conflict I have described upon the general question of ecclesiastical control of theological seminaries; and also to point out some of its lessons in regard to the special design of the Union Seminary.

(*a*) *Is direct ecclesiastical control essential to the efficiency, sound teaching and usefulness of a theological institution?*

If the answer to this question were based upon the position maintained by nearly the whole body of the opponents of Dr. Briggs, who had been trained in the Old School branch of the Church, it would be an emphatic YEA. I do not recall an instance in which one of them recognized the fact, that for a third of a century Union Seminary was under no ecclesiastical control whatever. They seemed to shut their eyes to this fact as not of the slightest importance. And also to the fact that the New School branch of the Church, to which the seminary belonged, never attempted, or desired, to exercise any authority over it, or over the other institutions where Presbyterian ministers were in training.

In taking this ground with regard to Union Seminary there was no thought of casting any censure upon seminaries founded upon a different plan and in different circumstances. Individuality is an element of utmost importance in the life of institutions, as well as in personal and national life. Unity in diversity is a fundamental law of the Providential system; unity in essence and spirit, endless diversity of outward form and manifestation. It is so in poetry and painting and all the other grand spheres of art; why should it not be so in the great sphere of learning and divinity? Institutions of lasting power grow; they cannot be improvised or manufactured. How little, for example, of the vast and beneficent influence of Princeton, as a theological institution, has been the product of mere ecclesiastical control? The hiding-place of that influence has been not in the supervision or in the votes and deliverances of the General Assembly, but in the minds and hearts and learning and enlightened piety and inspiring memories of Archibald Alexander, Samuel Miller, Charles Hodge, Addison Alexander, and others like them. And how little the best possible ecclesiastical supervision would have added to what such scholars and men of God as Edward Robinson, Thomas H.

Skinner, Henry B. Smith, W. G. T. Shedd, William Adams, Roswell D. Hitchcock and Philip Schaff did to make Union Seminary a fountain of spiritual light and benediction to our country and to the world! No ecclesiastical authority supervised its birth or controlled it during the first third of a century of its existence. And yet the New School Presbyterian Church, as I have said before, cherished Union as one of her most precious jewels, and delighted to honor it by choosing from its professors several Moderators of her General Assembly. Annual collections were taken in some of her wealthiest congregations for their worldly support. I was privileged to be the pastor of one of these congregations; a third of the first endowment of the seminary was its free gift; and yet I never heard a whisper even, that, in addition to the control of its Board of Directors, it ought also to be under the control of the General Assembly.

Let me now note some important lessons taught the friends of Union Seminary by its struggle with the Assembly—lessons which ought to be marked, learned and inwardly digested. Conflict, when based upon good, solid reasons and inspired by the right spirit, is one of the most potent educating forces in the world. It tends to awaken, stimulate and call into play dormant or latent capabilities. It drives men back into themselves, acquaints them with the full meaning of things, helps them to understand better their own real aims and ends, widens their outlook, and so trains them to wise and successful action. Our country, even while I write, is furnishing a wonderful illustration of this truth.* A long, trying conflict of public opinion about our relations and duty, as a nation, to the island of Cuba has of a sudden ended in a terrible conflict of arms far off on the other side of the globe. How fast it is educating the American people to a distinct consciousness of their providential calling and mission as a world-power! What an eye-opener it has been to them touching their possible duty as a leader in the glorious march of Christian civilization, freedom and humanity! Dewey's victory at Manila has all at once set the "universal Yankee nation" not only to a diligent study of the geography of the Phillipines, but to deep pondering of coming events throughout the farthest Orient that already cast their shadows before.

To return to the conflict between Union Seminary and the General Assembly. What useful lessons it has taught thousands of Christian men and women, both in and outside the Presbyterian Church! Including the "Briggs case," it has taught them more than in all their lives they had known before about theological seminaries, Biblical study and learning, "higher criticism," and the close connection of all these with human life and progress. But in referring to the lessons of this conflict I had in mind those chiefly which specially concern the friends and guardians of Union Seminary. It almost shames me to compare

* This was written in May, 1898.

what I knew about the far-reaching design of the institution when the conflict began with what I know to-day; and, doubtless, my own experience is not at all singular. What then, interpreted in the light of its recent struggle, was the design of the founders of Union Theological Seminary in the city of New York? That they themselves regarded it as of the very highest importance is evident from the opening sentence of the preamble to their plan. Here it is:

> *That the* DESIGN *of the founders of the seminary may be publicly known and be sacredly regarded by the directors, and professors and students, it is judged proper to make the following preliminary statement.*

Let us look closely at this statement and consider well its weighty clauses. And, first of all, it tells us that,

(*b*) *The design of the founders of Union Seminary was* WORLD-WIDE.

> A number of Christians, both clergymen and laymen, in the cities of New York and Brooklyn, deeply impressed with the claims of the world upon the Church of Christ to furnish a competent supply of well-educated and pious ministers of the Gospel, RESOLVED, in humble dependence on the grace of God, to attempt the establishment of a theological seminary in the city of New York.

Its founders were a number of Christians, both clergymen and laymen; and their attempt was not merely in response to the claims of the Presbyterian denomination, or of their own country, but of all nations. How vast, even unto the ends of the earth, was their spiritual outlook! From what a vantage-ground and in what an exalted mood they contemplated "the claims of THE WORLD upon the Church of Christ"! A new Acts of the Apostles could not open more fittingly. There is not a touch of sectarianism; not a sectarian note. And all that follows is in full accord with this beginning.

(c) *The design of the founders of Union Seminary was comprehensive, generous and ideal in the breadth and completeness of its plan.*

"In this institution it is the design of the founders to furnish the means of a full and thorough education in all the subjects taught in the best theological seminaries in this or other countries." Such was their language; and just that, I do not doubt, was in the mind of Erskine Mason, when after much thought and consultation, he conceived and thus defined the plan. It is the language of wisdom, foresight and strong convictions touching the high office of Christian learning and scholarship. One is surprised, to be sure, to hear such words at that day from a modest young Presbyterian minister. But Erskine Mason's father, the renowned John M. Mason—whose sermon at Bristol on Messiah's kingdom, is said to have wrung from Robert Hall the exclamation: "I can never preach in that pulpit again!"—was an intimate friend of Alexander

Hamilton, and not wholly unlike Hamilton in statesmanlike sagacity. The son inherited the spirit of the father, "Nothing, my brethren, is great in this world but the kingdom of Jesus Christ; nothing but that to a spiritual eye, has an air of permanency." This grand sentiment, uttered in one of his sermons, seems to have inspired him in setting forth the design of the new school of divinity.

How beautiful is such aspiring, prophetic thought, united, as it was here, with such practical, every-day wisdom, good sense and piety! "A full and thorough education;" what does that mean? It means that the young men trained in this seminary are to be genuine scholars, putting their whole mind and soul and strength into their studies. They are, each in his measure and all together, as far as possible, to become accurate, conscientious, self-centered and able to teach others also, in their knowledge of the Hebrew and Greek Scriptures, of the old English Bible, of the history of the Christian Church, life and doctrine, and of every other branch of theological instruction and science needful to render them thoroughly furnished for effective, fruitful labor in the varied service of the blessed Master, whether at home or abroad. That is the aim of the institution. "*In* ALL *the subjects taught in the best theological seminaries in this or* OTHER *countries.*" Why not? Shall American students in New York, who follow Christ and are preparing for the ministry of His Gospel, be in their advantages one whit behind students of divinity at Oxford and Cambridge, or at Halle and Leipsic and Berlin? Ought they not to have as good a theological education as Christendom affords?

So much on the intellectual side; but this is not all. Here is the design of the founders on the practical side:

> Being fully persuaded that vital godliness, a thorough education, and practical training in the works of benevolence and pastoral labor, are all essential to meet the wants and promote the best interests of the kingdom of Christ, the founders of this seminary design that its students, remaining under pastoral influence, and performing the duties of church members in the several churches to which they belong, or with which they worship, in prayer-meetings, in the instruction of Sabbath-schools and Bible classes, and being conversant with all the benevolent efforts of the present day in this great community, shall have the opportunity of *adding to solid learning and true piety the teachings of* EXPERIENCE.

(*d*) *The hope and expectation of the founders in the carrying out of their sacred design.*

> By the foregoing advantages the founders hope and expect with the blessing of God to call forth and enlist in the service of Christ and in the work of the ministry genius, talent, enlightened piety and missionary zeal; and to qualify many for the labors and management of the various religious institutions, seminaries of learning, and enterprises of benevolence which characterize the present time.

This seems to me a remarkable passage. What does it say? It says that in laying their plans for a theological seminary as good as could be found in the wide world, their first hope and expectation was to call forth and enlist in the service of Christ and in the work of the ministry *genius.* It is a strange word to use here; there is no other quite like it; and yet how fitting and in its right place is the word! Genius is something far deeper and higher than talent; it is inspiration and creative power; in the religious sphere, especially, it is the enthusiasm of holy intelligence, thought and passion for souls. It is what gives talent, enlightened piety and missionary zeal, resistless energy. All great theologians, preachers, evangelists and saints have possessed it, or rather been possessed by it; Paul and John among the apostles; Augustine and Chrysostom and Bernard; Luther, Calvin, Hooker, Jeremy Taylor, Leighton, Bunyan, John Wesley, Jonathan Edwards, Eliot, Swartz, Brainerd, Zeisberger, Livingston, they were all endued with the genius of faith and unbounded devotion to Jesus Christ; and, thank God, Union Seminary knows well in her own history what this sort of genius is and can do!

(*e*) *The design of the founders was crowned with the peace and charity of the Gospel.*

Let me quote yet once more their own admirable statement:

It is the design of the founders to provide a theological seminary in the midst of the greatest and most growing community in America, around which all men of moderate views and feel-

ings, who desire to live free from party strife, and to stand aloof from all extremes of doctrinal speculation, practical radicalism, and ecclesiastical domination, MAY CORDIALLY AND AFFECTIONATELY RALLY.

(*f*) *The special fitness of the charter of the Union Theological Seminary to fortify and carry out the design of its founders.*

"The government of the seminary shall at all times be vested in a Board of Directors." Of this brief but comprehensive enactment I have spoken already. Another provision of the charter is as follows:

Equal privileges of admission and instruction, with all the advantages of the institution, shall be allowed to students of every denomination of Christians.

There are some one hundred and fifty theological seminaries in the United States. As far as I have been able to learn there is not another among them all, whose charter contains an enactment so large and generous as this. Had not the founders of Union Seminary been men of extraordinary breadth of vision and been inspired by one overmastering, gospel-like design, never would they have framed, or accepted, such a charter and organized their new school of divinity in harmony with its catholic spirit.

(*g*) *A few words in conclusion.*

Before closing this chapter a few words about

schools of divinity in general will not be out of place. The simple fact that not far from one hundred and fifty such institutions have grown up in the United States—mostly within the last half century—may serve to show how highly they are valued by the various denominations of the country. They are related to its spiritual interests somewhat as West Point and Annapolis stand related to its great military interests. As the latter are training schools for leaders of our army and navy, in fighting the battles of the Republic on sea and land, so the theological seminary is a training school for leaders in the greater world-wide conflict of truth with error, of social right with social wrong, of humanity and its sweet charities with all forms of vice, cruelty and barbarism. Let me repeat on this subject what I said to my old Mercer street flock once, when urging them to be generous to Union Seminary: "Theology and theological institutions have something of the dignity and importance which belong to fundamental principles in ethics, or to universal laws in nature. These may vary greatly in their forms of working and of manifestation; but they themselves are permanent and immutable. Light, for example, is an element or force which conditions all our seeing; where there is no light, there can be no vision; yet in how many different ways it fulfils its kindly office? *Truly, the light is sweet, and a pleasant thing it is for the eyes to behold the sun;* but it is pleasant also to behold the moon and stars, the clear sky, the gleam from a distant home, the fire on the hearth.

> And storied windows, richly dight,
> Casting a dim, religious light.

So also with inspired theology, 'the sabbath and port of all men's labors and peregrinations,' as Lord Bacon calls it. How its precious, life-giving truth diffuses itself far and wide, embodies itself in song and parable, as well as in doctrine, precept and story, irradiating with its saving grace alike the souls of little children and the souls of learned divines and philosophers!

'Where there is no vision' said the wise man—and 'vision' in his day was prophetic insight and foresight; it was truth revealed first to the inspired seer, and through him, shining forth upon the face of the Nation—'*where there is no vision* THE PEOPLE PERISH.' The saying is for all time. Where, in our day, there is no genuine theology, no vital science of God and His government of the world; where the popular mind, opinion, literature, domestic and social habits, business and institutions are not in some degree informed and ruled by its holy, benign influences, there, sooner or later, the people will perish. This is at bottom one of the chief reasons of the sad spectacle which meets our eyes as we survey the moral state of Christendom; the spectacle, I mean, of dead and dying nations.

Never was there a time in all its history when Union Seminary was summoned to more strenuous work, or had a better opportunity to fulfil its noble office in teaching and in training others to teach the truth as it is in Jesus than to-day. Never had it stronger or more inspiring motives to call forth and enlist genius, talent and the best learning in carrying out its grand design. Some appear to feel that as society and knowledge advance, and we draw nearer to the millennial ages, the race of great theologians is going to die out. But I cannot think that the growing triumph of the Church is to be purchased by dwarfing the souls of her teachers. On the contrary, I believe the coming days will not be one whit behind the best days of her history. As she rises to greater heights of piety and holy intelligence; as she turns her back upon the world and fixes her expectant eye more steadily upon her risen Lord and Redeemer, I doubt not she will be blessed with preachers and divines worthy to have sat in the council of the Apostles. I doubt not that Jesus Christ will then hold in His right hand, stars as resplendant in their kind and measure as any that ever shone there in ancient or modern times! May it please Him to raise up many such preachers and theologians to be stars in the crown of Union Theological Seminary."

To these words of my own, uttered more than seven and forty years ago, I cannot refrain from adding the following sentences from a striking letter of my dearly beloved old friend, Dr. Thomas H. Skinner, written to Mr. Norman White, in February, 1865:

There is not in the entire church a theological school of higher promise than the Union Seminary. New York is the American centre of every human interest, secular and sacred; and it is doubtless, since our Nation is resolved not to die, the centre, prospectively, of the influences which are, under the Divine Will, to have the chief control of the world's future history. Not in Europe, but in the United States, is to be the seat of the Empire of the East, as De Tocqueville has told us; and no one can doubt that our already wonderful city is to be, to the end of our Nation's career, the imperial locality in this new world. A power for supreme good,—the dominion of Christianity,—cannot be established among men, of greater efficiency than *a first-rate School of the Prophets,* in New York City. The "Merchant Princes" of this metropolis who, with others, have undertaken to make our seminary what it ought to be, have put their hand to a business of infinitely higher moment than any enterprise of trade, real or conceivable; or any other interest which does or may solicit the application of their immense means. I use no hyperbole in thus speaking; given the continuance of our National life, and only prophecy itself is more certain of accomplishment, than what I have just predicted. Standing as I am, upon the verge of "nature's confine," it would be presumptuous in me to expect to see its accomplishment, but only the Nation's death can hinder it, and, except as this may by possibility happen, there are some living who will not die before they will have seen it. So far as "material" means are required for the perfection of our school, it is already provided for, virtually; these means are in the possession of our friends, in superabundance; and earnestness in prosecuting the work cannot but preclude the possibility of their not being applied on the largest scale of liberality; it cannot, will not, rest until edifices, and books, and the best accommodations for students and teachers, as far as they may be needed, shall be supplied, as largely as the completest execution of the undertaking can require.

Part Second.

THE CASE OF DR. BRIGGS.

ITS BEARING ON THE JUDICIAL SYSTEM OF THE PRESBYTERIAN CHURCH.

DR. R. W. PATTERSON'S VIEWS ON THE SUBJECT, AS EXPRESSED IN LETTERS TO DR. HASTINGS, WRITTEN AT THE TIME.

Part Second.

DR. BRIGGS AND HIS TRIAL FOR HERESY.—SOME OF ITS LESSONS.

The main design of the present volume, as was stated at the outset, is to give an account of the agreement of 1870 between the Union Theological Seminary and the General Assembly, and to explain the causes which led, in 1892, to the annulling of that agreement by the Board of Directors of the seminary. In carrying out this design, it has been necessary to refer frequently to the address of the Reverend Charles A. Briggs, D.D., on taking the new professorship of Biblical Theology in Union Seminary, and to the consequent action of the General Assembly at Detroit, vetoing his transfer to that chair. It is only incidentally, therefore, that the trial of Dr. Briggs for heresy by the Presbytery of New York, and, later, by the General Assembly of the Presbyterian Church in the United States of America, has a place in my narrative. Dr. Briggs was the occasion, though not the cause, of the struggle between the Assembly and Union Seminary. And as the occasion—the providential occasion—of this struggle, he rendered, perhaps, as great a service to Christian scholarship and theological freedom as in any other act of his remarkable career. It is due to him, therefore, due likewise to the claims of friendship and justice, that I should here put on record a brief expression of my opinion of him, as also of his trial and condemnation as a heretic.

Charles Augustus Briggs was born in the city of New York, January 15, 1841. His ancestors on the father's side were English Puritans, and on the mother's side, partly Huguenot and partly German Reformed and Scotch Presbyterian; all early settlers of New York and the New England colonies. It would be hard to see how, naturally or spiritually, he could have inherited a better mixture of solid qualities than belong to these renowned old stocks. An early letter, written by him to a younger brother of his father, shows the ancestral spirit that was in him:

> I am going back to school to prepare for college. I intend to finish Cæsar and Virgil, and get along considerable in Greek. . . . I intend to go right at it, when I get back to school. I am going in strong. When I start once, I am going to finish. My mind is made up.

I am going in strong; when I start once I am going to finish. There was the coming man in the boy. At the age of sixteen he entered the University of Virginia, where he pursued his studies for three years. He is said to have taken much interest in the "Washington Society," and to have been active in the prayer meeting, and the "Ragged Mountain" school. In his second year at the University, he united with the Presbyterian church in Charlottesville, and decided to give himself to the Christian ministry. He was one of the founders of the Young Men's Christian Association in the University, said to have been the first of these associations established in a college.

The outbreak of the Civil War, in 1861, cut short his course. He belonged to the celebrated Seventh Regiment of New York State Volunteers, and marched with it to the defense of Washington. In the same year he entered the Union Theological Seminary to study for the ministry. Here he came at once under the powerful and inspiring influence of Edward Robinson, Henry B. Smith and Roswell D. Hitchcock. After his graduation he became for several years his father's assistant and a hard-working, skilful man of business. In 1866 he went abroad, accompanied by his wife, and spent some three years in Germany, mostly at Berlin; making vacation trips also to Italy, France, Russia, Egypt and the Holy Land. In Berlin he was in very close relations with Dr. Dorner, both as a pupil and a friend.

Here is an extract from a letter to Dr. Henry B. Smith, written at Berlin, in November, 1868:

> I had thought of sending you an article on Biblical theology. It is a difficult subject, and as in some things, I must go an independent way, I have concluded to hold back for the present. It is one of my favorite studies. I have sometimes thought I would like a position in a theological

seminary; but I fear I could do little more with the languages—so little attention is paid to exegesis with us—and I would not devote my life even to the Biblical languages. I would use them as means and not ends.

In another letter from Berlin, dated January, 1867, he wrote:

We have religious services in the chapel every Sunday. We take turns in preaching. Sunday evenings at half past seven, we have a Bible circle on exactly the same plan as the one I organized in New York. I organized this here last winter, with the help of two brethren at the outset. It has become a great success and a standing institution of Berlin. . . . We all meet on pure Christian principles: Methodists, Baptists, Presbyterians, Congregationalists, English, Scotch and American; and there is entire harmony.

Shortly after returning home, Dr. Briggs accepted a call to the First Presbyterian church of Roseville, New Jersey, where for several years he labored with marked devotion and success. In October, 1876, he was inaugurated as Davenport professor of Hebrew and Cognate Languages in Union Seminary. His inaugural address was on Exegetical Theology, and in this address he claimed liberty of opinion on all questions of the higher criticism.

In November, 1890, the Board of Directors of the Union Seminary transferred Dr. Briggs to the new chair of Biblical Theology. His memorable address upon taking it, was delivered on January 20, 1891. This address led, a few months later, to the first exercise of the veto power by the General Assembly and to the conflict between the Assembly and Union Seminary already described. The subject of the address was *The Authority of Holy Scripture.* Dr. Briggs discussed it without fear, or favor, and with great ability.

The main positions of the address were by no means new. Dr. Briggs himself had asserted them for years in his various writings. But in this address he presented them in a somewhat novel form and with concentrated force of thought and learning. He pointed out, too, their vital relation to some of the burning questions of the day ; and that in a very positive tone. The consequence, naturally enough, was a violent disturbance of the religious atmosphere, more especially within the Presbyterian pale. His treatment of the subject offended many good men and was well adapted to stir up both theological and ecclesiastical prejudices, as he himself, doubtless, foresaw would be the case. And then impregnable as was the strength of his main argument in favor of the Church and the Reason as, along with Holy Scripture, fountains or channels of divine authority, he did not, perhaps, sufficiently consider how easily, how almost inevitably, important points and distinctions, clear as day to him, would be likely to puzzle and confuse plain Christian people, unversed in the knowledge that comes of books and scholastic studies. Had Dr. Briggs' real, honest meaning, born of his deep reverence for the Word of God, been as obvious to other minds as to his own, I feel quite sure that the number of his opponents would have been very much smaller than it was. In reference to one point in particular it always seemed to me that he made a mistake, which led to not a little needless suspicion and misunderstanding. I refer to his selection of Dr. Martineau as an example of those who, not finding God in the Scriptures or in the Church, do find Him in and through the Reason. If the example was to be sought within the bounds of Christendom, no better choice could have been made than Dr. Martineau. But in any case how much of what is best and most admirable in the writings, as in the life and character, of this noble Christain thinker, came to him through the old English Bible and the Church, as well as through the Reason. The power of reason as a fountain, or channel, of divine authority should have been illustrated, it appears to me, by taking a case *outside* Christendom, beyond the reach of the Bible or the Church. Socrates, or Plato, or even Epictetus, would have been a better example than Dr. Martineau; occasioning far less theological prejudice and furnishing a much stronger illustration.

During the conflict, that grew out of his address, very bitter charges were made against Dr. Briggs. In consequence of these charges he was regarded by tens of thousands of good men and women as an errorist of the worst sort. To decry him as an enemy of the Bible and an arrant heretic seemed to be considered by not a few as doing God service. Was he really such a man as his enemies depicted him? Or did they bear false witness against him? I might answer these questions by giving the testimony of eminent Christian scholars, at home and abroad, who knew him well and some of whom strongly dissented from much of his teaching about the higher criticism. But I do not think that, at this late day, he is in need of any such testimony. He can stand securely on the testimony of his own character, writings and services. The best answer to the charges brought against him by his enemies was his whole-souled, courageous devotion to the Divine Master whom he loves and adores. It has been my privilege to enjoy the friendship of very many good, learned and true men at home and abroad, and I have ever counted Dr. Briggs among them. Those, who knew him best, liked and loved him best. He was not, to be sure, altogether perfect; nor did he ever pretend to be. He was, undeniably, very positive and even aggressive, both by constitutional temperament and by force of conviction. If no good men were positive and at times even aggressive, who would be left to fight the perilous battles of truth and justice in such a world as this? Even granting that Dr. Briggs' tone and manner did not always tend to soften, or conciliate, hostile feeling, his intense earnestness rather than any personal ill-will was at fault. I have rarely known a man of such positive and strong convictions who was so little obdurate or selfish in his opinions.

To speak unadvisedly, or very positively, with one's

lips, or with one's pen, is no strange thing in the annals of American Presbyterianism. It did not come in with higher criticism. Dr. Briggs did not invent it. If in his Presbyterian days he sometimes sinned in that line, he followed the example of other famous Presbyterians of the 19th century. I have expressed my honest respect, not to say admiration, for Dr. Robert J. Breckinridge. But what shall be said of the tone and manner in which he was wont to express his mind about his New School brethren—and, as for that, his Old School brethren, also, when they differed with him—in 1834, 1837–38, at the Philadelphia Union Convention in 1867, and in the General Assembly at Albany in 1868? What could have been more provoking than his biting criticism upon the report of Dr. Adams and Dr. Beatty on reunion—a report so seasoned with the meekness of wisdom—pronouncing it unworthy of the great Presbyterian Church and "deficient in style, literature, grammar, and rhetoric from one end to the other!" The truth is, that Presbyterians, even if now and then the Lord's "silly people," as they have been often called, are also, undeniably, among the Lord's fighting people. Their Calvinism makes them bold and determined, but it tends also to make them somewhat pugnacious, not to say domineering. They hold a high doctrine of original and indwelling sin; and I have wondered whether, in His permissive will, the Lord did not, perhaps, allow an unusually large share of the latter to remain in them in attestation of their doctrine, as also to keep down their pride of orthodoxy.

When I consider what were Dr. Briggs' services to the Presbyterian Church, and to Christian truth; how far they exceeded in variety, amount, and quality those of most other Presbyterian scholars of his own day, at least in this country, and with what fidelity and zeal he rendered them, I am little in the mood to complain of his faults or to hear others do so. At his urgent request I consented to serve on the Executive Committee of the Association in charge of the *Presbyterian Review*, of which he was the principal founder and senior editor. He consulted me, both as a friend and as a member of that committee, year in and year out. He talked to me with absolute freedom respecting the *Review*, its policy, his colleagues, and his own plans, labors and trials in its management. He was restrained by no fear that anybody would ever know what he said to me. I do not believe he ever hesitated to give vent in my ear to his inmost thoughts, or doubts and suspicions and grievances about persons and things, so far as he had any, and yet as I now look over the record in my memory of those ten years I see nothing dishonoring to Christian scholarship; nothing that did not betoken one, whose devotion to sound doctrine, the best interests of the Presbyterian Church, the cause of sacred learning, and, above all, to the King of Truth, was an absorbing passion. Again and again I said to myself, "How this man loves to work for his Master and his Master's kingdom!"

This is not the place to speak at length of Dr. Briggs' trial for heresy by the Presbytery of New York and by the General Assembly of the Presbyterian Church in the United States of America. It has always seemed to me a very sad story, alike in its initiation, in its processes and incidents and in its final issue. I agree fully with those—and they formed a host of learned, wise and good men—who viewed this trial with profound regret, as involving not merely a great wrong to Dr. Briggs, but as also a heavy blow and dishonor to some of the most sacred principles of American Presbyterianism. As to the rasping tone, style, manner and language of not a few of his brethren, both ministers and elders, in opposing him and his views, it is hard to speak without some impatience. Harsh words, on both sides, usually accompany religious quarrels; that is one of the worst things about them. And they were often used, no doubt, in the Briggs case, as in all other cases of theological contention, with far less personal motive than their severity seemed to indicate. The best men and women are tempted to indulge in them; and are apt afterward to be sorry for it. Nothing is ever gained for a good cause by bitter, angry words. Still, the treatment of Dr. Briggs, bad as it was, might have been worse. I have examined with considerable care the records of his case as presented in the religious and secular press, and in the official proceedings of Presbytery and General Assembly, and find that so far as the printed accounts show, much that was most bitter had been weeded out, and that what is left was more fair, manly and of good report than I expected to find in them. Take, for example, the minutes and reports of speeches in the Washington Assembly, when it had been solemnly transformed from an ordinary business meeting into what is called a "Court of Jesus Christ." After years of heated conflict and discussion, the main question was now to be decided: Is Dr. Briggs GUILTY OF HERESY? Each commissioner, at the calling of his name, rose to "explain his vote" and give his judgment. A great hush, of a sudden, came over the whole Assembly. It was a wonderfully impressive scene. Almost everybody seemed to be awed by it, and a large number of the commissioners, who declared Dr. Briggs guilty of heresy, did it, apparently, not without regret, in entire honesty, quietly, and in the fear of God. There were, to be sure, a good many explanations loaded with partisan feeling and theological rancor; one in particular caused a pious shudder to pass over the whole vast audience. When the name was called of a ruling elder, who had been specially prominent in the organization and proceedings of the Assembly, he rose and explained his vote by a charge* against Dr. Briggs so terrible that

*"If it be in order in this Presbyterian General Assembly, in this court, permit me to direct your attention to the character of Almighty God and the Lord Jesus Christ for omniscience, veracity and absolute truthfulness. Almighty God said that Isaiah said thus and so; Dr. Briggs says to Almighty

the late Rev. Dr. H. M. Storrs—a splendid pattern of Christian manliness—sprung to his feet and exclaimed:

> Mr. Moderator: I rise to a point of order, and I wish it taken down. This man has been before us; is the charge now made against him true? Is it veracious? Has Dr. Briggs said any such thing? That is the question, sir. My point of order is that any man here has a right to the defence of his personal character against unwarranted statements. This is a charge of BLASPHEMY upon Dr. Briggs.
>
> Mr. McDougall— It is that matter I am going to discuss.
>
> Dr. Storrs—Mr. Moderator, before a man can say anything of this sort, he must locate particular language and statement; otherwise it is a general statement, and becomes an accusation of blasphemy for which there is no pardon.

This is not pleasant reading. But the majority, I repeat, of those who at Washington declared Dr. Briggs guilty of heresy, did it in a wholly different style and temper. One may easily respect them in spite of their unwise and wrongful verdict. Indeed, I go even further. Some of them in explaining their votes displayed, without knowing it, fine qualities of Christian sensibility and manhood. And along with the noble loyalty and devotion of the steadfast minority to Presbyterian law, liberty, justice and truth, these

God, 'Isaiah did not say so.' Which will you believe? This is not a question of finance, not a matter of science, not a matter of history; but the Almighty God, the Eternal Jehovah, said in His Written Word, in Luke, in John, in Romans, that Isaiah said thus and so; Dr. Briggs says, 'Almighty God, Isaiah never said it; he never wrote it; he was not living when it was written.' This is not a formal or technical question, it is a direct issue as to the veracity of the Eternal God."

qualities helped greatly to relieve the darker aspects of the scene. For, at the best, an American heresy trial, like that of Albert Barnes, or like those of Charles A. Briggs and Henry Preserved Smith, is a pitiable thing in the sight of heaven and earth.

This is not the place, as I have before said, to deal at length with the case of Dr. Briggs, to narrate the successive stages and incidents of his trial, to state the arguments for and against him, or to discuss the bearing of this trial upon public opinion, both in and outside the Presbyterian Church, in regard to the character and practical working of its judicial system. And yet the case was so full of impressive lessons, especially on the latter point, that I cannot wholly pass them over. Instead of my own reflections on the subject, however, I will give those of a much wiser man—one of larger experience and singularly gifted with ecclesiastical prudence. I refer to the late R. W. Patterson, D.D., the patriarch of American Presbyterianism in the great Northwest.

While engaged in writing this chapter Dr. Hastings put into my hands a parcel of letters, written to him by Dr. Patterson during 1891–1894. The following extracts from these familiar but weighty letters will explain some of the lessons taught by the case of Dr. Briggs, to which I have referred.

MAY 30, 1892.

I see that the Portland Assembly has decided to sustain the appeal of the committee and has reversed the action of the New

York Presbytery, but did not go on with the trial on the merits. This last the only sensible thing so far. I am not surprised, after witnessing the spirit of the Assembly at Detroit. Our judicial system must be reformed, or we shall as a Church lose all credit for decency in the trial of men accused of heresy, or, indeed, of any offence. Only think of five or six hundred men acting as a court!

It seems three members of the last Assembly's Committee of Conference were allowed, as individuals, to make a supplementary report, giving their pretended understanding of the "*status quo*," directly opposite (as Dr. Johnson tells me) of the fact that your board *declined* (very properly, I think) to consent to settle the question at issue by arbitration! I hope Union Seminary will resume her original freedom. The Assembly is on the high road to a tyranny that will divide the Church into worrying factions, and that will not be permanently endured in this free age, and all this outside of any provision of our constitution. Such usurpations are always smuggled in under the guise of *inferences* from constitutional provisions.

You will not infer from anything I say that I swear by Dr. Briggs. I dissent firmly from some of his views. But he is not a heretic, and his critical conclusions cannot be set aside by clamor, nor by the ignorant and prejudiced votes of an Assembly. He must be met, if at all, by patient discussion. The day for settling critical questions by fire and banishment is past, although I heard a high opponent of Dr. Briggs say (some years ago, it is true) that "Servetus *ought* to have been burned."

JUNE 1, 1892.

I do earnestly desire a thorough reform in our judicial system, which is the worst, I believe, in any Protestant

Church. A court of five or six hundred men, chosen with a view to the questions they are to adjudicate, and open to all outside influences and prejudiced appeals while they are acting in a judicial capacity! Of course a heresy-hunting committee would like to carry their case directly to such a body, passing over all intervening courts.

JULY 4, 1893.

I was not disappointed by the action of the Washington Assembly. The spirit of the leaders of 1835–1838 is again in the ascendant. But it is too violent to hold its present undisputed control. I know of strong dissent among conservative men, even at Princeton, and in the far West. The warriors, as in 1837, are led on by Kentuckians and Philadelphians. In spite of misrepresentation and attempts to repress discussion, thought and open speech will go forward and be felt. Union Seminary will live and be a great power in this struggle for liberty.

My greatest concern pertains to the *remoter future* of our Church. Can progressive men wait *long enough* to escape at last from the ecclesiastical tyranny that has fortified itself by misconstructions of Presbyterian law, still remaining in the Church? I fear many will get tired of the delay and go out in one direction or another—many of our best, ablest men. I feel the tendency myself. In fact, I begin to question *Scriptural authority* for such a system of government as ours has always been. Has a Christian church a right to build up such fences as we claim for safeguards against error?

SEPTEMBER 24, 1893.

The assumption now is that having a majority the extremists have a right, as a human organization, to construe or make laws as they please, without regard to the limitations of a *Christian church*, restricted by the teaching of its Divine Founder and the precedents furnished by the inspired apostles. I agree with you that if the church is a mere club, with authority to make or un-make its own laws, it is an instrument of despotism worse than Romanism. We are bound by a long confession, all of which we are confessedly not required to accept, but the majority can at any time fix the limits of "essential and necessary articles" as wider or narrower, and construe those articles by a court of six hundred men, the greater number of whom have no clear knowledge of the questions at issue. And then our rules of order can be stretched by forced interpretations of the same unwieldy majority to any result the leaders may desire. And, finally, if we complain, we are coolly invited to "get out," or be held as covenant breakers. The limits of *church* authority must be more discriminatingly settled if we are to hold our ground as Protestant Christians and churches. Many acute thinkers are inquiring in this line.

The theory of Presbyterian church polity, to which Dr. Patterson here refers, was very clearly defined by the Rev. Dr. William H. Roberts, Stated Clerk of the General Assembly, in explaining his vote at Washington in favor of condemning Dr. Briggs. It was as follows :

The foundation principle of Church organization held by the Presbyterian Church is that of a voluntary association. Without intruding on the rights of others, Presbyterians have voluntarily associated themselves into a denomination and have agreed to maintain a certain system of doctrine and form of government. The system of doctrine is composed of the fundamental doctrines contained in the Confession of

Faith. The Presbytery of New York by finding charges 1 to 3 in the case of Professor Briggs sufficient to put the accused on trial, approved as fundamental doctrines of the Presbyterian system these three, viz., that the Reason and the Church are not fountains of divine authority, and that the original Scriptures did not contain errors. The evidence given in Presbytery and the statements made by the parties on this floor have shown clearly, in my opinion, that the Presbytery has made a mistake and committed an injustice by its verdict of acquittal; and, further, that the Assembly, in order to maintain our system of doctrine intact, must so act that liberty of scholarship and opinion shall be given in the future as in the past only in matters non-essential. We must hold our ministers strictly to our system of doctrine in all fundamentals, or our Church will become something other than the clear-cut and thorough-going Calvinistic and Presbyterian Church which it has been for two centuries.

OCTOBER 20, 1893.

I do not see how we are to escape from the centralizing tendency of our Church. Your Synod of New York is largely governed by it, and so are all of our Synods. They must vindicate their loyalty to the Assembly by humbly bowing to all of its decisions. And the Assembly is governed by a dozen men, chiefly of Princeton antecedents. All the powers of the Church are concentrated at last in the Assembly, even to the creation of new constitutional provisions, which are easily made by new interpretations. Then each new decision of the Assembly is in the direction of stringency and narrowness.

NOVEMBER, 1893.

Hardly anything is surprising in these days. But it does seem past belief that Robinson and Booth should propose the refusal of license to the students of Union Seminary. That was beyond the Old School extremists of 1835–1837. No such ground was ever taken in regard to the students of Congregational seminaries, who have always been licensed without question on examination. Romanism could do no more. Union Seminary was always absolutely independent of ecclesiastical control up to 1870. It now stands on its original ground. . . . The truth is, our Church is more and more becoming a despotism. It needs a radical revision in polity as well as doctrine. I do not wish to die in such a Church as ours now is.

It is not my purpose, I repeat once more, to give in this volume a history of Dr. Briggs' case, but I am unwilling to pass from it without a word from Dr. Briggs himself. Here is a brief but very lucid statement on the subject, prepared by him at my request:

STATEMENT OF DR. BRIGGS.

In the autumn of 1879 I went to Princeton as a representative of the Union faculty to ask the co-operation of the Princeton faculty in the re-establishment of the *Presbyterian Review*. The W. Robertson Smith case was still in debate in Scotland, and it was supposed that I was in general sympathy with him; although I had not expressed my opinion in public any further than to claim his liberty of opinion in matters of the Higher Criticism, in my inaugural address as Professor of Hebrew in October, 1876. The Princeton faculty asked my views of inspiration and of the Higher Criticism. I stated that I did not accept Verbal Inspiration and Inerrancy and that I was in accord with the movement of Higher Criticism. The Princeton faculty agreed to unite with the Union faculty in the enterprise, and consented that Dr. A. A. Hodge and I should be the managing editors of the *Review*. The *Presbyterian Review* was started in January, 1880. The introductory article was written by myself and signed by Dr. Hodge without the change of a word. It was agreed that we should avoid questions in debate between us and endeavor to discuss all questions in the interest of the peace, harmony and unity of the Presbyterian Church. The other theological seminaries cordially united with us on this platform. Toward the close of 1880 the Princeton representative stated that it was necessary that the W. Robertson Smith case should be discussed in the *Review*, and that the conservatives demanded the right to speak their minds upon it. It was then resolved that both sides should be heard on the Higher Criticism. Dr. Hodge was to open and close the debate. I was to follow him at the beginning and precede him at the close. Dr. Hodge was to choose two intermediate writers and I two. I selected Dr. H. P. Smith and Dr. Willis J. Beecher, the representatives of the Auburn and Lane faculties, supposing that Dr. Hodge would choose representatives of the Alleghany and Chicago faculties, so that the six faculties represented in the *Review* would all be heard from. Instead of doing that, Dr. Hodge chose Dr. Green, of Princeton, and Dr. S. Ives Curtiss, of the Congregational Seminary of Chicago. To this plan of discussion we agreed. Subsequently the Princeton representatives insisted upon joining Dr. Warfield to Dr. Hodge in the opening article on Inspiration and of substituting Dr. Patton for Dr. Hodge in the closing article. The unfairness and partisanship of this proposed change of agreement was pointed out; but I consented to this violation of the original compact, under the advice of my colleagues in Union Seminary, in the interest of peace and harmony.

At the close of the discussion in the *Review* in April, 1883, there was little further discussion of the subject of Higher Criticism in the *Review*, except incidentally in the notices of books; and the excitement in the Church on the subject was gradually abating. It was revived only by partisan efforts in connection with the movement for the revision of the Westminster Confession in 1889.

The General Assembly in May, 1889, to the surprise of the great majority of the Church, sent down overtures to the Presbyteries, proposing the following questions: Do you desire a revision of the Confession of Faith? If so, in what respects, and to what extent?

These questions greatly agitated the whole Presbyterian Church. Three parties sprang into existence: One in favor of revision; one opposed to revision; and a third in favor of a new and simple consensus creed. The last two parties co-operated in the revision movement and won the victory, the result of which was the appointment of two committees; one to prepare a revision; the other to prepare a concensus creed. Union Seminary led the party of revision; Princeton the anti-revision party. At first I was opposed to the revision movement, as premature and impracticable; and expressed my views to this effect in the *Presbyterian Review* for October, 1889; but subsequently, seeing that the movement was an earnest and powerful one, and that it was necessary for me to take sides, I could not refrain from joining the party of progress.

The Presbyterian Union of New York invited Dr. Patton and myself to represent the two sides of the question before them December 2, 1889. This debate drew the fire of the entire anti-revision party on me. The very next evening, December 3rd, *The Mail and Express* published a bitter editorial attack on Union Seminary and on me, inspired by the anti-revisionists; and this attack continued in a most shameful way from that date onward.

These articles in *The Mail and Express* were sent to Presbyterian ministers and laymen especially in the West and Southwest, stirring up the Presbyterian Church against Union Seminary, the Presbytery of New York, and myself by false statements and misrepresentations. As this was done secretly, and was unknown at the time to the friends of Union Seminary, there was no opportunity of counteracting them. In the interest of peace and harmony, the friends of Union Seminary refrained from making any reply to these attacks in New York and vicinity, except by a few dignified articles by the late Henry Day. For the same reasons I refrained from making any reply to the attacks upon me. This situation continued for an entire year, waxing worse and worse.

In the autumn of 1890 enemies of Union Seminary employed a student in the Junior Class of the seminary to act as their spy. He made such false reports of my lectures that the entire student body arose in indignation and demanded his retirement from the seminary. The faculty, under the advice of the Board of Directors, called him to account, and after a careful investigation of the case expelled him from the seminary for his false statements in the public press.

When this situation was most acute, November 11, 1890, the directors of Union Seminary unanimously transferred me to the chair of Biblical Theology, just established by Mr. Charles Butler, president of the board. My induction into the new chair took place on January 20, 1891. The chair was entitled the Edward Robinson Chair of Biblical Theology. Inasmuch as Edward Robinson had been my teacher, and his name was more identified with Biblical Geography than with any other subject; the theme selected by me for my address was Biblical Geography. The donor of the chair, who was at the same time president of the Board of Directors of the seminary, was consulted as to the theme. He said that under other circumstances the theme would be most appropriate; but, under the circumstances forced upon us at the time, it was necessary to select a theme that would vindicate the seminary and myself in the matters under debate. I said to him that the result would be a very great increase in public excitement and bitter hostility on the part of the ultra conservatives, but he replied that it was necessary to meet the issue forced upon us, whatever the result might be. When one considers that it was Mr. Butler who aided Dr. Robinson in his journeys to Palestine, in the investigation of Biblical Geography; one can understand the significance of his opinion that I should abandon the theme of Biblical Geography and select the burning question. Yielding to his advice, which was reinforced by the faculty and other members of the board, the theme selected was the *Authority of Holy Scripture.* The aim of the address was to maintain and to assert in the strongest terms the divine authority of Holy Scripture in connection with a full recognition of the results of modern Biblical criticism and modern thought in all departments. No position was taken in that address which had not previously been taken in articles in the *Presbyterian Review* and in printed books many months before. The limits of the discourse required the condensation of a vast amount of material and the concentration of a very great many points of difference, which in the nature of the case were exceedingly disagreeable to the ultra conservative section of the Church, and the situation exacted of the speaker that his rhetoric should be fired to some degree of passion in view of the defense of himself and the cause that he represented, after more than a year of unjust attack. After several years of reflection I do not see how I could have done otherwise; but there is not a word of the address that I see any reason to change. There can be no reasonable doubt that this attack upon the seminary and myself was the result of the bitter feelings engendered by the revision controversy, and that it was organized and carried on as an anti-revision conspiracy by a very small body of active and unscrupulous partisans, who used *The Mail and Express* and affiliated organs and also an extensive pamphlet literature, and expended a large sum of money in order to fire the Presbyterian Church against the Higher Criticism and to persuade them that the Bible and the evangelical faith were in peril. In fact, the Presbyterian Church was deliberately thrown into a panic about the Bible in order to defeat the revision movement and to discredit Union Seminary. I was only an incident in this warfare. Circumstances made me the convenient target on which to concentrate the attack. In all respects this conspiracy was successful. The revision movement was defeated; Union Seminary was discredited; and I was suspended from the ministry of the Presbyterian Church.

It ought to be said that I was taken ill with a severe attack of the grippe, which confined me to my house and to my bed at the time when the movement against me began in the Presbytery of New York and the General Assembly. It was entirely contrary to ecclesiastical usage that action should be taken against a minister in his absence, when it was impossible for him to make such public statements before the bodies as might have satisfied them that no process was necessary. The directors of Union Seminary endeavored to overcome the panic by submitting a series of questions to me, the answers to which were signed from my sick bed. This action by the Board of Directors had no appreciable effect on the situation.

It should also be said that I proposed to the directors, through the officers of the board, to resign my chair in the seminary and relieve them of the necessity of defending me. The reason why I have remained in my chair is that I was requested not to resign because the directors felt that the rights and liberty of the seminary were inseparably bound up in my case.

It should also be said that it was my desire, in accordance with my best judgment, to withdraw from the Presbyterian Church after my acquittal by the Presbytery of New York, and that I yielded my desire and judgment to the unanimous advice of the faculty and the pillars of the seminary. I went on to sure defeat at the General Assembly, as was well known beforehand; and then suffered the humiliation of the unrighteous and illegal sentence for five years. At the close of this time, having made up my mind that I could change my ecclesiastical relations without any damage to the seminary or the cause that I represented, I carried out my desire and judgment, expressed several years before, and severed my connection with the Presbyterian Church and was received into the ministry of the Protestant Episcopal Church.

In closing this brief notice of the case of Dr. Briggs I will add a word touching the effect upon public opinion of his suspension by the General Assembly, as also of that of his friend, the Rev. Dr. Henry Preserved Smith, who on essentially the same ground was not long afterwards condemned as a heretic and punished in the same way. How were these two gifted Christian scholars, after they had been declared guilty of heresy, regarded and treated by their brethren outside the Presbyterian Church? The following extract from a letter of Mr. D. Willis James, dated Pasadena, California, March 30, 1899, may serve as a partial answer to this question:

Rarely has any ecclesiastical action met with such prompt and well-nigh universal condemnation as that of suspending the Rev. Dr. Charles A. Briggs and the Rev. Dr. Henry Preserved Smith from the sacred ministry. A large and, as I believe, the most intelligent part of the Presbyterian Church disapproved of this action. Dr. Briggs was warmly welcomed into the Episcopal Church and endorsed by some of its ablest leaders, such men, for example, as Bishop Potter and the Rev. Dr. Huntington; while the Rev. Dr. Henry Preserved Smith was unanimously elected by the trustees of Amherst College (composed of leading Congregational clergymen and laymen, also leading Episcopal clergymen and laymen, and at least two Presbyterians, one a prominent clergyman of New York City) as Professor of Biblical History and Interpretation and associate pastor of the college church. Dr. Smith was also received into the Congregational body by a unanimous vote of the local association and council. In what way could these eminent representatives of Episcopacy and of New England Congregrtionalism—differing so widely in forms and polity, agreeing so strongly in the liberty wherewith Christ has made us free—have expressed more emphatically their feeling and conviction that Dr. Briggs and Dr. Smith, judged by the great rule of the Gospel, are no heretics but brethren beloved in the Lord?

Part Third.

INTERNAL DEVELOPMENT AND EXPANSION OF THE SEMINARY SINCE 1886.

BY

THE REV. FRANCIS BROWN, Ph.D., D.D.,
Davenport Professor of Hebrew and the Cognate Languages.

THE COURSES OF STUDY AND SCHEDULE FOR 1898–99.

THE LIBRARY AND THE ALUMNI,

BY

THE REV. DR. CHARLES R. GILLETT,
Librarian.

THE INAUGURATION OF A NEW PRESIDENT AND GLANCES AT THE FUTURE.

Part Third.

THE INTERNAL DEVELOPMENT AND EXPANSION OF THE SEMINARY SINCE 1886.

BY PROFESSOR FRANCIS BROWN, D. D.

The internal development of the seminary, during the last twelve or thirteen years, has been gradual and quiet. The advance is, however, considerable.

Increase in the teaching force. Since the establishment of the Edward Robinson professorship of Biblical Theology, in 1890, not only have three new professors been chosen to fill vacancies,* but in the present year (February, 1899) two additional professors have been elected: the Rev. Thomas Cuming Hall, D.D., a graduate of Princeton University, in 1879, and of this seminary in 1882, as professor of Christian Ethics, and the Rev. George William Knox, D.D., a graduate of Hamilton College in 1874, and of Auburn Theological Seminary in 1877, as professor of the Philosophy and

*These are: The Rev. Arthur Cushman McGiffert, D.D., a graduate of western Reserve University in 1882, and of this seminary in 1885, on the resignation of Dr. Schaff, in 1893, was appointed Washburn professor of Church History; the Rev. Charles Cuthbert Hall, D.D., a graduate of Williams College in 1872, and of this seminary in 1875, on the resignation of Dr. Prentiss, in 1897, was appointed Skinner and McAlpin professor of Pastoral Theology, Church Polity and Mission Work, and also president of the faculty, on the resignation of that office by Dr. Hastings, in the same year; and, in 1878, the Rev. William Adams Brown, a graduate of Yale University in 1886, and of this seminary in 1890, was appointed Roosevelt professor of Systematic Theology, to fill the vacancy caused by the death of Dr. Worcester, in 1893.

History of Religion. These gentlemen will begin their regular work in the autumn of 1899.

With the transfers of Dr. Briggs to the Edward Robinson professorship of Biblical Theology, and of Dr. Francis Brown, to the Davenport professorship of Hebrew and the Cognate Languages (both in 1890), the position of instructor in Biblical Philology, as assistant in the Old Testament department, was revived. It was held for one year, 1891–92, by the Rev. Owen Hamilton Gates, Ph.D., a graduate of Dartmouth College in 1883, and a Fellow of this seminary in 1889–1891. When Dr. Gates left to accept the Old Testament professorship at Oberlin, O., the position was taken by the Rev. Charles Prosper Fagnani, D.D., a graduate of the College of the City of New York in 1873, and of this seminary in 1882, who still occupies the place. In 1897, the New Testament department was strengthened by the appointment of the Rev. James Everett Frame, M.A., a graduate of Harvard University in 1891, and Fellow of this seminary in 1895–1897, as instructor in that department, a position he still holds. In addition to these, the Rev. Charles Ripley Gillett, D.D.,L.H.D., librarian of the seminary, has, since 1893, given regular instruction in Theological Encyclopedia, Methodology and Bibliography.

Relations with the Columbia University and with the New York University. A much greater practical enlargement of the teaching force to whose instruction students of this seminary have access, is due to the special relations of mutual academic courtesy maintained since 1890 with the Columbia University and with the New York University, under which relations well qualified students of the seminary are admitted upon proper recommendation, and without fee, to the courses offered by the faculty of Philosophy at Columbia, and in the University Graduate School at New York University. These courses include advance work in Psychology and Philosophy, Anthropology, Political Science, Economics and Sociology, Greek, Latin and Semitica, Sanskrit, German and English, History, Comparative Religion, and other important subjects. A large proportion of the students of the seminary, avail themselves of these privileges.

Seminary Curriculum. Until 1894, there had been but three lectures daily in the seminary; since that date the number has been increased to four. The course of study in the seminary has been modified in several particulars. While a professional school can never adopt a purely elective system, it is recognized that, after a solid foundation has been laid in those studies which ought to form a part of the furnishing of every minister, some degree of specialization is possible, and, for thorough work is highly desirable, if not necessary. Changes in the curriculum have been made with this end in view. In 1894, there was announced a division of courses into *required* (in particular years or terms), *variable* (as to year or class, although required for graduation), and *elective.* In the junior or first year, the opportunity for electives is least, it is greater in the middle year, and greater still in the senior year; while graduate students and special students have a free range of electives. A certain proportion of the electives may be taken at the Columbia University and at the New York University.

There has been an increase in the number of seminars or classes for Special Research. In the year 1898–99, there were four seminars carried on in as many departments, to which only students of high grade are admitted, after personal application to the professor. Besides these, there are various seminars at the universities, open to the students of the seminary.

The practical use of the English Bible has been recognized as a distinct branch of instruction. In 1894–'95, Dr. Fagnani offered a special course in this subject, and since 1896, he has given two courses each year; an additional course is announced for 1899–1900, by Thomas C. Hall, to whom the subject has been specifically assigned.

Students entering the seminary with a good elementary knowledge of Hebrew have, since 1884, been put in a class by themselves, and have had opportunity for advanced work. Since 1897, a similar advanced class in Greek has been instituted, open to those who pass an entrance examination in that subject, and the result has been gratifying.

In 1896, an Honor Course was established for students of the higher grades, with somewhat severer requirements than the Regular Course. There is an Honor Course for graduates as well as for undergraduates. Special students who take at least fourteen hours a week, are upon the same footing with undergraduates and graduates in the matter of recommendation to the universities, but are not eligible for the Honor Course in the seminary.

Degrees. Under an agreement made in 1896, with the regents of the University of the State of New

York, students who successfully complete the Honor Course, are recommended by the faculty to the regents for the degree of B. D. Students have the further opportunity of working for the degrees of M. A. and Ph.D., at the Columbia University or at the New York University, and certain courses at this seminary are accepted by these universities in partial fulfilment of the conditions of these degrees.

Scholarships. Since 1893, four prize scholarships have been offered each year to college graduates of high rank who pass a special entrance examination. In 1898, a plan was adopted by which all scholarships are awarded on the basis of merit, and the scholarships are divided into classes varying in amount and corresponding to different degrees of merit. "Merit" is understood to include both scholarship rank and practical Christian efficiency.

In addition to the scholarships with stipend, an order of honorary scholarships without stipend, was established in 1898, for the further recognition of merit, called the Edward Robinson Scholarships.

Christian Work. For years past, a large number of the students of the seminary, have engaged in many forms of Christian work, under various methods of appointment and control. In 1898, this work was reorganized, and placed under the direction of the faculty as a department of Christian Work. The following branches of work are maintained under the rules of the department: work in churches and chapels; work as pastors' assistants; work in connection with the city mission society; settlement work; work in public institutions; regular and occasional preaching; choir service (for the advancement of the worship life within the seminary, and for occasional choir work in public institutions). Suitable measures are taken to secure supervision of the men, and reports of their work sufficiently definite to base upon them estimates of rank which estimates are considered in the award of the merit scholarships.

Almost the entire student body is engaged in some kind of Christian work under this scheme.

Student Societies. In addition to the historic "Society of Inquiry Concerning Missions," a branch of the Young Men's Christian Association was formed in 1898, and by means of it, membership was secured in the "World's Student Federation of Christian Workers."

Religious Services. The established services have long been daily morning prayers, students' prayer meetings and a monthly devotional meeting of faculty and students. In February, 1898, a vesper service, with sermon, was begun at 4:30 on Sunday afternoons, and has been continued. During the year 1898–99, a series of ten sermons on "The Holy Spirit," has been given on alternate Sunday afternoons, by specially invited preachers. Attendance by the students upon all the religious services of the seminary has been made voluntary.

The Union Settlement. A social settlement was established in 1895, by alumni and friends of the seminary, known as the "Union Settlement." It has a residence house in a needy district of the city—at 237 East 104th Street—with separate quarters for club rooms and kindergarten, a large hall for Sunday services, and a large free playground. The Head Worker is a graduate of the seminary, and members of the Board of Directors and of the faculty belong to the governing body. Its influence is rapidly increasing, and it offers valuable opportunities to students desiring to engage in this form of Christian work. Its relation to the seminary is close, though unofficial. It is supported by private subscription, and representatives of nearly all the Protestant Communions are united in its maintenance.

The Alumni Club. The Alumni Club of the Union Theological Seminary was formed in 1890. It was an outgrowth from a club maintained for some years by the members of the class of 1875. Its members are alumni of the seminary, for the most part settled in and near New York. Its purpose is social fellowship, the discussion of important questions, and co-operation, whenever practicable, in the interest of the seminary. It holds four meetings each year, with a luncheon, usually in November, January and March, and a dinner at the anniversary in May. Papers and addresses by specialists in many fields, form a prominent feature of the meetings. The number of members is about 250. The alumni, generally, are invited to the annual dinner in May. It was at a meeting of this club in 1894, that the Union Settlement Association was formed, which now carries on the settlement referred to above.

THE COURSES OF STUDY.

It may interest some readers to see, in addition to Dr. Brown's comprehensive and instructive paper, the Courses of Study for 1898–99. Here they are arranged by departments.

PROPÆDEUTICS.

Lectures on Theological Encyclopædia, Methodology and Bibliology, Dr. Gillett; First Term, Fri., 12 M.; required of Juniors.

BIBLICAL PHILOLOGY AND EXEGESIS.

Old Testament.

Hebrew A (1) Introductory Hebrew Grammar, with exercises in reading and writing Hebrew, followed by the reading of selected chapters of the Old Testament, Dr. Fagnani; First Term, Mon., Tues., Thurs., 9 A. M.; Wed., 10 A. M.; Fri., 11 A. M.; required of Juniors not taking B.

Hebrew A (2) Readings in the Pentateuch, with Exposition, Dr. Fagnani; Second Term, Thurs., 9 A. M., Fri., 10 A. M.; required of Juniors not taking B.

Hebrew B (1) Readings in I. Samuel, with exercises, Prof. F. Brown; First Term, Tues., 9 A. M.; Wed. 10 A. M.; Fri. 11 A. M.; required of Juniors advanced in Hebrew, elective for Graduates and qualified special students.

Hebrew B (2) Unpointed Text; Old Hebrew Inscriptions, Prof. F. Brown; Second Term, Fri., 10 A. M.; required of Juniors advanced in Hebrew, elective for all other qualified students.

Hebrew C. Hebrew Etymology and Syntax; Sight reading of Hebrew Prose, Dr. Fagnani; Second Term, Mon., 10 A. M.; required of Juniors.

Hebrew D. Readings in Kings, with Exposition, Prof. F. Brown; Second Term, Tues., 11 A. M.; Wed., 10 A. M.; required of Juniors.

Hebrew E (1) Isaiah i.-xii., Prof. F. Brown; First Term, Tues., 10 A. M.; Wed., 9 A. M.; variable, Middlers or Seniors.

Hebrew E (2) Psalms of Books I. and II., Prof. F. Brown; Second Term, Tues., Wed., 9 A. M.; variable, Middlers or Seniors.

Hebrew F (1) Zephaniah and Jonah, Prof. F. Brown; First Term, Fri., 9 A. M.; variable, Middlers or Seniors.

Hebrew F (2) Micah, Prof. F. BROWN; Second Term, Fri., 9 A. M.; variable, Middlers or Seniors.

Hebrew G (1) Exegetical Class; Judges, Prof. F. BROWN; First Term, Wed., Fri., 2.15 P. M.; elective for all qualified students.

Hebrew G (2) Exegetical Class; Isaiah xl., *ff.*, Prof. F. BROWN; Second Term, Wed., Fri., 2.15 P. M.; elective for all qualified students.

Hebrew H. Seminar; Haggai, Zechariah and Ezra, Prof. F. BROWN; two hours weekly through the year; open to a limited number of Graduates, Seniors and Middlers of high standing, after personal application to the Professor.

Biblical Aramaic. Dr. FAGNANI; Second Term, Thurs., 11 A. M.; elective for all qualified students.

(See also Semitic Courses at Columbia and New York Universities.)

NEW TESTAMENT.

Greek A (1) Grammar of the N. T. Greek; Synoptic Gospels; the Narrative of Mark and his Parallels; the Logia and other sources of Luke and Matthew; Mr. FRAME; First Term, Mon., 12 M.; Tues., Wed., 11 A. M.; Fri., 10 A. M.; required of Juniors not taking B.

Greek A (2) Synoptic Gospels, with Grammar, continued, Mr. FRAME; Second Term, Mon., 11 A. M.; Wed., 9 A. M.; Thurs., 10 A. M.; required of Juniors not taking B.

Greek B (1) Epistles of John, Prof. VINCENT; First Term, Tues., 11 A. M., Fri., 10 A. M.; required of Juniors advanced in Greek.

Greek B (2) Gospel of John, Prof. VINCENT; Second Term, Wed., 12 M.; Fri. 11 A. M.; required of Juniors advanced in Greek, elective for Middlers, Graduates, and qualified Special Students.

Greek C (1) Exegetical Class; Galatians, Mr. FRAME; First Term, Wed., Fri., 2.15 P. M.; elective for all but Juniors taking *Greek* A.

Greek C (2) Exegetical Class; Acts, Mr. FRAME; Second Term, Wed., Fri., 2.15 P. M.; elective for all qualified students.

Greek D (1) Epistle to the Romans, Prof. VINCENT; First Term, Tues., 10 A. M.; Wed., 9 A. M.; variable for Seniors or Middlers.

Greek D (2) Epistle to the Hebrews, Prof. VINCENT; Second Term, Tues., Wed., 9 A. M.; variable for Seniors or Middlers.

Greek E (1) General Introduction to the New Testament, I., Prof. VINCENT; First Term, Fri., 9 A. M.; variable for Seniors or Middlers.

Greek E (2) General Introduction to the New Testament, II., Prof. VINCENT; Second Term, Fri., 9 A. M.; variable for Seniors or Middlers.

Greek F. I. and II. Peter and Jude, Mr. FRAME; Second Term, Tues., 2.15 P. M.; elective for all qualified students.

Greek G. Seminar; I. Corinthians, Prof. VINCENT; two hours weekly through the year; open to a limited number of Middlers, Seniors and Graduates of high standing, after personal application to the professor.

(See further courses in Greek at Columbia and New York Universities.)

BIBLICAL THEOLOGY.

A. General Introduction to the Study of the Bible, Prof. BRIGGS; First Term, Tues., 10 A. M.; Wed., 9 A. M.; required of Juniors.

B (1) Biblical Theology I.: The Biblical Doctrine of God, Prof. BRIGGS; First Term., Tues., Thurs., 9 A. M.; Wed., 11 A. M.; variable, Middlers or Seniors.

B (2) Biblical Theology II.: The Biblical Doctrine of Man and of Redemption, Prof. BRIGGS; Second Term, Tues., Thurs., 11 A. M.; Wed., 10 A. M.; variable, Middlers or Seniors.

C. Special Introduction to the Old Testament, Prof. BRIGGS; Second Term, Tues., 10 A. M.; Wed., 11 A. M.; elective for. all students.

D. The Ethical Teachings of Jesus, Prof. BRIGGS; First Term, Thurs., 11 A. M.; elective for all students.

E. The Apostolic Church, Prof. BRIGGS; Second Term, Thurs., 12 M.; elective for all students.

CHURCH HISTORY.

A (1) History I.: History of Primitive, Catholic and Protestant Christianity, Prof. McGIFFERT; First Term, Mon., 11 A. M.; Wed., Fri., 10 A.M.; variable, Middlers or Seniors.

A (2) History II.: Continuation of A (1); Second Term, Mon., 11 A. M.; Wed., Fri., 12 M.

B (1) History of Christian Doctrine I., Prof. McGIFFERT; First Term, Mon., Thurs., 12 M.; elective for all students except Juniors.

B (2) History of Christian Doctrine II.; Continuation of B (1), Prof. McGIFFERT; Second Term, Mon., 12 M.; Fri, 10 A. M.; elective for all students except Juniors.

C. History of the Reformation in Western Europe, Prof. McGIFFERT; First Term, Thurs., 2.15 P. M.; elective for Seniors and Graduates.

D. Origin and History of the Apostles' Creed, Prof. McGIFFERT ; two hours weekly through the year ; Seminar for a limited number of Graduates, Seniors and Middlers of high standing, after personal application to the professor.

SYSTEMATIC THEOLOGY.

A (1) Dogmatics I.: The System of Christian Doctrine ; The Christian Doctrine of God, and of the World ; The Kingdom of God, Prof. WM. ADAMS BROWN ; First Term, Mon., 11 A. M.; Wed., Fri., 10 A. M.; variable, Seniors or Middlers.

A (2) Dogmatics II.: Continuation of A (1); The Person and Work of Christ ; The Trinity ; The Christian Doctrine of Man, of Sin, and of Salvation ; The Christian Doctrine of Redemption ; Second Term, Mon., 11 A. M.; Wed., Fri., 12 M.

B. Introduction to Dogmatics. This course is designed as an introduction to the fuller (dogmatic) Course A (1) and (2), and will discuss such practical questions as the *idea* and *sources* of Christian Theology, the nature of Revelation and Inspiration, and the Authority of the Scriptures, Prof. WM. ADAMS BROWN ; First Term, Wed., Fri., 12 M.; elective for all students except Juniors; especially recommended to Middlers.

C. The Westminster Standards. (Informal reading and discussion of selected passages from the Westminster Confession and Catechisms), Prof. WM. ADAMS BROWN ; Second Term, Tues., 10 A. M.; Wed., 11 A. M.; elective for all students except Juniors.

D. The Doctrine of the Person of Christ, Prof. WM. ADAMS BROWN ; two hours weekly through the year ; Seminar for a limited number of Graduates, Seniors and Middlers of high standing, after personal application to the professor.

PHILOSOPHY OF RELIGION, APOLOGETICS AND ETHICS.

A. *Philosophy of Religion.*—Introductory, the Rev. GEORGE WILLIAM KNOX, D.D.; First Term, Mon., Thurs., 10 A. M.; elective for all students; especially recommended to Juniors.

B. *Philosophy of Religion.*—Historical Development, the Rev. GEORGE WILLIAM KNOX, D.D.; Second Term, Mon., Thurs, 10 A. M.; elective for Middlers, Seniors and Graduates.

C. *Apologetics.*—The Conflict with Modern Doubt (not given in 1898–99).

D. *Christian Ethics.*—The Moral Principles of Christianity, and their Application to Human Life and Conduct (not given in 1898–99).

E. *Sociology.*

PRACTICAL THEOLOGY.

Homiletics A (1) Introductory instruction as to Methods of Pulpit Preparation, with practical exercises, Prof. HASTINGS; First Term, Mon., 11 A. M.; required of Juniors.

Homiletics A (2) Lectures with Practical Exercises, Prof. HASTINGS; Plans of Sermons are submitted not only for criticism by the class but also for private criticism by the professor; Second Term, Mon., 9 A. M.; required of Juniors and Middlers. Thurs., 9 A. M., required of Middlers.

Homiletics B (1) Lectures on the Composition and Delivery of Sermons, with practical exercises, Prof. HASTINGS; Sermons delivered by each student both in private and before the class; First Term, Tues., 11 A. M.; required of Seniors.

Homiletics B (2) Continuation of B (1), Prof. HASTINGS; Second Term, Fri., 11 A. M.; required of Seniors.

Homiletics C. Private Criticism of Sermons, through the year, Prof. HASTINGS; Mon., Tues., Thurs., Fri., 2.30 to 3.30 P. M.; required of Seniors. Four students in succession each week take their sermons to the professor for private criticism. At least two sermons must be thus submitted during the year by each member of the class.

Pastoral Theology A (1) Lectures on the Calling, Qualifications and Work of the Christian Pastor; on Hymnology and Psalmody, Prof. HASTINGS; First Term, Thurs., 9 A. M.; variable, Middlers or Seniors.

Pastoral Theology A (2) Continuation of A (1), Prof. HASTINGS; Second Term, Tues., 11 A. M.; variable, Middlers or Seniors.

Catechetics: Principles and Methods of Religious Teaching for Young People, Pres. HALL; Second Term, Wed., 10 A. M.; variable, Middlers or Seniors.

Church Polity: The New Testament Idea and Constitution of the Church of Christ: the ecclesiastical polities of later ages, Pres. HALL; Second Term, Thurs., 11 A. M.; variable, Middlers or Seniors.

Missions I.: City Evangelization and the Institutional Church, Pres. HALL; First Term, Thurs., 12 M.; elective for all students.

Missions II.: Home and Foreign Missions in the Nineteenth Century, Pres. HALL; Second Term, Tues., Fri., 9 A. M.; required of Juniors.

Missions III.: Geographical Distribution and Race Problems of Missions. Pres. HALL; First Term, Tues, Fri., 11 A. M.; elective, especially for Middlers (not open to Juniors).

Liturgics: I.: Historical Forms of Christian Worship; II.: Practical Administration of Christian Worship, Pres. HALL; First Term, Wed., Fri., 12 M.; elective for all students except Juniors.

Conferences on the Spiritual Life of the Minister: Themes invited from students, Pres. HALL; Second Term, Thurs, 9 A. M.; elective for Seniors.

Practical Use of the English Bible A (1) The International Sunday-school Lessons, Dr. FAGNANI; First Term, Sat., 9 A. M.; elective for all students.

Practical Use of the English Bible A (2) Continuation of A (1); Second Term, Sat., 9 A. M.; elective as above.

Practical Use of the English Bible B. Selections from the Old Testament practically expounded, Dr. FAGNANI; Second Term, Tues., 3.15 P. M.; elective for all students.

VOCAL CULTURE.

The exercises in this department are under the direction of Prof. ROBERTS. They are obligatory, unless otherwise stated, but do not count toward the required number of lectures specified.

A. *Juniors.*—The class is divided into sections; each section has exercises once a week for the developing, strengthening and management of the voice, and in the principles of expression in elocution as applied to the reading of extracts in Prose and Verse; Second Term, daily, 4.15 to 5.15 P. M.

B. *Middlers* (1)—Exercises in the reading of the Scriptures and Hymns; each section once a week; First Term, daily, 4.15 to 5.15 P. M.

C. *Middlers* (2)—Exercises in Pulpit and Platform Speaking. Individual drill and criticism; Second Term, daily, 5.15 to 6.15 P. M.

D. *Seniors* (1)—Exercises in Pulpit and Platform Speaking. Individual drill and criticism; First Term, daily, 5.15 to 6.15 P. M.

D. *Seniors* (2)—Continuation of D (1); Second Term, daily, at hours privately arranged.

SACRED MUSIC.

The exercises in this department are under the direction of Prof. SMITH. They are obligatory, unless otherwise stated, but do not count toward the required number of lectures specified. Most of them continue through the year.

A. *Elementary Class* (First Term), Thurs., 5.15 to 6 P. M.

B. *Choir Drill and Rehearsal,* Thurs., 4 to 5 P. M.

C. *Solfeggi Class,* Thurs., 5 to 5.15 P. M. (First Term).

D. *Elementary Class,* Section I., Thurs., 5.15 to 6 P. M. (Second Term).

E. *Elementary Class,* Section II., Fri., 5.15 to 6 P. M. (Second Term).

THE LIBRARY, GENERAL CATALOGUE AND THE ALUMNI.

BY THE REV. CHARLES RIPLEY GILLETT, D.D., L.H.D.,

LIBRARIAN.

The library of Union Theology Seminary contains an aggregate of about one hundred and fifteen thousand titles and volumes. It stands first in size among the collections belonging to theological seminaries in the country, and tenth in the list of libraries connected with educational institutions. It has grown by purchase, special gift and the endowment of departments. It came into existence almost as soon as the institution itself, and it has continued to increase with steady growth from the start, in spite of the lack of an adequate endowment.

The nucleus of the library was formed by the purchase of the Van Ess collection in 1838. This collection consisted originally, it is said, of about thirteen thousand volumes, and it has been characterized by Professor T. F. Crane of Cornell University, as "the most valuable library which has ever been brought into this country." The beginning of the collection is to be traced back to the library of the Benedictine Monastery of St. Mary, at Paderborn, where it constituted the collection of *libri prohibiti* under the charge of Brother Leander Van Ess. When the peace of Luneville, in 1801, threatened the sequestration of the property of the religious houses, the Benedictines of Paderborn divided the books and other property of the order among themselves and removed the same to places of safety. Van Ess went to Marburg, where he became professor of theology in the Roman Catholic faculty. Later he embraced Protestantism, and devoted himself to the translation of the Bible into the vernacular. At a later date the collection, which had grown much in the interval as a result of later studies, was offered for sale, and was finally acquired by the "New York Theological Seminary."

The collection is particularly rich in Incunabula or "cradle-books," printed before 1500, when the art of the printer was in its infancy; in patristic literature in the original editions, and in the early collections made in the 17th and 18th centuries; in Roman Catholic theology, liturgies, Canon law, and Casuistry, and in the writings of Luther and other reformers in the original editions; in early German, Latin, Greek, Hebrew and Polyglot editions of the Bible; in the exegetical works produced by post-reformation writers, and printed in great tomes; in collections of councils and of lives of saints, such as the Acta Sanctorum; in early theological systems; and in the German theological periodicals of the early part of the present century. Taken in its entirety, the collection justifies the remark of the eminent specialist quoted above.

For many years the library was under the charge of the renowned scholar and famous professor, Dr. Edward Robinson. To it he devoted much of his unbounded enthusiasm, and to it came, after his death, the valuable library which he had gathered in the pursuit of his archæological and exegetical studies. Next it passed into the charge of the late Dr. Henry B. Smith, professor of Systematic Theology. The catalogue of the library, which has survived in four great folio volumes, is a maze to the seeker after information, and the tradition still lingers that the gifted librarian's wonderful memory and his exhaustive knowledge of the treasures under his charge, constituted a far better index to the collections than this manuscript catalogue on many pages and in various styles of handwriting.

All this time the growth of the library had gone on

steadily. During Dr. Smith's incumbency, the late Dr. Ezra H. Gillett, had given much pains and labor to the increase of the department of British theology of the latter part of the 16th and the early portion of the 17th centuries. The result of this labor is seen to-day in an almost absolutely complete collection of the works which appeared in the Deistic controversy, and in an almost as complete representation of the Trinitarian and Non-Conformist controversies. It was by the generosity of Mr. David H. McAlpin, that the gathering of these books was made possible, and it was through the efforts thus made that Mr. McAlpin's interest in the library was lastingly aroused, an interest which led in 1884, to the endowment of the "McAlpin Collection of British Theology and History," and the "Gillett Collection of American Theology and History," by that generous donor. This interest was continued after the death of Drs. Gillett and Smith, and by it Dr. Charles A. Briggs, who succeeded Dr. Smith as librarian in 1876, was enabled to begin the acquisition of the collection of the works of the Westminster and Puritan divines of the 17th century, and of the religious and controversial works which preceded and followed the period of the Westminster Assembly, which are so essential to the proper comprehension and exposition of the Presbyterian standards, and of the other historical documents of this period of British history. In the same way have been gathered large and valuable collections of books bearing upon the early Baptist, Brownist and Independent connections, and upon the Family of Love, Muggletonians and other sects. The Roman Catholic controversies of the 16th and 17th centuries are also well represented by many scarce books and tracts. The importance of these special departments may be judged by the fact that the McAlpin collection is third in size only to the British Museum and the Bodleian

Library so far as the first two thousand titles in Dexter's "Bibliography of Congregationalism" are concerned. The collection will ever remain as a lasting monument to the enlightened generosity of the donor, and to the scholarly enthusiasm, the persistent and tireless zeal, the wide knowledge and the deep scholarship of Dr. Briggs, without whom the collection could never have been made. To-day it stands as one of the greatest treasures of the library which it adorns. The foregoing collections are all component parts of the greater collection which bears Mr. McAlpin's name. But besides them it contains also a large number of general and local secular histories of Great Britain and its parts; the most important histories of the Churches of England, Scotland and Ireland; a large number of biographies, and the collected works of British divines of all periods.

The Gillett collection of American Theology and History stands as another monument to the generosity of the same donor, and to the memory of his early pastor and manhood's friend. It is rich in general and local histories, both secular and ecclesiastical, and in biography in all its phases and branches. Ecclesiastical bodies are well represented by large and valuable collections of minutes and proceedings, and the early theological controversies of New England can be studied in the original writings which they produced.

Important additions were made also to the pamphlet department of the library through the efforts of Dr. Gillett. Most important among these are the early American titles contained in the extensive collection made by Dr. David Dudley Field, which constitute a veritable mine for the study of early American religious history. In this branch of the library are also the collections made by Dr. Gillett, Dr. Samuel Hanson Cox, Dr. William B. Sprague, and Dr. John Marsh, most of them being bound in book form, in manilla paper covers, placed there by Dr. Gillett himself. This pamphlet collection, which has been growing steadily for many years, and which has been further enriched by purchase from the library of Dr. Henry B. Smith, and by gift from the families of Dr. William Adams, and Dr. Edwin F. Hatfield, is regarded as a part of the department of American History and Theology, and is named in honor of Dr. Gillett.

Another section of the pamphlet department contains a large assortment of titles from the 17th, 18th and 19th centuries, bearing upon the religious controversies and history of Great Britain. These naturally form a portion of the McAlpin Collection, and are so counted. Recent purchases have added materially to the collection especially in the later periods.

When Dr. Briggs became librarian in 1876, he at once undertook a re-classification of all departments, and began a card catalogue which has grown ever since, till it covers practically all the books in the library. Under his successor the work in both departments has been continued, and a subject index, corresponding in the main to the shelf classification of the library, has been prepared. This catalogue resulted in more than doubling the use of the library. The original classification made by Dr. Briggs was a very large task, embodying an application of the current principles of Theological Encyclopædia, and representing an advance upon any scheme that had been employed previously in any theological library.

The most notable addition to the library in its more recent history was that from the library of the late Dr. Edwin F. Hatfield, so long the Stated Clerk of the General Assembly of the Presbyterian Church. This addition was rich in many departments, particularly in Americana and periodicals.

It was the richest gift ever made to the seminary library, aggregating about seven thousand volumes. A considerable portion of the books was incorporated in the Gillett collection, and the rest were distributed through the library by topics, in accordance with the settled policy. The periodical department, in recognition of the notable additions thus made to it, deserves to be called in honor of Dr. Hatfield.

When the construction of the present buildings was proposed, the late Governor Edwin D. Morgan endowed the library in the sum of one hundred thousand dollars, one-half of which was expended in the construction of the library building, and the other half was retained as a permanent fund. A further addition was made to the permanent fund by the gift of twenty thousand dollars by the late Mrs. Elizabeth Fogg in 1892, as the "William H. Fogg Memorial." The income of this fund is recommended to be expended for the purchase of books, pamphlets, and maps. For several years past the fund originally subscribed by the alumni and professors as an endowment of the Reference Library, has been known as the "Henry B. Smith Memorial: Philosophy," the change of object having been approved by the Associated Alumni of the seminary. The collection for which it is used has already been greatly enriched from the library of Dr. Smith, thus making the new designation of the fund particularly appropriate. The fund is small and inadequate for its purpose, but so far as it goes it insures a steady growth to the collection.

Another notable feature of the library is found in its hymnological department. This was a result of growth through many years, and it had been enriched by the addition of many volumes bearing the names of Dr. Robinson, Dr. Hatfield, and others. But the largest addition was that of the library of Professor Frederic M. Bird, bought through the liberality of the late Henry Day, Esq., prompted by Dr. Thomas S. Hastings. The combination of all these collections resulted in the exclusion of a remarkably small number of duplicates, and constituted a department of over five thousand titles, the largest collection of English hymnology to be found in any institution in the land.

The general library of the seminary is divided into four main divisions in accordance with the current scheme of theological classification. The department of Exegetical Theology contains valuable works which represent each separate topic of the general subject. With the acquisition of the Van Ess collection came many polyglots, texts and versions. Within the past year, through the munificence of Mr. David H. McAlpin, the valuable collection of Greek Testaments, made by the late Dr. Isaac H. Hall, was added to the library. It forms a unique collection of about eight hundred volumes, and it cost the collector years of patient and untiring search. In the departments of criticism and exegesis the library is well supplied, both with the older and newer literature. Here again the name of Edward Robinson is found upon the fly-leaves of many volumes.

The Historical Department is also large and valuable, being particularly rich in the matter of sources. Patristic literature, which was well represented in the Van Ess collection, has been supplemented as the years have passed, and it now constitutes one of the most valuable departments upon our shelves. The history of doctrine occupies considerable space. By the kindness of Charles W. Hassler, Esq., the library came into possession of a remarkable collection of books bearing upon the dogma of the immaculate conception of the Virgin Mary. These books found their place in the department of the history of Roman Catholic doctrine. The library also contains in this department a large number of important works in the field of general and local ecclesiastical and secular history, with many numbers in the field of Reformation history and literature. The writings of the Reformers are available both in the original editions and in the scholarly collections of learned societies and associations. Oriental history and antiquities, European history and general biography occupy much space.

Systematic theology covers a number of cognate topics: symbolics, polemics, irenics, apologetics, the systems of the various confessions, and monographs on the separate doctrines. The side-lights upon these doctrines are cast by the various controversies which have rent the churches, the literary results of which are classed with the history of which they are a part. The whole collection shows evidences of the formative hand of that master of theological science, Dr. Henry B. Smith. Unfortunately the department has not experienced a proportionate growth in later years. Nevertheless to the student of past phases of theological discussion as well as of present problems the collection is most valuable.

The department of Practical Theology is fairly well supplied. There is an abundance of works on various phases and experiences of personal religion, but the most used portion deals with the various phases of the activity of pastor and preacher. Homiletics and sermonic literature, the doctrine of the Church, the sacraments, missions and applied Christianity are all quite well represented, but they are by no means beyond the necessity of continued growth.

There are some departments in which the library needs to be supplemented, and the necessity is sore. Indeed, the size and growth of the collections are remarkable, in view of the meagreness of its endowment. An income is demanded which shall enable the library to keep abreast of the latest and best literature, and which shall provide also for efficient administration. A total endowment of two hundred and fifty thousand dollars would place it in this enviable position; its present income does not fully cover running expenses and fixed charges.

THE GENERAL CATALOGUE AND THE ALUMNI.

Within the past year the third general catalogue of the seminary has appeared, bringing the record down to include the class of 1898. The first was prepared by Dr. Edwin F. Hatfield, formerly the Stated Clerk of the General Assembly, and was published in 1876. The second appeared in 1886, and the third in 1898, both the latter being the work of the present writer. Appended to the third edition is a table, showing some interesting facts in regard to the student-body. It includes the classes from 1837 to 1897, sixty-one in all.

The total number of students during this period was 2,896, or, including the class of 1898 also, 2,955. Of these, 1,836 (or, with the class of 1898, 1,871) were graduates in the regular course, and 1,060 (or 1,084) were partial or special course students. The record shows the decease of 817; 58 others are returned as "unknown," that is, no amount of enquiry has sufficed to trace them. It is probable that at least forty of them are dead, bringing the total necrological list to nearly 860. This would indicate that about 2,100 alumni are now living.

The statistics as to ordination are interesting and instructive. Of the total of 2,896 students, 431 never were ordained, 83 of them having died at so early an age as to prevent their entry into the ministry, 57 having become physicians, 97 lawyers and 38 business men. The 58 "unknown" nearly all belong here also. The Presbyterian Church (Old

School) received 69, the New School, 514, and the reunited Church, 735, making an aggregate of 1,318, out of a total of 2,465 ordained men, or 51½ per cent. The other Presbyterian Churches received 110, and the Reformed Churches, 98, making a total of 1,526 holding the Presbyterian system; almost 62 per cent. There were 691 who went into the Congregational Church (a little over 28 per cent.), and 101 entered other denominations holding the Congregational polity, making a total of 792 such, or 32 per cent. of all. Up to 1897, Union had graduated 21 Lutherans, 59 Episcopalians, 61 Methodists and 6 Moravians.

The record of the seminary as a missionary educator is also enviable. The record shows that no less than 209 were engaged in labor under one or other of the various Foreign Mission Boards or other agency. This was a total of almost 8½ per cent. of those who were ordained. As a trainer of educators it holds a remarkable place also, having sent out no less than 84 teachers in theological seminaries, 72 college presidents, 196 college professors, 105 principals of academies or superintendents of education, and 124 teachers in schools. Many of these had been ordained and had engaged at some time in the work of the ministry.

To some extent the quality of the alumni of a seminary is indicated by the learned degrees which have been conferred upon them. The doctorate of philosophy belongs to 92, of divinity to 444, of laws to 44, and of literature to 10.

The list of abbreviations shows that through its students, the seminary has had relations with about 250 institutions of learning, in this and other lands. The edition of the General Catalogue, issued in 1886, showed that over 91 per cent. of the students of Union had had college training, and it is probable that the present edition would not have shown any lowering of the proportion if the statistics had been compiled. In fact there is a growing tendency to raise, not to lower the requirements and the proportion.

In his preceding volume, "FIFTY YEARS OF UNION THEOLOGICAL SEMINARY" (published in 1889), Dr. Prentiss spoke of the wide distribution of the original homes of the members of the student-body. The same statement remains true to-day, and the seminary remains constant to its name, for it is still a place where men meet from all parts of the United States and of the world. Irrespective of storm and tumult without, and unwounded by the shafts leveled at it, Union is a place of studious calm, where there is that union with God and man wherein is strength.

THE INAUGURATION OF A NEW PRESIDENT—GLANCES AT THE FUTURE.

I am unwilling to close this narrative without an allusion to the happy auspices under which Union Seminary has entered its seventh decade, and will shortly cross the threshold of another century. The growth of a theological seminary, like that of all great educational institutions, is largely a succession of new departures and involves ever-increasing cares, perils and responsibility; nor is anyone wise enough to foretell what errors or false steps may lie hidden in the future. The transition period through which Union Seminary has been passing is a case in point. Still, the prospect appears, to me at least, to be bright with promise. *We are saved by hope: but hope that is seen is not hope.* Distinct signs seem already to foretoken what the future is likely to be; and I cannot think these cheering signs are going to prove delusive. The inauguration of my old pupil and well-beloved friend, CHARLES CUTHBERT HALL, as president of the seminary and successor to my chair, with some passages from his address on the occasion, will best show what they are.

I.

THE INAUGURATION SERVICE.

The inauguration of the Rev. CHARLES CUTHBERT HALL, D.D., as Skinner and McAlpin Professor of Pastoral Theology, Church Polity and Mission Work in the Union Theological Seminary, and president of the faculty, took place, by appointment of the Board of Directors, in the Adams Chapel, on Tuesday evening, February 8, 1898, at a quarter past eight o'clock.

The procession entered the chapel in the following order: 1. Ushers. 2. Choir, followed by Dr. Gerrit Smith, the musical director. 3. Faculty of the seminary. 4. Representatives of other institutions. 5. Directors of the seminary. 6. Officiating persons.

The representatives of other institutions present were:

From Columbia University, President Seth Low, LL.D.; New York University, Chancellor Henry M. MacCracken, D.D., LL.D.; Harvard University, Professor Francis G. Peabody, D.D., and Professor J. Winthrop Platner, M.A.; Yale University, Professor Edward L. Curtis, Ph.D., D.D.; Princeton University, Professor Charles W. Shields, D.D., LL.D.; Wesleyan University, Professor Andrew C. Armstrong, Jr., Ph.D., and the Rev. Henry A. Starks, D.D; Cornell University, Professor Charles M. Tyler, D.D.; Johns Hopkins University, Dean Edward H. Griffin, D.D., LL.D.;

Williams College, President Franklin Carter, LL.D.; Rutgers College, Professor Jacob Cooper, D.D., S.T.D., LL.D.; Whitworth College, President Calvin W. Stewart, D.D.; Vassar College, President James M. Taylor, D.D., LL.D.; Barnard College, Dean Emily James Smith, B.A.; Auburn Theological Seminary, President Henry M. Booth, D.D., LL.D.; German Theological Seminary of Newark, President Charles E. Knox, D.D., and Professor Henry J. Weber, Ph.D.; Hartford Theological Seminary, President Chester D. Hartranft, D.D.; Chicago Theological Seminary, Professor Emeritus George N. Boardman, D.D., LL.D.; Pacific Theological Seminary, President John K. McLean, D.D.; Drew Theological Seminary, President Henry A. Buttz, D.D., LL.D. The Divinity Schools of Harvard University and Yale University were represented, respectively, by Professor Platner, and Professor Curtis, named above.

Courteous messages of regret were received from many institutions.

The organ voluntary was played during the entrance of the procession by Mr. R. H. Woodman, organist of the First Presbyterian Church of Brooklyn, whose pastorate Dr. Hall resigned to accept office at the seminary. At its conclusion, the hymn, "The Church's One Foundation," was sung by the choir and congregation; the Scripture lesson, Ephesians iv: 1–16, was read by President Franklin Carter, LL.D., of Williams College; after this Mr. John Crosby Brown, vice-president of the Board of Directors, and its acting president since the death of Charles Butler, LL.D., December 13, 1897, spoke as follows:

On the seventh day of February, 1897, the Board of Directors of the Union Theological Seminary by a unanimous vote elected the Rev. Charles Cuthbert Hall, D.D., to fill the Skinner and McAlpin Chair of Pastoral Theology, Church

Polity and Mission Work, made vacant by the resignation of the Rev. Dr. Prentiss. At the same time and by the same vote they elected Dr. Hall to the presidency of the faculty, made vacant by the resignation of the Rev. Dr. Hastings.

Both of these honored professors are with us to-day, Dr. Prentiss, as Professor Emeritus, enjoying the well-earned leisure to which his age and years of service entitle him, and Dr. Hastings, relieved at his own request, by the advice of his physician, from the onerous duties of president of the faculty, but retaining and discharging with unabated vigor the full work of his professorship.

One familiar face we miss. The president of the Board of Directors, the late Charles Butler, one of the original founders of this seminary, its devoted friend, counsellor and benefactor, who was spared to welcome Dr. Hall to his new work here, was taken from us too soon to preside as the official representative of the board on this as on so many other similar occasions for the past twenty-eight years. We mourn his absence to-day.

Under ordinary circumstances the inauguration of Dr. Hall would have taken place last autumn at the opening of the term. Gifts of friends, however, made possible some much needed improvements to the seminary buildings, and the completion of the chapel according to the original design of the architect, which contemplated a beautiful and appropriate place of worship and a memorial worthy of the man whose name it bears.

The time required for the completion of this work necessitated the postponement of this service.

Some here present may remember the old chapel on University Place, cold, forbidding and cheerless, and they may also remember that the late Dr. William Adams, after his election as professor and president of the faculty, at once undertook, through the liberality of a friend, its reconstruction. Some of us look back with special interest to those occasions, when professors, students and friends of the seminary met with graduating class in that renovated chapel for a last communion service before entering upon their life's work. The memory of those services lingers with us still; they have proved an inspiration to many a life.

Standing as this seminary does, and as I believe always will, for thorough scholarship, and aiming to give its students the best and highest intellectual training, I think I may venture to say for my colleagues in the board, that we hope that this chapel may become to all connected with this institution—directors, professors, teachers, students, and even to the neighborhood—a house of God and a very gate of Heaven, and that the services held here, where all will be cordially welcomed, whether morning prayer, Sunday service or the communion services with the graduating classes, may bring us all into closer fellowship, and above all into closer personal touch with our Lord and Saviour Jesus Christ, without Whose presence here all the beauty and outward adornment of this chapel and all its services will be utterly valueless.

Prayer was then offered by the Rev. Henry Van Dyke, D.D., of New York City.

Mr. John Crosby Brown then spoke further, as follows:

The constitution of this seminary requires each professor when entering upon the duties of his chair, and periodically thereafter, to make a certain declaration prescribed by that instrument. I now call upon the Rev. Dr. Hall to make the constitutional declaration.

Thereupon Dr. Hall made the declaration, as follows:

In the presence of God and of the directors of this seminary, I solemnly affirm that I believe the Scriptures of the Old and New Testaments to be the Word of God, the only infallible rule of faith and practice; that I receive and adopt the Westminster Confession of Faith, in all the essential and necessary articles thereof, as containing the system of doctrine taught in Holy Scripture; that I approve of the principles of the Presbyterian Form of Government; and that I will not teach anything which shall appear to me to be subversive of the said system of doctrine, or of the principles of the said Form of Government, so long as I continue to be a professor in this seminary.

Mr. John Crosby Brown then said:

Having been elected by the Board of Directors a professor in this seminary and president of the faculty, and having made in this public manner the declaration required by the constitution, on behalf of the Board of Directors of the Union Theological Seminary I now pronounce the Rev. Charles Cuthbert Hall, D.D., duly inaugurated as Skinner and McAlpin Professor of Pastoral Theology, Church Polity, and Mission Work, and president of the faculty, and as such entitled to discharge all the duties of these respective offices in this seminary.

Mr. Brown added:

It is the custom of this board to appoint one of its own members to deliver on its behalf a charge to a professor at his inauguration. Acting upon the authority conferred upon them by the board, the executive committee has asked the Rev. Dr. Hastings to deliver the charge to Dr. Hall.

Technically, this appointment is slightly irregular. At the present time Dr. Hastings is not a member of the board, having declined to allow us to retain him as a member of our body, lest thereby a precedent might be established that might possibly embarrass this institution in the future. We could not, however, release him from the duty of representing us this evening, and he will now deliver the charge to Dr. Hall.

The charge was then delivered by the Rev. Professor Thomas S. Hastings, D.D., LL.D., L.H.D., former president of the faculty.

Thereupon the inaugural address was delivered by the Rev. Charles Cuthbert Hall, D.D.

At its conclusion a hymn, "We give Thee but Thine own," was sung by the choir and congregation; prayer was offered and the benediction pronounced by the Rev. Professor Francis G. Peabody, D.D., of Harvard University, and the procession retired during an organ voluntary by Dr. Gerrit Smith.

II.

CHARGE.

BY THE REV. PROFESSOR THOMAS S. HASTINGS, D.D., LL.D., L.H.D.

On behalf of the Board of Directors I am called upon to address you, my brother, in recognition of the important office you will henceforth occupy.

First of all, permit me to congratulate you upon the singular unanimity with which you were called to the presidency of the faculty. No other name than yours was considered in the board or mentioned in the faculty. A common conviction and a common feeling seemed at once to possess all minds and hearts. We feel, and, I am sure, you feel that the hand of Providence was peculiarly clear in the matter from the beginning. This is a great comfort to us all and should be also a great comfort to you. If God has called you, as we all believe, to this high trust, He will certainly help you to fulfill its obligations.

Let me congratulate you, also, upon the *time* of your induction into the presidency. The autonomy and position of this seminary have been secured: its self-governing power and its catholic independence have been settled; and now "forgetting those things which are behind," we are all, with one heart, "reaching forth unto those things which are before." We are eager to enrich our curriculum, and in every way to enlarge and to improve our work. The beautiful catholicity, which has characterized this institution from the beginning up to this sixty-second year of its life, is demanding a fuller expression than that of open doors as toward students of all denominations of Christians. We look and long for a theological university, broad and comprehensive, which shall be the natural evolution of the spirit and aim of our honored founders.

Our doctrinal basis must and will be maintained inviolate. We are anchored to the Westminster Confession of Faith, though some of us deeply regret that it was not revised when two-thirds of the church desired revision. Yet, while holding to that confession, and *held by it*, we receive on equal terms students of every denomination of Christians, and must provide for them, as our charter says "*Equal privileges of admission and instruction,*" and this cannot really be done unless our institution expands into a true theological university. The way seems to me to be opening before you, my brother, for such expansion. It may not be effected at once, but the morning glow is already gilding our horizon, and, though I may not live to see the noontide splendor, I trust devoutly that this may be your high and happy privilege. What we want is not *revolution*, but only *evolution.* One of the finest mills in the British manufacturing districts is the oldest. The machinery has always been kept even with the progress of improvement and of invention; and yet the mill has never been closed for a single day. The proprietor explains it thus: "I am always altering, but never changing." *Always altering, but never changing;* that is the true progressive method. We cannot be content with what has been accomplished; we must move on to higher and better things; progress is the necessity of healthy life. Our teaching should be as broad as our charter is, and as comprehensive and catholic as is our student body, within which are always found representatives of all the Evangelical churches. God forbid that we should try to make them all Presbyterians. To make a good Methodist or Baptist into a poor Presbyterian would be a dreadful waste of consecrated force, besides being a dishonorable betrayal of our high trust. We must aim only to make our students better in and for their respective denominations than they can be made anywhere else. We scorn the low work of proselyting, and aim only at the high and holy work of a truly Christian education,—scholarly, spiritual, practical and catholic. We delight always to stimulate our students to think for themselves, only with such guidance and help as we may be enabled to give them. We crave the free development of sacred and consecrated individuality. Traditions and conventionalities and shibboleths in Union Seminary have always been put aside, that, in the love of the truth, we may all be emancipated from every kind of small and degrading bondage, and so may study God's Holy Word with reverent and open hearts, and with free, trained and enlightened minds. I know, my brother, that you are in cordial sympathy with this controlling and characteristic spirit of our seminary life, and I am sure that you will seek to promote its unbroken continuance.

Permit me also to congratulate you that you are called to preside over a united faculty. Of course I do not mean to say that we always think alike on every question which comes before us: each one of us thinks his own thought and speaks his own word frankly and freely. We are decidedly finite men, and so we differ and discuss; but we are united by strong and delightful ties, and we reach our conclusions harmoniously, and we stand by one another and by our president with affectionate loyalty. The faculty is accustomed to being considered and consulted in all things which pertain to the welfare and the growth of the seminary; but you may be assured that they will right loyally sustain you, and faithfully honor your leadership. After nine years of experience, I say to you,—*you can trust them,* and the more you trust them, the more can they and will they help you.

Again, I congratulate you that you have with you a united Board of Directors, composed of the noblest collection of men with whom it has ever been my privilege to work. I cannot think or speak of them without deep emotion and a thrill of enthusiasm. They have proved their love for this seminary by a noble and a generous devotion to its best and highest interests. I am sure that Dr. Adams and Dr. Hitchcock, if, from out the great cloud of witnesses, they could speak to you to-night, would join me in saying—You can trust this board; they will support you to their uttermost ability in all your efforts to promote the welfare and the growth of this seminary. They will carefully guard the financial interests of the institution, and if they do not always move as fast as you could wish, be assured that they will move as fast as they can, and as fast as is best. I doubt whether there is an educational institution in the country whose finances have been managed with such consummate skill and success as have the finances of this seminary. You should be happy that you have with you such wise and such safe supporters. Progress and enlargement or expansion require money, and that necessity is a constant and a painful limitation. Unfortunately this seminary has the reputation of being wealthy, and that misapprehension needs to be corrected before we can hope to receive such gifts as our plans and hopes require. When the Lord's stewards know that this institution is *really poor,* and can improve and expand, grow better and more useful, only as fast and far as the noble generosity of the friends of sacred learning will permit, then we shall have the help we need. All good educational institutions, are always wanting money; they are perennially poor because they are good, and are so eager to do better. But we must be thankful for the past, and try hard to be patient for the present.

In all our forward movements you, my brother, are to be our leader. May you be enabled to lead us wisely and safely. A passenger on one of our coastwise steamers said to the veteran pilot at the helm,—" I suppose you know where every rock is, and every sand-bar on this coast." "No," said the pilot, "but I know where they are not." We believe you, my brother, know where the rocks and the sand-bars *are not*, and we trust you to *steer our course just* THERE! We have no desire to hunt for rocks or sand-bars!

You have already made your mark upon our seminary life. You are aiming to get near to the student-body and to reach its heart. You will do it. The students will love you because you love them. You are aiming to promote their spiritual development, and to prepare them for practical, divine and human service. You are seeking to cultivate among our students a high Christian manliness, which will fit them to command the respect and to win the love and the confidence of those to whom they will be called to minister. The amplitude and the comprehensiveness of the Skinner and McAlpin chair, which you occupy, will give you abundant opportunity to carry out your high purpose, and to realize your cherished ideal. Permit me to assure you that in all this you will have the cordial cooperation of the faculty, as well as the earnest and the prayerful sympathy of the directors. May God bless you, my dear brother, and endue you richly with His grace, for the high and holy service upon which you have entered.

III.

PASSAGES FROM THE INAUGURAL ADDRESS.

Union Seminary has exercised an engaging fascination over the minds that have known it best. It is doubtful if any institution of theology was ever more beloved of men. A singular charm of perpetual youth and freshness abides upon it. The years of its history multiply, yet it grows not antiquated and feeble. It renews its youth. It keeps pace with the changing thought of the changing generations, that it may the better bear witness to Him Who through all changes is the same yesterday, and to-day and forever. It turns itself hopefully to the new problems of the new times, that it may help men to hold with braver hearts the faith once for all delivered to the saints. It seeks to understand the thought and the temper of the current age that it may exalt amidst new conditions the eternal and indestructible Gospel of the Lord Jesus Christ.

As to-night, I seem to stand where two ways meet, looking backward over two generations of the seminary's history, and forward into a new time throbbing with new and vast problems—problems that involve the most precious interests of the Church of Christ and the moral health and safety of society, I need not attempt to conceal the profound and sacred solicitude that fills my mind as I ask myself: To this new time, with its new interests and its new problems, in what relation shall this seminary stand? Shall it be but as a surviving institution of the past, honored and loved for the good it has done, cherished still for the unworldly calm of age that shall brood over it, but bearing no real relation to the thought struggles of the twentieth century, and to those social movements of Christianity that are even now advancing as in a mighty crusade of love to grapple with the sorrows and the oppressions and the ignorances of the human race? Shall this seminary in that new time, the thunder of whose coming is in our ears like the boom of the rising tide, be but a seat of cloistered repose, or shall it be a centre of power consecrated to the service of humanity? Questions like these fill my soul as I stand to-night at the parting of the ways. This is not an hour in which it is given me to make any official announcement of the means and methods by which the expansion of the seminary is to be accomplished, and I make no such announcement. But speaking as one whose love was long since given to this seminary and whose life is now given for whatsoever form or duration of service it may please God to indicate, it is my privilege, if not my duty, to describe an expansion of the seminary which would be at once concurrent with the ideals of the founders and adapted to some great needs and great opportunities of the times into which we are moving. Circumstances may postpone for a season the accomplishment of this expansion (I pray God it may not be long postponed!), I may not survive to see upon the earth the fruition of this fond desire; nevertheless I would record myself, in this hour which binds me to this work, as having believed these things, hoped these things, and (so far as one man may do) as laboring to accomplish these things. Not that the lines of expansion I am about to indicate are devised by myself: not that I am the author of this scheme of expansion—some of the features of which have been for years discussed by my colleagues in the faculty and in the board, and I doubt not by others. But there is a sense in which one who gives his life to an undertaking appropriates, incorporates as of the very substance of his own thought, affirms as the true expression of his own mind, the principles and ideals to which he unreservedly commits himself. In such a sense I speak of the expansion of the seminary, committing myself to that ideal in all fullness of faith, in all seriousness of hope and expectation. But this ideal whereof I speak is not the pleasureable dream of an unsanctified ambition, seeking great things for the sake of worldly glory ; it is not the vain conceit of an unspiritual rivalry, straining to outdo its competitors in the field of theological discipline—this ideal is but the yearning hope that in the time to come this honorable foundation, over which the prayers and labors of the holy dead were lavishly expended, may still be worthy of Christ's use, and fruitful of good in the great world for which Christ died.

The expansion of the seminary presents itself to my mind not as a one-sided development, an overgrowth in one direction, but as an expansion on every side, a quadrilateral expansion. For there are four lines which are susceptible of an extension perfectly concurrent with the plans of the founders and with the constitutional rights and liberties of the institution.

There is the *Academic Line.* There is the *University Extension Line.* There is the *Line of Social Service.* There is the *Line of Spiritual Power.* This is a quadrilateral which would represent an immense expansion of the seminary, but which would not by one jot or tittle deflect the plans of those wise and far-seeing men to whose courage, generosity, and faith the seminary owes its existence. This expansion would indeed bring the seminary into close and irenic relation with the various branches of the Christian Church, but it would not weaken nor change in any way its relation to that particular branch of the Church, in the communion of which the founders lived and died. This expansion would indeed bring the seminary into warm and practical touch with some of those most broad and most earnest sociological movements which are seeking to purge and uplift and bless with gladness the lives of the poor, but it would not confuse nor obscure in any way the chief end of the founders which was, to use their own language, "to furnish a competent supply of well-educated and pious ministers of the Gospel." This expansion would indeed bring this seminary nearer perhaps than it has ever been to the spiritual life of the community at large; would involve it, more perhaps than it has ever been involved, in the responsibility of offering the comforts and encouragements of worship to human souls; would emphasize more strongly perhaps than has ever been emphasized the supreme necessity for an ardent, profound and progressive spiritual experience in students for the ministry; but nothing in this spiritual expansion would diminish, by so much as the least degree, the height and stability of that academic standard which from the first days until now has been the honorable and continuous tradition of this seat of learning.

In language which shall be as calm as may be when the heart's love is uttering itself with the mind's conviction, I shall endeavor in this closing portion of my address to describe the nature of this expansion upon what I have called the lines of the Quadrilateral.

1. The Academic Line. To me, who am but the humblest student of contemporary thought and feeling within the Church of Christ, the time seems ripe for a noble and irenic extension of the academic work of this seminary. Two influences, beneficent and broadening, appear to be at work in the minds of many men who having finished their earlier courses are thoughtfully engaging in post-graduate study; or who, whether by choice or by necessity, having gone into the pastorate are eagerly and anxiously ponder-

ing, in the scant leisure of their daily round, problems of belief and problems of Christian brotherhood. One of these influences is theological and ethical—the other is ecclesiastical. Theological and ethical thought in the minds of the younger ministry is to-day like the full, swift, impetuous, torrent of a springtide flood, when the ice gorge is broken and the stream runs free. It is a great and glorious time wherein to be young, wherein to be standing on the threshold of one's ministry, or to have moved but a little way along its course. The Christianity of the cross is being seen in new light—which is also old light—the light of the knowledge of the glory of God in the face of Jesus Christ. New co-ordinations are being made of truth with life, of life with truth; the Gospel, fresh with eternal youth, is vindicating its power to deal with social difficulties, and everywhere young men of consecration are awaking to the thought that he who holds the truth holds power if he but learn to use the truth aright.

Ecclesiastical thought in young, brave and unfettered minds is also like the springtide flood speeding into sunlight below the gloomy gorge. The Church of which the one Lord Jesus Christ, God of God, Light of Light is the sovereign and enthroned head is awaking to conceive of her own oneness in Him. From remotely separated points of view, on lines sometimes deflected, it may be, by prejudice or by un-wisdom, yet with hearts glowing in the warmth of truly Christian purpose many younger men are following many older men in love's unconquerable search for a self-revelation to the whole Church of her own essential oneness in the one Lord Jesus Christ. Men of various polities are yearning for a better understanding of one another.

I believe that for these post-graduate men and for these young pastors, upon whom the theological and ecclesiastical progress of the time is bringing a new sense of the value of calm and careful study of these mighty themes, the seminary may, by an expansion of its scope upon the academic line, provide an incalculable blessing. By establishing a series of University lectureships outside the faculty, and by appointing to those lectureships, in accordance with its well-known constitutional right, representatives of the various branches and polities of the Christian Church, who in the spirit not of controversy but of peace shall luminuosly present the history and the distinctive principles of their respective polities; by providing other lectureships for the most advanced study of Christian ethics, canon law, symbolics and comparative religion, the seminary can meet and answer comprehensively, irenically, and on the highest grade of academic discipline, that fundamental need of a clearer faith, a more intelligent ethics, a more catholic and Christlike churchmanship, of which all over the land many of our finest and ablest men are conscious.

2. The University Extension Line. "University Extension" has become a technical term in the modern educational system. As applied to the college and to the university, it signifies the arrangement of special lectures outside of the ordinary curriculum, by means of which a measure of collegiate advantage is supplied to those who, for any reason, cannot have the privilege of collegiate training. As applied to the theological seminary, "University Extension" would mean the sharing with lay-workers of those advantages of Bible study and other preparation for Christian usefulness which are secured to ministers by the ordinary curriculum. With new intensity and a fresh baptism of social love the Church is everywhere making a practical application of Christianity for the betterment of

society. It is seeking to offset the evils and sorrows of poverty; to supplement the deficiencies resulting from sin, neglect or ignorance; to reduce the melancholy alienation of class from class. And the Church has found out that this practical application of Christianity can never be accomplished by the unassisted work of the ministry. The progress already made would have been impossible but for the splendid earnestness of men and women of the laity. But the value of lay-work can be indefinitely augmented by means of training; training in the principles of a popularized and purely evangelical theology, training in the practical and facile use of the English Bible, training in the history of missions throughout the world, training in the true and harmonious relation of various church polities to each other, training in the uses and values of sacred music, training in the principles of civics and in the economic side of social reconstruction; training, in short, in whatever makes for the complete efficiency of the lay-worker. I believe that the seminary, by an expansion of its scope on lines well within its constitutional rights, may place itself in an attitude toward lay-training which shall be related to its ordinary curriculum for ministerial training as the University Extension Lectures are related to the college course. Steadily, as I believe and as I pray, the distinction between the ministry and the laity, in so far as it is an artificial distinction, is receding from view; and in its place is rising a new brotherhood between all, ordained or unordained, who are working, in the one Sacred Name, to upbuild and to unify a fallen and dismembered social fabric. Why should the ministry have a monopoly of that learning which may be supposed to exist in the faculty of such a school as this? Why may not the same knowledge be communicated to any and to all who are to labor side by side in the great world-field of human life? If the subjects taught in the theological seminary are of any real value as an equipment for practical usefulness, why should not those teachings be shared by all men and women who love the Lord Jesus Christ in sincerity and who are purposing to spread Christ's influence in the earth?

3. The Line of Social Service. On the upper East side of New York, particularly the thirty-second and thirty-third Assembly Districts, a new and densely populated city has sprung into being within the last ten or fifteen years. Far more than one hundred thousand persons are dwelling in that quarter, the greater part of them being industrious and self-supporting toilers. They represent many nations and many forms of faith. Earnest ministers and missionaries, Protestant, Catholic, and Jewish, are laboring in that quarter to supply the comfort and guidance provided by their social faiths. But all existing means of religious teaching and social elevation in that crowded district are, up to this time, far less than the conditions require. Three years ago, in the very heart of that populous territory, a social settlement was planted in faith and hope. It sustained then, and it sustains now, no organic relation to this seminary, although it bears the name of "Union." But it was a direct emanation from this seminary; an expression of the spirit of social love which prevails within this institution. An honored and dearly loved member of this faculty was at the head of the movement, and his colleagues have given freely of their time and strength to promote its interests. An alumnus of the seminary became the head worker; many undergraduates have done manful service there, and the friends of the seminary have been the friends of the settlement. Its history thus far has been a sweet and simple

chronicle of work done in Christ's name and spirit to make life brighter, purer, and more hopeful for men, women, youths, and little children, who, because they are poor and must toil painfully for daily bread, cannot otherwise possess those inspiring and educating influences which are provided in the settlement. And now the time has arrived when the preaching of the Gospel has become a part of the Union Settlement work, and when week by week one of God's servants offers to the dwellers in those crowded homes "the life which is life indeed."

I believe that this seminary by the expansion of its scope along the line of social service, and by using the Providential opportunity afforded in the Union Settlement, may take one of the most advanced positions that has yet been taken by a divinity school in showing that high Christian scholarship and intense evangelistic and social effort truly and properly go together. I pray for the day when in the heart of that neighborhood which I have described, some far-visioned Christian man or woman shall build for the Union Settlement a great and complete establishment, as great as Mansfield House in the east of London; making that house, consecrated to the service of humanity upon the basis of the Gospel of the Cross, a perpetual expression of the true spirit and intention of this seminary toward the problem of social reconstruction. I would have that house a centre of physical, intellectual, and spiritual education for the people of that district; an open portal, a gate beautiful into a wider and happier life than the life of Christless ignorance. And I would have that house and the district about it a sublime opportunity for the students of this seminary to learn all the new, loving, generous methods of helping mankind to a better life, and of coming near unto, yes, of immersing one's self into that deep sea of humanity which heaves in restlessness around the walls of the Church and knows so little of what Christ intended that His Church should mean in this fallen and disordered world.

4. The Line of Spiritual Power. In many quarters of the Church to day (and I speak now of all branches of the Church) the deepest longing of the most thoughtful hearts is for a return of Christians to that spirituality of mind and of life which prevailed among the believers of the Apostolic Age. Gratefully do I quote the devout words of one of my colleagues who has recently written concerning this primitive period of Christian history. "It is not enough to speak of the ethical principles and practice of the early Christians; their life was above all else religious and it was that dominant religiousness which gave it its peculiar and distinctive character. The controlling fact in their life was the consciousness of being citizens of a heavenly Kingdom and heirs of a heavenly inheritance. They might go about their ordinary occupations as they had always done and might mingle with their neighbors as before, but they were conscious all the time that they were living in another world, and that the forces and influences which controlled them were from above. The consciousness found concrete expression in the belief that the Holy Spirit was in the church, guiding and inspiring the followers of Christ and endowing them with power far beyond their own." Words like these represent that for which the most thoughtful men within the Church are praying; the deepening of the spiritual sense of Christ's person, of Christ's work, and of Christ's ideal for His church which alone can prevail to banish controversy, quicken faith, and promote personal consecration.

I believe that this seminary may and must expand its scope along this line of spiritual power. The chapel in which we gather to-night, and which loving and filial hands have adorned in memory of one whose life and whose teachings bore witness to the value of a spiritually minded ministry, ought to be a place where those of all branches of the Church who desire to worship in the spirit and to ponder the principles and objects of the life which is hid with Christ in God may come together, free from the saddening influences of controversy and far from the dark shadows of doubt, to sit together in heavenly places in Jesus Christ and commune in the unity of the spirit and under the bond of peace. The whole effect and influence of this seminary upon those who study within its walls in preparation for the ministry ought to be to exalt Jesus Christ in His eternal Godhead, in His atoning sacrifice, in His risen and enthroned glory, in His future advent; and so to nourish and to strengthen the powers of the spiritual manhood that all who go forth from this place to lead the Living Church into the new opportunities of a new century shall bear upon their lives the seal of God and shall utter with their lips that ageless mystery, revealed in Christ, of grace, mercy and peace, through God the Father, God the Son, and God the Holy Ghost.

Part Fourth.

BIOGRAPHICAL SKETCHES

OF

DIRECTORS AND PROFESSORS.

Part Fourth.

BIOGRAPHICAL SKETCHES OF DIRECTORS AND PROFESSORS.

WILLIAM AGUR BOOTH (1860–1895) was born in Stamford, Connecticut, 1805, and died in Englewood, New Jersey, on the 28th day of December, 1895, in the ninety-first year of his age. Mr. Booth was one of the foremost citizens of New York, eminent alike in the world of business, in the whole sphere of religious activity and service, in patriotic devotion, and above all, in weight of personal character and influence. His name will always be associated with that remarkable succession of Christian laymen of New York, to whose wisdom, energy, foresight, liberality and pious zeal, home and foreign missions in all their varied forms and societies owe so great and lasting a debt. To do full justice to this part of his life-work would require a volume. His own "Reminiscences," prepared for the gratification of his wide family circle, and printed after his death, furnish indeed such a record. It is an old man's story, told to his children and grandchildren, and told with a modesty and simplicity of style most attractive. The following minute was adopted by the Board of Directors of Union Theological Seminary:

On the 28th day of December, 1895, at his home in Englewood, New Jersey, surrounded by his immediate kindred, our revered father, associate and friend, Mr. William A. Booth, in the ninety-first year of his age,

> Meekly gave his being up and went
> To share that holy rest which waits a life well spent.

The Board of Directors of Union Seminary, bowing submissively to the divine visitation, hereby do record their sense of bereavement and their high appreciation of the many and rare qualities of mind and heart which easily placed Mr. Booth among the foremost in Christian citizenship; a human standard of human excellence.

Mr. Booth was elected a director of this institution on November 14, 1860, filling the place of Mr. Caleb O. Halsted, then recently deceased. Of those who then composed the directorate, only three survive, viz., Charles Butler, LL.D., Rev. George L. Prentiss, D.D., and Mr. Salem H. Wales.

With characteristic zeal and fidelity, Mr. Booth addressed himself to the active duties of his office. He was at once made a member of the Finance Committee, where his large experience, sound judgment and wise counsels enabled him to render eminent service in the management not only of the financial, but of all other departments through the Civil War period and continuously thereafter.

By reason of his advanced age and distant residence Mr. Booth's personal intercourse with the board in later years has been subject to these limitations, but to those who through long years of close intimacy have walked with him in the marts of commerce, amid the rugged scenes of public alarm and of national peril, in the more congenial fields of benevolence and philanthropic enterprise, or in the tranquil paths of Christian beneficence, his exemplary life and symmetrical character combining in such degree and beautiful proportion the gentleness and grace of a Christian spirit with the sterling qualities of a vigorous and forceful manhood, will be an abiding inspiration; and his uniform courtesy, his habitual self-command, his genial fellowship and his generous friendship will all be cherished in grateful and affectionate remembrance.

John Hall D.D., LL.D., (1870–1892) belonged to an old Scotch-Irish family. He was born in the county of Armagh, Ireland, July 31, 1829. He was a graduate of the Royal College and of the General Assembly's Theological College in Belfast. Licensed to preach in 1849, he labored for the next three years as the "students' missionary" in the west of Ireland. In 1852 he became pastor of the First Presbyterian church at Armagh, and in 1858 collegiate pastor of St. Mary's Abbey in Dublin. In 1867 he accepted a call to the Fifth Avenue Presbyterian church in the city of New York. Here he labored with extraordinary zeal, fidelity and success for the next thirty years. His congregation was one of the largest, most influential and most noted for its varied and munificent charities in all the land. In addition to his work as a preacher and pastor Dr. Hall rendered valuable service to the cause of missions, both domestic and foreign, and to other great Christian interests. For several years he was chancellor of the University of the city of New York. As an author also he was highly useful. He died suddenly while on a visit to his sister at Bangor, County Down, Ireland, on September 17, 1898. Others may have surpassed him in pulpit oratory, in theological learning, or as leaders of religious thought and action; but in solidity of personal character, in the simplicity, depth and earnestness of his piety, in preaching the old Gospel of salvation through the grace of God in Jesus Christ, in the abundance and sweetness of his pastoral care, Dr. Hall was among the foremost Presbyterian ministers of his generation, whether at home or abroad. "If I could only preach the Gospel like that!" wrote Dr. Henry B. Smith in 1871, referring to a sermon he had just heard from Dr. Hall.

JOHN TAYLOR JOHNSTON (1870–1893) was born in New York, April 8, 1820. He graduated at the University of the City of New York, with the class of 1839, and was admitted to the bar in 1843. The chief business of his life, however, was the management and control of railroads, rather than the practice of law. Before his thirtieth year he became president of the Central Railroad of New Jersey, and remained for many years at its head, directing its affairs with rare skill and ability. He took an active interest in education, especially as represented by his Alma Mater, and was president also of the Metropolitan Museum of Art. He died after a wearisome illness.

Mr. Johnston furnished a fine example of an American man of business, who at the same time was a man of scholarly tastes and of high culture both in literature and art. No one could meet him in the Board of Directors, in the committee room, or in social intercourse, without feeling himself in the presence of a refined and high-minded Christian gentleman.

JOSEPH TUTTLE DURYEA, D.D., (1868–1874) was born at Jamaica, Long Island, December 9, 1832. He graduated at the College of New Jersey in the class of 1856, and was also a graduate of Princeton Theological Seminary in the class of 1859. In the same year he was ordained pastor of the Second Presbyterian church, Troy, New York. Three years later he became a pastor of the Collegiate Reformed church, New York City. In 1867 he accepted a call to the Closson Avenue Presbyterian church, Brooklyn, New York. In 1879 he became pastor of the Central Congregational church, Boston, Massachusetts. After a ten years' ministry of varied activity and power in Boston, he was called in 1889 to the First Congregational church in Omaha, Nebraska. His last pastorate was of the First Reformed church in Brooklyn, New York. He resigned on account of physical weakness in February, 1898, and died suddenly in Boston, a few months later.

My acquaintance with Dr. Duryea began soon after his settlement in New York. He was then thirty years old, very winning in his manners, and full of intellectual and spiritual energy. I thought him one of the most interesting and gifted young ministers I had ever known. How high he stood in the public estimation was shown a few years later by his appointment to deliver the opening address at the memorial jubilee of Dr. Charles Hodge in 1872. During the Civil War he rendered invaluable service in the work of the Christian Commission, while as an orator at patriotic gatherings, both in New York and at Washington, he touched the popular heart with the skill of a master. I never met him again after his removal to New England, but often heard of his indefatigable labors and usefulness, both as preacher in Boston and as a favorite lecturer at Andover, at Wellesley, and elsewhere. Here is an extract from a notice of his departure in *The Evangelist* of May 26, 1898, written by an old friend:

The highest encomium we can pay him as a preacher is to repeat the words of Phillips Brooks, "I cannot afford to miss one of Dr. Duryea's sermons." Brooks was his near neighbor in Boston and always attended Duryea's afternoon service. He had grown up to a stature that made him easily a superior intelligence and authority. He was too independent for a prescribed professorship; he was sometimes too philosophical for the comfort of his congregation. But he was a man so richly endowed and so rarely furnished that it was a privilege to listen to him, which the best men and the best furnished minds found especially grateful and desirable. He grew in wisdom and knoweldge to the end.

HENRY DAY (1870–1893) was one of the most ardent and influential friends of reunion among the laymen of the Old School Church. In the General Assembly of that branch, held at Albany in 1868, he took a leading part in advocating the cause. He was sent as a special messenger to bear the greeting of the Albany Assembly to that of the New School Church, then in session at Harrisburg. I was a member of that New School Assembly and remember well the fine impression he made upon the entire body. Hardly had the reunion been accomplished when he was unanimously elected a director of the Union Theological Seminary. Of his invaluable services to the institution no one is so well entitled to speak as his friend, Dr. Hastings, to whom I am indebted for the following truthful sketch:

MY DEAR DR. PRENTISS:—You asked me to write you concerning the life and services of our friend, the late Henry Day, Esq. I accept this task as a labor of love, since I have special reasons for holding Mr. Day in grateful and affectionate remembrance, though I cannot hope to say how much he was to me as a counsellor and a cordial supporter through the most trying years of the seminary's history.

Henry Day was born in South Hadley, Massachusetts, December 25, 1820. He was graduated at Yale College in 1845, and was admitted to the New York bar in the fall of 1845. He married, January 31, 1849, the daughter of the late Daniel Lord, and was associated with the distinguished firm of Lord, Day and Lord throughout his professional career. It was said of him at his death that "he had drawn more wills, involving millions perhaps, than any other lawyer in New York City," and he was one of those practitioners who could never be induced by a retainer, or by any other influence, to bring his great legal abilities to bear in favor of corporations or individuals who sought to avoid legal responsibility by legal subtlety. He was a director and the counsel of the Equitable Life Insurance Company, of which he was one of the founders, and of the Mercantile Trust Company, and of the Lawyers' Title Insurance Company.

Mr. Day united with the church in South Hadley in 1840 before entering college, and in New York was made an elder in the Fifth Avenue Presbyterian church under the pastorate of the late Dr. James W. Alexander, which office he held until his death. In 1865 he was made a trustee of Princeton Theological Seminary. He took an active interest in promoting the reunion of the Presbyterian Church, and was a member of the committee of the Assembly of 1867 which prepared the overtures of peace of the New School Church, and he also had a hand in drafting the articles which formed the basis of reunion. He published two books of travel, "A Lawyer Abroad," and "From the Pyrenees to the Pillars of Hercules."

In 1870 Mr. Day was elected a director of Union Theological Seminary, in which capacity he served for twenty-three years until his death. It would be difficult to overestimate the zeal, devotion and fidelity with which he discharged his duties as a member of the Board of Directors and of the Executive Committee. Far seeing and fearless, he was always ready to bear responsibility, and to meet difficulty with an enthusiastic faith in the future of our seminary. In the controversy with the General Assembly he never faltered or weakened for a moment, but bravely and yet in the best spirit contended for the liberty of our institution. There were two other lawyers in the board, but Mr. Day was the first to contend that the agreement of 1870 was an illegal surrender of the rights and responsibilities of the seminary to the General Assembly. He obtained from Judge Noah Davis an elaborate opinion confirmatory of this view. It was then that the board secured the opinion of James C. Carter, Esq., bearing upon this point, and I well remember the satisfaction of Mr. Day in the conclusive impression which Mr. Carter's opinion made upon the board. He rejoiced to see the seminary recover its original independence, and to the last, even when weakened by illness, he attended the meetings of the board and aided its counsels. He proved himself in many ways an ardent friend of free and high scholarship, and a fearless advocate of Christian liberty. He was genial and courteous and generous, and in my judgment rendered distinguished service to the cause of higher theological education, aiding us in bearing heavy burdens and in meeting special exigencies.

He died in New York City on the 9th of January, 1893, in the seventy-third year of his age and in the twenty-third year of his service as a director. Surely his name should be held in grateful and loving remembrance by all the friends of Union Seminary and of what it represents.

Always affectionately yours,

THOMAS S. HASTINGS.

JONATHAN FRENCH STEARNS, D.D. (1850–1888) was one of the worthiest representatives of two very old and eminent ministerial families of New England. His father, the Rev. Samuel Stearns, pastor for thirty-seven years of the Congregational church in Bedford, Massachusetts, took a leading part in the controversy, which early in the century led to a sharp division between Orthodoxy and Unitarianism; while his grandfather on his mother's side, the Rev. Jonathan French, was closely identified with the establishment of the Andover Theological Seminary. Both were men noted in their day for weight of character, personal excellence, and wide influence in the revival of religious faith and learning among the Congregational churches of Massachusetts. Three sons of the Rev. Samuel Stearns, all graduates of Harvard College, and inheriting the best qualities of their Puritan ancestry, left behind them honored names as pastors and preachers of the Gospel. Samuel, the eldest, after a short ministry in the Old South church, Boston, passed away in early manhood, greatly beloved and lamented by the whole community. William, after a most useful pastorate, became president of Amherst College, and did a noble work in strengthening and widening its influence. Two other sons, Josiah and Eben, spent their lives in teaching; the former in Boston, the latter in Portland, Exeter, Albany and Nashville. They were among the most successful and noted educators of their day.

Mr. Stearns was born at Bedford, September 4, 1808, and educated, as I have said, at Harvard College. He belonged to the class of 1830. Shortly before the death of the late George Ripley, so long identified with the literary department of the *New York Tribune,* I accompanied Dr. Stearns on a visit to that accomplished scholar, and listened with delight to their charming talk and bright anecdotes about college days. Charles Sumner was in the same class with Jonathan F. Stearns, was his room-mate during a part of the course, and the friendship then formed between them continued unbroken to the last. In 1835 Mr. Stearns was ordained and installed pastor of the first Presbyterian church, Newburyport, Massachusetts; the church in which George Whitefield often preached, and beneath whose pulpit his dust is still sleeping. Here he continued to labor for fourteen years, endearing himself more and more to the people and to the whole city. In 1849, he accepted a call to the First Presbyterian church in Newark, N. J.; the venerable church whose annals form no small part of the earlier history of the town and of the region round about. Henry B. Smith, then professor at Amherst, preached the installation sermon. Dr. Stearns' Newark pastorate, was crowded with work and usefulness. Newark in 1849 was remarkable, as indeed it always had been, for the high character of its ministers and its Christian laymen, and as a centre of the religious life and culture of New Jersey. Dr. Stearns' labors and influence both at Newark and in New York, for more than a third of the century, were very great; greater far than was known to the general public. He was a modest man, and a good deal of his best work was that of a wise counsellor and helper; he got oftentimes no credit for it because he sought and desired none. As a director nearly two score years of Union Theological Seminary, for example, his advice was at critical times simply invaluable; but it was usually given by request and followed without any mention of his name. I myself owed him a heavy debt for such advice; and Henry B. Smith, I feel sure, would have said the same thing. My own opinion is, and has always been, that but for him Henry B. Smith would never have been connected with the institution, nor would the Washburn chair of Church History have been founded or Roswell D. Hitchcock called to fill it. How much of the most effective service to the cause of God and humanity is rendered in just such quiet, unknown ways! Dr. Stearns' best influence in the Church at large, was of this unobtrusive sort. And if to such influence be added that of his open, strong advocacy of important principles and measures bearing upon the order, faith, progress, peace and unity of the Churches of Christ throughout our land—more especially of the Presbyterian and Congregational Churches—we shall have as the total result a kind and degree of usefulness worthy of the highest praise. I have never known a man who seemed to me to look at great questions of duty with an eye more single, or a judgment less biassed by sectarian or personal narrowness and prejudice. The Presbyterian Church showed her estimate of his character by placing him year after year upon several of her most important committees or boards, and by electing him Moderator of her General Assembly at Harrisburg, in 1868. He was also for many years a trustee of Princeton College, from which he had received his doctorate of divinity. Owing to failing health and infirmities of age, he resigned his charge in April, 1882, and was made Pastor Emeritus, the congregation providing very generously for his worldly comfort. His last days, though sadly darkened by loss of memory and mental weakness, were not without hours brightened by the old smile, by flashes of happy and tender recollection, by a child's delight in the books and toys of his boyhood, by the sweetest expressions of old household affection, and by the wondrous reverence with which he still bowed his knee to the name of Jesus. He passed into rest at the home of his son-in-law, President Scott of Rutgers College, New Brunswick, November 11, 1889. He left three children, two of whom still survive—Seargent Prentiss Stearns, Esq., of Montreal, for several years United States Consul-General in Canada, and Mrs. Austin Scott, of New Brunswick. His youngest son, Lewis French, was professor of Theology at Bangor, Maine, and died suddenly in 1892, greatly lamented by Christian scholars throughout the country.

Dr. Stearns wrote a good deal for the religious press, especially for the New York *Evangelist*, on questions of the day, theological and ecclesiastical; and besides published a a very able sermon on "Justification," preached before the Synod of New York and New Jersey, a centennial discourse in memory of Whitefield, and various occasional addresses. He also published a history of the First Church of Newark, which is a model of its kind. Not long after his death his successor, the Rev. Dr. Frazer, delivered in the First Presbyterian church at Newark, a very affectionate and discriminating discourse, in which the leading traits of Dr. Stearns' life and character were delineated in the happiest manner.

About the same time a special memorial service was held in the First Presbyterian church at Newburyport, which was attended by the mayor and other leading citizens, and by a crowded assembly composed largely of the children and children's children of Dr. Stearns' New England flock. The tribute both to the old pastor and pastor's wife could hardly have been more beautiful or more touching had only five instead of forty years passed away since their departure to Newark. A single extract from an address of the Rev. Dr. Fiske on the occasion will show its spirit:

I esteem it a privilege to join you this morning in paying some fitting tribute to a former pastor of this church, whom to know was to love. Dr. Stearns had been your pastor nearly twelve years when I came to reside in the city and first made his acquaintance. Yet he seemed and was quite a young man beside his venerable ministerial neighbors, Dr. Daniel Dana, Dr. Leonard Withington, and Dr. Luther F. Dimmick. At my ordination he was selected to give me, in the name of the Congregational churches in the vicinity, and in the name of the Congregational churches at large, the right hand of fellowship. It may seem strange that this duty should have been assigned to the pastor of a Presbyterian church. But Dr. Stearns was a Congregationalist before he was a Presbyterian, and enough of a Congregationalist afterward to be in heartiest sympathy with Congregational churches and Congregational ministers. Indeed he was a man of such broad views, large heart and catholic spirit that he could fitly represent both of these denominations, which have always been one in all the great essentials of Christianity. So hearty was the right hand of fellowship which he gave me—more than forty-two years ago—that I seem to feel the warm pressure of his clasping palm still; and so chaste and classic was his diction, and yet so throbbing with life and emotion, that my heart was touched and I felt assured that I should find in him a true friend and brother. Nor was I disappointed.

Dr. Stearns was a man of scholarly and refined tastes, of urbane manners, of sweet and gentle disposition, of warm sympathies, of firm convictions, of earnest purposes, of tempered enthusiasm and of a devout and reverent spirit, an able and instructive preacher, a faithful pastor, a worthy citizen, a kind neighbor, always and everywhere a cultivated Christian gentlemen. His removal to Newark was a great public loss; a great loss to this church, to all these churches, to our whole city where he was universally esteemed both as a man and a minister.

Let us to-day devoutly thank God for the life of such a noble man as Jonathan F. Stearns. His influence still lives among you. The record of his ministry here forms a bright chapter in your history. His very name is to you a perpetual benediction.

It may not be unfitting to add a word respecting the wife, so tenderly referred to in the memorial services at Newark and Newburyport, and also the son, who quickly followed his father to the better country. How much of the finest and most effective work of the American pastorate is wrought unconsciously by the woman behind the throne, and then reappears in a son of her right hand! It was so in the present case. Mrs. Stearns was a sister of the great lawyer, orator and patriot, S. S. Prentiss, whose name is still a household word throughout the South. The relation between them was wonderfully beautiful and had all the charms of romance.

Her youngest son, Lewis French, on the retirement of Dr. Shedd from the chair of Systematic Theology in Union Seminary, was unanimously chosen to succeed him. He had just given an original and striking course of Ely lectures on *The Evidence of Christian Experience*, and was already regarded as one of the very foremost of the younger theologians of the country. The veto power had something to do with his declining the call to Union. A few months before his death he had won the admiration of Christian scholars, both at home and in England, by his masterly address before the Congregational Council held in London in 1891.

Here follows an extract from the minutes of the Board of Directors of Union Theological Seminary, on the death of Dr. Stearns. The minute was prepared by Dr. Frazer, his successor at Newark:

In 1850, Dr. Stearns, then in the full maturity of his powers, was elected a member of this board, devoted himself enthusiastically to the advancement of the best interests of the seminary, rendered faithful and efficient service for nearly two score years and ended his official relation only when disease made him incompetent to serve.

He was one of the prompt, regular and diligent attendants upon the meetings of the board. He was a wise counsellor, being singularly free alike from that abnormal conservatism which refuses to recognize the exigences of the present, and from the excessive radicalism which insists upon repudiating the past simply because it is past.

By reason of his long and intimate acquaintance with the men, he was able to render and did render distinguished aid in securing the invaluable services of Henry B. Smith and Roswell D. Hitchcock to this institution. He was a man of strong mind, large culture, broad views, warm sympathies and courtly manners; in a word, a Christian gentleman.

With gratitude to God that he gave and so long spared Dr. Stearns to us, we record this minute as an expression of the respect which we have long cherished for the man, as an exponent of our appreciation of the zeal and the fidelity with which for thirty-eight years he discharged the duty of director, and also as an embodiment of our sympathy for those who mourn a father beloved and whom we tenderly commend to the all-sufficient grace of the great and gracious Father above.

John H. Worcester, Jr., D.D., (1891–1893). Dr. Worcester was a member of the Detroit Assembly and took a prominent part in the discussion, which followed the report of the Standing Committee on Theological Seminaries recommending a disapproval of the transfer of Professor Briggs to the new chair of Biblical Theology. Not long after the adjournment of the General Assembly, he was unanimously elected to the chair of Systematic Theology in Union Seminary. Having known and highly esteemed him while a student in the institution, I watched his career as a pastor, both in the East and in the West, with lively interest; and it would afford me heartfelt pleasure to make this sketch my own tribute to his memory. But a tribute much better and more worthy than I could write was paid to him by his friend the Rev. Simon J. McPherson, D.D., of Chicago, in a discourse delivered by invitation of the Board of Directors of the Union Theological Seminary in Adams Chapel, April 13, 1893. Here follow extracts from this very interesting and beautiful discourse:

We are a company of bereaved brethren. We at once lament and celebrate, a pastor, a colleague, a teacher, who was a faithful lover and friend to us all. For myself I can truly say that I never had, and I never expect to have, a more valued fellow in the ministry of the Gospel than he. From the day on which I was ordained, through twelve happy years to the day when he became a professor in this honored institution, it was my favored lot in Providence to serve parishes which immediately adjoined his own. I became intimately associated and acquainted with him. The better I came to know him, the more highly I estimated him as a rare type of Christian manhood, and the more warmly I loved him as a great-hearted companion.

He was of English and Puritan lineage, but in the eighth of the generations who have been at home in the New World. Four of his seven American forefathers were ministers. His name, which, under two or three different forms of orthography, is widely scattered amongst Anglo-Saxons, is said to have etymologically, a martial meaning; but the family coat of arms, we are told, "signifies the first bearer to have been a priest, or some religious person; or else one that had done much for the church." The family itself has certainly favored both the church and the school.

The original settler in New England, Rev. William Worcester, is mentioned in the Magnalia of Cotton Mather. "A fugitive from persecution and tyranny;" he came, apparently, from Salisbury, England, in 1637 or 1638. He was at once appointed pastor at Colchester, which, in 1840, became Salisbury, the oldest town north of the Merrimac river. Its church was the eighteenth in the Massachusetts Colony, of which he was made a freeman in 1639. A man of liberal education, he is described as "learned, wise, meek and patient,"—attributes distinctive of his descendants.

The next three in the line lived in Massachusetts; godly, industrious men, of stalwart character, devoted to the public weal, and loving, as one of them said, "to see a man, manly." Francis, of the fourth generation, after being some ten years a pastor, became an evangelist and did thorough work in revival meetings, part of the time with Whitefield. Noah, his son, a farmer and shoemaker, who settled at Hollis, New Hampshire, entered the army of the revolution with two of his sons, but lived to gather around his table eighteen children, of whom five were ministers. When he died he left seventy-eight grandchildren.

Throughout these five generations, we are credibly assured, "one and the same character, essentially, appeared from first to last . . . There may be ascribed to each an enlightened belief in God and His Word; a confiding recognition of His Providence in all things; a fervent spirit and a constant habit of devotion; an undeviating reverence for the Sabbath and every institution of the Gospel; an irreproachable veracity and honesty: an exact manliness and an undaunted moral courage; with an inflexible adherence to convictions of duty, and a benevolent forwardness to multiply and extend, in every appropriate and practical manner, 'the glory and virtue' of the Church of God." What an index to the personality of Professor Worcester, and, indeed, to the Pilgrim race of New England!

In the sixth generation, two members of the family are of special interest to us. One of them, Dr. Samuel Worcester, a graduate of Dartmouth and a famous preacher of the day at Salem, was among the most active of the organizers, and for about twenty years the first corresponding secretary, of the American Board of Commissioners for Foreign Missions. The other, Rev. Leonard Worcester, was the grandfather of our friend. He was a trustee of the University of Vermont. At first an editor, he was afterwards, for nearly half a century, the pastor at Peacham, Vermont, where his memory is still reverently cherished.

Four of his sons, as I make it out, were ministers. One of them, Rev. John H. Worcester, D.D., whose namesake and only child your professor was, still lives in Burlington, Vermont, a noble and most venerable figure. He was the pastor, first, at St. Johnsbury, where his son was born, and, later, at Burlington. For some years subsequently he was occupied in teaching. Burdened with defective hearing at his great age, he has passed his most recent years largely within his spacious and well-filled library, in refined and studious retirement. His patriarchal form, cast in the heroic mould which has been common in the family, his intellectual head and attractive face, his gentle and dignified manner, and his pathetic and controlled sorrow, too deep for tears and too great for words, would win and touch any heart, especially if it loved his son. His is a gifted and cultivated mind, stored with select and classified knowledge, and trained to think upon high and difficult themes. Withal, its forces are marshalled by a reverent and independent judgment, conservative of ascertained realities and hospitable to fresh aspects of truth from any quarter. We need not wonder at what Professor Worcester was when we remember that he was not only the son, but also, for a third of a century, the close companion of such a man.

To this heritage and family John Hopkins Worcester, Jr., was born April 2, 1845. Clean, stimulating blood flowed in his infant veins. When self-consciousness dawned, he could look backward with a sense of privilege and indebtedness, and forward with a sense of opportunity and high obligation. He found himself tenderly welcomed in the membership of a respected, refined and unostentatiously affectionate Christian home. He had parents to whom he could look up, and who led his youthful vision towards the Father in heaven. His mother, Martha P. Clark, was the daughter of Deacon Luther Clark, of St. Johnsbury. She was the youngest of three sisters, and the only one that is not now living. One of her sisters married the late Judge Redfield, for many years Chief Justice of Vermont. The other became the wife of Rev. Joseph S. Gallagher, once the skillful and efficient treasurer of the seminary. All accounts agree that Professor Worcester's mother was a lovely woman, with fine intellectual endowments and a sweet Christian spirit. She died when her son was three years old, entreating him with her latest breath to love the dear Saviour. As he was carried away from her grave, he burst into tears with the bitter cry: "Now, I shan't have a Mamma any more." But it was otherwise ordered. He was favored as few orphans have ever been. When he was less than seven years old, the present wife of his father became a genuine mother to him. Of Scottish extraction, high attainments and beautiful Christian character, her training was invaluable to him.

In Burlington, as in St. Johnsbury, he was surrounded by a quiet, cultivated New England town. The glories of the Green Mountains and of the Adirondacks beset him round. The picturesque and historic Lake Champlain lay beneath his eyes. Temptations, like those of a great city, were nowhere obtrusive, and there was a wholesome inspiration alike in the human life and in the natural scenery environing him. The climate, like the moral standard of his home, was honestly severe, but the impulses of domestic, social and religious life were warm, true and inviting. It was a favored, happy lot, whose good influences abounded in him to his latest hour on earth.

As a boy, he appears to have been precocious, as he certainly was remarkably handsome. He knew the alphabet from picture-blocks when he was only two years old, and by the end of his third year he had, with a little occasional help, taught himself to read. But his native capacity, industry and modesty, coupled with wise training, kept him from being spoiled. The intellectual and moral atmosphere of his home were unusually stimulating, in some particulars, perhaps, too stimulating for an entirely symmetrical development of his boyish nature. It was at first a parsonage and afterwards a school. He was constantly in the company of older minds. It may be a question whether his early years had enough either of playtime or playmates for jovial mental health. At any rate, there are indications that he attained uncommon maturity in his youth. He became a member of the church in his seventeenth year. That step, however, was by no means forced upon him. It was the natural thing for him to take it, for he never knew when he became a Christian. His faith blossomed out like a flower in spring time. Its fruits, too, were prompt to follow. While still young, he was one of the original founders of the Young Men's Christian Association in Burlington, and an effective leader in Sunday-school and mission work. Nevertheless, his powers and his useful activities continued to grow and to increase their harmonious adjustments to the end of his life.

After completing his preparatory courses under the eye of his father, he entered the University of Vermont, from which he graduated in 1865. It was one of the small colleges, set upon the Acropolis of the Athens of Vermont. He was not only well-known to the unconventional students, but he enjoyed also the advantages, peculiar to a small college, of intimate association with ripe professors who gave him individual attention. He improved his opportunities and became truly educated. Indeed, he has added distinction to the institution. The honored president tells me that all who have known it intimately for the last thirty years would be sure to name him among the score, or even the ten, who have had the most brilliant and promising collegiate careers. As attesting her continued regard, the University of Vermont gave him his doctorate degree in 1885.

He entered upon his theological course here in 1867. At the end of his middle year he went abroad and spent a year or more in traveling and in studying at Berlin and Leipsic. Returning, he graduated from this school of the prophets in 1871; and up to the 5th of last February, on every day of his life, he was both an honor to Union Seminary, and an exalted type of the ministers whom she has trained for the Church of God.

The chief work of his noble life was done in the pastorate, preaching the living Christ to dying men—to my mind the holiest and sweetest vocation on earth. In these days of frequent pastoral changes, occasioned in part, no doubt, by the exacting and exhausting demands of the work, but far more, I fear, by the restlessness of ministers and churches, let it be noted both that in almost twenty years he had but two charges and that he left neither of them because he would or because he must, but solely in response to an imperative summons of conscience. He was installed pastor of the First Presbyterian Church of South Orange, New Jersey, January 10, 1872, and left it in January, 1883, to become pastor of the Sixth Presbyterian Church of Chicago. His work as preacher and pastor was of a uniform quality throughout, and the quality was uniformly high. It was all done on his honor as the servant of Jesus Christ. None of it was slighted, whether it was public or private; his study and his prayer-closet were as faithfully devoted to their purposes as the pulpit or the platform. Every minister is master of his own time. Every minister is likely to hear the effusive praises of the friendly flatterer, and to be left out of hearing by his average critic. Consequently, the besetting sins of weak ministers are laziness and egotism. But my brother was neither lazy nor egotistical, for he was not weak; he was faithful, sincere and virile. For genuine fidelity towards God and man, he was well-nigh matchless.

His preaching, as some of you know, was distinguished for thoroughness; whether he read from manuscript, or spoke extemporaneously, as he could do with admirable completeness, clearness and finish, he always brought beaten oil into the sanctuary. His published sermons on "Womanhood" are in evidence. Unusually intellectual, yet with the white light of great emotions, and with a passion for saving the whole of a man, he made large demands upon his hearers, at the same time that he gave them large supplies of thought, feeling and purpose. Partly for that reason, he was not, in the common apprehension of the word, a popular preacher. He dwelt in rather too high and rare an atmosphere for that. He appealed especially to the somewhat select class of thoughtful and educated minds. Yet he left indelible lines of life upon the souls of all regular attendants, even when they were unconscious of the fact. He was singularly unselfish in preaching. It was not a great name nor a conspicious place that he was seeking, any more than it was a fat salary. His first desire seemed to be to fill the place assigned to him, to make Jesus Christ conspicious in truth and love, and to leave permanent gracious impressions.

He was a "house-going" minister, and he did not confine himself to houses of any class, rich or poor, personally friendly or personally indifferent. To his great personal regret he could not easily win an entrance into the affections of a stranger or acquaintance. He was too thorough for that; at a time when much of our pastoral visitation consists largely of small talk, he had no small talk at all. He had to make his way on his genuine merits, which he was not facile in exploiting. But in times of stress and burden, when death stood at the door or devastated the home, he was most welcome. There was enough of him to meet a crisis, and souls in critical situations had faith in him, and found strength and peace in his ministrations. I have often felt that if I were on my death-bed, I should prefer his ministry to any other. He would have told me the truth honestly, completely, simply and affectionately.

A good general test of his pastoral efficiency may be found in the condition in which he left each of his churches. I fancy that one of the surest tests of any pastor's career comes to light after he goes away. If a church then has parties who say I am of Paul, Apollos or Cephas, you may almost take it for granted that there was something radically defective or selfish in his teaching. For some pastors seem to brand the Master's sheep with their own initials. But our friend left the Master's high, unifying name in his parishioners' hearts. They thought of Christ rather than of him. They remained united and prepared to offer a common welcome to the succeeding under-shepherd.

Such a man needed human sympathy—he got it. His brethren learned to love and trust him, and he had a sweet and hallowed domestic life. On October 29, 1874, he married Miss Harriet W. Strong, a daughter of Edward Strong, M. D., of Auburndale, Massachusetts. Four children, two boys and two girls, were given to them, all born in Orange and all living still excepting little Martha, who is with her father. Let him who can, believe in the celibacy of the clergy. Our friend found almost an ideal of the kingdom of God on earth in his family. Strenuous man as he was, with deep-seated convictions, he was so tolerant of the rightful opinions of others that, as I believe, he never once, during their eighteen years of married life, crossed any real independent judgment of Mrs. Worcester's. Nor was he ever dictatorial, unreasonable or merely suppressive towards his children. A strong man will be considerate and fair, if he be only strong enough. He was strong enough, and he had sufficient reason. His children are worthy of him. His wife was like-minded with himself. With the same Puritan blood and New England culture, with almost equal gifts of mind and heart, she loved to be in his shadow, but, more than she will ever acknowledge or even know, she directed and inspired his life. He owed her much and, through him, so do you and I.

It is not strange that such a man, with such gifts, such a pastoral experience and such a home, should come to love with unspeakable ardor the ministry of the Gospel. He often said to his nearest intimates, that he thought no other work in life comparable to it. He left it, therefore, with as much reluctance as he entered it. When he was called in May, 1891, to the chair of Systematic Theology in Hartford, he was in actual distress until he concluded that it was his privilege to decline it. He loved the pastorate, and although he was from a Congregational family, he had an intelligent and discriminating love for the Presbyterian Church. Two months later came the call from you. He appreciated the great honor of it, as his friends did; but he shrank from it, with characteristic diffidence, and the acceptance of it required no small degree of personal self-denial. It was not the line of life which he had chosen, nor the department of theological instruction which he preferred. He consulted his close friends and they, in spite of their wishes to keep him in the pastorate, advised him to accept, because they regarded him as an ordained leader of leaders and because they hoped that he, with his conservative temper, non-partisan theological attitude and independent yet progressive mind, might do something to aid a beloved institution, and to heal the existing lamentable breach between brethren in the same church. Now, that he has gone home, shall we not hope and pray that the breach will be closed?

During the last eighteen months of his life, as his strength was failing and his life was fading away, some of us have wondered whether his coming was not a mistake. But he did not feel any such questioning. Trusting to no human counsel for the final decision, he had prayed fervently for divine guidance; he fully believed that he had been led by God's spirit, and that the transfer was a part of the gracious Father's plan for him and for us all. He died as he had lived, better than submissive,—acquiescent. Filial hearts, therefore, will not be impatient or complaining that his work here ended when it seemed only to have begun. Its influence, I am sure, will not be transient. I know his work among you was rapidly growing in interest to him. You know, as I cannot, how gifted, cultured, genuine, devoted and open-hearted it was becoming. It would naturally have special attractions for strong, candid and manly students. Doubtless, he was in the main a disciple of your epoch-making teacher, Dr. Henry B. Smith; so true a disciple that he could be independent of his teacher in important particulars. He had the same reverent, discerning spirit, the same firm, conservative and delicate grasp of generic essentials, the same undisturbed sense of liberty as to all undetermined and incidental matters. Equally with that master, he spent his strength in strenuous seeking after truth, and he would dare encourage his pupils to think for themselves, and to besiege him with all sorts of honest questions. If he had lived, I am sure he would have filled his place with ever-increasing power and with indubitable adequacy and renown.

No one could accurately measure his intellectual processes without noting his predominant moral qualities. Remembering both, I call him a great man. But, lest my own estimate of him may be partial and faulty, let me adapt the words of another friend. His greatness consisted in his surpassing perspicuity of mind, in his rare capacity to separate a complex problem into its simple elements, in his wonderful power of thorough and convincing statement, in his supreme loyalty to truth and his courageous advocacy of it, under all circumstances, in his genuine humility of soul, which enabled him to see the truth easily, yet never permitted him to seek prominence for himself, in his sincere and unpretentious candor, in his loving catholicity of spirit and in the complete consecration of his unusual powers and acquirements to the Light of the World.

The key to his character, I believe, will be found in the fact that moral considerations controlled him. The chief defect which I have heard ascribed to him was an apparent reserve of manner. His exterior gave to the average person meeting him the impression that he was cold. A few acquaintances have thought that he was even haughty. But his intimate friends knew that this view of his character was radically mistaken. His heart was always warm. He had an ample capacity for true friendship. He depended upon the love of friends, hungered for the good-will of all, and suffered often because he could not facilely show his own good-will. He could not tell you to your face that he loved you. If his life did not show it, he was powerless. It was one of his heavy burdens that he had to force his way where many another could win an entrance to the human heart. He was utterly unable to wear his heart upon his sleeve.

As conscientious a man as I have ever known, he was hard upon himself, but gracious and tolerant towards the sincere moral postures of others. For this reason questions which belonged to the pure ethical realm appeared to give him unusually little trouble. He was simply above the reach of many of the ordinary temptations of life. When he perceived that a thing was right or obligatory, his doubts about it were settled.

If, in matters of expediency or questions of the reason, he would sometimes hesitate, you might be sure that conscientious scruples were at the bottom of his hesitancy, and that he could not as yet make out his moral bearings. The moment that he discerned distinctly what he ought to do, he became as bold as a lion. It was a curious combination, timid as to his own personality, even as to his judgment; perfectly fearless as to duty. The historic speech at Detroit is an instance in point. To his intimates it has always seemed characteristic rather than exceptional in its intellectual power, its Christian spirit, its moral weight. For days he had been urged to speak. But he shrank from the conspicuous responsibility. Though he passed almost sleepless nights over the matter, he still refused to say a word. But things appeared to him to be going wrong. Finally, alone, upon his knees, it became plain to him that the Master summoned him to the task. Then his lips were touched with fire, and, even if the whole world had been against him, nothing could have swerved him, more than Isaiah, from the purpose to utter his convictions boldly, tenderly, mightily, under the resistless inspiration of the sense of duty. This is why my friend's speech will live and quicken after the mere controversies of that hour are the forgotten dust of logomachy.

Contrary to the opinions of some acquaintances, he had an enthusiastic nature. His later boyhood in Burlington furnishes a typical illustration. It seems that one evening, shortly after dark, fire broke out in a building down near the lake shore under the little bluff. The boys started for it instantly on a run. He outran the others, and, in going over the side of the bluff, he made a misstep, fell and broke his leg. When the others overtook him, they wanted to carry him home at once. But he said: "No, no, leave me here; go and help put out the fire; take me home afterwards."

Under that calm manner and controlled temper, there was an intensity of conviction, of purpose, of feeling, of courage, of ideal vision, which explains apparent anomalies in his finished career and which promised heroic achievements in the withheld second half of his life-time. It will teach us why he was constant and tireless in every form of faithfulness, to his conscience, to his father, his wife and children and his friends, to the churches which he served, to the seminary, to the Lord Jesus Christ. He was faithful in the least and faithful also in much, faithful alike in service and in suffering.

What is all this but to say, by way of summary and preeminence, that he was a gifted, manly, true-hearted Christian. His life amply exemplified the title of one of my favorites among his sermons, "Christianity, a Virile Religion." He exemplified it also in the supreme hour. He died at Lakewood, New Jersey, alone with his wife and his Saviour. When it became plain to the physician about nine o'clock on that Sabbath evening that he was soon to enter into rest, she went to him and said: "Well, dear, you won't need to suffer much longer." "Then," said he, "you think I am going?" "Yes," she answered, with the simple truthfulness of their life. He waited half a minute, and then replied: "We should send some telegrams;" that is, to his children and father and nearest friends. Brave, self-forgetful, resolute to the end! A kind-hearted lady in the hotel came to the door to ask them if she should not stay with them during that awful ordeal. But it was he who, looking towards her with a grateful smile, answered: "No, we will watch it out together." Love was sufficient and triumphant. Presently, Mrs. Worcester asked if he felt ready to go. Observe the reply of that man of white character and noble life. He just said: "Only as I trust in my Redeemer." They prayed together—he for patience, and she that he may be released from physical agony. I shall never think of that man and that woman, their children absent, sitting alone, hand in hand, before the King who waited with the crown, not a tear in their eyes, but praying with unbroken voices to God their Father, without rejoicing that heroism still lingers upon earth.

Henry Jackson Van Dyke, D.D. My first acquaintance with Dr. Van Dyke goes back to the summer of 1856. I met him at Sharon Springs and we made an excursion together to Howe's Cave. It was a charming day and he ran over with high spirits and good fellowship. Although he was Old School and I New School, we at once took a liking for each other, which grew stronger and more affectionate as the years went on. After the reunion we served together on an important church committee and thus learned to know each other better. With the exception of Dr. Briggs, he sympathized with me in special fondness for the old mystical writers of the 17th century more than any one else. He was a noble specimen of Christian manhood and all my recollections of him are most pleasant. I used to admire the beautiful relation which existed between Dr. Van Dyke and his two sons. He was their comrade and dear friend, as well as their loving father. One of my last recollections of him is his look of honest pride and joy, as he sat on the platform beside ex-President Cleveland and Mr. Choate, listening to a glowing address by his son Henry, on the public charities of New York. To this son the reader is indebted for the following vivid and truthful sketch:

A life of great simplicity, directed by a steady purpose towards a simple aim, the preaching of the Gospel of Jesus Christ; a character of rare strength and tenderness, earnestness and generosity, frankness and force; a career of large and tranquil usefulness as the bishop of a Christian church in the Presbyterian communion, this is what we have to recall in making a brief memorial of Henry Jackson Van Dyke, who was elected in the spring of 1891, to the professorship of Systematic Theology in Union Theological Seminary, but died on May 25th of the same year, before he had entered upon the labors of his new office.

He was born on March 2, 1822, at Abingdon, Pennsylvania, and was the favorite son of Frederick Augustus Van Dyke, M. D. From boyhood he was marked by the firmness of his religious faith and the directness of his moral purposes. He was not a waverer. He was a straightforward believer and a fearless follower of his creed. He was the first member of his immediate family to take an outspoken and unreserved stand for Christ. Many years afterwards he had the joy of welcoming his father and mother to the full communion of the Lord Jesus.

Educated at Yale College, the University of Pennsylvania, and Princeton Theological Seminary, he was licensed to preach by the Third Presbytery of Philadelphia in June, 1845, at the age of twenty-three years, and immediately afterwards became the pastor of the Second Presbyterian Church of Bridgeton, N. J. He was married in the same year to Miss Henrietta Ashmead of Philadelphia, who bore him six children, of whom four died in early childhood and two sons are still living.

His pastorate at Bridgeton lasted seven years, and was followed by a brief but fruitful work in charge of the First Presbyterian Church of Germantown, Pa. From this place he was called in 1853, to the First Presbyterian Church in Remsen Street, Brooklyn. Here he remained for thirty-eight years, with only a short interval of tentative labor as pastor-elect of the First Presbyterian Church at Nashville, Tenn., from which he returned, after six months' absence, to his Brooklyn parish in 1872.

The place which he occupied in the city where his life-work was done, was distinctive and honorable. There were many storms and conflicts in church and state during his long pastorate. His strong and definite convictions often forced him to take a position which was opposed to that of his associates and unpopular with the majority. He was an old-fashioned State rights democrat in his political views, and an open-minded conservative in his ecclesiastical preferences. He never made any secret of his opinions, nor did he modify them for the sake of expediency. But through all the controversies and struggles of these tempestuous years he kept his temper sweet, his affections warm, his courage clear, and his honor clean by living in the kindliest human fellowship with men and women of his flock and in the closest personal communion with his Divine Master. He won the admiration of opponents by his candor and fairness, the love of friends by his loyalty and unselfishness, and the respect of all men by his unquestionable integrity and devotion to duty.

He was characteristically a manly man. Fond of the free intercourse of comrades, he cared little for the forms of artificial society. A great lover of children, he refreshed his mind and his heart by joining in their sports without restraint. The boys and girls of Brooklyn knew him as a good friend and a merry comrade. The dignities of life rested lightly upon him; he was not indifferent to them, but he never let them chain him to a ponderous solemnity. He had a lively sense of humor and was always ready to laugh at clean fun. His short, vigorous, active frame, fitted him for out-of-door life. He loved nature, and was always at home in the woods or on the waters. Angling was his favorite recreation. He was a man whom Izaak Walton would have loved.

In his study he was industrious and systematic, a wide reader, with a taste for the substantial and profitable, rather than for the brilliant and sensational. The strongest influence in his intellectual development were the English poets, of whom he preferred Milton and Shakspere, Wordsworth and Tennyson, and the Puritan divines, in whose works he was profoundly versed. He did not care much for metaphysics except as he found it in the form of theology. He preferred history to fiction, though he frequently delighted to read the greater objective novels, which deal more with the real facts of life, than with subtle speculations about them. He never succeeded in reading through a novel of society, or a psychological romance. When he was tired, if it was not possible for him to go a-fishing on a mountain stream, he would turn to "Paradise Lost," or to "In Memorium" or to Wordsworth's poems, for rest and refreshment. But all the other reading that he did was less, in amount and in interest than his reading of the English Bible.

He published but two books; a small volume of sermons on "The Lord's Prayer," and a larger volume of lectures on "The Church: Her Ministry and Sacraments." The former may stand as representative of his method of preaching; dignified, earnest, Scriptural, authoritative, and specifically directed to the inward experience of religion. The latter presents his matured views on theological subjects. There was an unmistakable change in his convictions in this region, between his earlier and his later ministry, a change which was not in the nature of a revolution, but of a growth, an expansion. His theology did not become more loose, but did become more simple. He worked it out in the school of practical ministry to men. His attachment to the old doctrines of divine sovereignty, atonement by the cross of Christ, regeneration by the Holy Spirit, and salvation through faith in the Divine Christ, was strengthened as the years went on. But he learned also to set these truths in larger relations with life, and to welcome the interpretation which was given to them by men of different schools, and to rejoice in the substantial unity of the evangelical faith. The sacraments became more dear to him as the universal signs and seals of spiritual grace, and the oneness of the Christian ministry as a divine institution was an article of his belief in which he found great comfort and strength.

In 1876 he was elected Moderator of the Presbyterian General Assembly, which met in Brooklyn. In 1877 he went to Edinburgh as a delegate to the First General Presbyterian Council. On several occasions he was elected to the chair of Systematic Theology in various seminaries—among which Alleghany and San Francisco may be mentioned. But these invitations he always declined, until the election came in 1891, which called him to Union Seminary in New York. He rightly regarded this election as a great honor. Coming unanimously as it did, from a Board of Directors representing many shades of theological opinion, and in a time of controversy and strife in the Presbyterian Church, it was a tribute to his reputation as a man of thought as well as of action, a recognition of the soundness of his faith and the fairness of his spirit, a sign of liberty and peace within the Church.

It was in this spirit, with many unnecessary misgivings as to his own fitness for the place, but with a clear, strong desire to serve the Church and the seminary as one in their interests and one in their allegiance to Christ, that he accepted the invitation.*

He closed his fruitful and blessed ministry in Brooklyn in his sixty-ninth year, in the fulness of his powers, with a long and beautiful record of work behind him, and with the love and reverence of his people crowning his labors in full measure.

He turned his face with cheerful courage toward his new task. He was confident that the evangelical theology in which he was grounded by years of practical preaching as well as of earnest study, was a living theology. He felt that it could be presented simply and directly, on a Scriptural basis, in such a way that students for the ministry would see its moral reasonableness, its Biblical authority, and its adaptation to the needs of mankind. He believed that such a presentation was entirely consistent with the freedom of scholarship and Biblical research, and that it would promote the purity and peace of the Church. He looked forward to this work with the interest, the enthusiasm, the courage of

* The following letter was written at the time:

BROOKLYN, April 26, 1891.

MY DEAR DR. HASTINGS:

If the Board of Directors confirm the judgment of the Nominating Committee in regard to my fitness for the Chair of Dogmatic Theology in the Union Seminary, it is my desire and purpose to accept the position.

I am not without great misgivings in coming to this conclusion. But I dare not allow my fears to oppose the judgment of such friends as you and the rest of the committee. God seems to be leading me in the direction to which you point. In Him I put my trust. May he guide us all to do the best for His glory and the peace of the church. To be thought worthy of the position to which you purpose to call me is a crown to my life-work such as I have never dared to hope for.

Affectionately yours in Christ,
HENRY J. VAN DYKE.

a young man, and with the steadiness, the breadth of mind, the patience of a veteran.

But God's plan for him was different. On Monday, the 25th of May, after preaching twice in his old church on the preceding Sabbath, he was suddenly attacked by *agina pectoris*. Almost without a warning God's finger had touched his large heart, and he fell quietly asleep. His last words were, "I am ready to go."

The University of Wisconsin gave him the degree of Doctor of Divinity in 1860. He was a member of the Presbyterian Board of Home Missions and a Director of Princeton Theological Seminary for many years.

William Greenough Thayer Shedd (1863–1893) was born at Acton, Massachusetts, June 21, 1820. He studied at the University of Vermont and was graduated in the class of 1839. A year later he entered Andover Theological Seminary, and not long after his graduation was ordained and installed as pastor of the Congregational church of Brandon, Vermont. In 1845 he was appointed professor of English Literature in the University of Vermont. In 1852 he accepted a call to Auburn Theological Seminary as professor of Sacred Rhetoric. The next year he took the chair of Ecclesiastical History at Andover. Here he remained until 1862, when he became co-pastor with the venerable Gardiner Spring of the Brick Church in the city of New York. The next year he accepted a call to the chair of Biblical Literature in the Union Theological Seminary, and in 1874 was transferred to the chair of Systematic Theology, occupying it until 1893, when he resigned and was made Professor Emeritus. His few remaining days were spent in congenial literary work.

The University of Vermont gave him the honorary degree of D.D. and the University of the City of New York that of LL.D.

Dr. Shedd was one of the ablest and most accomplished theologians our country has produced. In pure literary culture he had few equals. Among American divines Dr. Charles Hodge, Professor Park of Andover, Henry B. Smith, Philip Schaff, and several others may have surpassed him along certain lines of theological scholarship, both in study and action; but no one surpassed him as a master of lucid and vigorous English style, or in the high quality of his thinking. Books, especially the best books, were his utmost delight. He came early under the influence of Coleridge; and, after President Marsh of the University of Vermont, did more than any other man to render the writings of that great Christian philosopher a power in the intellectual life of New England. He was indeed, after Dr. Marsh's death, the foremost disciple of Coleridge in this country. His memory is fairly entitled to this honor. Among the leaders of theological opinion in his day no one could be compared with Dr. Shedd in intimate knowledge of Coleridge's teaching, or in effective labor to spread it. No better evidence of this is needed than his edition of Coleridge's prose writings, and the very able essay which introduced it to the public.

Dr. Shedd's connection with the Union Theological Seminary in the city of New York lasted nearly a third of a century. He brought to it both as teacher and preacher a high reputation; and his long service in it carried his influence far and wide over the country and the world. He was a man of profound convictions, a lover of truth for truth's sake, ardent and fearless in asserting what he believed, and armed with a logic which never flinched under the pressure of any difficulties. His orthodoxy was of the old Augustinian and Calvinistic type; and it grew stronger, I think, with the advancing years. His colleagues in Union Seminary by no means agreed with all his premises or with all his conclusions; nor did all of his pupils. But his colleagues and his pupils alike honored and loved him for his manly qualities, his simplicity and godly sincerity, and the many charms, both natural and spiritual, which adorned his character. In the unhappy conflict between the seminary and the General Assembly, which grew out of the case of Dr. Briggs, he took little or no part, so far as I know. But in the whole matter of the so-called higher criticism as represented by Dr. Briggs he took an active part, writing and speaking against it with great decision. And surely nobody that knew him well, could doubt for a moment that he did it all as a painful duty and in the fear of God.

Among Dr. Shedd's more important writings are "History of Christian Doctrine," New York and Edinburgh, 1865, 2 volumes. "Homiletics and Pastoral Theology," 1867. "Sermons to the Natural Man," 1871; "Theological Essays," 1877; "Literary Essays," 1878; "Commentary on Romans," 1879; "Sermons to the Spiritual Man," 1884; "The Doctrine of Endless Punishment," 1885; "Dogmatic Theology," 1889, 2 volumes.

PHILIP SCHAFF (1870–1893) was born at Coire, Switzerland, January 1, 1819. He studied at Coire, in the gymnasium at Stuttgart, and in the universities of Tubingen, Halle and Berlin; later, he traveled as tutor to a young Prussian nobleman through Italy, returned to Berlin in 1842 and lectured in the university there as *privat-docent* on Exegesis and Church History.

In 1844 he was called to a chair in the Theological Seminary of the German Reformed Church of the United States at Mercersburg, Pennsylvania. The next year he was tried for heresy before the Synod of York and acquitted. His labors at Mercersburg were most abundant. Besides lecturing on all branches of theology, he served as chairman of two committees to which was entrusted the task of preparing a new liturgy and a new hymn book. Both were chiefly written by him and passed into general use in the German Reformed Church. During the civil war Mercersburg was drawn into the struggle and the seminary turned into a military hospital. Late in 1863 Dr. Schaff removed to New York and became secretary of the New York Sabbath Committee. During this period, in addition to his indefatigable labors among the German population in behalf of a better Sabbath observance, he gave courses of lectures on Church History, at Andover, Hartford and New York. In 1870 he became Professor of Theological Encyclopedia and Christian Symbolism in the Union Theological Seminary. In 1872 he was transferred to the Hebrew chair, and in 1875 to that of Sacred Literature. In 1887 he succeeded Dr. Hitchcock as Professor of Church History. He was one of the founders and also the honorary secretary of the American branch of the Evangelical Alliance. He crossed the ocean many times in the service of the Alliance and of the Alliance of the Reformed Churches. He was president of the American Bible Revision Committee, which he organized at the request of the British Committee. His labors of this description were extraordinary, as also the skill, ability and generous self-devotion with which he performed them. He surpassed all the men I ever knew in the extent, variety and fruitful results of his practical, literary, and theological activities. One is fairly staggered in reading over a list of the books he wrote, the journeys he made, the societies he founded, the plans he formed, the addresses he delivered, the funds he raised, and the solid, lasting effects he produced in furtherance of good learning, Christian union and fellowship, and other vital interests of the cause and kingdom of

Jesus Christ. Of all his books, as I often told him, "The Creeds of Christendom" seemed to me the most valuable. I doubt if any other Christian scholar on either side of the Atlantic could have written it. I had the privilege of being his oldest American friend. From our first meeting under Tholuck's roof at Halle, in 1839, to our last walk together through the Central Park in New York a few days before his death, in 1893, our attachment to each other and our fellowship in Christ and His truth grew ever stronger and more full of mutual comfort and good cheer.

Dr. Schaff was greatly favored in leaving behind him a son to walk in his footsteps, and to give to the Christian public the story of his life.

Among the many tributes which crowned the fiftieth anniversary of Dr. Schaff's theological course, and which followed his death, I select a single one as fairly representing all the rest. The following are the main sections of a congratulatory address sent to him by the theological faculty of the university of Berlin, which, it is understood, was written by Professor Harnack. In his acknowledgment Dr. Schaff declared he could not "have wished for a nobler and more honorable testimonial to his labors."

BERLIN, November 16, 1892.

MOST WORTHY SIR, MOST HONORED COLLEAGUE:

On this, the anniversary of the day when fifty years ago you won in our high school the *venia legendi*, the Theological Faculty of the Frederick William University would present to you, most honored colleague, their heartiest good wishes and prayers. You entered upon your work as academical instructor in our high school at the time when the study of church history, under the lead of Neander and Baur, had taken on a marked impetus. Erbkam, Piper, Kahnis and Jacobi were among your immediate predecessors; Reuter following two months later; these, with yourself, all grateful pupils of Neander and filled with the noble spirit that animated him, were one in their determination to seek the welfare of the church by mastering with loving zeal the distinctive features of Christian life and thought in order faithfully to impart the results to others.

You have introduced into your new fatherland in English translations an array of valuable and weighty works of German theology, thus naturalizing there that science and causing it to be appreciated. This however, forms but a small part of your great and fruitful work. You have advanced the science of theology by works both in German and English, particularly by your great works, the "History of the Apostolic Church," the "History of the Christian Church," *Bibliotheca Symbolica Ecclesiae Universalis* ("The Creeds of Christendom"), together with numerous treatises on subjects pertaining to church history, which are the fruits of your own independent studies. Your Church History in particular has taken a most honorable rank among the church histories of the day, by virtue of the thoroughness of its execution and the clearness of its style. It is the most notable monument of universal historical learning produced by the school of Neander.

In addition to this, and thereby resembling the great mediator between the Greek and the Latin Churches in the past, you have shown the most lively interest in both the original text of the New Testament and its translation into English. Your "Companion of the Greek Testament and the English Version," has become a most useful hand-book. And as president of the American Bible Revision Committee in co-operation with the English committee, you have played a most prominent part in bringing that great work to a happy conclusion. But, unlike Jerome, your aim was not to introduce into one country the theological conflicts of another, nor to draw party lines of doctrine as strictly as possible, but, on the contrary, you have ever made it your task to promote reconciliation, to draw together the various parties in the Church, and everywhere to bring about "the speaking of the truth in love." If the signs of the times do not deceive us, your work in this regard also has been crowned with special blessing. The various evangelical denominations of your new home are indeed drawing nearer to one another, and their ecclesiastical and scholarly emulation no longer minister to strife, but to mutual recognition and co-operation.

The Lord Almighty has vouchsafed to you, most honored colleague, to pass the threshold of your seventieth year with activity and strength undiminished. Within the past few years you have begun two great undertakings, the founding of an American Society of Church History, whose president you have become and in the forefront of whose work you stand, and the editing of an English translation of a "Nicene and Post-Nicene Library of the Fathers."

That your health and strength may long abide unimpaired in order that you may bring to a successful issue all you have undertaken, is our most heartfelt wish.

THE THEOLOGICAL FACULTY OF THE ROYAL FREDERICK WILLIAM UNIVERSITY.

B. WEISS, *Dean.*

Since these sketches were written and in print two other ministers, once directors of Union Seminary, have passed away. They were known and honored throughout the country alike for their high personal qualities, and for the eminent services which they rendered, each in his own peculiar sphere as preacher or teacher and author, to the cause of the Divine Master. I refer to the REV. CHARLES SEYMOUR ROBINSON, D.D., LL.D., (1860–1869) and the REV. JAMES ORMSBEE MURRAY, D.D., LL.D. (1869–1882).

Part Fifth.

A SKETCH OF

THE LIFE AND PUBLIC SERVICES

OF

CHARLES BUTLER, LL.D.

Part Fifth.

A SKETCH OF THE LIFE AND PUBLIC SERVICES OF CHARLES BUTLER, LL.D.

I.

BIRTH AND PARENTAGE.—EARLY YEARS.—ADMITTED TO THE BAR.—SETTLED AT GENEVA, N. Y.—A JOURNEY TO THE GREAT WEST AND WHAT CAME OF IT.—CHICAGO IN 1833. —REV. JEREMIAH PORTER.—REMOVAL TO NEW YORK CITY.—ENLARGEMENT OF HIS CAREER AS MAN OF BUSINESS AND CHRISTIAN CITIZEN.—ENTERS AT ONCE UPON HIS LIFE-WORK AS ONE OF THE FOUNDERS OF THE MERCER STREET PRESBYTERIAN CHURCH, THE UNIVERSITY OF THE CITY OF NEW YORK, AND THE UNION THEOLOGICAL SEMINARY.—BECOMES, LATER, THE AUTHORIZED AGENT AND REPRESENTATIVE OF NEW YORK AND LONDON CAPITALISTS IN ADJUSTING THE FINANCIAL INTERESTS IN THE STATES OF MICHIGAN AND INDIANA.

Charles Butler was born at Kinderhook Landing, now Stuyvesant, Columbia County, New York, February 15, 1802, being the fifth son of Medad Butler and Hannah Tyler, in a family of twelve children. His father, well known as a merchant and as a judge of the county of Columbia, was a descendant of Jonathan Butler, an Irish gentleman, who settled in Saybrook, Connecticut, in 1724, and who married Temperance Buckingham, daughter of the Rev. Daniel Buckingham, one of the founders of Yale College. A younger sister, still living, recalls characteristic scenes and incidents of Charles' early years. Here is one of them:

The Fourth of July, 1821, was a memorable day for our little town. Franklin came from Albany to deliver the oration. Charles and Walter were very active in making the occasion a success. We were just through with the oration and refreshments when a great excitement was caused by the arrival of the famous steamboat *Richmond*, on its way to Albany, bringing the news of Napoleon Bonaparte's death. As mother always had a great horror of Bonaparte, Charles congratulated her on the news as a forerunner of the millenium! His love and veneration for his mother was very beautiful and touching, even to his ninety-sixth year.

Charles received his education in the district school of Kinderhook Landing and in the academy at Greenville, New York. On leaving school he entered the office of Judge Vanderpool at Kinderhook, and, later, went to Albany to pursue his law studies in the office of Martin VanBuren, then Attorney-General of New York, and afterwards President of the United States, in whose family he was for some time an inmate. His elder brother, Benjamin Franklin, had already been taken in by Mr. VanBuren as junior partner. The relations between the two brothers seem to have been already very close and beautiful. Here is an extract from a letter of Franklin to Charles, while the latter was in Judge Vanderpool's office. Charles was then seventeen and Franklin twenty-three years old:

I need not say anything to you about the importance of clear and vigorous attention to office duty and reading. Don't make too many acquaintances, and be cautious in those you do make. Above all things never be ashamed of being more virtuous or less gay than the rest of the world. Endeavor to retain as much as possible the scrupulous regard to truth, honesty and virtue you had when a child, and try to be as ignorant of everything that opposes them as you then were. Let conscience do her office fully and faithfully, and be careful never to resist her dictates, or ever to reason with her supposed absurdities. The moment you begin to think her over-nice that moment your integrity is in danger.

Charles Butler was admitted to the bar in 1824. In 1825 he married Eliza A. Ogden, of Walton, Delaware County, New York. Before his marriage he removed to Geneva, New York, and there formed a partnership with Bowen Whiting, later a justice of the Supreme Court of the State. Shortly after settling in Geneva he became Assistant District-Attorney of Genesee County, and as such took part in the noted prosecution of certain persons prominent in Masonic circles, which grew out of the mysterious disappearance of Morgan. His recollections, sixty years later, of this celebrated case, as also of the man and the incidents, which so stirred political and popular feeling throughout New York and all over the country, were exceedingly vivid and interesting. Mr. Butler practiced law in Geneva for ten years, acting as agent and attorney in western New York for the New York Life Insurance and Trust Company—said to have been the first of modern trust companies—on whose behalf he loaned the farmers of that part of the State large sums of money, which enabled them to improve and develop their properties, and particularly to convert the leasehold interests, which they held from the so-called Holland patent and other land grant companies, into estates in fee simple. He was thus largely instrumental in building up that section of western New York.

In June, 1833, Mr. Butler left Geneva with his friend, Mr. Arthur Bronson, of New York City, to make a visit to Chicago, known then chiefly as Fort Dearborn. This journey was a turning-point in his life and his life-work. It brought him face to face with the Great West and opened his eyes to the immense resources and possibilities of that vast region. In letters and a journal, written at the time, is a minute account of his journey. A few passages from this record will show with what an observing eye he watched the signs of coming greatness, which before his death was to transform the rude little settlement on the Chicago River into one of the foremost cities of the world:

I approached Chicago in the afternoon of a beautiful day, the sun setting on a cloudless sky. On my left lay the prairie bounded only by the distant horizon like a vast expanse of ocean; on my right in summer stillness lay Lake Michigan. I had never seen anything in nature more captivating. There was an entire absence of animal life, nothing visible in the way of human habitation or to indicate the presence of man; and yet it was a scene full of life, for there, spread out before me in every direction, as far as the eye could reach, were the germs of life in earth, air and water. But what was this Chicago to which I had come? A small settlement, a handful of people all told, who had come together mostly in the last year or two. The houses, with one or two exceptions, were of the cheapest and most primitive character for human habitation. A string of these buildings had been erected without much regard to lines on the south side of Chicago river. On the west side near the junction a tavern had been improvised for the entertainment of travellers and there we found lodgings.

On the morning after our arrival, in walking out I met a gentleman of whom I inquired where the Rev. Jeremiah Porter, the chaplain of Fort Dearborn, to whom I had a letter of introduction, could be found. Upon exhibiting my letter he said he was the person and that he was then on his way to attend the funeral of a child. He asked me if I would accompany him, and I did so. On going to the house, which was new and cheap, we found the father and mother; the dead child lay in a rude coffin. There was no one present except the parents, Mr. John Wright, Dr. Kimball, Mr. Porter and myself. It became a question how the remains of the child should be conveyed to the cemetery, which was on the west side of the north branch of the river. While we were attending this simple service we were interrupted by the noise of the hammer of a workman outside, engaged in putting up a shanty for some new comer. Mr. Porter went out and secured the assistance of this workman. We acted as bearers in conveying the remains of the child from the house across the river to the grave and assisted in burying it.*

*The Rev. JEREMIAH PORTER was a great-grandson of the renowned New England theologian, Jonathan Edwards. He pursued his college course at Williams, while the missionary enthusiasm aroused by the memorable

At this time there were perhaps from two to three hundred people in Chicago, mostly strangers to each other. The tavern was filled with emigrants and travellers, many of whom could only find a sleeping place on the floor, which was crowded with weary men at night.

Mr. Butler spent some time in studying the condition and prospects of the place. As a result, he purchased a large amount of land in what is now the city of Chicago, and held a small portion of it to the day of his death. In September, 1833, the U. S. government by treaty with the Indians extinguished the Indian title to lands in the Northwest and advertised a great land sale in this section to take place at Chicago in June, 1835. This sale attracted a large concourse

scene at the hay-stack consecration was still in full tide. In the very spirit of Samuel J. Mills and his ardent associates, young Porter "went West" and became one of the most useful home missionaries that ever labored in that field. He organized the First Presbyterian church in Chicago in 1833. "On May 30th of that year I preached at Fort Dearborn," he wrote, "the first sermon ever preached within one hundred miles of Chicago by any other than a traveling Methodist preacher." He died in 1893, greatly beloved and revered throughout the whole Interior as a patriarch of all the churches. In a journal, kept by him in his early years at Chicago, there are repeated allusions to Mr. Butler. Here is an extract from this journal:

AUGUST 5, 1833.

Mr. Butler, a lawyer from Geneva, New York, made remarks in the Sunday-school and at our evening prayer-meeting. Afterwards, he came to my room with three of the brethren of my church and a young man just come in from Dr. Cox's church; and we had a pleasant prayer-meeting. Mr. Butler says this is the most important point in a religious and commercial view west of Buffalo.

A few months later he records the arrival of a fine Sunday-school library of two hundred volumes, sent to him from New York by Mr. Butler and his friend, Mr. Bronson. To show how land values had increased in Chicago, he states in a letter to Mr. Butler, written in 1856, that a section of public school land sold, not long after Mr. Butler's visit in 1833 for $40,000, was sold some years afterward for $12,000,000.

of people. In May of that year Mr. Butler induced his brother-in-law, William B. Ogden, then a young man and just elected to the Legislature of New York, to go to Chicago for the purpose of looking after and offering for sale the lands in which he had invested. Mr. Ogden was afterwards known throughout the country as the first mayor of Chicago and one of its most eminent citizens. Mr. Butler subsequently became interested in several great railroad enterprises having their inception or terminus at Chicago; among them the Michigan Southern, Chicago and Rock Island, and Chicago and Northwestern Railroads.

In 1834 Mr. Butler removed to New York, which became his home until his death. Just at that time three very important movements were about to begin, in each of which he was to take a leading part. I refer to the founding of the Mercer street Presbyterian church, the University of the City of New York, and the Union Theological Seminary Here, too, he still represented financial interests that long had occupied much of his time. But in New York he soon became identified with far more important interests, which had their centre in London, involved many millions of dollars, and for years tasked to the utmost both his physical and mental forces. This chapter of his life is highly interesting for the extraordinary ability and wisdom, of which he showed himself master in the conduct of great and very difficult financial operations. But it is far more striking on account of the rare moral and personal qualities it brought into action.

The period to which it especially relates formed one of the most critical in the commercial history and character of the country. For the first time the hideous doctrine of *repudiation* had seized control of several States of the Union and threatened to subvert the very foundations of public credit and justice. In meeting and contending with this peril Mr. Butler stood among the foremost men of the nation. His record relating to it, had he done nothing else worthy of praise, should keep him in lasting remembrance. I recall no other name of that trying period that was, and still is, entitled to higher honor in this regard. I refer particularly to Mr. Butler's service in effecting an adjustment of the public debt of the State of Michigan in 1843, and to the still more important services, rendered by him later, in restoring the credit of Indiana and relieving that State from the embarrassments caused by the building of the Wabash and Erie canal and other internal improvements. In both cases he acted as agent of the domestic and foreign bondholders of these States. During his absence in Detroit and Indianapolis on these errands of professional and public duty Mr. Butler carried on a constant correspondence with his wife, in which he communicated to her in detail the nature and progress of the negotiations. His letters to her cast much light upon his character and his training for the work to which he was later called in the service of the Union

Theological Seminary; they bear directly upon turning-points in the moral, as well as financial, history of two great States of the Union; and they are full also of interesting personal incidents or allusions; I shall, therefore, offer no apology for giving here somewhat copious abstracts of the most important of them.

II.

THE FIGHT WITH REPUDIATION IN MICHIGAN IN 1843.

I.

Arrival in Detroit and entrance upon his mission.—Preliminary steps.—Message to the Governor and the Legislature.—Difficulties in the way and uncertainty of the issue.—Comfort in prayer and thoughts of home.

DETROIT, January 28, 1843.

MY DEAR WIFE:—It is now twenty minutes to twelve, but I cannot close the day without writing to you. I have been at Chancellor Farnsworth's all the evening in conference with him over our business, and returned only a few minutes since, and found your letter to welcome me. I could not but follow up the reading of it with the 8th of Romans, our chapter in course, and then on my knees acknowledge the goodness and grace of our Heavenly Father for His preserving care and for all His mercy towards us.

Yesterday and to-day have been very, very busy days. It is a regular lobbying campaign. The authorities from the Governor down have received me with the greatest cordiality. I arrived here in the very nick of time, neither too early nor too late, and they all say it will do good. I will not be too sanguine, for there are many difficulties in the way, which no one can understand or appreciate, who is not on the spot. On Monday morning I am to meet committees of the Legislature. This morning I had a long, uninterrupted conference with the Governor and went over the whole ground. Yesterday I conferred with no less than twenty persons on the subject. Talking is my special business, and of that I shall have a great deal to do. The contents of your letter interested me very much. The death of Captain Stoddard was not unexpected, and I rejoice to learn that it was peaceful and happy. By this event another is added to the list of widows, and other orphans are thrown upon the sympathy of Christian friends. *Pure religion and undefiled before God is to visit the widow and the fatherless in their affliction.* How the benevolence of the Gospel shames us for our selfishness! Oh, that we could break the fetters that bind us to earthly interests and go forth in the love of Christ, doing good as we have opportunity, every day and every hour of every day!

SUNDAY, January 29th.

I remained at home this afternoon as well to rest as to write to you. Sunday is a day of home feelings, a day to think of those dear ones that cluster around its hearths and altars more than at any other time. What a faculty is the memory; how vividly it brings up every expression of the face, the manners and the very tones of voice of those we love. And then imagination comes in and completes the picture, and enables us to see them arranged around the table at tea, in the parlor or nursery, in the church or on the way to it. I know that at this moment you and the children are occupied in thinking and talking about me. Your account of our dear boy delighted me. I cannot bear to have Ogden any other than one of the *best* of boys. I look forward to the time when he will be a young man and when, if we live, our hopes and happiness will be bound up in him. A good boy is certain to make a good man, and a bad boy is equally certain to make a bad man and to bring disgrace and unhappiness upon his parents. Witness poor S. Let us pray to God fervently and frequently to give us the wisdom we need to train up our children to His service and glory; and let us, above all, often, very often, pray for them. We are called to exercise towards them the utmost patience, forbearance, gentleness, kindness and firmness in their management. We must regard the weakness and infirmity of their natures, as well as our own; while we reprove their faults and errors, whether of a negative or positive character, we must not fail to encourage and cherish all their endeavors to do right and to please us. The real difficulty is *in the heart*, and God alone by His grace can change that. Ogden is getting to such an age that he is becoming a companion for us. This will give us more influence over him and we must exercise it in the best possible manner.

DETROIT, Saturday evening, 4th February, 1843.

I was rejoiced this afternoon to receive your and Ogden's letter. Ogden's letter was particularly gratifying. I read it aloud to Mrs. Governor Barry and Mrs. Taylor, and they both said it was a good letter. To hear that you were all so well and happy made me feel very happy; and I could not refrain from expressing my gratitude on my knees. The week has been one of great labor, day and night. I have not made a single call till this evening, or been out except on Thursday evening. Mrs. Farnsworth gave a party to help our business on. I went of course. This afternoon I gave Mrs. Barry and Mrs. Taylor a sleighride; and as I had not had one for nine years I was quite willing to get the relaxation. We had a delightful drive down the river, eight miles and back, in quick time.

I shall send you next week my message to the Governor and the two houses of Legislature, and you will then see how I stand and what ground I have taken. It has excited a great deal of interest, and I bid fair to be quite a lion, or rather a stripling bearding the lion in his den. It is queer business all around, and a Legislature here is a queer body, and they have queer notions of matters and things. I entertain strong hopes of success, but cannot possibly predict what the result will be. It is *all* a lottery. I find many old friends among the members of the Legislature. I have really laid myself out to bring about something, and they give me credit for urging sound doctrine and insisting on reasonable terms. Still, the idea of any one coming here and insisting on Michigan fulfilling her obligations is *monstrous* in the estimation of some; it involves the honor and dignity of a sovereign State! My communication was read in the Senate with profound attention, and an extra number of copies ordered to be printed unanimously. In the afternoon, however, they reconsidered, and by a majority of one decided not to print. The main argument was that they did not want it to go to the people without an antidote. It will, however, be printed, and will, I think, do good. The Legislature is a very impulsive body, and no reliance can be placed on a large majority. I shall have to see every man, and to omit one may lose the bill. Mr. Taylor and Mr. Farnsworth, my coadjutors, keep entirely in the background and are not known at all in the premises. I, coming all the way from New York, through the mud, *on purpose*, can say and do things which no one here would dare to say and do without being charged with treason. It is now precisely twelve o'clock at night and I will lay aside all business cares for the coming Sabbath. Before commencing this letter I had read the fifteenth chapter of Romans in course. What a beautiful epistle it is! Oh, for the spirit of Paul! I went to prayer-meeting last night just to kindle up a spark of love in this "cold heart of mine," and we had a pleasant meeting. Ten days will bring me to another era in my life and another revolution of the wheel. How true it is that life is but a hand breadth.

II.

A bill prepared by him passes the Senate 14 to 1.—The prospect clouded by the repudiators.—Bill finally passes the House and is sent to the Governor.—What it is and will do for Michigan.—Sabbath rest.

FRIDAY EVENING, February 24th.

I have but a moment to say that God seems to be prospering me in my business here. The Senate by a vote of 14 to 1 have passed a bill which *I had prepared in the very form in which I had prepared it;* and it will pass the House next week, as I hope, by a unanimous vote. It is wonderful. Patience, hearty good will and hard work, night and day, have brought it about. . . . My prospects [he writes a few days later] are not so bright as they were on Friday. I then thought the trouble was over, but in the House it has just begun, I fear. Demagogues and repudiators there are who resist every honest measure, but the hearts of all men are in the hand of God and He turns them which way He will like rivers of water.

MONDAY EVENING, February 27th.

I find that there is an opportunity of sending to New York by private conveyance, and so I will make a double letter. It is now eleven o'clock and I have had another hard day's work. The prospect now is that I shall carry my business through triumphantly and settle a great question, to the honor and prosperity of a great State, and secure a great object to the bondholders. And I am confident that I say but the simple truth, and what is apparent, that it would not have been settled if I had not come; and that no one else could probably have effected it in the same way. I have as much as I can do to follow it up, being obliged to go and see every man and talk it over with him plainly and fully. You could have seen me this evening in a room with half a dozen members seated around a table, laying down sound principles of democracy in relation to the *payment of the public debt* and the maintenance of the public credit; telling them that whereas a good citizen should be ready always to lay down his life in defence of his country against an invading foe, so he should always be ready to give up his property to preserve and defend the honor of his country and pay its debts.

DETROIT, March 7, 1843.

In the morning of Monday it was ascertained that the enemies of the bill had been so active during Sunday that they had a fixed majority. I and my friends went to work and in the afternoon when the bill came up, there was a very animated debate pro and con. I had not conceived of such violent opposition and at times it seemed as if the bill would certainly be lost. We carried one question only by a vote of 25 to 24. We finally carried the bill by a vote of 28 to 20. To-day it is in the hands of the Governor for his signature and is safe. But I have scarcely ever in my life passed through a more exciting scene. The question was in fact, repudiation, or no repudiation; and the debates were very exciting. General Cass turned out in the evening to hear. The opponents of the bill appealed to passion rather than to reason, and in the course of the evening the yeas and nays were taken seven times. Thus has ended my mission here after six weeks of toil and anxiety, and in the result I recognize the hand and blessing of God. It is all His work and not mine. It has settled a great question on just and honest principles, redeemed the credit of Michigan, and done justice to her creditors. The law grants precisely what I asked for, and was prepared by me, and you will see what that is by looking at my letter to the Governor. The only change is in funding the interest up to July 1, 1845, instead of January 1, 1844. The time I regarded as of secondary importance. The great question was whether the debt would be recognized and secured by taxation. I desire to place these things on record for my own benefit, if spared for many years; and if not, then for the benefit of those who may come after us. I desire it from a conviction that Michigan, if this law is maintained from this day forward, will go on prosperously as a people and that this act will constitute one of the most important events in her history. It is to give shape and character to her future Legislation: it will redeem the honor and credit of the State. It will be a landmark to steer by; a sheet anchor to hold on to; and a star to guide, and by it the policy of the State in coming time will be established. Had I known, before coming to Michigan, what I *now* know, I would not have ventured an opinion in favor either of the recognition or the payment of the debt. Ninety-nine persons out of a hundred did not feel that there was any *obligation* resting on them to recognize, or pay, any of the bonds; and though they said that the State would acknowledge and pay what she had received, still that even was considered a matter of grace rather than of legal and equitable liability. This ground was quite broadly taken in so important a document as the report of the joint committee of the two houses—a committee composed of eight individuals constituting the very best and most influential men in the Legislature.

I shall now leave Detroit by Friday of this week. I cannot close up sooner. Then I shall be at Toledo one week to finish up there; and then it is an even chance whether I set my face steadily southwest or right about towards New York. I am tired out now, and can hardly look my south-western jaunt in the face; still my duty may urge me on, and I cannot well resist the monitor within. I thought of, and prayed for, you and our dear children on Sunday a great deal. It was communion Sunday in Dr. Duffield's church, and he was very interesting. It was a lovely day for March, and though my mind was harassed and distracted by the business of the week, and my bill had come up just at the close of Saturday, yet I was enabled to preserve a good degree of composure and to enter, I trust, somewhat into the spirit of the day and its ordinances. What a blessed day the Sabbath is! I enjoyed our concert at the twilight and could think of you and Ogden and Emily and our domestics and our family altar and all its blessings, and thank my Heavenly Father for the intelligence that you were, just one week before, in life, health and comfort. May He keep you thus, and sanctify unto each of us all the trials, cares and temptations of life, and finally bring us into His heavenly rest, with all whom we love, to the praise of the riches of His grace in Jesus Christ our Redeemer. Kiss Ogden and Emily thrice each for me.

III.

Sudden pull-back and consternation.—A VETO *threatened.—How the friends of public honesty and good faith rallied to save the bill and persuade the Governor. Captain Purdy and other helpers.—A noble object-lesson in the art of political management and doing the right thing in the right way.—The bill signed.—Letter from the Auditor General of Michigan in praise of Mr. Butler.*

TOLEDO, O., March 14, 1843.

I left Detroit on the eleventh, and arrived here the same evening, with another cold fastened on me. I have been out to-day but a few minutes, to the post-office and printing office, both near by. I wrote you on the passage of the bill through the House, after a very stormy debate, by a vote of 28 to 20. I will now relate what followed; and this letter I wish you to carefully preserve, as it contains the record of important events, which in coming times I may desire to refer to. It is the only full history which I shall give in writing; and this is not full either, for it would take me a week to write all out.

The bill, having passed the House on Monday evening, was returned with a slight amendment to the Senate, where it originated, the same evening, the Senate being in session. It again passed, the ayes and noes being called for, every member but one voting in the affirmative, although leading senators had made speeches against it on the ground that *no tax should ever be levied to pay the debt;* that the only security of the bond holders was a lien upon the income of the railroads; and if that proved insufficient, then their security failed altogether; that it has never contemplated to *tax* the people to pay the debt; and the pledge of the faith of the State did not involve any such consequences. They took the ground, in a word, of open repudiation. The bill was sent to the Governor for his approval on Tuesday at noon. I then felt that the crisis had passed, and that the bill was safe. It never entered my mind that the Governor could, or would, veto it. It was a question of policy to be settled by the Legislature and it did not involve any constitutional principles. On Wednesday morning the Governor had not returned the bill, and a good deal of solicitude began to be expressed. This was increased by the declaration of Bush and others that Governor Barry would veto the bill. Still its friends did not yield to any serious fear. In the afternoon I was in my room, about half-past two, and had just finished a letter to my brother Franklin, giving an account of the results of my mission, rather a crowing letter, too (I shall never crow again till I get out of the woods!) when Mr. Wells, the commissioner, a friend of the Governor, and known to be intimate with him, came in with a good deal of anxiety depicted in his face and said that he had called to see me about the bill, and that something must be done right away. I expressed my astonishment and inquired whether the Governor had any hesitation on the subject. He replied that he was not authorized to say that the Governor would not sign the bill with the tax clause in, but unless that clause was stricken out, he thought the bill would be in danger. He then urged me to consent to this alteration. If the tax clause was not stricken out it would ruin the Governor and the party, and I ought not to place them in such a position. I replied that this was the only feature of the bill worth saving; the Governor must take the responsibility, and I had rather have the bill vetoed than signed without the tax clause. Mr. Wells left me, saying that if I changed my mind I must let him know within half an hour, as time was passing. After he had gone I could not but muse on the uncertainty of all human affairs. Here was I, after having secured, as I supposed, beyond any question the passage of a bill, which would reflect honor on the people and do justice to the creditors of the State, rejoicing in the victory and reposing on my laurels, when lo! a veto! I was almost driven in desperation to take ground with Clay against the *veto power* ALTOGETHER. A little reflection, however, brought me to my senses and to my knees. I had forgotten God in this business, and taken to myself the praise, which belonged to Him and to Him alone. Surely every man is vanity, as the psalmist says. Such a rebuke, such a *break down,* I had never before realized. But, my dear wife, when I arose from that prayer I felt such a calmness, such contentment, such submission and resignation to the will of God as to be willing, I had almost said desiring, that He would cause the Governor to veto the bill and thus humble my pride, self-confidence and conceit into the very dust.

I thought, however, that duty to my employers and duty to an upright cause and a sincere desire to promote what I certainly conceived to be for the true interests, moral, political and financial of Michigan, required of me to use all honest means to prevent so great a disaster and injury to these interests as such an event would produce. It would be a death-blow to the character and credit of the State, and fatal, of course, to the hopes of the bondholders. It would be to encourage and strengthen the open repudiators and stimulate them in their appeals to the people against the recognition and payment of the bonds; and it would be in the very face of Governor Barry's messages; while to him personally it would be utter political ruin, and to the Democratic party of the State division and ruin. Above all, it would encourage the people in their unwillingness to pay, and open a wide field for demagogues and hold out an invitation to them to come and occupy it. They had already declared that if the Governor should sign the bill, they would take the stump against him next summer throughout the State. A veto would give such men great power and influence with the people; and the standard of moral feeling being very low and the real inability of the people to pay falling in with it, it was obvious to any reflecting mind that the most important interests, individual and collective, were involved in the crisis and dependent on the single act of the Governor. I never estimated the moral force of the veto power, for good or evil, as I did then, and as I shall ever hereafter, when any great question is involved. I knew that Governor Barry was an honest, just and prudent man; that he would act cautiously; but I saw in the fact that his most confidential friend and adviser regarded a veto inevitable, unless I consented to strike out the tax-clause, the strongest evidence that such was the meaning, if not the conclusion, of his mind.

But I went out to see what I could do. I first called on a leading Democrat, resident in the city, and asked him if he knew that the bill was in danger. He replied that he did. He had been up to the Legislature, and he heard there that the Governor would veto the bill. He had come down to see Dr. Houghton (the Mayor and State Geologist) a personal and political friend of the Governor, also to see Chancellor Farnsworth, and if possible, prevent a measure, which, in his opinion, would be ruinous to the credit of the State, to Governor Barry and to the Democratic party. He had been unable to find either of the three gentlemen. He said he would go again immediately to the House and see what could be done. As I left the office I met Chancellor Farnsworth and communicated to him the intelligence, which affected him as strongly as it had me. A few minutes later we met Dr. Houghton, who was also alarmed, having heard it from another source. We all started for the Capitol, those two to see the Governor, and I to see what I could see, and to do what I could do.

On getting to the Capitol, I went immediately to Captain Purdy. Now Captain Purdy is a man about fifty years of age, a sound, intelligent, upright man; remarkable for his good sense, good temper, and conciliating manners, and withal a pure and devoted Christian; one of the best men in a Legislative body I ever knew. He had from the beginning taken a very deep interest in the bill, not only because it was honest and just towards the creditors, but because it was the duty of the State and would reflect honor upon the people and do them good. He has exercised more influence in the Legislature than any other man in it, and to him Providence directed me. I told him what I had heard and what I feared. He expressed surprise that the Governor should hesitate, said he had heard such a rumor but supposed it had been circulated by the enemies of the bill. But now, he would go at once and see the Governor, as his friend, and tell him what his fate would be if he did veto it. He started off for the Executive chamber. I then passed round among the members and found that the rumor was beginning to excite a deep anxiety and feeling. I traced the rumor to the Lieutenant Governor Richardson, and in a few moments met him and he stated to me that to pass the bill with the tax clause would be death to the Governor and the party. I then went up into the Senate and found the rumor of veto rife there. I went to Judge Bell, the chairman of the joint committee, who said if the Governor did veto the bill it would kill him, if it did not destroy the party and ruin the credit of the State.

After a brief conversation he said he would go in and see the Governor and tell him what he thought of it. I then spoke to Mr. Wakefield, another leading member of the Senate, who said he would go and see the Governor and tell him, too, what the consequences would be of such an act. On passing through the Senate I spoke consecutively to about every senator and found that they had all heard the rumor and, with a single exception, spoke of it as a most extraordinary thing. If vetoed, the bill, they said, would still pass the Senate by a unanimous vote save one; but in the House the result would be doubtful. Shortly after I was sent for into the library and there met Mr. Wells, who, with the Secretary of State, had just come from the Governor. He again urged and begged of me to consent to strike out the tax clause, and thus save the bill. I refused utterly on the ground that the Legislature had passed it, and that it would be improper for me to interfere in any way. And if I could change it I would not, as it was the only feature in the bill that furnished any security to the bond holders. He seemed to think it very cruel in me to place the Governor and the party in such a situation, and was firmly persuaded that we should lose the next election on this ground, and that the next Legislature would repeal the law, leaving the bond holders worse off than ever.

Mr. Wells left me to return to the Governor. It afterwards turned out that the Governor had called his cabinet around him and was then discussing the question. There were four besides the Governor; two, the Auditor General and the State Treasurer, were firm and decided friends of the bill: and two, the Secretary of State and Mr. Wells, the Commissioner, were opposed; and the Governor inclined to go with the latter. In the course of the afternoon and evening the Governor had a series of calls from his personal and political friends, who remonstrated with him most plainly against so suicidal an act, and I had reports from Houghton, Purdy, Hall, Wakefield and others, of the results of their various interviews. As time was pressing, this being the afternoon of the last day of the session, the gentlemen had no time for compliments. It was plain talk all round, and I was amused at the report which an eye witness gave of Judge Bell's mission. When the Judge entered, the Cabinet were in session deliberating on the bill, and he addressed himself directly to the Governor, "talking with him like a father." As the Governor is probably ten years older than the Judge, it struck me with more humor.

After tea the Cabinet again met to deliberate further and I went to the Capitol again to see how things stood. I found very great excitement prevading both Houses and an increasing confidence that the bill would be vetoed; and it was said, that if vetoed it would be passed through the House even by a constitutional majority of two-thirds. Perhaps the wish was father to the thought. It was evident, however, that the current was setting with overwhelming force against the veto. The enemies of the bill had made extraordinary efforts to bring an influence to bear upon the Governor through his trusted friend, Mr. Eldridge, the Secretary of State. They said that his signing it would be a deathblow to his administration, and to the ascendancy of the Democratic party in the State, and he had, no doubt, been brought to believe this. The counteracting influences, however, in support of an honest and just cause, were too powerful to be resisted and at nine o'clock in the evening the Governor signed the bill. This result was brought to me confidentially in the Senate chamber, where I was patiently awaiting the veto message, the moment it occurred. It was soon circulated among the members and the congregation of by-standers who were lookers-on in Vienna. Well was it for Governor Barry and for the honor and credit of the State of Michigan that unwise counsels did not prevail with him; that God so overruled things that he was kept from falling into a snare and inflicting an irreparable injury on his own character and upon the character and good name of the State. And thus ended this chapter and this day of the 8th of March, 1843, at 10 o'clock P. M., when I left the Capitol.

Here are passages from a letter of Hon. C. J. Hammond, Auditor General of the State, addressed to Mr. George Griswold, one of the most distinguished and highly esteemed citizens of New York in that day:

I avail myself of the opportunity presented by the return of Charles Butler, Esq., to say what simple justice to him requires you should know. You will be advised by him of the result of his mission more perfectly than the limits of a letter will permit me to do. Of his agency in producing this result I cannot say too much. He has accomplished all that man could do and more than almost any other gentleman you might have selected. You are aware that when the present executive took the gubernatorial chair repudiation was ready to burst forth, and if they had been led in that direction a large majority of the people of this State would have followed. In his first message the Governor gave tone to the then forming public sentiment, which led to the legislation of 1842. In his last annual communication to the Legislature he advanced a step and public opinion sustained him. But many even of our most valuable citizens had not dreamed of *taxation*, and the Executive did not think public opinion would warrant a present enactment embodying that principle. Although it was fast approximating to that high and honest stand, still it seemed a task beyond the powers of any man to lead a majority of the representatives of the people to that point, at this time. Mr. Butler, by his address, amenity of manners, and powerful arguments, has succeeded and procured an enactment based on high moral and political principles; one that reflects great credit on him and, I think I may justly say, great credit on the State. . . . Discretion will require that the agency of Mr. Butler in producing this result should not be *trumpeted.* Our people are jealous of foreign and out-door influence, and the people should have all the credit that can be bestowed upon them consistently.

The readers of this history, which turns so largely upon the veto power conceded by Union Seminary to the General Assembly in 1870, can hardly fail to have been struck by the following passage in one of Mr. Butler's letters to his wife:

I never estimated the moral force of the VETO POWER, *for good or* EVIL, *as I did then, and as I shall ever hereafter, when any great question is involved.*

It is also noteworthy that in the midst of this severe, all-absorbing struggle for public honesty in Michigan Mr. Butler did not forget Union Theological Seminary, then carrying on a struggle scarcely less severe with poverty and discouragement. Dr. Peters was financial agent of the institution.

I wish you to pay Dr. Peters the balance of my subscription to the theological seminary, and to say to him that if I live and prosper, I shall pay as much more the next year. I want to know how they get on in the seminary, and if you see Dr. Peters, or Professor Robinson, do ask them to write me at Cincinnati and let me know. I have not heard a word on the subject since I left New York.

In the same letter he thus alludes to his New York pastor, Dr. Thomas H. Skinner:

I am afraid Dr. Skinner will think me a faithless elder. Tell him I have endeavored to do my duty here, and that I have not failed to remember our dear church. Oh, what great privileges we enjoy in New York! All other ministers seem so tame and languid as compared with Dr. Skinner! Our chapter I fail not to read and with continued interest every night. Kiss Ogden and Emily for me.

III.

THE FIGHT WITH REPUDIATION IN INDIANA IN 1845–6.

Let us pass now to Indianapolis and watch the Detroit struggle repeated on a larger scale. The political scene and the incidents change, but the same principles are at work. In Indiana, as in Michigan, it was still a deadly fight between public faith and public dishonesty; and the signal triumph of the cause of honesty forms one of the noblest chapters in the history of that great commonwealth. In 1840 the State had defaulted on the payment of interest on the public debt. It was an ominous year in the moral and financial annals of the country. Early in 1840 Gov. McNutt had sent forth his notorious proclamation, announcing to the world that Mississippi would not pay the bonds issued under her great seal and signed by himself, in her name, on account of the Union Bank. Repudiation was in the air and threatened to become a veritable epidemic of dishonesty over a large portion of the land. The creditors of Indiana were among leading capitalists and financial institutions in New York and London. Mr. Butler's struggle, as authorized agent of the domestic and foreign bond-holders, culminated in the winter of 1845–6. A full account of the situation and of the plan proposed for its relief may be found in a letter addressed by him to the Legislature. This letter is admirable alike for strong argument, for the wise moderation of its claims, and in the dignity and gentleness of its tone from beginning to end.*

Mr. Butler's letters to his wife, written at Indianapolis, like those from Detroit, are full of details respecting the character and progress of the negotiations he was carrying on, as agent of the domestic and foreign bond-holders of the State. I proceed now to give copious passages and abstracts of these very interesting letters. Aside from the valuable information stored away in them, they furnish lessons in the art of dealing with difficult questions bearing upon public morals

* Letter of Charles Butler, Esq., to the Legislature of Indiana and other documents in relation to the public debt. Indianapolis, printed by Morrison & Spann, 1845, p. 107.

and appealing to the public conscience, which are good for all time.

I.

Mr. Butler arrives in Indianapolis and finds the situation almost hopeless.—The question of public honesty to be settled now or never.—The Governor's position.—Good preaching and Sabbath rest.—No man dares to use the word PAY *or* TAX.—*Still a faithful remnant stand up for the honest cause.—A letter to the Legislature written.*

INDIANAPOLIS, November 29, 1845.

MY DEAR WIFE :—

I have been incessantly engaged, night and day, and hardly find time to eat or sleep. The prospects are altogether discouraging and almost everybody says that *nothing* can be done. Politicians, on both sides, are afraid to move. It is really amazing to see what a paralysis hangs upon this people. Everything is merged in the most trifling local politics. The Governor is a prominent candidate for the United States Senate and dare not open his mouth as he should, lest it might affect his election to that office. His friends are in the same predicament; and so with all the other candidates and their respective friends. My mission is a hard one and *no mistake.* Still, it is not fair to judge altogether from present indications. I must take a week or more to find out how the land lies. It is hardly possible but there will be found some good men, and some men who will take right ground. I must try my hand and see what I can do. Perhaps the very discouragements which meet me at the outset may be useful, and prepare the way for ultimate success. It is certain that if the question is not now settled it never will be; the people will go into repudiation. I have had two interviews with the Governor, one at my room and the other at his own house, and they have been quite satisfactory. He is one of the most cautious and timid men in the world; at the same time he is, I think, entirely honest and would be glad to have right done. He told me what he should say in his message, and if he adheres to this intention, it will be *all I could desire.*

INDIANAPOLIS, December 7, 1845.

The last week has been one of great excitement and pressure with me in my business, and I am glad to have the Sabbath come with its sacred rest. This morning I heard a sound, practical discourse in Mr. Gurley's church, and this evening another like it from Mr. Beecher. What a different world this would be if all its inhabitants were influenced by the simple principles of the Gospel! What a beautiful world it would be, and how sweet would be our existence in it! The Sabbath has come to me as a thing to be coveted. My spiritual nature was famishing and wearied, and needed food and rest. I find that I am engaged in a great undertaking, involved in the most complicated and, perhaps, insuperable difficulties. I am fully persuaded that it is only by addressing myself to the conscience of the people, stirring that up, and bringing that to bear, that I stand the slightest chance of success; and this cannot be done in a day. A revolution, a reformation, is required to be wrought. The whole population has got to be, in a sense, made over again, before justice can or will be done to the holders of the pledged faith of the State. Who is sufficient for these things? I am sure I am not. The difficulty in the way is radical; it lies at the very heart of the people. Such is the sentiment produced by the efforts of heartless, unprincipled politicians, that it has become a question whether it would be honest and right to pay the debt! No man dare take the responsibility in the Legislature of advocating payment. The Governor, even though he went very far for him, yet dare not use the word *pay* or *tax*. I consider his message a great triumph and as preparing the way for my mission; yet he has thrown the whole responsibility on me. I am preparing my letter but it requires great labor and reflection. I have to weigh every word and get it exactly right, or else I shall stir up such a hornet's nest about my ears that I shall be glad "to cut and run" out of the Hoosier State as fast as possible. I transmitted by mail yesterday four sheets of it, the first part, in manuscript, to Mr. King to be forwarded to Mr. Palmer, by the steamer on the 16th instant, and shall finish it to-morrow. I mean to make an issue between the bond-holders and the State in a way that the people shall understand it, and lay the foundation, I hope, for future success if I fail now. I find myself backed up by a few good and strong men of both parties, and a great change has certainly been wrought since I came. The little leaven may leaven the whole lump. I have reason, certainly, to be encouraged with the indications around me, and the revolution I speak of is certainly within the power of Him who holds all hearts in His hand. It is a great question, intimately connected with religion and morals; and that connection is what I rely on. Last night I did not get to bed till one o'clock. I am run down with engagements and scarcely get out of my room all day.

DECEMBER 10th, 7 P. M.

I have only this moment finished my letter to the Legislature. To-morrow, or day after, I expect to read it *in person* at the bar of the House of Representatives. I do not know how it will be received. It will kill or cure. The letter is very much complimented by the few to whom I have submitted it, among whom there are the best men I can find here; they think it will save the debt and the people. The fact is, the State is on the verge of repudiation, but they have not known it.

Having eased my mind of my message to the people of Indiana, I am going to a party at the Governor's this evening. My task seems a mountain but it may be removed in one way. The hearts of men are not in their own hands, and well it is, they are not. I am aided by Mr. Dodge of Terre Haute, who is at my elbow constantly, and then I have a young man to aid also in copying.

II.

Delivers his letter to the Governor.—Invited to read it to the Legislature.—Its surprising effect.—A letter to his son Ogden.—A restful Sunday.—His letter referred to a Joint Committee of Twenty-four.—His authority to act for bond-holders questioned by the repudiators.—His troubles fairly set in.

INDIANAPOLIS, December 11, 8 P. M.

I delivered my letter this forenoon to the Governor, who transmitted it by special message to the two Houses this afternoon. I was there, and the Speaker, by the unanimous consent of the House, invited me to read it in person, which I did. The lobby was pretty full, and they all listened with profound attention. When I finished—it took just an hour—they immediately ordered a thousand copies to be printed for the use of the House, which shows their estimate, as one hundred is the usual number. It seems to have met with universal approbation. The Rev. Dr. White, president of Wabash College, met me as I came out, took me by the hand, said that he had heard the whole of it, and that it was a most able and statesmanlike document. He seemed perfectly delighted. The Governor was present; and though he had, of course, read it through before sending it in, yet sat throughout and listened with the deepest attention. He and the Speaker expressed great satisfaction, and said that the temper and spirit of it were most unexceptionable, and compliments are pouring in on every side. Indeed, I am myself surprised at the manner in which it has been received and the effect produced.

My bark is now fairly launched, and though I have scarcely a hope of its weathering the adverse blasts which I hear and see driving all around me, yet I feel persuaded that I have done enough *to save the question in Indiana* at another session. I will send you the document itself to-morrow and you will read and judge for yourself. All the compliments which I have embodied in this letter are meant for you, my better half, and I hope they will not make you vain. My head is not quite turned, but it aches terribly from excitement, and labor, and fatigue. Kiss the dear children for me.

Before proceeding further, I will give a few extracts from this Letter, addressed to Governor Whitcomb, and through him to the Legislature and people of Indiana. Let the reader judge for himself whether I have praised it too highly:

According to the most reliable estimates, the people of Indiana will realize an advance on the productions of the

State for the year 1845, over the value of the same products in the year 1844, of not less than four millions of dollars—a result as gratifying to your bond-holders as it can be to any resident citizen of the State; and this, taken in connection with other concurring and favorable circumstances, renders the present a most auspicious time for the disposition of this subject.

I may be permitted with propriety to allude not only to the great internal prosperity of the State, over which you have the honor to preside, for encouragment; but also to the prosperous condition of all the States in the Great Valley, and constituting at this time the granary whence are drawn, I might almost say, the supplies of the world, and with which States Indiana is so interlocked, as to make *their* prosperity *hers*; and especially would I direct the attention of the Legislature to the brilliant example of your sister State of Ohio, whose citizens have borne without murmuring the burdens necessary to sustain their credit throughout a period of great pressure and gloom, and where a tax is collected for the year 1845 of *seventy-five cents* on the hundred dollars for the specific purpose of paying the interest on her public debt. Here is a noble example, illustrating the integrity of a free people, who regard the maintenance of plighted faith as the true foundation of State character and the seal of their prosperity. Indiana, with a soil equally fertile and a population equally industrious and enterprising, has opened to her a career as brilliant. She has only to restore her credit—that *greatest* element of national wealth—to render it certain.

I would refer also to the progress which other States have made for the restoration of their credit, to Pennsylvania and Maryland, to Michigan and Illinois, in each of which steps have been taken for the restoration of their credit, and the satisfactory relief of their bond-holders; and in these efforts we see the recuperative energies of the American character and the sense of justice prevailing over every obstacle. It is a movement which enlists the sympathy of every American citizen, wherever his residence may be, and which should challenge the admiration of the world.

I cannot close without availing myself of the occasion to present a few of the considerations which belong to this great subject, involving, as it surely does, the honor of the State, and the prosperity, interests and welfare of its eight hundred thousand population, and which, it would seem, should prompt the Legislature to take immediate steps, to the extent of her ability, for the relief of her foreign bond-holders. It will be remembered that they have held their bonds for a long period, without receiving any payment from the State, and the effect of such delay is to render their property comparatively valueless in their hands. In many instances parties have held on without submitting to the enormous sacrifice which a sale would involve, hoping for speedy relief from the State; and in such cases, if they can only be re-assured by the payment of a small portion of the accruing interest, and by certain provision for the future, it would save them from ruinous sacrifices, and enable them to preserve their property. Next to the payment in full of all arrears, is the *fixing* the time when it will be paid; in other words, *certainty* is the thing desired—it is the uncertainty in which the whole subject is involved, and the consequent inability of needy holders to make any certain calculations, that adds to their unhappiness—as in the case between man and man. An examination would show that the bonds of Indiana, like those of Pennsylvania and New York, are to be found extensively in the hands of trustees, guardians, retired and aged persons, widows, and others whose object was investment, and whose reliance for support is on income. Such, with scarcely an exception, is the class I represent. The State cannot be constrained to make payment, in any manner, at the will of the holders of her bonds, however pressing their necessities may be; they are left to depend entirely for the fulfilment of obligations, upon her own sense of honor and justice. In the exercise of her sovereignty, she is the sole judge of her own ability, and it might be deemed presumption in any one, even a creditor, to question her integrity and disinterestedness in deciding on the question, however it might disappoint his expectations, and however variant it might be from his own estimate.

The highest evidence which can be given of the reliance of those whom I represent, on the honor and faith of the State, is to be found in the fact already mentioned, that they have continued to hold the bonds from the period of their purchase, prior to the default of the State, down to the present time. It is true, they have been encouraged from time to time by the solemn assurances of the people of Indiana, speaking through their Executive and Representatives, of their intention to do justice to them as soon as they should have the ability; and especially by the emphatic language of the joint resolution, adopted by the Legislature of 1844–45, which is—"that we regard the slightest breach of plighted faith, public or private, as an evidence of the want of that moral principle upon which all obligations depend: that when any State in this Union shall refuse to recognize her great seal, as the sufficient evidence of her obligation, she will have forfeited her station in the sisterhood of States and will be no longer worthy of their confidence and respect"—and while they ought not to doubt that such is the sentiment of the people of Indiana, still, they are painfully concious that time is running against them, that the interest is accumulating, and with the increase of the debt the difficulties in the way of payment will also naturally increase, and they are impressed with the serious conviction that the neglect, or refusal on the part of the State, to provide for the payment of its just debts, for an unreasonable length of time, does involve all the practical consequences of repudiation to the holders of its obligations and to the people themselves, and will be so regarded by the world at large; and the danger of this *tacit* or *passive* repudiation is increased with the delay; for the longer it is suffered to remain, the further removed it is from the time when the obligation was incurred, and when the sense of it was fresh; and when we consider the changing character of the population of all the new States it is not surprising that the sense of obligation should grow weaker and weaker with the lapse of time. Nor is it surprising, in this view of the subject, that the most lively apprehension should be indulged by persons situated like those I represent, nor that they should be importunate with your Excellency and the Legislature, to save them from such a possible fate. And in the communication which I have the honor to make, if I have expressed myself too strongly on any point, or if I have seemed to fail in any particular in the respect which is due from me, either to your Excellency or the Legislature, or the people of Indiana, I beg once for all most earnestly to disclaim any such intention, and that you will attribute it to my anxiety to represent faithfully the rights and expectations of those who have sent me on this mission, and who cannot be presumed from the relation they sustain to the State, to entertain any other than feelings of the utmost respect for its public authorities, and a sincere desire to see its credit established on the most enduring basis, and its prosperity thereby secured.

These passages, as indeed the whole letter, remind me vividly of the speeches made by my renowned brother, S. S. Prentiss, a few years earlier, while carrying on his memorable fight with Repudiation in the State of Mississippi. The disease was much more virulent and frought with consequences vastly more disastrous there than in Michigan or Indiana. But the remedy urged upon the people of Mississippi with matchless eloquence and moral power, was precisely the same in principle as that depicted in Mr. Butler's admirable letter to Governor Whitcomb. What an unspeakable blessing it would have been to Mississippi had she applied the remedy as it was applied in Michigan and Indiana! This was what her ill-fated creditors urged in season and out of season. In a letter to me, dated Rydal Mount, March 23, 1843, Mr. Wordsworth, the illustrious poet, wrote, in regard to bonds of that State held by his only daughter and an aged brother and sister of his wife:

"In matters like this time, as in the case of my relatives, is of infinite importance, and it is to be feared that the two individuals for whose comfort payment is of the most consequence, may both be in their graves before it comes. *Let but taxes, to amount however small, once be imposed exclusively for discharging these obligations,* and that measure would be hailed as the dawn of a coming day; but until that is effected, the most sanguine must be subject to fits of despondency."

Unhappily, it was never effected.

TO HIS SON OGDEN.

INDIANAPOLIS, December 12, 1845.
Friday evening, 7 o'clock.

MY DEAR SON:

I was truly gratified to receive your affectionate letter and read it with deep interest. I have scarcely a moment to write to you. I think of you constantly and so I do of dear Emily and Anna. I am delighted that you are all so happy. You can make each other so happy if you only try. Your school report was a famous one; such a character is more to be desired than gold. I am very busy. My letter to the Governor will be printed to-morrow. I was amused at a remark of one of the plain country members, who said to Mr. Bright that there "was first a little sugar, then a little soap, then sugar, and then soap, and it was sugar and soap all the way through." Another said that I had "molassoed" it well. You will think from this it was a strange document, but the critics were real Hoosiers and "no mistake," as they say here. At any rate, they liked it well,—for maple sugar and soap and maple molasses, you will understand, are three of the greatest staples in this country. They don't make much use of the soap, but they do of the sugar and molasses, so I infer from it that they were pleased. Take good care of dear mother and Emmy and Anna. I will see if I can find anything curious for you in this country. I go out this evening to the Governor's party. I go as a matter of business, to meet with the people and form acquaintances.

INDIANAPOLIS, December 19, 1845.

MY DEAR WIFE:

To-day I attended a communion service in the Rev. Mr. Gurley's church, which was deeply interesting. Mr. Gurley is a very spiritual man and a man of uncommon sweetness, mingled with great manliness and boldness. . . . My nature is truly social, and needs constant exercise to preserve it from the withering influence of corroding care. The weighty business which seems to fall to my share is too great a burden, and I am conscious of it. Still, it might be borne, and without injury, if only I could keep my heart in the right place; for then I could cast it off on One who is able and willing to bear it. I was never engaged in any undertaking, in which I felt such utter impotence and feebleness as I do now. God only knows how it will end. I am in the midst of it, I voluntarily placed myself there, and the interests of hundreds of thousands are bound up in the result. I have unwittingly become conspicuous before the eyes of the people of this State, and they will look to all my movements with the greatest circumspection and solicitude. But I will not allow my thoughts to run into my business; the devil has all day been tempting me with it, and I have tried to resist him. He had great advantage over me in the circumstances which occurred yesterday afternoon, and which left my business in a way calculated to make me think more about it to-day. Nor is it possible to avoid intrusion altogether to-day, in such a place. People will come in and ask questions, and it is difficult to keep myself entirely out of the way. As I think my business has an intimate theological connection, I endeavor to turn it in that channel. Mr. Gurley will, probably, give us a sermon yet on the subject. For repudiation and Sabbath breaking ought to go together as national sins.

My letter has been referred to a Joint Committee of Twenty-four, to confer with me on the whole subject, and this committee are now in session, and adopting their preparatory organization. In so large a committee there are, of course, friends and foes, and the latter, I fear, are the strongest, not in numbers, but in power. It is an easy thing to make mischief and they are now trying, as I understand, to embarrass the question by objecting to my authority to act at all, which is quite ludicrous, after receiving my communication and ordering 1,000 copies to be printed. This is the beginning of trouble of which I shall have enough, before I get through. But I mean, if my life is spared, to represent the bond-holders faithfully to the end. The people have now got the matter presented to them in a form it never was before, and they cannot prevent the effect of it. I expect to-morrow to go before the Sanhedrim in person, and the discussions are to be oral. That is, I am to be permitted to make my propositions and accompany them with oral explanations, which gives me the chance to say all I want to say, and to lay all the reasons before them. It will probably be public also; and the matter is so novel and of such deep public interest that everybody is looking to the proceedings of the committee with great curiosity and interest.

III.

His authority recognized and the discussion with the Committee of Twenty-four begins.—A Sunday evening with two strong friends of public honesty, one a Cumberland, the other a New School, Presbyterian.—His entire reliance is in the moral power of the question.—Bids his desponding friends to be of good courage and go ahead.—Popular interest in the subject throughout Indiana.—Converts the wife of a leading anti-bond Senator.

INDIANAPOLIS, December 18, 1845.

MY DEAR WIFE:

Your letter of the 11th inst. was received last evening, just as I came in from my first meeting with the committee.

The question of authority is yet unsettled. They had a very violent debate and fight over it. I declined entering into any conference with them till they had settled that question, laying before them such credentials as I could, and then I withdrew. The committee decided by a strong vote in favor of my power and adjourned to meet to-morrow evening, when I am to appear and enter on the discussion. This morning the repudiators raised the same question in the Senate and an angry debate was the result. They finally adopted a resolution, by consent of the friends of public credit, calling on the Governor for information. The Governor was present during the discussion and will send in the message to-morrow. This will, I presume, settle their point; but then they will raise others, as fast as possible, in the hope, by reason of the shortness of the session, to bluff off all action.

INDIANAPOLIS, December 21, 1845.

MY DEAR WIFE:

I intended to devote this whole evening to you and our dear children, but two gentlemen came in, who have this moment left me. One of them is a Cumberland Presbyterian, and the other a New School Presbyterian. The first is a plain farmer from the country, but a most lovely Christian. Our conversation took a religious turn and he gave me a history of his conversion in such simple and affecting language that, in connection with the circumstances, it interested me very much. What fine characters we meet with often under the roughest exterior and the plainest manners, and how refining, purifying and elevating is the influence of the blessed Gospel on the man! What a different being it makes of him. This good man has come up on purpose to help me settle the public debt. He says that his people sent him on that business and he pledged himself to them that he would not leave a single stone unturned, to effect it. He is a man of most excellent good sense. The other gentleman is one of the first men in the State and also a lovely Christian; he, too, is here on that business exclusively, and with such aids I feel strong in the Lord. My entire reliance is in the moral power of the question, the force of truth. If God sees fit to make it go, it will go. If not, it will not. There is enough to discourage the stoutest heart, and my friends out doors have been most desponding and unhappy, at the prospect. Strange to say, I have *not* been, but have worked on as though it were certain and have animated them to the conflict, and said to them, "keep cool, be of good courage and go ahead, and we shall come out right in the end." The opposition is boiling over and furious; it is out and out repudiation with many, and politics with others; but I have a sure conviction that if I can only keep the Legislature together long enough, I shall succeed. I feel calm and prepared for any result. I had the first conference with the committee on Friday evening, and addressed them two hours in connection with the proposition which I submitted. I succeeded in making a decided impression; they listened with the deepest interest. The result was better than I anticipated. It is a formidable business, I assure you, to address a body of twenty-four men on so great and grave a subject, and with the eyes of the whole State fixed on us. Our meetings are private. I am allowed a reporter and clerk and shall have every word reported. We meet again to-morrow evening. I expect to occupy about three evenings this week, and about three hours each evening in order to go over *all* the points, and submit all my views. I have been so much absorbed in this business that I have not heard the war rumbling in the East.* I cannot believe

* Referring to the trouble with Great Britain on the Oregon question.

that war will take place. It would be an awful calamity, and may God in his mercy avert it from our land! Oh, what folly, and what an awful responsibility would rest somewhere. Still, I regard the arrogance of Great Britain with distrust, and it may be the only way to check it. She is too ambitious. She must let the American Continent alone. It is the proper soil for free institutions, and such only can, or will, be tolerated.

INDIANAPOLIS, December 22d.
Monday evening.

MY DEAR WIFE:

I closed a second conference with the Joint Committee this evening, having addressed them just two and a half hours. The impression was evidently very favorable. The meeting was held in the Senate chamber and was altogether interesting. The truth is, the subject is a very great one with the people of Indiana, and this proceeding has given to it great prominence. All eyes are now directed to the result of the conference pending between the State and its public creditors, the latter represented by me. The momentous question of the public debt is to be settled, and the foundations laid for the future prosperity and greatness of the State. The theme is a noble one and the occasion extraordinary. Every evening thus far I have made converts in the committee to my views, so that the friends of public credit say they now consider the House safe, and the only difficulty is in the Senate. I do not know how this is, and can hardly credit it. In the committee we have a number of out and out repudiators, violent and unreasonable men, and yet they have listened to me with much respect and attention. One only has abandoned the committee, and does not pretend to come. The other twenty-three are there to a man, and a minute.

TUESDAY AFTERNOON.

We meet again this evening, when I proceed with the argument. To-morrow evening I appropriate especially to the consideration of the bonds which it is proposed to repudiate, amounting to some $3,000,000 or $4,000,000. This brings up the whole subject of repudiation, and is the most important point involved in the discussion. It is profoundly interesting, and I feel oppressed with the weight and burden of it. On the result depends the question whether the State will or will not repudiate. The committee will decide that question, probably. If they decide against me, I shall then protest and ask to be heard at the bar of the House, and if the House decide against me, I shall withdraw the proposals and shake the dust from my feet and go home.

The enemy will rally again. My committee meet again this evening. The Governor helped me this afternoon, by a message to the Senate in reply to a resolution. He and Mr. Bright go in for me strong, head and shoulders, and now I have a strong team, in-doors and out. My room is run down with people constantly, and to-day I have done nothing but see company, and make one call on *two ladies*. One of them is the wife of a leading Senator, whom I have not seen yet, but who is dead against me. His wife I got all right, in an hour's talk devoted exclusively to the subject, and she goes in strong for my plan. I made the call this morning, and this P. M. the Senator gave a vote in my favor. So, you see what a good wife can do in an important affair. This morning he voted against me. You must know that in the Senate they have had me on the coals, for about a week, hot enough. The Legislature will adjourn by the 15th of January. Wishing you all a happy New Year, and commending you to the care of Him whose blessings we have enjoyed for the year, so profusely bestowed upon us, let us enter on another year with a purpose to serve Him more faithfully, and thereby secure our own happiness, both temporal and eternal. Do give my love to all my friends, and the compliments of the season. If for a fortnight you do not hear much from me, do not be uneasy. Next week we enter in the regular battle, and up to the end I shall have my hands full.

IV.

Last conference with the Joint Committee of Twenty-four.—He talked to them for three and a half hours with REPUDIATION *as his theme.—This question raised in regard to over $3,000,000 of the State bonds.—The mode of procedure.—One or more converts to the cause of honesty every evening.—The repudiators wish to stay all actions; but the movement "will go on by its own mighty moral power."—A day of great excitement: he submits a final proposition and his hotel is on fire.—The fire a blessing in disguise.—Electric effect of his ultimatum.*

INDIANAPOLIS, Christmas Eve.
After 10 o'clock.

MY DEAR WIFE:

I have at this moment returned from the fourth and last conference of the Joint Committee. I spoke with entire freedom for a period of three and a half hours, and the committee listened with deep attention and interest during the whole time. The theme was repudiation. That is the question raised distinctly in regard to from three to four millions of dollars of the State bonds. I never satisfied myself better in speaking than I did this evening, and I was gratified to find that my remarks seemed to be received with the most decided favor. The meetings are held in the Senate chamber, and this evening the committee allowed a number of gentlemen to come in to listen to the discussion. The mode of procedure is for the chairman to take the president's chair in the Senate and call the committee to order, the minutes of the last meeting are then read over, the names of the Joint Committee called, and if all appear, then the chairman announces to me the organization of the committee, and their readiness to hear me proceed in my remarks. The committee occupy seats directly in front of me and my address is to them. Last evening I spoke about an hour and a quarter. Thus far, every evening I have made one or more converts to our side, and this evening I was informed by the chairman of the House committee that there was but one man on his committee now wrong, and that one was Mr. Carr, who has been an out and out repudiator. He remarked, when I got through this evening, that he could not have believed that he ever would sit so long and hear a speech, every word of which rasped his feelings. Still, he did it, and evidently was greatly interested. I can hardly credit it, that such a change has taken place in the House committee. A week ago it seemed incredible, nor do I now believe it. My friends were completely down at the heel, and thought the Speaker had given them the worst committee he could possibly have made up. I think it will turn out a good committee yet. There are seven farmers on it, and five lawyers and doctors. The Senate is now the hardest body; they have a set of low blackguards in it, who have, ever since I came here, made a dead set at me, and are constantly raising questions. They want to prevent all action, some from one cause and some from another. They wish to stifle the movement, but it will go on by force of its own intrinsic, mighty moral power, and I yet have hope. It is indeed a missionary enterprise.

DECEMBER 25, 1845, quarter past 11 P. M.

MY DEAR WIFE:

This has been no holiday to me; the Joint Committee met this morning at nine, and again this afternoon at three, and we have been hard at work all day, diplomatically passing notes. What the result will be I do not know. Governor Whitcomb and Mr. Lane, the chairman, spent some time with me this morning. I have yet another proposition to be submitted in the morning, which I hope will be accepted. It is a desperate business all around. Nobody can tell anything about it, or form any correct opinion, who is not familiar with the whole ground. I do not know that anything satisfactory can be done, and if it goes on, the danger is that it will be worse than it now is. My speech last evening did good and made friends, and stirred up enemies, and the two parties are arranging themselves actively for a real cat fight. They get so angry at each other that I have to keep advising them to keep cool. Yesterday P. M. they had a most angry debate in the Senate, and I came in for a full share, one Senator calling me a Wall Street broker, etc.

I was rejoiced last evening to get your letter, with one from my dear Emily enclosed. I was glad to see a letter from her; it made me laugh out loud, I was so happy. She must write me again, and you must give her and dear Ogden and sweet Anna each a New Year's present for me. I shall have nothing but hard work, and hard knocks, and hard times, during the holiday season. It makes me sick to think of it, but I have embarked, and I mean to follow it up to the last thoroughly. I have had a chance to talk plain to the committee anyhow, and they have listened attentively. These Hoosiers are made up from the Carolinas, Kentucky, Tennessee, Virginia, Ohio, Maryland, Pennsylvania and New Jersey, and at the north there is a mixing of New York and New England people. They are the strangest mixture I have ever seen.

FRIDAY EVENING, 10 o'clock.

I could not find time to finish my letter and send it off by the mail this evening, which I regret, as I fear you will not get it by New Year's day. I am so driven night and day that I hardly know how the time runs. This has been a day of great excitement. In the first place, the Joint Committee adjourned over to this evening at six, to receive a final proposition from me,—an ultimatum. At the same time a desperate movement was made in the Senate to *revoke* the powers of the committee. The repudiators, it was feared, would carry the point this afternoon, and my friends were speaking against time, so as to prevent its coming to a vote to-day. Just then, about 3 P. M., while the war was going on hot in the Senate chamber and I was busy in my room at the hotel preparing my ultimatum, an alarm of fire was given on the floor on which my room is—third story. At the other end of the hall a gentleman had gone out, leaving a large fire and it had caught and actually burned through the floor, and dropped down into the room below, which led to its detection by some ladies of the family, who were occupying an adjoining room below. It is a large house and has one hundred and fifty people in it, and the alarm went like fire itself, from room to room through the house, in the street, and up to the Capitol, where it found

Mr. Lane, chairman of the Joint Committee, on the floor, making a beautiful speech on my business. Of course the Senate and House adjourned in a panic, for half of them stay at the Palmer House. I had my papers, books and clothes all strewed about, and was alone. As the prospect was threatening,—indeed, I scarcely doubted that the house would burn up,—it put me in a panic, too, and I out with my trunk and tumbled in my papers first, and then such clothes as were most convenient, all in a heap and a mess, and dragged my trunk down stairs; and then got out the balance of my clothes.

The fire was extinguished, but it made a terrible muss and confusion all the afternoon. It saved my friends, however, in the Senate, and this evening I proceeded to meet the committee in the Senate chamber, and to deliver my ultimatum in person. You can have no conception of the interest felt on the subject; the friends of the canal and the friends of public credit all hanging in the deepest suspense upon the issue. The committee had rejected my proposition yesterday (which I enclose that you may know how the business is done) and now they were apprehensive that nothing would or could be done, and a feeling of despondency and restless gloom was creeping over them. I found a large number of spectators present, to my surprise, expecting to have a secret session with them, and entertaining doubts as to the propriety of submitting my proposition to any except the committee in private,—for its rejection might be injurious, equally to the public credit and the public creditors. I hesitated about going on, for the step I was about to take involved a great personal responsibility. The result I had come to, had not been without inward groans and conflicts, but it was the only chance, and the time had come for a bold step, that would settle it one way or the other—for weal or for woe. I concluded to take no exception to the presence of others, and proceeded in introducing my proposition with remarks which occupied half an hour, and then read and explained it. The effect was electrical; and if I can judge, it really routed the last hold of the enemy. One man, a Senator who has been exceedingly bitter and personal in his opposition, so much so that my friends have christened him with the nick name of "Tallow Face"—said that he could not go against that.

The friends of public credit and the canal are now in ecstacies. I think the blow has been struck that will sweep the opposition and save the great object, to wit, the restoration of credit and payment of the debt. They ordered a large number of copies to be printed and adjourned. Now, I cannot tell whether it will go or not, but it looks promising. I have made great concessions, but they are indispensible. If it were to go over to another session, with the war feeling springing up among the people, and the bond-holders being foreigners, and with the other difficulties operating on it, the debt would be lost. By the proposition I have made, I have no doubt but it will be ultimately paid to the last farthing. The friends of the canal and public credit, on the committee, had not one of them anticipated the proposition I submitted, and it took them by surprise. It met their most sanguine expectations—indeed, they had not dreamed that I would make one so liberal and fair, and they were overwhelmed, whilst the enemy were scattered in every direction. They may rally, however, again, for it is impossible that it should pass in any shape without a great fight. But I think I have placed its friends on the vantage ground. On coming from the committee, I found among my mail a letter from Mr. Palmer, under date of London, 2d December. "Thinks I to myself, now, what if the letter should contain something adverse decidedly to the very movement which I have just made,—it is too late to back out." On reading the letter, however, I found it all right, and judging from its spirit I feel confident that I can rely on being sustained when I come to explain to him my reason. This has been truly a busy and exciting day with me.

SATURDAY EVENING, 27th December.

I add a few words at the close of the day and week. I can scarcely realize that we are so near the end of the year, and that this will reach you not till the year 1846. I am so driven and hurried with important matters that I cannot think. To-day the friends of the canal and the public credit have been in a perfect glee,—as though the question were now settled, Indiana redeemed and the canal finished. They already talk of illuminations, bon-fires and cannon, but I tell them to keep cool, the battle is yet to be fought.

V.

An anxious Sabbath day.—The time short and the work pressing.—The Lord only knows when or how it will end.—The strength of popular feeling in favor of the bill.—An anti-bond paying Senator rebuked by his town and county.—A sermon on the subject by HENRY WARD BEECHER.—*The bill reported to both branches of the Legislature by unanimous consent of the Committee of Twenty-four.—Friendly attitude of the little country papers.*

INDIANAPOLIS, December 28, 1845.

MY DEAR WIFE:

At the close of the last Sabbath in the year! It is now nine o'clock and I am alone in my room. I have been out all day; this morning to Mr. Gurley's, in the afternoon to the Sabbath school, and this evening to Mr. Beecher's. After Sabbath school I went home with Mr. Ray and took tea. He is a cashier of the bank, a very fine man, and has a fine family. The Misses Axtell live with him, and now their brother Charles is also spending a little time with them. All very nice people, and forming quite a Geneva circle, and as they are all associated with my first impressions of Geneva, it was pleasant to go there and get out of the noise and confusion of my hotel, which is a perfect bedlam. I have been under such high pressure, both mental and physical, the last week, that I felt the need of the Sabbath very much. I have just been interrupted by a member, coming to talk about the great business. I fear this day has been devoted to it altogether, by the members of the Legislature. It excites such a deep and thrilling interest, they can't talk or think of anything else. And the time is so short that they say they must keep at it on Sunday. I was amused last Sunday when a Senator came to see and talk with me and I declined talking with him about it, and he remarked that *he* thought "that it was like lifting the ox out of the gutter," and that it was a work of necessity and mercy; and so, in truth, it is. I have thought and felt so myself, and this rough Hoosier is right.

Governor Whitcomb came in this morning and spent an hour with me on the subject, regarding it in its moral aspect. He goes in, heart and soul, for me, and so does Mr. Bright. They are in fine spirits, and it really looks as if Providence designed that it should be settled. Still, I can hardly realize it, and I do know that there must be a terrible fight over it, for the opposition is very violent and active. "The lot is cast into the lap, and the whole disposing thereof is of the Lord." It is with Him, and He only knows how and when it is to end. I do not want to be puffed up about it, for if I am, I shall very likely be disappointed, and so it is best to keep low, lie flat, and wait.

INDIANAPOLIS, January 1, 1846,
Thursday, 10 A. M.

MY DEAR WIFE:

I had just taken up the act to settle the public debt of Indiana, and to finish their great canal, for examination and correction, but laid it aside, to devote the first business moments this morning to you, and our dear children. The day here is anything but a holiday. The Legislature sits, the Joint Committe sits, as on any other day. It was the intention to introduce the report of the committee and the bill accompanying it, into the House to-day, as an auspicious coincidence,—the beginning of the New Year and of a New Era in the history of the State. God has wonderfully blessed me and prospered my labors. Still, I do not count on entire success. The time is too short for so great a work. A wonderful change is coming over the people and public sentiment is rolling in from every quarter in favor of the settlement, on the plan last proposed by me, and the demagogues are getting dreadfully frightened. My letter, I find, meets the feelings of the people. They like it, and it is interesting to read the comments of country papers on it. Mr. Chapman, the Senator who has been so violent and vindictive against me and the object, has been instructed, by an overwhelming meeting of the Democrats in his town and county, to support the bill, and they have rebuked him terribly for his course. I received the paper yesterday containing the proceedings and sent it to Mr. Palmer (England). The editor came out in a very able article dead against him. But I can hardly realize that we have entered on another year. I hope you and our dear children are well and enjoying the social pleasures and gratifications of this day. It is a good custom, that of our city—a noble custom, and worth a great deal—I feel it now and esteem its value. May this year be one of renewed zeal and devotion to the greatest, best and noblest of causes—the service of our Redeemer, to whom we are indebted for all our blessings, both temporal and spiritual. The past year has been one of extraordinary temporal mercies—health and life and every needed blessing—ourselves, our children, and relatives, and friends—*all*—*all* have been preserved and blessed. What a year of mercies it has been.

I am anxious to hear from father and mother. How glad I am that Walter is there to cheer and comfort them, and Walter, I hope, is getting on with his business. I am anxious he should, and say to him that I will help all I can, and if I can settle the debt of Indiana, I shall hope to be able to help him pay his, and help myself, too. But it is a great business, this getting out of debt; and if I had not been very deep in and had a great deal of *hind-cast* in it (as the Dutchman said) I shouldn't have been at all fitted for the work I am engaged in, so that every man is prepared for his calling by his experience. My power here, I find, is in my *personal* experience, which enables me to hit the true chord of every man's heart on that subject. Wish all my friends a Happy New Year for me. Kiss our dear children, and wishing you all a Happy New Year and commending you all to the care of God, I am,

Your affectionate husband,

CHARLES BUTLER.

P.S.—I now close my letter and go to the bill to finish it. The bill and report will come in to-morrow, 2d of January, and then comes the tug of war. The time, I fear, is too short to carry it.

INDIANAPOLIS, January 4, 1846.

I returned an hour since from the evening meeting, and then took a walk for exercise. On my return to my room, Governor Whitcomb came in, and has this moment left, so that I shall write you very briefly to-night. Mr. Beecher preached an admirable sermon, bearing on the great question pending before the Legislature, to a full house containing a large number of members. I was up till twelve last night at work on the bill. It was reported yesterday to both branches of the Legislature by the unanimous consent of the committee. Still, I regard its final success as involved in doubt. The Legislature has passed a resolution to adjourn two weeks from to-morrow, and there does not seem to me to be time enough to get so great a measure through the Legislature. And yet there may be. It is now the absorbing topic with all parties. My only reliance is in the paramount moral obligation involved in the question, and the discreet manner of pressing it. If the moral feeling be only rightly stimulated, the pecuniary relief will soon and cheerfully follow. It is not the mere question of dollars and cents, nor have I ever so regarded it. If I had, I should have failed, utterly, in awakening any interest. My labors have been very great and my anxieties, corresponding to the magnitude of the subject which I have had to grapple with. Thus far, Providence seems to have wonderfully favored me, and the people here cannot comprehend how it is that such a commotion and change have been brought about. They at first seemed to feel that it was useless to talk about it; now they regard it as a most urgent subject and one that may be disposed of notwithstanding the shortness of the session. The intelligence from the country all around is very favorable, as much so as I could possibly expect. My letter has been extensively published by the little country papers with very approbatory remarks. I have not seen one dissenting or complaining criticism on it.

This is the first Sabbath in the year, but I can hardly realize it. I have had no holiday here and nothing to impress on me those reflections which the season ought to inspire. On the contrary, I have been so driven as not to find time to think at all. I feel that I have sustained great loss in this respect, and the absence from home and its dear ones at this time, is an occasion of real grief when I do think at all, for which money cannot compensate. The consciousness of doing good may. And I trust that the latter feeling has been predominant with me since I got fairly embarked in it. Looking around and seeing the great number of persons interested, and the intense solicitude for the success of my mission and their warm hearted encouragment, has changed the whole motive power in my bosom. I feel that I am working to accomplish a great moral object, dear to the hearts and hopes of hundred of thousands, and affecting a great State and its prosperity for all coming time. The object seems to be a great and good one, and my heart is in it, and God seems to regard it with favor, and why should He not? Is it not the cause of the widow, and the fatherless and the needy, thousands of them? I will send you the memorial of the savings bank, which is one of the most beautiful things of the kind I have ever read. It was drawn up by Mr. Daniel Lord at my suggestion and transmitted to the Governor.

VI.

The extraordinary character and pressure of his labors, especially "to keep my temper, the hardest work of all."—Renomination of Governor Whitcomb.—"The war rages hotter and hotter."—A Democratic caucus called by the Governor.—In the House only forty-five certain; must have fifty.—The battle on.—He is charged with selling out the people of Indiana, land and all, to the British bondholders.—The bill passed through the House by a vote of 61 to 33, but will be killed he thinks, in the Senate.—Amended at the last moment; it is ordered in the Senate to a third, by a vote of 31 to 18.—The Governor taken very ill.

INDIANAPOLIS, January 9, 1846.
Friday evening, 11:30.

MY DEAR WIFE:

I am almost fagged out with the excitement and labor of the week, and cannot realize that it is Friday evening. I console myself with the reflection that in a few days more my work will be at an end, as the Legislature will have closed its labors. A week from Monday next they adjourn. My bill will probably come up to-morrow (Saturday). It has been in the hands of a select committee for amendment, and I have just closed my labors with them and agreed to the amendments. I cannot give you any idea of my labors here. They are greater than anything I ever before undertook and more various. I have to talk with and see the members, have to take care of the printers, superintend the press, for I am printing a book on my own hook, attend on committees, keep in with the Whigs and Democrats, counsel and advise both parties, and all parties, and be all things, to all men. Above all, I have to keep my temper, which is the hardest work of all. My friends give me a great deal of trouble about the bill, some of them; they quarrel about the details and kick out of the traces. I have had at least a dozen serious flare ups, among its friends, on one point or another, then I had to go to each one and reason with him or get them all together, and make a speech to them. Sometimes one thing, and sometimes another. Yesterday the Democrats held their convention, and to-day the Whigs.

Well, I have had to manage with the leaders of both to get them to go right on the State debt, and last night I gave up almost in despair at the result of the Democratic convention. They nominated Whitcomb again unanimously and by acclamation, but quarelled about the resolutions and address on the State debt. However, it passed off finally pretty well, and this morning I waked up feeling that, on the whole, it had done good. To-day the Whigs held their convention and nominated, and took decided ground on the State debt, by way of gaining on the Democrats, and to-night Whigs and Democrats feel pretty strong on the subject and things look better. Both parties are pledged to the proposition, and my hope is that now the Legislature will act. Still, the time is short and they are afraid, and I think the only form in which it can be carried will be to agree that the act itself shall be submitted to the people at the next election, to vote on, law or no law. It is now precisely twelve and I go to bed. These conventions have brought into the city a vast number of country people and a great number are in the hotel I am staying at, and have rendered it dreadfully uncomfortable.

Saturday evening, January 10th.

My bill is set down for Monday certain, when the discussion comes on. The war rages hotter and hotter, one day up, the other down. I am pressed to death with engagements and only wonder that I can endure so much. The prospect seems to be more favorable, but I regard the result as altogether uncertain. Indeed, I have very little confidence that the bill will pass, the time is so short and the difficulties so great. One week from Monday the Legislature adjourns. The weather is very fine indeed. The winter has seemed no winter, it has been so moderate for a long time. The roads have been bad but are now hard and smooth. My health keeps good, and I rejoice that in one week more all will be over, as far as this great measure is concerned. My friends are in the highest state of anxiety and excitement and can hardly keep their senses. I have just closed a conference with the Democratic nominee for Lieutenant-Governor, of two hours, and had a similar conference with Governor Whitcomb to-day, of more than two hours, adjusting proceedings. Now I have to go and look after my Whig friends, and see how they stand. I never was quite in such a fix as I am here. The country papers, with one or two exceptions, speak out manfully, and I am encouraged by good men of both parties.

SATURDAY, 10th January, 12 o'clock.

It is now exactly 12 o'clock, and Gov. Whitcomb has this moment left me. He called a private caucus of the Democratic Senators this evening, for the purpose of getting them to agree to go as one man, for the Bill, and took very decided, indeed very earnest and pressing ground, and told them that he was committed for it, that it was a great and honest measure, and one which the Democrats should go for as a party. That he was willing to go to the stump on it, and to peril his political fortunes on the issue, and wanted his friends to take bold and decided ground, and go shoulder to shoulder. That it was a question of simple honesty, and they could not, as honest men, resist it; they must go for it. It had a very happy effect and some of the most stubborn were melted down, and came in at once and agreed to go for it. They finally agreed to have another meeting on Monday evening, and my hope is that nearly all, if not all, the Democratic senators will go in for it. The candidate for Lieut.-Governor is equally anxious, and will attend the meeting on Monday evening and take the same ground. If this movement succeeds, it will insure the passage of the Bill next week. I have been all the evening engaged with the Committee again on amendments, and have now settled all so that on Monday the battle will come off. But I will not count on it. "*Sufficient unto the day is the evil thereof.*" I fear that I am placing too much reliance upon an arm of flesh, and not enough upon an Almighty Arm. I ought to see the hand of God in it all, and labor in dependence on His blessing alone.

SUNDAY EVENING, January 11th.

It is now precisely 12 again, and I have this moment parted from Gov. Whitcomb and Mr. Bright, with whom I have been engaged the last hour. As in Revolutionary times there are no Sabbaths, so it seems to be here in "debt paying" times. I would not have you think that my Sabbath has been spent *in* the business, as this morning I went to Mr. Gurley's, and this evening to Mr. Beecher's, and after meeting went and spent an hour and a half with Mr. Beecher and a friend, very pleasantly. The business is, however, so pressing, and the time is so short, and the object so great that the day has been spent by its friends and its enemies in great activity, I understand. Gov. Whitcomb and Mr. Bright work night and day, day in and day out; the Governor said he could not sleep at all, and as the question may be decided to-morrow and must be next day at the furthest, and the difficulties are so great, that it demands the uttermost exertion from the friends of public credit to carry it, the Governor called a caucus this evening of all the *opposing* Democratic members of the House to confer with them, and see if he could n't get them to agree to support it, and he and Mr. Bright discussed it all the evening. The meeting had a good effect, but they are very stubborn and the result is uncertain. They say it is proper Sunday work, that it is lifting the ox out of the gutter. To-morrow—I might say to-day, for it is now 20 minutes after 12—the question will be taken, probably to decide it. I cannot but admire Gov. Whitcomb's decision and effort—he has taken the only true ground. He is resolved that it shall go, if any effort or influence of his can insure it, and he is a host when he takes hold.

MONDAY EVENING, 7 P. M.

I threw down my pen this morning to go and see the Governor. The day has been a busy one. The Bill was put off till to-morrow *10 o'clock*, and referred back to the Committee, and is now in my hands for amendments. It will certainly come on to-morrow (13th); its fate is doubtful. This evening the Governor has called all his Democratic friends together to a caucus to confer with them again, and its fate will be sealed one way or the other. He and Mr. Bright have just left me to go to the meeting. The Governor seemed completely worn out and complained of indisposition, and I sent out for a bottle of champagne for him, and gave him a glass, which he said tasted good, and revived him. I told him to take the bottle along to the Capitol, which he did. You will laugh at this, I am sure, I could n't help laughing myself. I shall in this campaign lay up a fund to serve me for a life-time. It is the queerest and still the *greatest* business I ever had on hand. It is a regular *set-to*, and calls into exercise the most skillful tactics and diplomacy. I think that the Governor, Mr. Bright and myself make a strong team, still we may not be able to carry it. We can only count on, as yet, forty-five certain in the House; we must have fifty. It is close counting, and of course the result is uncertain. Gov. Whitcomb has taken the most manly and decided course throughout, and more than sustained his pledges to me, and so has Mr. Bright. I have no time to add more.

NOTA BENE. *Keep all my letters from here carefully, as part of my journal and memoranda.*

INDIANAPOLIS, Monday night,
12th January, 1846.

It is now half-past twelve, and Mr. Bright has just come in from the Democratic caucus and reports that they have, by a very large vote, decided on passing the bill, with a proviso to submit it to the people to decide at the August election, whether it shall be a law or not—the people to vote directly for it. This course of the Democrats will ruin the party, and put the bill in jeopardy, and devolves on me a terrible responsibility. The question with me is, am I at liberty to incur so great a risk as the loss of the entire public debt by this course? Ought I not to withdraw my proposal, and thus let the bill fall to the ground? Suppose the people should vote against it; that would forever destroy the hopes of the bond-holders; and as the members of the Legislature distrust the people, ought I not to distrust them? The great objection, that strikes my mind, is that it is impossible for the people in so short a time to make themselves acquainted with the details of the bill, and they will quarrel about the details.

"Through all the various shifting scenes,
Of life's mistaken ill or good,
Thy hand, O God, conducts unseen
The beautiful vicissitude."

Tuesday, 13th, 2 P. M.

The battle commenced this morning at ten, and is now on. Have had six or seven speeches, pro and con. The discussion is on the amendment to submit it to the vote of the people at the August election. I cannot predict the fate of the amendment; I hope it will not prevail. If it does, I may feel constrained to withdraw my proposition altogether. I dare not risk the loss of the whole.

7 P. M.

The battle is closed for to-day; the House has just adjourned. The vote on the amendment was taken and rejected, *49 to 41.* This weakening insures the passage of the bill through the House to-morrow. The debate to-day was very exciting, and some good speeches made on both sides. Some very fine ones on our side, and some very bad ones on the other side. The minority are very much excited, and a violent effort will be made yet to defeat it, on its final vote to-morrow. The time is very short and we may lose it. I had made up my mind to withdraw the proposition if they had added the amendment. I dared not take the responsibility of the risk, involved in the submission,—though it might be small. I have no time to add more, I am too pressed to think. Kiss the children.

This has been a most exciting day, and yet I have been cool. The ememy made a terrible assault on me, as the representative of the British bondholders. One man said the bill sold out the whole people, land and all, to the British. The oldest gentleman in the House, Father Pennington, made a most excellent speech in my defense, and vindicated me from the attacks, in a very manly and gratifying manner. I cannot give you any idea of the events of to-day.

INDIANAPOLIS, January 14, 1846.
7:15 P. M.

MY DEAR WIFE:

After a most desperate battle all day, we closed this evening with a complete victory, 56 to 30. The question taken last evening was reconsidered to-day by a very large vote, and the bill was in great danger, under a furious debate, till 6 P. M. when the vote was taken as above. At 3 P. M. I had to make a further concession, which was thrown in at the very crisis of its fate, and created a terrible commotion. To-morrow, we shall have another fight, and a final one, and then we have to go through the Senate. The Governor and Mr. Bright and several others have just come in and my room is thronged. My friends are in fine spirits, but I do not yet count on success. The vote of last evening was revolutionized so suddenly this morning, as to preclude certainty. I have no time to write. Kiss the dear children.

January 15th.

The bill passed through the House to-day by a vote of 61 to 33, nearly 2 to 1,—after another furious onslaught on me. The bill will be killed in the Senate, in spite of every effort, by the *unreasonable* and absurd notions of some Senators, and the shameful conduct of others.

INDIANAPOLIS, Friday evening, 7 P. M.
16th of January, 1846.

MY DEAR WIFE:

At the close of one of the most exciting and trying days of my life, I am happy to say that the bill was ordered to a third reading in the Senate this evening by a vote of 31 to 18. The debate was most violent and exciting, and the conflict a long time doubtful. I had to yield to some amendments again, which are, to some extent, objectionable, but not fatal. The great question is settled. The bill is now, I think, beyond danger. Will be concurred in by the House to-morrow, and signed by the Governor on Monday, the last day of the session. The Governor, by the way, was taken very sick this morning in my room, and was obliged to go to bed, and has been unable to leave since. He has been removed this evening into an adjoining room, where he lies very ill with a pleuritic attack. I verily believe that his labors and anxieties for this measure have made him sick. I am almost sick myself with a severe cold which has come within the last thirty-six hours, and just during the most trying crisis of my business.

On Wednesday evening, the fight closed in the House, and the bill was ordered to a third reading, and on coming home I found your letter of the 6th, with Ogden's enclosed, and also a good, long letter from Cornelia, giving me the most gratifying news respecting father and mother. I thought that I had too many mercies and favors heaped on me at once. To know that you are all well, and to get letters so frequently is most gratifying, and is a cordial under the most trying burdens. Tell dear Emily that I hope she and dear Anna are both good girls, and that I do want to see them very much. There is a little orphan boy, about four years old, in the house who comes up every day to see me. He is a great favorite and loves me very much. He is a generous little fellow. If he gets any candy or cake he is sure to bring it to me and insist on my sharing it with him. He is a noble hearted, manly little fellow. As for Ogden, he gives me great comfort by his industry and progress. I hope he will keep his *heart* right before his Maker, and be sure to set a strict guard upon his tongue. Kiss the dear children for me.

VII.

The final passage of the bill nearly prevented by a characteristic demagogical pledge and trick of the repudiators: an object lesson in subterranean politics.—Another anti-bond paying trick met and thwarted by a new concession in behalf of the creditors.—The bill signed by Governor Whitcombe while still lying very ill in bed.—Joy at Terre Haute and all over the State at the passage of the bill.—Henry Ward Beecher and Mr. Gurley.

INDIANAPOLIS, 17th of January, 1846.

My labors have been crowned with complete success. The public credit of Indiana is restored and her bond-holders provided for. The progress of the measure, from its inception, has been wonderful and sure, but every step has been contested inch by inch, and every possible measure has been resorted to, to defeat it. The last and most desperate took place on Thursday night, when 11 Senators met and entered into a solemn pledge, in writing, with each other, that if the question was forced on them, on the passage of the bill, they would leave their seats in the Senate and break up a quorum, and so defeat the bill. This pledge was signed by 11, taking in leading men in the Senate, chiefly Whigs. A friend of the bill, an honorable Whig Senator, happened to go into the room where the caucus had been held at a very late hour, and just as it had broken up. Taking his seat by the table, his eye, unwittingly, rested on the paper, which had been signed and incautiously left on the table. He seemed not to notice it, but read it over carefully with the names, and when he retired from the room, immediately committed to paper the substance of the pledge, with the names of the Senators. While he sat near the table, and after he had thus become possessed of the facts, Mr. Holloway (the Senator in whose room it took place) noticed the paper lying there, and slyly put out his hand and turned it over, Mr. Coffin not seeming to notice it. The detection of this conspiracy gave our friends a decided advantage; they kept it strictly to themselves, and when the discussion came on yesterday, they watched the movements of the conspirators closely. The latter interposed every possible obstacle and amendment, and bye and bye one of the leading Senators got up and, in the course of his speech, alluded to the combination which produced a great sensation. He was called upon to give names, the principal parties being the most vociferous. The Senator on the floor said the information had been given to him confidentially by a Senator who was within sound of his voice, and with *his* consent he would give the names. Mr. Coffin immediately arose and promptly cried out, *"I am the boy!"*

Of course, this electrified the Senate and audience, and he then told the story most inimitably and let the cat out of the bag. Such a scene of confusion and excitement followed as was both amusing and distressing. The object of the exposition was to save those Senators who were really honest and knew nothing of the desperate intentions of the party, from being drawn into them, and this effect it had and saved the bill. Every amendment was voted down, and the bill passed by a vote of 31 to 18, and to-day by a larger vote, 32 to 15, and one friend out. Another exciting passage occurred on Thursday afternoon. Mr. Buel, a leading Senator in opposition, offered an amendment, requiring *one-half of all* the bonds to be surrendered and cancelled before the act should take effect. This amendment I was unwilling to assent to as it came from the extreme left, that is from the ultra-opponents of the bill, and the object was, of course, to defeat it. This amendment was offered to the Senate bill, which they had under discussion when the House bill was reported. This last bill was then agreed to be taken up yesterday morning, and when it came up Mr. Buel offered what was stated and supposed to be the *same* amendment, (it was not read) to the House bill. The discussion on it was very warm, and I had, at the instance of Mr. Bright, told Mr. Lane that he might agree to the proposition of Mr. Buel, especially as it appeared that it would satisfy nearly half the Senate and disarm opposition. Mr. Lane had just risen to speak, as I had whispered it to him, and he announced it. It was received with a shout of applause and stamping and clapping of hands, by the whole Senate, as a compromise.

The reading of Buel's amendment was then called for and behold, on hearing it, I instantly said that it required not half, but that *every single bond* should be surrendered before the act should take effect. It was so artfully drawn that a superficial reading of it left the impression that only half was required. This led to another scene of excitement, and when Coffin exposed the caucus intrigue the history of this amendment was unravelled. The enemies of the bill had all rallied, on Buel's amendment, Thursday afternoon, and every one of them said, "If you will only adopt that, we will go for the bill," and when I finally assented on Friday forenoon, it was to catch all and take them at their word. They found, it seemed, that the amendment offered on Thursday afternoon did not go far enough to defeat the bill, and the amendment offered yesterday was shaped accordingly. It was handed to the clerk and not read, with a remark that it was the same as had been previously offered. The explanation helped us, and put the parties to shame. The Senators who were in the secret, when Mr. Lane agreed to adopt the substitute, were elated and shouted because they thought they had trapped us, while the other part of the Senate were elated because they received it as a *compromise* and would secure harmony in the passage of the bill. The error was corrected by a Senator, offering the very amendment which had been first proposed, and to which I supposed I had agreed, and then these men (the leaders) all turned around and hotly opposed it! It rendered them so ridiculous that they lost their strength, and though they fought desperately to the last they were completely foiled. There are a great many incidents connected with the progress of the bill, equally exciting at the time, but it is impossible to give any idea of them on paper. I rejoice that it is over. Since I commenced writing a friend has come in to inform me that the amendments have been concurred in by the House with only two dissenting votes. Everybody is now friendly to the bill. On Monday the Governor (who, by the way, is very unwell and in bed yet) will put his signature to it, and that will be the last act in the business, and my mission will be closed. I cannot say yet when I shall be able to leave. I have a great deal to do. Love to all and kisses for the children.

INDIANAPOLIS, 19th of January, 1846.

MY DEAR WIFE:

I am happy to say to you that the bill to redeem the credit of Indiana and finish her great canal, has this day received the signature of the Governor. He signed it in bed in my presence, saying that it was one of the most gratifying acts of his life. He is yet very sick and confined to his bed, not being able to be removed to his own house. The necessary tax bill, and all other needful bills to give effect to the measure, have also passed. Thus my mission is accomplished, and God has smiled on me and on all my endeavors. It has been the more remarkable because, as you will see from my letters, I never counted a day ahead on anything certain. Every day found and left me uncertain as to the probable issue. I am sure now that the bill is passed, though it seems like a dream. The friends of public credit are overjoyed. They are now taking leave of me. I assure you that I have become so attached to some of these people, who have stood by me through thick and thin, that I feel sorry to part with them. I feel as if with them I have gone through a protracted scene of trial and conflict. Adversity sweetens friendship and binds the tie more closely. I shall never forget them and I am sure they will not me, and if I should want to leave for the West I should now find warm hearts and honest hands to give me a welcome in Indiana. The people are warm hearted and hospitable.

I cannot say yet when I shall leave. I am suffering from severe cold and sore throat, and shall give myself up to rest for a few days after the Legislature adjourns. They hold on to-morrow in consequence of the Governor's sickness, and then we shall be quiet enough. I have a great deal to do to make up my report to the bondholders, which I must do, before I leave.

INDIANAPOLIS, January 22, 1846.

The Governor is convalescent. I rode out with him this P. M. By next week I hope that both of us will be well enough to finish up our business. I cannot yet say when I will leave. I have a great deal of hard labor yet to perform, to prepare my report to my constituents. The feeling about the bill is excellent. On receiving the intelligence of its passage at Terre Haute, about eleven o'clock at night, its friends fired cannon and illuminated, and the people came together and they had a jubilee. Such will be the feeling throughout the State; at the same time, there will be a desperate effort made to raise opposition to the bill. The politicians are pondering what they shall do, especially the Whigs.

I have received a very complimentary letter, signed by the leading members of the Legislature, and leading citizens of Indianapolis, to which I shall reply next week. Tomorrow will be my last day to write for the steamer of first of February. I have kept up a very thorough correspondence with Mr. King, having written him every day during the whole session, and it has been no small job, I assure you.

I have had an excellent assistant in Mr. Dodge, of Terre Haute, a most estimable gentleman, who has been my secretary, and is yet with me. His wife scolds a little at my keeping him so long, but she is reconciled to it, as she thinks he is engaged in a good work. Give my love to all. Kiss the dear children.

INDIANAPOLIS, Feb'y 7, 1846.

Colonel Blake and the Governor are the only boys left to keep me company. Everybody here is a *boy*. A member of the Legislature in speaking of it will say "the boys." The Colonel is an old widower "boy" of 55, and the Governor a bachelor "boy" of 48.

SUNDAY EVENING, Feb'y 8.

This morning I heard Mr. Beecher on Luke 12 : 47: *And that servant which knew his Lord's will and prepared not himself, neither did according to His will, shall be beaten with many stripes.* The subject was the nature and effect of mere neglect upon moral character, and it was a very pungent, solemn discourse. He is an extraordinary young man, highly gifted as to talents, a remarkably fine speaker—eloquent, indeed—a wonderful knowledge of human nature and a *tact*, if I may so speak, of exhibiting it, which carries you along irresistibly with him. He is an able reasoner, too. Old Dr. Beecher more than lives in this son again. He seems deeply exercised in his work and his feelings are very tender. Often his face is suffused with tears in prayer and in preaching with the weight and pressure of his subject. He touches the deepest chord of the human heart and wakes you up powerfully. He is deservedly popular and draws full houses. Mr. Gurley, from whose prayer-meeting I have just come in, is also a most solemn preacher; always without notes, but always methodical and logical. He, too, is a fine young man. He is of the Old School. Mr. Beecher is of the New School. I love them both and there is a kind, Christian feeling among them. They work together and so do all the churches here.*

CINCINNATI, Sunday Evening, February 22, 1846.

I thought that in this business I was doing good and promoting the welfare of a State and its hundreds of thousands of people and of generations yet to come. The influence of my operations is not limited to Indiana itself, but will tell on the destiny of other States and the country at large. The measure is not yet sufficiently estimated, nor, indeed, can it be. A few years will develop its fruits and effects more strikingly, and it will be regarded with admiration.

* The Rev. HENRY WARD BEECHER was settled at Indianapolis as pastor of the New School Presbyterian Church in 1839. He was then twenty-six years old. In 1847 he was installed as pastor of the Plymouth Congregational Church in Brooklyn, N. Y., where his name and influence soon became world-wide.

The Rev. PHINEAS DENSMORE GURLEY, D.D., was a native of Hamilton, N. Y. His father was a Quaker, though descended from Scotch Covenanters; his mother was a Methodist and he seemed to combine as an Old School Presbyterian, the best qualities of all three. On the recommendation of "Old Dr. Alexander," of Princeton, he was called to the First Presbyterian Church in Indianapolis, being then in his twenty-fourth year. In 1854 he accepted a call to Washington, where he labored with great success for many years. Mr. Lincoln was one of his warmest friends and admirers. No better or truer man could be found in the Presbyterian ministry of his day. He died in 1868.

IV.

MY EARLIEST ACQUAINTANCE WITH MR. BUTLER.—HIS INFLUENCE IN PROCURING THE FIRST ENDOWMENT OF UNION SEMINARY. WHAT HE WAS TO THAT INSTITUTION AND TO THE UNIVERSITY OF THE CITY OF NEW YORK.—EXTRACTS FROM DR. VINCENT'S MEMORIAL ADDRESS.—DEATH OF HIS SON OGDEN.

Mr. Butler's work at Detroit and Indianapolis attracted wide attention and at once marked him out as a man of extraordinary wisdom and force of character. This cannot, perhaps, be more clearly shown than by referring to a meeting of the council, faculties and friends of the University of the city of New York, held on the evening of December 13, 1886, to commemorate Mr. Butler's fifty years of service to the institution. Mr. John E. Parsons, the eminent lawyer, delivered an address on behalf of the council and faculties. In this address Mr. Parsons thus alluded to Mr. Butler's legal course:

As a lawyer you reached distinction among your compeers at a period from which there is scarcely a survivor in active life; you had the holders of the public debt of sovereign States for your clients, and gained early renown in the settlement of legal and financial questions by which, as the result of your ability, the rapid progress of those States was promoted. In the development of the great West, from highways and waterways to railways, you have had a conspicuous part, and your statesmanship gave you great power in your constant purpose for the welfare of the University. . . . An occasion like this is rare in human history, still more unmatched for the promise your unbroken energy gives us that you will continue to be wise in counsels, and foremost among us in efforts.

Soon after Mr. Butler's settlement in New York another chapter in his remarkable career opened before him—the chapter which records his invaluable services to the cause of the higher education. These services were rendered mainly in helping to found and build up two great institutions of Christian culture and learning, viz.: the University of the City of New York and Union Theological Seminary. It was in connection with the latter institution that my own intimate acquaintance with Mr. Butler may almost be said to have begun. I first met him in the spring of 1851, on my becoming pastor of the Mercer street Presbyterian church, of which he was then a ruling elder. In October of that year I made an appeal to my people for the immediate endowment of the Union Theological Seminary. Mr. Butler seconded my appeal with all his soul and strength. Early in 1852 he gave in furtherance of this object a reception at his house in 14th Street. Many of New York's foremost citizens—men of national reputation—were present on the occasion. At this meeting—largely through Mr. Butler's quiet but potent influence—it was resolved that an effort should at once be made to raise $100,000 for the endowment of the seminary. Speedy success crowned the effort. This was the beginning of the long succession of special efforts and benefactions by which the institution has attained its present high position; and at every step of the progress Mr. Butler's devotion only grew stronger and more helpful. A few extracts from the address at his funeral by the Rev. Marvin R. Vincent, D.D., one of his old pastors, will show how abundant and faithful were his labors along not only this but many other lines of humane and Christian activity:

It has been truthfully said of Mr. Butler that a prophetic instinct dominated all his acts, and that each act was so conceived and so fulfilled as to insure increasing usefulness with the increasing lapse of years. This was manifest in that work by which he is best known and by which he will continue longest to be known—the promotion of liberal education. It was not only that he desired to see literary institutions established to meet immediate needs; it was also that he was anxious to see these inaugurated on lines which would admit of their expansion and ready adaptation to future and larger needs. Work of this character has an eternal quality which is wanting to material achievement. The gray old obelisk looks down on the throngs in Central Park to-day, as it looked down on the Egypt of the Pharaohs and of Moses; yet in all the centuries in which it has been toilsomely transported from city to city, it remains only a stone, a huge, unproductive bulk, while the words and the story of Moses whose burial place no man knoweth, have wrought themselves as living forces into the life of generations. By his labors, his counsels and his gifts in the cause of education Mr. Butler has set in motion influences which are wrought into the society, the ideals, the morals and the culture of this city and of this and other lands, and which are asserting themselves with ever-growing emphasis. These influences are deep-lying, silent, unrecognized by the general public, but they are none the less real and potent.

He was one of the earliest patrons of the New York University, and became a member of its council six years after its organization. He completed the fiftieth year of his service in the council in December, 1886, and was its president to the day of his death. During all those years, by the example of his character, by his wisdom and energy, and by his generous gift he helped to prepare the way for that new and larger career upon which the institution has entered, the beginnings of which he lived to witness and rejoice in.

He was one of the founders of Union Theological Seminary and was a member of the first Board of Directors, a position which he continued to hold for the remainder of his life. At the time of his death he had been the president of the Board for twenty-seven years. I think that no interest lay nearer to his heart than that of Union Seminary. It was not only that he deeply felt the necessity of such an institution, and thoroughly believed in the principles for which it stood, but he had for it the affection which one acquires for an object which he has helped to carry through and struggle for. Through the first thirteen years of its history, when its very existence was threatened by commercial panic, when its treasury was empty, when its building and library were mortgaged, and its instructors unpaid, he was its steadfast friend and benefactor, never relaxing his efforts to free it from its embarrassments and to place it upon a permanent basis. And after the peril was over, and the success and prosperity apparently assured through the baptism of fire which followed, he never flinched, never lent an ear to half-way measures, never forsook the men whose reputation and position were at stake, never dreamt of surrender, and never lost faith in the coming of that brighter morrow whose dawn lent its lustre and its joy to his last days. Notwithstanding his advanced age he continued to preside at the meetings of the board until less than two years ago. He was always present at the annual alumni meetings, and until the seminary commencement in May last, he regularly appeared at the graduation exercises, and presented their diplomas to the class, with either a formal address to the entire body or a few appropriate words to each graduate. For years it has been his custom to give a reception to the senior class at his house, on some evening shortly before their graduation, and to add to his elegant hospitality words of ripe wisdom and fatherly counsel.

The reach and the fruit of work such as he has done through these two institutions, it is not possible to compute. It is not too much to say that if he had accomplished nothing else, he would have richly served his day and generation. When one thinks of the graduates of the University during nearly seventy years,—of two full generations which have struck out from that centre upon so many and such widely diverging lines, and are represented in numerous positions of honor and influence,—when one thinks of the hundreds of men whom, in a period of sixty-one years, Union Seminary has sent into pulpits from Maine to California, and from Canada to the Gulf,—into teachers' chairs in colleges and theological schools and academies, into mission fields in Asia, Africa and America,—when one tries in vain to reckon the rate at which their work multiplies itself in the interest of religion and morals, of learning and culture, of social order and social betterment—one may well thank God for a man whom He has inspired and empowered to open the fountain-heads of these streams, and count the man himself blessed in having been the agent of such fruitful ministries.

These are not all. It would be pleasant to speak of his ministrations to the orphan, the friendless child, and to the tiller of the soil; but there is not time for these. We give the honor of these ministries of his where it is due; and that is not to mere natural kindness and generosity.

Conceding the most that can be claimed for his possession of these as natural traits, the natural traits were elevated, widened, intensified and guided by the spirit of that gospel in the faith of which he lived and died. What he was to other secular institutions, in his interest, and activity, and efficiency, he was to the church. He was, if I am not mistaken, one of the original members of that congregation so notable in New York Presbyterianism, the congregation of the old Mercer street Presbyterian Church, and he and his family were among those who, in 1862, organized the Church of the Covenant. His means, his counsel, his labors were freely given to the church. He was an efficient church officer, an attentive, reverent and appreciative hearer, an affectionate and faithful friend to his pastors. The general tone of his religious life was quiet and equable. His faith was simple, and he had little interest in theological subtleties. He was sorely chastened in the school of affliction, but he accepted the trials without murmuring, and appropriated and bore them like a man of faith.

He was remarkable for his love of life. He lived in readiness for death, which came very near him more than once, but he had no desire to die, even at his great age. He rejoiced in living almost up to the very last, and to a degree which one rarely sees equalled he kept himself in touch with the world and with the current of events.

He had a pride in appearing at his post in the different offices which he held; many of us have seen him in his official chair when most other men with his years and weakness would have been in their beds. He delighted in the society of his friends, and in dispensing the hospitalities of his pleasant homes in the city and at Fox Meadow.

He was fond of books and of works of art, and numbered among his friends and guests some of the most eminent literary men of England. He was always the finished gentleman, not of mere polish of manner, but in the shining of a genuine kindliness through his peaceful dignity, and his fine courtesy was noticeable even in his intercourse with children. Yet with all his suavity and peace and real heartiness, he was positive in conviction, definite in opinion and tenacious of purpose, and a determined antagonist when his convictions were assailed.

One of the sore chastenings in the school of affliction, to which Professor Vincent alludes, was the death of Ogden, his only son. Ogden was a graduate of the University, very dear to his father, and full of promise. Chiefly for his sake the splendid domain of Fox Meadow had been purchased; and some of its earliest improvements were planned and started by him. How well I recall the June morning in 1856, when, in company with his uncle Franklin, I went out to Fox Meadow on a pastoral visit to this fine young man, then on his death bed. Shortly after I tried to comfort the stricken parents and sisters as he lay upon his bier in the old city home on Fourteenth street. It was a very touching and impressive scene; for in the large company of mourning friends were William C. Bryant, Samuel J. Tilden and a score more of the most eminent citizens of New York. Even from beyond the sea came tender messages of sympathy. Here is one sent by THOMAS CARLYLE:

Alas, I can too well understand what a blank of utter sorrow and desolation that sad loss must have left in your household, and in the heart of everybody there. Your one son, and such a son, cut off in the flower of his days; so many high hopes for himself and others, suddenly abolished forever! It is hard for flesh and blood—and yet it must be borne; there is no relief from this; and all wisdom of all ages bids us say, "good is the will of the Lord," though that is hard to do.

You do well not to slacken in your labors: to keep doing so long as the day is, the duty of the day. I know no other remedy so sure of ultimately helping in all sorrow whatsoever. Let us work while it is called to-day. In a very little while we too shall follow into the silent kingdom the loved ones that have already gone; and one divine eternity will hold us all again, as God may have appointed for them and for us. I will say no more on this sad subject; upon which you feel at present all speech to be mostly only idle.

V.

LETTERS FROM MR. FROUDE, GOLDWIN SMITH AND THOMAS CARLYLE.

Mr. Butler went abroad repeatedly, both on business and for recreation and pleasure. These visits to the old world brought him into close acquaintance not only with some of the most eminent European financiers and capitalists but also with leaders in society and literature in London and on the continent. His acquaintance with Mr. Carlyle in particular ripened into a beautiful and lasting friendship. Their correspondence with each other, while relating to business, related also to higher interests and was full of expressions of mutual esteem and affection. Mr. Butler corresponded also with other noted men of letters abroad, who had enjoyed his hospitality while visiting this country. No one crossed his threshold without a restful feeling. His hospitality, indeed, was almost unique in its heartiness and good cheer. Froude, Goldwin Smith, Charles Kingsley, Matthew Arnold, Hon. Lyulph Stanley, Mr. Olyphant, the traveler, Prof. Bruce of Scotland, and I know not how many others all joined in praising it. In their letters to him his hospitality is constantly referred to. Some of these letters are very interesting and reflect a bright light upon his own character. A good test, indeed, of a man's quality is, often-times, the sort of letters written to him by his friends. Certainly, this was the case with Mr. Butler. A number of letters from Mr. Froude have been preserved. I will give some passages, expressive of his political sentiments and of his regard for the American friend whom he esteemed above all others. Here is the larger portion of a letter dated No. 5 Onslow Gardens, January 1, 1892:

My dear Mr. Butler:

This is the first letter which I write in the new year, and I write it with peculiar pleasure to an old and honored friend; first to thank you for the pamphlets which you have so kindly sent me, and then to wish you continued peace and happiness in this fresh period on which we are entering.

As to the pamphlets, I read them without the enthusiasm which I should once perhaps have felt. The discussions are the inevitable consequences of the eagerness of our forefathers to make truth truer than it is, but I have lived long enough to see with sadness how men rush along a new course, imagining they can fix the limit to which they will advance. The disintegration of an old established belief is always demoralizing. Religious problems are insoluble to the reason. The questions raised have no bottom either for logic or speculation, and those generations are happiest which inherit as a basis for morality a system of belief, like a system of laws which the opinion of mankind forbids them to take to pieces. Such systems no doubt will carry traces in them of the imperfect knowledge of the age in which they live. But a conviction of any kind which requires and encourages morality and submission to our Maker is so infinitely precious in itself, so hard to replace when broken up, that wise men will bear with small defects sooner than allow it to be disturbed. In the sixteenth century Catholic Christianity had become so corrupt and deformed that the reformation became an absolute necessity. It cannot be said that the belief in the infallibility of the Bible was doing similar harm, even if it is a pious mistake. I know that I am stumbling over the root of a tree that I helped to plant; but many things are clear to me now which I could not see forty-five years ago. The severe piety of the early Protestants could sweep away the faults and preserve the more tenaciously the essential principles of religion. But the temper no longer exists. Those who quarrel with such points in the Bible go on to larger, and they or their followers will continue till they reject its authority altogether. The hardy and consistent go on to Atheism. The timid fall back on the Roman Church. We have probably centuries of spiritual anarchy before us before any fresh and really pious conviction can grow up again.

You Americans are young and confident; you are not burdened with sentimental traditions. You are starting fresh and may meet a new era, but the character of it I expect will be something very unlike what broad churchmen affect to anticipate. I croak like an old man. You are an old man too, and will understand me if you do not sympathize. Anyway, these discussions are forced upon us and will not now be checked till the natural issue is worked out. It had to be and now it is come. You and I at any rate will soon be out of it.

Here in England; and indeed in all Europe, the year closes with universal uncertainty. The Great Powers are armed to the teeth and any accident may set free the electricity. Our own general election will be postponed if the government can manage it, till July, but it may easily be forced on by impatience and restlessness. There are many cross currents under the surface. I conclude myself that Gladstone will return to office, and will try to carry his Home Rule. Beyond that no one can venture a prediction. The majority in England will still perhaps be against him. It will be awkward and perhaps dangerous if England is to be outvoted by Wales, Ireland and Scotland. The Peers will resist, and who will prophesy what then may follow! . . . Prolonged life has many alleviations which when young we did not anticipate. I should find it tolerable and even pleasant but for the inseparable condition of the loss of our friends. Most of my own old companions have now disappeared. The club is full of new faces which I do not recognize. One forms fresh acquaintances, but cannot form new friendships; even one's own family shrink; some dead, some married. But the foolish anxieties and foolish ambitions are gone also; and the future (in this world) draws into so small a space that one ceases to worry oneself. Time has nothing more to give. There is not much which it can take away; and thus there is a degree of tranquility not possible in earlier years.

My Canada fellow subjects are anxious that I should go out next summer and pay them a visit. If I do go, not the least of the temptations will be the charm of seeing you once more.

The "pamphlets" sent to him by Mr. Butler related, no doubt, to the fierce controversy about revision of the Westminster symbols and the Higher Criticism, which was then in full blast. On January 13, he wrote:

A few days ago I inflicted an unwarrantably long letter on you in acknowledgment of those theological tracts. We are worried here by the same controversies, which steal into our houses and disturb the peace. . . . You say nothing of your own condition, but your firm and vigorous hand writing seems to show that age is dealing gently with you. May a life so useful as yours be long continued. For myself I wish only to last as long as I can work. When I can do no more I shall hope for my promotion. To the change, whatever it may be, I can look with increasing equanimity. Yours ever gratefully and truly,

J. A. FROUDE.

Here is another characteristic letter, dated December 7, 1892:

MY DEAR MR. BUTLER:

When the cask of apples arrived yesterday from America it set me speculating which of my kind friends thus had been so kindly thinking of me. Your letter tells me that I owe it to the one among them all by whom it is most gratifying to me to be remembered. There is a protracted enjoyment of such a gift as this which makes the giver continually present. All this pleasant Christmas season we shall have you constantly before our minds here. But indeed to me the valuable part of such things is the sense that I am not forgotten by those whose good opinion is precious to me. Let me add to this, that I, as a Devonshire born and bred, profess to be a judge of apples and find these particularly excellent.

There is much that is interesting in what is going on on both sides of the Atlantic. You have had your Presidential election and we have our eternal Irish scandal. We could extinguish it all with a stamp of the foot, and I suppose in the end it will come to that. But our own record is not clear. We are ashamed of our past neglect; we are not at all sure that we should do any better if we had it all in our hands again to do as we pleased. We are paralyzed by party government. Whatever one side proposes the other opposes; and so we go on, and shall go on, making ourselves a laughing stock to Europe, and forfeiting influence we ought to be exercising, till the situation becomes unbearable.

My two short books about the colonies, "Oceana," and "The Bow of Ulysses," have been a good deal read, and perhaps have had some influence. But as far as our West

Indies are concerned, I should be heartily glad to hear that there was a likelihood of your taking charge of them. For I see no other hope of their escaping a relapse into barbarism. When I plead with Cabinet ministers to give them an effective government they tell me that it is impossible in the immediate neighborhood of the United States. Americans will insist on their having her Constitution under which the black multitude must rule. In vain I say that there are probably not a dozen Americans alive who care the toss of a sixpence about it, and that those who do care wish only to see the islands well and wisely managed. It is all in vain. Their only chance lies in your taking them and you are too prudent to do anything of the sort.

I hope I may see you again in this world, my dear Mr. Butler. You will hardly cross the Atlantic again yourself; but I always feel so much refreshed by a stay in New York (unless I catch cold as I did the last time) that I think I shall run over myself when I can find leisure. I trust it may be so, and when I do I shall find you well and strong, and enjoying the well-earned rest of the seventh day of your life. Till then believe me,

Warmly and gratefully yours,

J. A. FROUDE.

Here are some sentences from his last letter:

Constitutional Government in England itself is at stake. When the mass of our people are made to see that the Liberal policy means disintegration of the Empire, there will be a wild and final, and probably uncontrollable reaction. The Conservatives are no wiser than their antagonists. Carlyle alone in my opinion really understood the signs of the present times.

You will be sorry to hear that my dear friend John Ruskin is very ill. He is a man of true genius, the most *gifted* perhaps of all his contemporaries. He started in life an only son, heir of a large fortune with splendid talents. At twenty-five he had made a European reputation. His life has been spotlessly pure. He has been generous to excess, nobly disinterested in thought and action. Yet few men have been more unhappy. His home has been desolate. He has instructed and delighted millions; and his own portion has been dust and ashes.

But I must not end in this melancholy tone. The sunlight will come around again, and the good seed which has been sown will then spring up and make itself seen. If it is dark here, there is light yonder in the American *Goshen.* May you live long and enjoy it.

Another of Mr. Butler's English friends and correspondents, held by him in the highest esteem, still survives; and yet I cannot help giving here part of a letter, in which he expressed his feeling about our Civil War and the issues and interests involved in it. I refer to one of the very few eminent Englishmen, who were strong champions of the Union in that awful struggle, GOLDWIN SMITH. The letter is dated OXFORD, April 23, 1865:

I need hardly tell you with what joy the tidings of these days have filled the hearts of all friends of the Union and of Freedom here. I thank God for this great deliverance of humanity, the greatest since the defeat of the Armada. At last, after four years of agony, it is decided that the hopes of man shall not die but live.

And now, the Civil War is over, and American blood will be shed by American hands no more. I should often have been a weak counsellor, if it had been my part to say whether the carnage, the suffering and the mourning shall go on. May the wounds of your nation be quickly and completely healed; may it now enter into a solid and enduring peace; may its sacrifices be repaid tenfold by the prosperity of the opening future—a prosperity pure and clear, untainted by complicity with evil, darkened by no shadow of impending retribution.

That you will be merciful and more than merciful to the vanquished—that conquest will be swallowed up in reconciliation—that your free institutions will be justified before the world not only by their military but by their moral results.—I know not only from the language of your people, which I am sure came from their hearts, but from their treatment of the captured enemies whom I saw in their hands. Your rulers in the midst of triumph, speak of peace and moderation; and their words shake the old stronghold of Feudalism here more than the thunder of victory.

Already England begins to feel the effect of your success. Already the Liberal party, half dead three years ago, feels the current of a new life in its veins. We, as well as you, shall date a new era from Gettysburg. It is the most glorious and beneficent victory ever gained in war. Only let us nor forget, while we thank Divine Goodness for it that the most glorious and beneficent victories of all have been won not in that but in peace. A long train of such victories, I trust, awaits your nation now.

Mr. Butler's correspondence with Carlyle in particular is altogether charming. It were not easy to decide which of the two it presents in the most attractive light, the sage of Chelsea or the New York man of business. Mr. Carlyle's letters are very characteristic of him in some of his strong and finest points. I cannot resist the temptation to add to the interest of this sketch by making a few of them a part of it. The allusions to money matters tell their own story and need no comment.

5 CHEYNE ROW, CHELSEA, LONDON,
January 17, 1854.

MY DEAR SIR:

Your very obliging letter came in due course of post, but except a silent record of thanks for your goodness, I was not at that time able to do anything with it. I had been called into Scotland; my dear and excellent old mother was passing away from me by the road we have all to go:—that unforgetable event took place on Christmas day; and ever since, there as here, I have been occupied as you may fancy. It was not till yesterday that I could get a proper copy of the Illinois bond; and to-day I hasten to send you the original, that you may dispose of it for me, according to your kind purposes, in the way you judge most advantageous.

The copy, so far as I can examine, is exact to the original now sent: Bond for $1,000. State of Illinois, No. 324 with thirty-warrants of interest of $30 each, attached to it, the first dated July, 1843, the last, July, 1860, by means of which, I suppose, the original could be replaced, should any accident happen to it.

As to management of the affair, I have only to say that the money is not at all wanted here at present; and that I will leave the matter wholly to your *skill* and friendliness, well aware that there can be no course nearly so good for me and it. Had I once got notice from you that the bond has arrived safe, I shall dismiss *it* from the list of my anxieties, and wait with very great composure indeed for what issue you will educe from it. So enough on that subject.

Miss B has gone away from us—soon after you went—to St. Albans, the great Chancellor Bacon's place: there we suppose her to be elaborating the Shakspeare discovery! but have heard almost nothing since, and have seen absolutely nothing. The painter whom my wife spoke of has at length, I believe, actually got to sea, and will probably be in New York the week before this arrives: he has a note to Miss Lynch and you from my wife; and as he is both a really superior artist, and a very honest, modest, kindly and interesting man, we doubt not you will be good to him as opportunity offers. A lively remembrance of that pleasant evening survives here, too; it is not always that one falls in with human figures of that kind either from our side of the water or from yours! I beg many kind and respectful regards to Miss Lynch, whom I shall long remember.

And so adieu for this time,

Yours sincerely,
T. CARLYLE.

CHELSEA, LONDON, 3rd March, 1854.

MY DEAR SIR:

A week ago I received your kind and pleasant letter, intimating to me, among other welcome things, that you had received the Illinois Bond safe, and would, as your beneficent purpose had been, take charge of it in due business form, which is all right and a real favor done me; which in fact, as it were, absolves my lazy mind from any farther thought or trouble about that matter; there being evidently nothing half so good I could have done with it, and therefore in the meanwhile, nothing further whatever that I *have* to do with it. With many sincere thanks, let it so stand therefore! I have only to add that the 3 coupons you inquire about are quite gone beyond my reach or inquiry. I suppose them to have been given off for 3 installments of interest, which were, (as I can remember) paid to me in regular succession, long years ago, when a worthy friend, a merchant in the city, now deceased, had charge of the Bond for me; if that was not their fate, I cannot form a guess about it; but in any case, they are to be held, these 3 coupons, as extinct for us, and finally gone. And this is now all I have to say upon the Illinois Bond. Requesting you only not to bother yourself with it, beyond what comes quite in your way in the current of far wider operations, I will leave that rather memorable Document now at length well lodged in your repositories, and dismiss it again quite into the background of my own rememberances.

We are struck with a glad surprise to hear you have been so supremely hospitable to our voyaging painter. To snatch him, the thin-skinned, sea-worn man, from the horrors of a stranger hotel or boarding-house, and bid him come and rest in safety, under soft covers and protection, in the house of a human friend; this is indeed a high and fine procedure; but it is far beyond what is demanded or expected in these later unheroic ages! I can only say we find a beautiful "politeness of the old school" in all this, and in the way all this is spoken of and done; and do very much thank Miss Lynch and yourself for all your kindnesses; and shall (if we be wise) silently regard the existence of such a temper of mind, thousands of miles away from us, as a real possession in this world.

Miss B. sends no sign whatever from St. Albans; we suppose her to be, day and night, strenuously wrestling down in her own peculiar way, that monstrous problem she has got; poor lady, I really wish I heard of her safe home again, and well out of it, on any terms. Your Minister here has done a notable thing the other day: entertained, or rather been partner while the Consul entertained,) the 6 or 5 select pearls of European Revolutionism, Kossuth, Ledru-Rollin, Mazzini, Garibaldi, etc., I do believe the most condensed Elixir of modern Anarchy that could have well been got together round any earthly dinner table, which has caused a preceptible degree of laughter, commentary and censure in certain circles; now pretty much fallen silent again. Undoubtedly a diplomatic mistake (in a small way) on the part of Mr. B.; which, however, it is expected he will amply redeem by and by.

Adieu my dear sir; with many kind regards, from both of us, to both of you, I remain,

Yours always truly,

T. CARLYLE.

CHELSEA, LONDON, May 28, 1854.

MY DEAR SIR:

It must be at once admitted, and ought to be always gratefully remembered, you have stood a real father to that poor down-broken bond; and have set it up triumphantly, with victorious kindness, on such a footing as it never had before! I think (so far as vague recollection serves), it bears now almost the value, and yields about twice the interest that was originally attached to it, which is a result valuable to me, in more ways than one. The money is worth something in this ever-hungry world; and as to the transaction which the money now comes from, that is one with a value in it higher, probably, than any money. I may long recollect that pleasant brief evening, and the chivalrous procedure that has arisen out of it.

By all means, leave the document where it is, if you will still be so kind as to trouble yourself with the keeping of it. If you continue to think the investment safe, I may send you some more in the course of years; the interest, in August or any time, will find uses for itself here. And so, with many thanks, let the matter lie arranged.

We are in our usual state here, little different from what you saw, except that I am dreadfully overwhelmed this long while with an ill-fated *Prussian* enterprise in the Book way, the ugliest I ever undertook, and the most thankless and hopeless, in which, except the unwillingness to be flatly *beaten* in one's old days, there is no adequate motive to persevere. This is really a sore job, and I have often fallen nearly desperate upon it. One needs "the obstinacy of ten mules," as I sometimes say, "in this world." However, I now do begin, in cheerful moments, to see promises of daylight here and there through the abominable black dust-whirlwind where my dwelling has so long been; and expect to get out of it alive after all, doing a *bad* Book, the best I can, since a good one is not possible in the case.

Of Miss B., I am sorry to report that I know absolutely nothing for many months past, perhaps above a year, when she made her last visit here, and promised to come back soon, but never came. She lives about four miles from us (in a street leading off Hyde Park Gardens, towards the Paddington region, at least there she did live, when I called long since and found her gone out). I am so held to the grinding-stone, I never, by any chance, get away to such distances, and indeed, hardly make visits at all, this long while. I have often asked myself, and ask all American friends, what poor Miss B. is about? but nobody knew her, nobody can tell. Her very address I have now lost; could find the place, I think, from the physiognomy of the street, were I there in person, and from some recollections of "twelve" as being the number of the house. Poor lady! I fear she is in a very abstruse condition; engaged in an enterprise which is totally without rational basis, and getting more and more exasperated that she does not (as she cannot by possibility) succeed in it.

Laurence need not write to me 'till his *demon* fairly bids him; I am satisfied to hear of his prospering so among you; for which, I doubt not, the good, meritorious man is thankful. Such "hospitality"—I have often thought of it with loyal wonder; it is like the hospitality of the heroic ages, and rebukes common mankind of our day!

My wife joins with me in kind regards to Miss Lynch (among others of the Chelsea party of that evening) whom I very well remember, and still like. My notion is the Sardinian professor may have done an extremely wise thing, in *staying* where he was on those terms. Easily go farther and fare worse.

What a narrow providential miss of the uttermost calamity was that of you and yours.*

We do well to recognise such things as mercies of a Special Power that has pity on us. Great pity withal is shown us in this universe, where so much rage and cruelty also are—the soil of it only getting arable by little and little. Accept our united regards. I remain always,

Yours sincerely,

(Signed) T. CARLYLE.

The last letter of Mr. Carlyle in regard to matters

*They had taken passage on the ill-fated *Arctic* and, at the last moment, were led by an unexpected incident to give up their staterooms and await the next steamer.

of business was preceded by one from his brother John. I give them both :

5 CHEYNE ROW, CHELSEA, May 6, 1868.

MY DEAR SIR:

Last week before leaving Dumfries I wrote to you, acknowledging receipt of your letter of the fourteenth of April, with notarial packages of eighteen bonds, for one thousand dollars each which up to that date you had purchased for Thomas Carlyle, my brother. These bonds are now lodged in his name at Dumfries in the British Linen Company's Bank. And since my arrival here I have got your second letter of April twenty-first, with notarial certificate (copy) of statement of account up to that time, and bill for £34, 8s. 6p. which balances it finally and which I have had paid to my brother's London banker. The statement is quite clear to me and corresponds with all earlier ones. I enclose that of August, 1865 (4), signed by you and declaring what bonds you had in trust at that time; and if there be any later declaration of the sort at Dumfries, I will have it cancelled at once.

I need hardly say that my brother feels extremely obliged for all your kindness and work on his behalf through so long a series of years. I find him looking at least as well as last year, and he is occupied at present in preparing for a new library edition of all his works. It will be a useful and not too severe occupation for him in the coming month. He may, perhaps, add a post-script to this, though to-day he is entangled with preliminaries for settling with printers as to the forms of that edition.

I remain,

Most sincerely yours,

J. A. CARLYLE.

CHELSEA, May 6, 1868.

DEAR SIR:

I cannot let my brother despatch this final document, and altogether satisfactory closure of the affairs, there have been between us, without testifying in my own words what a pleasant and grateful feeling I have now, and all along have had, for the whole of your conduct, from first to last, in regard to all that. I was a stranger, and I felt that you took me up as a friend; and, sure enough, you have throughout acted conspicuously in that character; caring for my interests with a constant loyalty, sagacity and punctuality, as if they had been your own; manifesting at all times the qualities of a perfect man of business, and of an altogether singularly generous, faithful and courteous benefactor:—in short, *making good* nobly, in all points, the *reading* we took of you here, that evening, long years ago, when, alas, it was still "we," not as now only one, who could recognize good men and love them!

Words of thanks are of little use, but it is certain I shall all my days remember you with gratitude, with honest satisfaction, and even a kind of pride, which will or may, whether talked of or not, be a real possession to us both. I do not yet renounce the hope of seeing you again this side the sea. Meanwhile, I enclose (by same mail) a little *bundle* of new *photographs*, which may gain a few glances from your ladykind on an evening, and occasionally bring me to mind. May all good be with you and yours, dear sir. I remain yours with lasting esteem and good will,

T. CARLYLE.

The reader may like to see the original letter. Here is a facsimile of it:

Chelsea, 5 May 1868

Dear Sir, — I cannot let my Brother despatch this final Document, and altogr satisfactory Closure of the affairs that have been betn us, without testifying in my own words what a pleast and grateful feeling I have now, and all along have had, for the whole of yr conduct, from first to last, in regard to all that. I was a stranger, and I felt that you took me up as a friend; — and, sure enough, you have throughout acted conspicuously in that character; caring for my interests with a constant loyalty, sagacity and punctuality, as if they had been yr own; manifesting at all times the qualities of a perfect man of busss, and of an altogether singularly generous faithful and courteous benefactor; — in short, *making*

Good nobly, in all points, the reading we took of you here, that Evg. long years ago, — when, alas it was still "we", not as now one only, who could recog-nise good men and love them! —

Words of thanks are of little use: but it is certn I shall all my days remember you with grati-tude, with honest satisfactn, and even a kind of pride, — wh will or may, whether talked of or not, be a real possessn to us both. I do not yet renounce the hope of seeing you agn, there side the Sea. Mean-while I inclose (by same mail) a little Bundle of new Photographs; wh may gain a few glances from yr Lady-kind on an Evg, and occasionally bring me to mind. — May all good be with you and yours, Dear Sir I remain

Yrs with lasting esteem & goodwill T. Carlyle

VI.

HIS HOME.—DEATH OF HIS YOUNGEST DAUGHTER AND OF MRS. BUTLER.—HIS LAST YEARS.—FOX-MEADOW. —A PICTURE OF HIM THERE AS DRAWN BY AN OLD FRIEND.—TRIBUTE OF THE BOARD OF DIRECTORS AND FACULTY OF THE UNION THEOLOGICAL SEMINARY.

Mr. Butler's home, both to its own members and to the stranger within his gates, was full of light and sweetness. All who were privileged to sojourn under his roof, whether for days, or for weeks and months, felt and said so. In the letters from Detroit and Indianapolis, written late at night, under the pressure of distracting cares and responsibility, one gets constant glimpses of the ever-thoughtful, devoted husband and father. And in the whole tone and character of these same letters, I may add, one gets glimpses also of the Christian wife and mother not less striking and attractive. The only son passed away in 1856, a score of years later followed the youngest daughter, and shortly after the mother herself; but the elder daughter was still spared to be her father's companion, staff and comforter during the rest of his long pilgrimage. A large circle also of loving nephews and nieces with their children and children's children grew up about him and helped to cheer his old age. When they all came together to celebrate one of "Uncle Charles'" birthdays, after he had passed into the nineties, and the time of his departure drew near, the sight was most pleasing and beautiful. Of Mr. Butler's hospitality I have spoken already. In the later years of his life a visit in the summer or fall to Fox Meadow was a special benediction. It was as if you were holding converse with one of the patriarchs sitting at the door of his tent and rehearsing the wonderful works of the Lord. How many delightful memories are associated with that summer home, its green meadows, its walks and drives through the fine old forest trees and along the rippling brooks!

Here is a pen picture of the scene, the place and the man so truthful that I cannot help giving it as a fitting close of this sketch. It was written by Col. William E. McLean, of Terre Haute, Indiana, some two years before the death of Mr. Butler:

Many of our older citizens will be pleased to learn that Mr. Charles Butler, the kind and courtly old gentleman, who, more than a quarter of a century ago, used to pay his semi-annual visits to Terre Haute, in discharge of his duties as chairman of the board of trustees of the Wabash and Erie canal, is still living, in quiet and dignified retirement, at his princely country residence, near the Hudson, some sixteen miles above New York. During a recent visit East, the writer called upon him, was most pleasantly received, and delightfully entertained as a citizen of Terre Haute.

Mr. Butler remembered with lively interest our earlier citizenship, many of whose acquaintance he made more than fifty years ago. He recalled the fact that all the men most intimately associated with him in the enterprise of the construction and management of that great work have gone to their final reward. Colonel Thomas H. Blake, Colonel Thomas Dowling, Jessie L. Williams, of Ft. Wayne, William J. Ball, Jacob H. Hager and others. He inquired very pleasantly of Colonel Thompson, Mr. McKeen, Harry Ross, the family of his old friend William J. Ball whom he esteemed most highly, and many others, surprising me by the accuracy of his memory and the interest he still takes in his old acquaintance of the Wabash. The day following he did me the honor to call at a neighbor's—a gentleman who was formerly a prominent young citizen of this city, whom I was visiting—and presented me with his photograph, a striking likeness, upon the reverse side of which he had written, in clear and excellent hand, betraying no sign of age, "With regards of Mr. Charles Butler, Fox Meadow, June 15, 1895." Upon the face of the photograph, which would be easily recognized by any of his former acquaintances, he had written "Charles Butler, February 15, 1895. Born February 15, 1802." Although past his 93d year, Mr. Butler is exceedingly well preserved for his years, enjoys greatly the society of his friends, and, in every respect, is a typical and cultured gentleman of the old school, one who has eminently known how to grow old, demonstrating the truth of the proverb that no old age is agreeable but that of a wise man.

He was surprised to be informed that Terre Haute now boasts a population of more than 40,000, and recalled his early visits to our straggling little settlement as it existed in the days of the tallow dip and the lumbering old stage coach, when it required two long weary weeks to make the trip from New York to the primitive hamlet on the Wabash.

Although never a citizen of Indiana, no man played a more important part in its early financial history than did

Mr. Charles Butler. A gentleman of the highest character for business ability and integrity, recognized as such both in Europe and this country, he became the American representative of the foreign holders of our bonds—the agent of Indiana's early creditors from 1840 to the final settlement of the affairs of the old Wabash and Erie canal. He discharged the duties of that great trust, difficult and delicate as they were, in a manner satisfactory to his principals and in a way that should have won him the everlasting gratitude of the people of Indiana. No one not gifted with the ken of prophecy, could have predicted that the construction of the canal would so soon be rendered practically worthless by the great railroad systems which were to spring into life almost before the last shovel of dirt was thrown upon its banks. Mr. Butler secured the passage after much labor and serious opposition, by the legislature of 1846, of the so-called "Butler Bill," by the provisions of which measure the State surrendered to her bond-holders all her interest in the canal, then unfinished and uncompleted, in consideration of the cancellation of several millions of her bonds, thus lifting from the shoulders of our people a load of indebtedness which, at that time they had found too great to bear. The "Butler Bill" preserved the credit and character of the State unimpared. In the end it proved a splendid contract for the State, but a hard one for the creditors. No human foresight could have predicted that the canal would go so quickly into "innocuous desuetude." The condition of the State at the time of the passage of the "Butler Bill" was truly critical. There had been borrowed by the State for internal improvement purposes, including the amount expended in the practical construction of the Wabash and Erie canal, more than $4,000,000, upon which the State, then a mere frontier State, with all her grand resources not only undeveloped and unavailable, but really not dreamed of, was paying an unusual interest of 5 per cent., which of itself was an unbearable burden. Governor Wallace, in a message to the legislature some years before the passage of the "Butler Bill," in describing the financial condition then existing in the State, said: "The truth is, and it would be folly to conceal it, we have our hands full, full to overflowing, to sustain ourselves, to preserve the credit and character of the State, we have not an hour of time, nor a dollar of money, nor a hand employed in labor to squander and dissipate upon objects of idleness, or taste or amusement."

Mr. Butler talks entertainingly of Indiana's prominent law-makers and politicians who figured in the old days of 1846. Governor Whitcomb, Oliver H. Smith, Caleb B. Smith, Colonel Thompson, Joseph J. Jernegan, Mr. James Farregan and others. Men of that marked individuality of character which stamped their impress upon our early legislation. To-day one of New York's best known philanthropists, his life redolent with good deeds, entrenched in old and congenial friendships, respected and honored by all who know him, he is still treading, with confident and cheerful steps, the brightening paths of duty. His friends, those who know him best, will bear testimony, that were every soul as free from guile as his has been, the world would be fairer to live in and heaven more easily attained.

The following minute, prepared by President Hastings, expresses the sentiment with which the Faculty and Board of Directors of the Union Theological Seminary regarded the departure to the "better country" of this eminently wise and good man:

MINUTE OF THE DIRECTORY OF UNION THEOLOGICAL SEMINARY IN REGARD TO CHARLES BUTLER, LL.D.

With sad hearts we record the death of the venerable and beloved President of this Board, Charles Butler, LL.D., who was taken from us on the morning of December 13, 1897. This event makes an epoch of the sixty-second year in the history of our Seminary, for Mr. Butler was the last of the twenty-four "Founders," who in 1836 constituted the first Board of Directors. Now all the names of the Founders are among the starred, and yet they shall ever be cherished here with veneration and affection by those who guard well this institution as the great monument to their memory.

We had hoped that our friend might live to celebrate his ninety-sixth birthday on the 15th of February, but that was not to be. During the first thirty-four years of our history this board had four Presidents, the Rev. Thomas McAuley, D.D., LL.D.; Richard Townley Haines; the Rev. Samuel Hanson Cox, D.D., LL.D., and Richard Townley Haines. In 1870 Mr. Butler was elected to this responsible position, which he has filled for twenty-seven years with so much wisdom and grace. We are devoutly grateful for the length of his service, but still more grateful for the character and quality of his service. He had rare sagacity, poise and balance, with inimitable grace and dignity as a presiding officer. His commanding presence was also and always an attractive presence. His fine countenance lighted by his beautiful faith and love, wore a peculiar radiance which was at once a doxology and a benediction. We loved him as much as we revered him. His mind and heart was full of the liveliest interest in all that pertained to the life and growth of this institution, to which he gave most liberally of his time and strength and means. He generously endowed the Edward Robinson Professorship of Biblical Theology intending it to be a monument to his honored friend whose name it bears, but it will be his own monument also.

It was wonderful in his old age to see how clear and how comprehensive his mind continued to be even unto the last. During the recent serious and protracted controversy growing out of our relation to the General Assembly, the finest qualities of Mr. Butler's character were conspicuously revealed. In all the trying conferences with the General Assembly's Committee he commanded in a marked degree the respect and admiration of the members of that Committee by the dignity, calmness and graciousness with which he presided over the protracted deliberations. In him with a noble courage and an unflinching resolution there were combined such gentleness and courtesy as to command the reverence even of those who differed most with him. His serene and charming spirit thus rendered admirable service to this board throughout the period of its severest trial.

But no words of ours can do justice to our appreciation of the personality, the character, and the service of our departed friend. His memory for many years to come, will be fragrant to the members of this Board, to the Faculty and to the Alumni, so many of whom have known him in the refined and generous hospitalities of his home.

We give him joy that he has entered the gates of the Eternal City, where he has been welcomed to the blessed fellowship of many who had loved him here and who have long watched and waited for him there.

In concluding this tribute of reverent affection we desire to express our deep gratitude and our profound sympathy to his noble daughter who has ministered with such tender and beautiful devotion to her father and our friend.

Appendix.

A.

THE ESTABLISHMENT OF THE EDWARD ROBINSON CHAIR OF BIBLICAL THEOLOGY.

I.

At the regular meeting of the Board of Directors of the Union Theological Seminary in the city of New York, held November 11, 1890, the following preamble and resolution were adopted by a unanimous vote:

WHEREAS, The Honorable Charles Butler, LL.D., president of the Board of Directors of this seminary, has made provision for a permanent fund for the purpose of establishing and endowing a chair in this seminary, to be called the Edward Robinson Chair of Biblical Theology:

NOW THEREFORE, *Resolved*, That a new professorship shall be and is hereby created, which shall be called the "Edward Robinson Chair of Biblical Theology"; that the income of the endowment of one hundred thousand dollars given to this seminary by the said Charles Butler in the manner mentioned in his bond, dated April 15, 1890, shall be applied solely to the support of the chair, according to the provisions of said bond.

The president of the faculty suggested that the board, in courtesy, should ask Dr. Butler to express to us freely his wishes with reference to the action just taken.

Thereupon President Butler addressed the Board of Directors as follows:

The formal establishment by the board of "The Edward Robinson Chair of Biblical Theology" fulfils the object desired in the provision which I have made for its endowment. I beg to express my satisfaction and gratitude for this action. It is in accord with the views of the distinguished

Christian scholar in whose memory the chair is founded. In a letter to the board, dated January 20, 1837, accepting the professorship of Sacred Literature, he said: "The constitution properly requires every professor to declare that he believes the Scriptures of the Old and New Testaments to be the Word of God, the only infallible rule of faith and practice. This is placing the Bible in its true position as the only foundation of Christian theology. It follows as a necessary consequence that the study of the Bible, as taught in the department of Biblical Literature, must be the foundation of all right theological education." This new chair of Biblical Theology seems to me to realize the sentiment embodied in this quotation, in a form which, if he were now present with us, would receive his benediction. It embalms his memory indissolubly with the life of this seminary, and will ever be an inspiration to its students in their "search of the Scriptures."

In regard to the incumbent of this chair, I avail of the courtesy of the board to express my wish that it may be one who sat as a pupil at the feet of that eminent teacher, and I regard it as a felicity to the seminary that there is one here who has been trained within its walls, and who, by his ripe scholarship and purity of character in Christian faith and practice, has won the confidence and affection of his associate professors, of this Board of Directors, and of the students who have come under his teaching during these years of faithful and devoted service.

From what I have said, you will anticipate that my wishes will be fully gratified in the appointment of the Rev. Charles A. Briggs, D.D., as eminently qualified to fill this chair. In this expression of preference, it gives me the greatest pleasure to say that I do but voice the views and wishes of our late revered president of the faculty, Roswell D. Hitchcock. Dr. Briggs was his choice for this chair.

I cannot doubt that the highest interests of this seminary, and, what is more, those of the Redeemer's kingdom on earth, will be promoted by this realization of the plans of these two Christian scholars, both as regards the foundation of the chair and the selection of the suggested incumbent.

THE APPOINTMENT OF THE INCUMBENT.

At the conclusion of President Butler's address, Henry Day, Esq., offered the following resolution, which was unanimously adopted:

Resolved, That Professor Charles A. Briggs, D.D., be transferred from the Davenport Professorship of Hebrew and the Cognate Languages to the Edward Robinson Chair of Biblical Theology.

Professor Briggs, having been duly advised of the action above recorded, addressed a communication to the board, under date of January 7, 1891, accepting the new chair to which he had been transferred. It was as follows:

120 WEST 93D ST., NEW YORK,
January 7, 1891.

Gentlemen of the Board of Directors of the Union Theological Seminary, New York:

I thank you for the mark of confidence expressed in your choice of me to fill the Edward Robinson Professorship of Biblical Theology. There is no chair that so well suits my tastes and my studies for the past twenty-five years. Under the advice of the faculty, I have been building up the department of Biblical Theology for some years past. But I had reached the limit of new work. I could not advance further until relieved of the Hebrew work. In accepting the new chair, I propose to push the work of the department rapidly forward, and to cover the whole ground of the chair at as early a date as possible. I give over the work of the Hebrew chair to my pupil, colleague, and friend, Dr. Brown, with confidence, that building on the foundations I have laid, he will make marked improvement upon my work.

Biblical Theology is, at the present time, the vantage ground for the solution of those important problems in religion, doctrine and morals that are compelling the attention of the men of our times. The Bible is the Word of God, and its authority is divine authority that determines the faith and life of men. Biblical scholars have been long held in bondage to ecclesiasticism and dogmatism. But modern Biblical criticism has won the battle of freedom. The accumulations of long periods of traditional speculation and dogmatism have been in large measure removed, and the Bible itself stands before the men of our time in a commanding position, such as it has never enjoyed before. On all sides it is asked, not what do the creeds teach, what do the theologians say, what is the authority of the church, but what does the Bible itself teach us? It is the office of Biblical Theology to answer this question. It is the culmination of the work of Exegesis. It rises on a complete induction through all the departments of Biblical study to a comprehensive grasp of the Bible as a whole, to the unity and variety of the sum of its teaching. It draws the line with the teaching of the Bible. It fences off from the Scriptures all the speculations, all the dogmatic elaborations, all the doctrinal adaptations that have been made in the history of doctrine in the church. It does not deny their propriety and importance, but it insists upon the threefold distinction as necessary to truth and theological honesty, that the theology of the Bible is one thing, the only infallible authority; the theology of the creeds is another thing, having simply ecclesiastical authority; and the theology of the theologians, or Dogmatic Theology, is a third thing, which has no more authority than any other system of human construction. It is well known that until quite recent times, and even at present in some quarters, the creeds have lorded it over the Scriptures, and the dogmaticians have lorded it over the creeds, so that in its last analysis the authority in the church has been, too often, the authority of certain theologians. Now, Biblical Theology aims to limit itself strictly to the theology of the Bible itself. Biblical theologians are fallible men, and doubtless it is true, that they err in their interpretation of the Scriptures, as have others; but it is the aim of the discipline to give the theology of the Bible pure and simple; and the inductive and historical methods that determine the working of the department are certainly favorable to an objective presentation of the subject, and are unfavorable to the intrusion of subjective fancies and circumstantial considerations. It will be my aim, so long as I remain in the chair, to accomplish this ideal as far as possible. Without fear or favor I shall teach the truth of God's Word as I find it. The theology of the Bible is much simpler, richer, and grander than any of the creeds or dogmatic systems. These have been built upon select portions of the Bible, and there is a capriciousness of selection in them all. But Biblical Theology makes no selection of texts—it uses the entire Bible in all its passages, and in every single passage, giving each its place and importance in the unfolding of divine revelation. To Biblical Theology the Bible is a mine of untold wealth; treasures, new and old, are in its storehouses; all its avenues lead, in one way or another, to the presence of the Living God and the Divine Saviour.

The work of Biblical Theology is conducted on such a comprehensive study of the Bible, that while the professor builds upon a thorough study of the original texts, his class must use their English Bibles. A thorough study of the English Bible is necessarily included in the course. If the plan of the work is carried out, the student will accompany his professor through the entire English Bible during his seminary course, and will be taught to expound a large number of the most important passages in the light of all the passages leading up to them.

In conclusion, allow me to express my gratitude to the venerable president of the Board of Directors for the interest he has ever taken in my work, for the honor he has shown me in nominating me for the chair he so generously founded, and for attaching to the chair, with such modesty and consideration, the name of Edward Robinson, my honored teacher, the greatest name on the roll of Biblical scholars of America, and the most widely known and honored of her professors. I shall regard it as my high calling and privilege to build on his foundations, and to advance the work that he carried on as far as it can be advanced in the circumstances of our time. The names of Edward Robinson and Charles Butler will be entwined into a bond of double strength to sustain me in the delicate and difficult work that I now undertake to do.

Faithfully,

C. A. Briggs.

II.

THE INAUGURATION.

Tuesday Evening, January 20, 1891.

President Charles Butler, LL. D., presided. After devotional exercises, at the request of Mr. Butler, the president of the faculty made a brief preliminary statement, as follows:

As has been announced, last May the president of the Board of Directors of the Union Theological Seminary, Charles Butler, LL.D., provided for the endowment of a new chair in the sum of $100,000.

On the basis of this munificent gift, at the recent meeting of the board, the new professorship was formally established, to be known, in accordance with the request of President Butler, as *The Edward Robinson Professorship of Biblical Theology*. This was designed by Mr. Butler to be a memorial of his long-time friend, the late Edward Robinson, D.D., LL.D., the first professor of Sacred Literature in this institution, who honored that chair and this seminary by his long and distinguished service from 1837 to 1863.

The president of the board suggested that it would be in accord with his own wishes and with those of his friend, the late President Roswell D. Hitchcock, D.D., LL.D., if the board should transfer the Rev. Professor Charles A. Briggs, D.D., to the new chair just established. By a unanimous vote the board at once adopted the suggestion of their president, and transferred Professor Briggs from the *Davenport Chair of Hebrew and the Cognate Languages* to the *Edward Robinson Chair of Biblical Theology.* Dr. Briggs, having signified his acceptance of this transfer, his inauguration will now take place.

President Butler addressed Professor Briggs as follows:

On behalf of the Board of Directors, and in accordance with the Constitution of the "Union Theological Seminary in the city of New York," I call upon you to "*make and subscribe*" the "*declaration*" required of each member of the faculty of this institution.

Thereupon Professor Briggs made the "declaration" as follows:

I believe the Scriptures of the Old and New Testament to be the Word of God, the only infallible rule of faith and practice; and I do now, in the presence of God and the directors of this seminary, solemnly and sincerely receive and adopt the Westminster Confession of Faith, as containing the system of doctrine taught in the Holy Scriptures. I do also, in like manner, approve of the Presbyterian Form of Government; and I do solemnly promise that I will not teach or inculcate anything which shall appear to me to be subversive of the said system of doctrines, or of the principles of said Form of Government, so long as I shall continue to be a professor in the seminary.

Thereupon President Butler said:

In the name of the Board of Directors, I declare that Professor Charles A. Briggs, D.D., is inaugurated as the Incumbent of the *Edward Robinson Chair of Biblical Theology.*

On behalf of the Board of Directors, the charge to Professor Briggs will now be delivered by the member of the board duly appointed for this service—the Rev. David R. Frazer, D.D., the pastor of the First Presbyterian Church of Newark, N. J.

THE CHARGE.

My dear Brother Briggs :—

Before attempting to discharge the duty which, by your kind consideration, has been devolved upon me, permit me to tender my heartfelt congratulations: first, upon the establishment of the Edward Robinson Chair of Biblical Theology; a consummation so devoutly wished for alike by yourself and by our revered Hitchcock. We all share in your joy, and recognize the new departure as a long and right step in advance in the history of our institution.

In the orderings of God's providence every age has its own peculiar problem to solve, the solution being wrought out from the standpoint of its own pressing needs. It is a marked characteristic of our day that the Bible is now studied as never before in the world's history, and the establishment of this new department is in the line of this development, and is answerable to this modern demand. For, if I understand aright the function of Biblical Theology, it does not conduct a simple, grammatical exercise; it does not discuss the various textual readings; it does not study the opinions of the fathers or the deliverances of the church; it does not formulate a body of systematic divinity grouped about some chosen central principle. These are important and legitimate topics of study, hence are properly cared for in our curriculum. They will doubtless be very helpful as external aids in the prosecution of the work of this chair, but the peculiar province of Biblical Theology is to study the Word; to determine what God intends to say in His Word, and then to formulate these hallowed teachings.

Such being its province, I need not pause to show that Biblical Theology is the normal response to that modern critical spirit which refuses to accept anything upon the basis of authority, and insists upon tracing everything back to its genetic principle and its efficient cause. Neither need I tarry to discriminate sharply and accurately between the functions of Biblical and Systematic Theology. If you, my dear brother, have any especial interest in or desire for information on this general subject, I would respectfully refer you to a work on "Biblical Study," which is published by the Scribners, and was written by one who has served long and well in, and has just been transferred from, "the Davenport Professorship of Hebrew and the Cognate Languages" in this institution; and, if you are not acquainted with the work, I can assure you that the time spent in its perusal will not be wasted, for you will find therein an admirable and exhaustive discussion of the subject.

But I want to congratulate you, secondly, upon the fact that *you* are to be the incumbent of the new chair, a position for which you are pre-eminently qualified by reason of the peculiar character of your past studies. I am very well aware that you would much prefer to have me discuss the general topic of Biblical Theology, and to dwell upon the claims it has to a place in our curriculum, rather than to hint the name of, or make any reference to the professor who is to occupy the new chair. But if anything of a personal character should be said, please remember, my brother, you have no one to blame save yourself, since, passing by abler men, you have kindly insisted that your old friend and classmate should deliver the charge, as you enter the awful responsibilities of your new position. And as the class spirit asserts itself, I will say, despite your unspoken protest, that the class of '64 is proud of its representative; that it rejoices in your well-deserved success, and that it appropriates to itself a peculiar glory by virtue of the events of this hour. Little did we dream, when we sat at the feet of that honored man whose name gives dignity to your new chair, as also at the feet of those other scholarly and godly men, Henry B. Smith, Thomas H. Skinner, Roswell D. Hitchcock, and Henry H. Hadley, men whose presence was a benediction, whose instruction was an inspiration, whose memories are revered and hallowed, that there was among us, going in and out just as we went in and out, one who was destined to sit in Gamaliel's seat and to honor the exalted position by his scholarly attainments. Yet such was the fact, and although you wish I would not say it, still, as your classmate and on behalf of the class thus signally honored, I tender you our warmest and heartiest congratulations.

And I propose saying further, since I betray no confidence by the declaration, that it would have greatly rejoiced your heart and would have wonderfully inspirited you for your work could you have heard the cordial, tender, and appreciative words with which our venerable and venerated president of the Board of Directors (who is also the kind and generous patron through whose munificence the new chair has been endowed, "Serus in coelum redeas"), placed your name, the only name placed in nomination for the position.

And I am sure you would have been more than pleased could you have witnessed the unanimity with which the directors ratified the nomination and transferred you from the Davenport Chair of Hebrew to the Edward Robinson Chair of Biblical Theology. I congratulate you that the honored and revered founder of the department wanted *you* in the department which he founded, and also upon the fact that you enter your new work in the enjoyment of the fullest confidence, respect, and love of the directors of this seminary.

But I may not forget that this is your hour. Inasmuch as I cannot hope to impart any instruction respecting the peculiar and practical duties of your new position, I would be content to let these congratulatory words take the place of the more formal charge. In order, however, to meet the requirements of my appointment, and to stir up your pure mind by way of remembrance, I charge you:

First. To have clear, well-settled, and accurately defined views of the nature, the scope, and the design of the Holy Scriptures.

The Bible is to be your text-book, and the Bible claims to be the book of God. If this high claim cannot be maintained; if the Bible be not the book of God, as verily as Jesus Christ is the Son of God, then is it unworthy of our confidence. That Word which was in the beginning with God and was God, and which in the fulness of time began to be flesh, was, as the Incarnate Word, the God-Man, very God and very Man. We do not understand this "great mystery of godliness, God manifest in the flesh." We do not attempt to explain it, but we accept it, we believe it, we rest our hopes of life, here and hereafter, upon it. And upon this same basis we can accept the Word written. It also is an incarnation. Great is the mystery of Revelation, God manifesting His thought in the forms of human speech. Since holy men of old spake as they were moved by the Holy Ghost, the divine and human elements are co-ordinated in the Word written as well as in the Word Incarnated. We must recognize the divine and human factors in the Scriptures and assign a legitimate place to each and to both, but I need not charge you, my dear brother, to bear in ceaseless remembrance the fact, that just in the proportion that the divine element is eliminated or is abnormally subordinated to the human, is the authority of the Bible circumscribed and the power of the Bible abridged. You will never forget that you have GOD'S WORD for your text-book, and you will never fail to teach it as the very Word of God.

The *scope* of biblical instruction is clearly set forth on the sacred page. Great mischief is often wrought by the notion that the Bible aims to cover the whole sphere of human knowledge, and that its authority is lessened by the concession that there are some things which can be comprehended without its aid. We surely do not need the Bible to teach us that two and two make four, or that the whole is greater than any of its parts. The Holy Word has a distinct mission and a definite aim. It does not come to us as a teacher of physics or of metaphysics, but as a revelation: as a revelation of God: as a revelation of God to man: as a revelation of God to man concerning the highest and the dearest moral interests of man, alike for time and for eternity. It comes to man, not primarily to reason, but to reveal, and to reveal those high themes, which, by necessity of being, transcend the ordinary processes of human thought. While pervaded with an air of simplicity and honesty and truthfulness, it comes not primarily to persuade, but to command, and to command, not in view of the deductions of human reason, or in the light of conclusions reached by the processes of a speculative philosophy, but upon that simple, yet sublime, basis, "Thus saith the Lord God."

The *design* of Revelation is summed up essentially in the Johannean statement, "these things are *written* that ye might *believe* that Jesus is the Christ, the Son of God, and that believing ye might have *life* through His name." As all roads led to Rome, so all Scripture leads to Christ. The poetry, the prophecy, the precepts, the biography, the history of the Bible, find their true centrality in Him who was at once dust and Divinity, the Workman of Nazareth, the Prophet of Galilee, "The Lamb of God which taketh away the sin of the world." The final end and ultimate design of the Holy Scriptures are "to make wise unto salvation, through faith which is in Christ Jesus;" hence it is your business, my dear brother, from the Word written to educe the Word Incarnate, and I beg you to so present Jesus Christ to all who come to you for instruction, that they may go from your class-room to their great life-work, not only impressed with an abiding sense of the matchless beauty and the mighty power of that Divine Saviour concerning whom the Scriptures so abundantly testify, but also, and as the normal outcome of your teachings, with a fixed determination "to know nothing among men save Jesus Christ and Him crucified."

But Paul forewarns "of things hard to be understood," of problems which must perplex the most acute mind and defy the grasp of the most profound intellect. Furthermore, in the interpretation of the Word, conflicting views respecting the exact significance of the revelation will arise. Who shall decide when learned doctors disagree? To whom shall the ultimate appeal be taken? Manifestly to the Spirit of the Living God by whom the declaration was prompted, and to whom the meaning is clear; hence, I charge you.

Secondly. Seek the aid of the Holy Ghost in your arduous and responsible work.

I attempt no solution of the mooted questions as to whether our Lord's promise of the Holy Ghost should lead believers in "the way of all truth," was restricted to the Apostolic College, and was literally fulfilled in the written revelation, or whether it pertains to believers in all time.

But the Scriptures most clearly require that all believers should "live in the Spirit," "walk in the Spirit," "be filled with the Spirit." Christian consciousness bears witness that the abiding presence of the Spirit begets deep and vital spirituality, and Christian experience abundantly confirms the assertion that vital spirituality ensures a large insight of that truth which must be spiritually discerned. A willingness to do God's will must precede the knowledge of the doctrine, and this willingness of mind and heart must be begotten by the Holy Ghost. Put peculiar honor upon the Divine Spirit and He will put peculiar honor upon you and your work. He will open your eyes to behold the wondrous things in God's law; He will give you the witness of His presence in your own soul, and will enable you, in all meekness and humility, yet with the highest Christian positiveness, to say: I know whom and what and why I have believed, and am persuaded that my confidence rests not upon the wisdom of man, but upon the wisdom of God.

And as you thus teach the Word of God under the guidance of the Spirit of God; as day by day you present the truth as it is in Jesus to those who are to preach a crucified Redeemer to dying men, may the Lord bless you and keep you; may He equip you for duty, help you in the discharge of it, and when your great work is finished may His "Well done" be pronounced upon His "good and faithful servant."

III.

QUESTIONS SUBMITTED TO DR. BRIGGS AND HIS ANSWERS.

In view of the general attack upon Dr. Briggs the Board

of Directors appointed a committee of three to prepare a series of questions for categorical answers from Dr. Briggs. That committee reported June 5, 1891, as follows:

Question 1. Do you consider the Bible, the Church, and the Reason as co-ordinate sources of authority? Answer. No.

Or, do you believe the Scriptures of the Old and New Testament to be the only infallible rule of faith and practice? Answer. Yes.

Question 2. When you use the word "reason" do you include the conscience and the religious feelings? Answer. Yes.

Question 3. Would you accept the following as a satisfactory definition of inspiration: "Inspiration is such a divine direction as to secure an infallible record of God's revelation in respect to both fact and doctrine?" Answer. Yes.

Question 4. Do you believe the Bible to be inerrant in all matters concerning faith and practice, and in everything in which it is a revelation from God or a vehicle of divine truth, and that there are no errors that disturb its infallibility in these matters or in its records of the historic events and institutions with which they are inseparably connected? Answer. Yes.

Question 5. Do you believe that the miracles recorded in Scripture are due to an extraordinary exercise of divine energy either directly or mediately through holy men? Answer. Yes.

Question 6. Do you hold what is commonly known as the doctrine of a second probation? Do you believe in Purgatory? Answer. No.

Question 7. Do you believe that the issues of this life are final and that a man who dies impenitent will have no further opportunity of salvation? Answer. Yes.

Question 8. Is your theory of progressive sanctification such that it will permit you to say that you believe that when a man dies in the faith he enters the middle state regenerated, justified and sinless? Answer. Yes.

IV.

RESOLUTIONS OF THE BOARD OF DIRECTORS SUSTAINING DR. BRIGGS, AS PASSED UNANIMOUSLY MAY 19, 1891.

Resolved, That this board has listened with satisfaction to the categorical replies rendered by Dr. Briggs to the questions submitted to him, and that it trusts that the manner in which he has therein dealt with the points that are in dispute will operate to correct the misapprehensions that are so widely current, and to quiet the disturbed condition of mind in which, as a communion, we are so unhappily involved.

Resolved, The directors of the Union Theological Seminary desire to express to Professor Briggs their high appreciation of his Christian courtesy in the consultations which he has had with the Committee of Inquiry in reference to the trying questions now under consideration.

They will stand by him heartily on the ground of this report, and affectionately commend him to the leading of our common Master, having perfect confidence in his honesty of purpose.

E. M. KINGSLEY, *Recorder*. JOHN CROSBY BROWN, *Vice-President*.

NEW YORK, May 19, 1891.

V.

STATEMENT OF THE FACULTY OF UNION THEOLOGICAL SEMINARY.

In view of the general comment and discussion called forth by the recent inaugural address of Professor Charles A. Briggs, D.D., the undersigned, members of the faculty of Union Theological Seminary, deem it their duty to make the following statement:

With the conviction that Christian courtesy, modesty and mutual respect for difference of opinion should characterize theological controversy, we distinctly recognize and deprecate the dogmatic and irritating character of certain of Dr. Briggs' utterances in his Inaugural and in others of his writings: while, on the other hand, we do not recognize, even in these, any warrant for persistent misrepresentations of his views, and for the style and temper in which he has in many cases been assailed.

1. The views propounded by Dr. Briggs in his Inaugural are not new.

They have all been stated by him in one or another of his published works, in articles in the *Presbyterian Review*, during his ten years' editorship, and in more recent contributions to other periodicals. Moreover, for the past ten years, Dr. Briggs has been teaching Biblical Theology in the seminary, and has been expounding to successive classes of students the statements for which he is now arraigned. The present excitement is, as we believe, due, largely, to the tone of the Inaugural Address, to certain unguarded expressions, and to an impression that the transfer of the author to the Chair of Biblical Theology would be subject to the veto of the General Assembly.

2. The address contains, in our judgment, nothing which can be fairly construed into heresy or departure from the Westminster Confession, to which Dr. Briggs honestly subscribed at his recent inauguration.

(*a*) His words concerning "Bibliolatry" are not aimed at humble and devout reverence for the Word of God, but at the error, rebuked by the Apostle Paul, of revering "the letter" above "the spirit."

(*b*) Dr. Briggs declares that, conjointly with the Bible, the *Church* and the *Reason* are *sources* of authority in religion. He uses the term "reason" as embracing the conscience and the religious feeling. We object to the term "sources," since there is but one source of divine authority—God himself. We prefer to say that the Bible, the Church, and the Reason are *media* and *vehicles* through which we recognize and receive the divine authority. This is the generally-accepted Protestant position. Every Church in Christendom admits that the church is a medium of divine authority.

The Confession of Faith declares that "unto the catholic, visible Church, Christ hath given the *ministry*, *oracles* and *ordinances* of God."

That the *reason*, in the broad sense in which it is explained by Dr. Briggs, is also an *organ* to and through which the divine authority is conveyed, is assumed in Scripture and in the Confession, and is the necessary postulate of a divine revelation to man. It is the only point in the natural man to which the qualities of God's character, the operations of His power, and the right-reasonableness of His claims can appeal: and it is distinctly declared and assumed by St. Paul to be the recipient of such appeals; to be the subject of the divine Spirit's illumination; and to become thus the proper instrument for discerning, comparing and judging spiritual truth. If the reason has no such function in religion, it is superfluous to assert that "Scripture is profitable for *teaching*, for *discipline*, and for *upbuilding in righteousness.*" Spiritual righteousness implies an *intelligent* and *rational* perception and reception of the law and truth of God. The *living* sacrifice which is "holy and acceptable unto God" is a "*rational* service."

But Dr. Briggs does not, with the Romanist, exalt the Church above the Bible and the Reason. He does not, with the Rationalist, place the Reason above the Bible and the Church. Neither does he, as has been often charged, *co-ordinate* the three sources. His position is the Protestant and the Presbyterian position, assumed in his subscription to the declaration of the Confession, that the Scriptures are "the only infallible rule of faith and practice," and asserted in his address in the words: "Protestant Christianity builds its faith and life on the divine authority contained in the Scriptures." That Protestant Christianity too often depreciates the Church and the Reason is an entirely distinct statement, involving a question of fact; and the statement and its discussion in no way affect Dr. Briggs' endorsement of the Protestant doctrine of the supreme authority of Scripture.

To assert, as has been so often done, that Dr. Briggs is aiming to undermine the divine authority of Scripture, is preeminently unfair. Not only this Inaugural, but all his published writings, teem with the most positive and uncompromising expressions of love and reverence for the Bible.

(c). The consistency of Dr. Briggs' position as to the supreme authority and divine quality of Holy Scripture, is in no way affected by his views of the nature of Inspiration.

While asserting the plenary inspiration of Scripture, he denies that inspiration involves *absolute inerrancy — literal, verbal accuracy,* and *perfect correspondence of minor details.*

In this view there is nothing original or new. It is the view of Calvin, and of an overwhelming majority of Protestant divines in Europe and America. It was propounded at least eight years ago by Dr. Briggs in his "Biblical Study."

Inspiration, in the sense of literal inerrancy, is nowhere claimed for Scripture by Scripture itself.

It is contradicted by the contents of Scripture in the form in which we have it. It involves, logically, a minute, specific divine superintendence of each detail of the entire process of transmission—copying, translating, printing—and the prevention of all errors. It confronts those who maintain it not only with discrepancies of statement in the present text, but with the innumerable textual variations in the Hebrew and Greek Bibles, and the variations between the Hebrew and the Septuagint. To meet these facts with the assertion of the inerrancy of the original autographs, is to beg the whole question in dispute, to lay down a purely arbitrary, *a priori* hypothesis, and to introduce into the discussion an entirely irrelevant factor, seeing that the errors and discrepancies remain and the original autographs cannot be recovered.

To make the inspiration of Scripture turn upon verbal inerrancy is to commit the Church to an utterly untenable position, and to place her apologists at the mercy of cavillers who are only too glad to evade broader and deeper issues and to shift the discussion to the region of mere verbal details, where they are sure to have the best of the argument.

Dr. Briggs holds and teaches the doctrine of the divine inspiration, infallibility, and authority of the Holy Scriptures in all matters of Christian faith and duty, which is all that any evangelical divine is bound to maintain on that subject. The Westminster and other Confessions of Faith clearly and strongly assert the *fact* of divine inspiration, but wisely abstain from defining the *mode* and *degrees* of divine inspiration. The former is a matter of *faith*, the latter of *human theory*, on which there must be liberty if there is to be any progress. To impose upon a Christian teacher any particular theory of inspiration not sanctioned by the Bible itself is tyranny.

(*d*). Dr. Briggs is further charged with a departure from the Westminster Eschatology in teaching *progressive sanctification after death.*

While we are not to be understood as accepting or endorsing Dr. Briggs' conclusions on this point, it is sufficient to say that he is here in an open field, where, having expressly repudiated the doctrines of future probation, universal restoration, and the Romanist purgatory, he is certainly entitled to the largest liberty in the attempt to elucidate a subject so little understood, and on which the standards are open to differences of interpretation. The phrase "progressive sanctification after death" admits of a sound and orthodox interpretation; but Protestant Eschatology, as defined in the Confessions of the 16th and 17th centuries, is generally admitted to be defective and in need of further development within the limits of that caution and reserve imposed by the comparative silence of Scripture on that mysterious period between death and resurrection. In the words of the late Henry B. Smith written not long before his death: "What Reformed Theology has got to do is to Christologize predestination and decrees, regeneration and sanctification, the doctrine of the Church and *the whole of Eschatology.*

III. After years of familiar acquaintance with Dr. Briggs and his teaching, we are moved to utter our emphatic protest against the spirit and language with which, in so many cases, he has been assailed. If, in any of his writings, Dr. Briggs, as is charged, has wantonly offended the honest convictions of good men, or has in any other way sinned against the ethical code of Christian scholarship laid down in the New Testament, it is not our business to defend him therein. He must answer for it to his own conscience and to God. But in the public discussion of matters of opinion, it is neither right nor decent that an earnest, learned, devoted scholar and faithful teacher, even though mistaken, should be attacked with virulence, contemptuous flippancy, and imputations of unworthy motive. In too many instances it seems to have been assumed that all the *sacredness* of personal conviction is upon one side; that a higher critic can have no convictions or rights which the lower critic or the uncritical censor is bound to respect; and that the fact of his differing with them justifies his opponents in laying aside in discussion the character of Christian gentlemen.

We know Dr. Briggs to be an earnest Christian, a devout student of the Bible, an indefatigable teacher and worker, and one who holds the standards of the Church with an intelligence based on an exhaustive study of their history and literature. The numerous testimonies of his students during seventeen years prove that he inspires them with a deep reverence and enthusiasm for the Bible.

In like manner we protest against the matter and temper of the assaults on Union Seminary. By its history of over half a century, by the character, standing, and services of its graduates, and by the amount and value of its contributions to Christian Literature, this Institution should be insured against such assaults. Its value to the Presbyterian Church needs no demonstration. From the days of Edward Robinson, the pioneer of Palestine exploration and the founder of American Biblical Lexicograghy, Union Seminary has steadily pressed forward on the lines of advanced Biblical study. Its Professors, in subscribing to the Westminster standards, have always been understood to do so with the concession of that measure of freedom which is the right of every Christian scholar. They honor the venerable Confessions of past ages, but they place the Bible above the Confessions, and hold themselves bound by their loyalty to Christ and to His Church, to follow the truth withersoever it may lead them.

We assert and must insist upon the liberty exercised by the Reformers and by the early Church, to discuss the Scriptures freely and reverently and to avail ourselves of all the light which may be thrown upon them from any source. It is in the interest of God's truth to set forth Scripture *as it is*, and not to expose its friends and teachers to humiliation and defeat by claiming for it that it cannot be substantiated. In the words of Ullman, "Not *fixedness* nor *revolution*, but *evolution* and *reform*, is the motto for our times." We maintain that human conceptions of the Bible and of its inspired teachings are subject to revision. To grasp the results of deeper research and to apply them with caution, reverence, and boldness is not only our *privilege*, it is our solemn *duty* in the discharge of the sacred trust committed to us by Christ and His Church. More light is yet to break from God's Word. We would be found ever upon the watch-towers to catch and to transmit its rays. No theological school can take any other attitude without neglecting its duty to the present age and losing its hold upon the rising generation of Biblical students. That such method may dissipate or modify certain traditional views as to the origin or date of the Books of Scripture; that it may expose and correct certain long-established errors of interpretation; that it may modify certain theological dogmas, is only what is to be expected from similar results in the past. But we have no fear for the Bible. The Word of God will come forth from the fire of reverent criticism as fine gold with a new accretion of testimony to its divine origin, and a new power of appeal to the world.

(Signed),

THOMAS S. HASTINGS, (*President*),
PHILIP SCHAFF,
GEORGE L. PRENTISS,
MARVIN R. VINCENT.

(Professor Francis Brown is at Oxford, superintending the publication of his Hebrew Lexicon.)

B.

Dr. Patton's statement referred to on page 132 was elicited by the following remarks of President Hastings:

DR. HASTINGS: May I ask a single question of you, Dr. Patton, as chairman of the late committee on Theological Seminaries? You may have noticed in the paper submitted that the action in the matter of the transfer, therein referred to, was taken by the Executive Committee and laid before the Board before the meeting of the General Assembly. But the Board did not communicate that paper to the Committee on Theological Seminaries, because it decided that it would not be respectful to the General Assembly to assume that the Assembly would undertake to do, under the Agreement of 1870, what we think it had not the right to do; but we sent to the Assembly Dr. White, who prepared the paper, Dr. Dickey and Dr. Parkhurst, saying to ourselves and to them that if the Committee on Theological Seminaries in the General Assembly desired information as to our views, that Committee will ask our representatives for such information. We learned that Dr. White offered such information. Dr. Patton courteously said he would call him before the Committee. Dr. White was not called before the Committee. That we have not been able to understand. If Dr. Patton, as chairman of the General Assembly's Committee on Theological Seminaries, could give us light about that it would relieve some of us.

DR. PATTON: It will give me the greatest pleasure in the world to tell all I know about it, Mr. Chairman. Soon after I was appointed I received a personal letter from Dr. White, stating substantially this: that he was a Director of the Union Theological Seminary, and that he was intimately acquainted with its ins and outs; that he knew everything that had occurred in reference to the matter that was likely to come before the General Assembly, in the case of Dr. Briggs; and, particularly, that he was one of the committee of three, who prepared the questions to which Dr. Briggs gave the categorical answers with which we are familiar, and that he would like to have the opportunity of a personal interview with me as chairman of that committee, because he thought he could put me in possession of some facts that I ought to know. Well, I received the letter. It was a personal letter to me, to be sure, but it was not a confidential letter and I happened to receive my mail, or I happened to have my mail with me, in the committee room over the gallery. I said: "Brethren, here is a letter from Dr. Erskine N. White, in which he says he would like an interview with me on the matter of Dr. Briggs. Now, I said, I feel that, in the first place, this committee should keep its own counsel and talk absolutely to no one (I think it was the most reticent committee in the Assembly—I never heard of any member of the committee telling anything to anybody); if there is to be any communication made it should be made to the entire committee. For myself I am unwilling to be burdened with any confidences from any source, in regard to any matter that is to come before us as a committee. If the committee wishes to hear Dr. White, I am entirely willing that it should do so. It may be best to hear him, but I simply wish to say that I am not willing to take information that is not the common property of every member of the committee." The committee agreed with me, and we said well, perhaps it would be better to hear Dr. White; and by a general consent, though I think no formal vote was taken, we agreed to hear him. After the committee had adjourned I went downstairs and happened to meet Dr. White. I said: "Dr. White, I read your letter to the committee; and to be frank with you, I am not going to talk with you or with anybody else on the case. We are charged with a very serious business, it is an immense responsibility put on us, and we are going to take it, but I think the committee will hear you." He said, "I shall be very glad to wait upon the committee." He did suggest—I don't know just in what form or how emphatically, whether in the form of a distinct preference, or in the form of a modest disclaimer of precedence in favor of Dr. Dickey—but, in all events, he did suggest that perhaps it would be better for the committee to hear Dr. Dickey. "Very well," I said, "I will see the committee." I went back to the committee at a subsequent meeting and reported substantially what Dr. White had said. We concluded that, perhaps, it would be better to hear Dr. Dickey. Then somebody raised the question, "Do we know that Dr. Dickey or Dr. White has been authorized by the Board to speak for it? Are we not assuming a great deal in that? How do we know that the Board would not prefer somebody else? Well," we said, "maybe we will leave it with the men who are here in the Assembly that really represent the seminary." That we left in the same informal and ragged way without any definite action, until my report was fully ready, had passed our sub-committee and had been adopted, word for word, by the sub-committee of five, and I was ready to read it in the full session of the committee. I read it, and we were ready to adopt it, when a member of the committee said, "Are we not going to hear some of the representatives of Union Seminary?" That, I said, was for the committee to decide. The Assembly was getting a little weary and wanted to know when the matter was to come up. It had been made the order of the day for Thursday morning, and we wanted to get the report in, in order that the members of the Assembly might have the benefit of reading it the night before, and that there might not be any needless delay the next day. Somebody said—I think it was Dr. Humphrey, who was a member of the committee—"Well, what is to be gained by having any one represent Union Seminary? We can only act on the light of official communication; private opinions and representations of a confidental nature—communications that are not in the nature of evidence, and that only show the sentiment or temper of the Board of Directors—ought not, and cannot, influence our judgement upon the square issues brought before us in the official report of the Directors of Union Theological Seminary. It may be a great deal more embarrassing to have that sort of communication than not; we cannot act upon it, and if we have it and don't act upon it, it does not look well; and let us remember that two Directors of Union Theological Seminary are themselves members of the Assembly and have all the privileges of the floor, with great facility of speech besides (meaning Dr. Parkhurst and Dr. Dickey). We may make mistakes in our report, to be sure, but we must take the responsibility, and if we are the subject of blame, why, we must bear the blame. We must take the responsibility of making the report in the light of conscience, and with the best guidance we can get, upon the basis of the facts officially before us. Then if the Assembly, under the guidance and with the new light, and the reinforcement that shall come through the medium of Dr. Dickey and Dr. Parkhurst, who undoubtedly will speak in behalf of Union Seminary, sees fit to modify the report, we will cheerfully submit to the modification. Of course, it will be in the Assembly's power to do what it thinks best when all the facts are before it."

Now, if we had known that our not hearing Dr. White would hurt the feelings of any member of this Board, we would have heard him, and anybody else connected with Union Seminary. I think there is no doubt about that. At the same time, if you ask the question, whether in the light of my sober judgment after these months of reflection, I think any rights were neglected by our failure to hear Dr. White, or to hear any representative of Union Seminary, I must very frankly say that I do not feel that there have been. I do not think that we took a single step upon which we ought to look back with regret. I am inclined to think that if I should ever be chairman of another committee (I trust it will not be of Theological Seminaries) but if I should ever be chairman of a committee, or a committee charged with serious responsibilities in the future, I should be very eareful how I recommended an action that would solicit *ex-parte* representations of an unofficial, and perhaps, of a confidential kind, that might enlist feeling, but that ought not to affect judgment. That is my present conviction, and if our committee seems to have erred in a matter of judgment, why, of course, we are sorry for that, but so far as the question of technical right and substantial justice is concerned, I do n't think we erred at all.

And now, while I am on my feet, if the Directors will bear with me, I will say another word apropos of what Dr. Hastings has said. I did not know it then, and have not known it until now, but I take it that the purpose of the interview between Dr. White and our committee was to present to our committee the view taken by this Board of Directors with respect to the construction of that arrangement of 1870. Now I want to say—and I will think aloud—that that view would not have taken us by surprise, for I knew it already. I am afraid I read the New York Evangelist on Sunday and the part of it that was not so distinctly devotional, more than I read some other things, that might have been more suited to the day. But I had that problem on my mind and heart the whole Lord's day, because I could not get rid of it, except while I was preaching. When I went into that committee room—I am thinking aloud again—I had never expressed in conversation, I had never expressed in writing, by signed article, or by anonymous communication, or by confidential letter, or by a letter less confidential, nor by oral utterance or communication, directly or indirectly made, anything whatever upon this whole question of Dr. Briggs and his relations to the General Assembly, and to the Presbytery; not a thing. My whole expression of myself has been in the report of the General Assembly's committee on Theological Seminaries. That I did write every word of it and that I am thoroughly ready to assume the responsibility of at any time. And to come back to where I was, the distinction that this Board adopted was fully before us, and it was thoroughly weighed, and we knew it, and I think we had read Dr. Prentiss' article (I had) very carefully, and the reason that we did not adopt the distinction contemplated by this Board (and that this Board has evidently seen its way to adopt), was because we could not do it. We looked at this matter, we went around the circle, we called upon every man to give his opinion upon the question, as to whether a fair construction of the language of the compact of 1870 made between the General Assembly and the Seminary would justify us in saying that a transfer is not an appointment within the meaning of that arrangement. We said no, it would not; and we said in our committee it would not. I reached that conclusion; and with all the facts before me, and with all deference to my friend Dr. White, I do not believe that it would have been possible, if we had talked four hours instead of one, for him to have changed our minds upon that question.

C.

MR. WILLIAM ALLEN BUTLER'S OPINION.

NEW YORK, June 4th, 1891.

CHARLES BUTLER, ESQ.,

President of the Board of Directors of the Union Theological Seminary,

DEAR SIR—As requested by you I have carefully considered the questions arising on the recent action of the General Assembly in reference to the Rev. Dr. Briggs and the Union Theological Seminary.

Without going into details I submit a summary of the conclusions, which it seems to me necessarily follow a fair view of the facts:

1. The Union Theological Seminary, being a corporation existing under the laws of New York, has full power to regulate the administration of its affairs pursuant to its charter, which was enacted March 27, 1839, and which vests the government of the seminary in a Board of Directors of twenty-eight members, one half of whom shall be clergymen and the other half laymen. The constitution adopted under the charter empowers the Board of Directors to appoint all professors, fix their salaries and determine their duties. These powers have never been surrendered or impaired, and are now in full force and effect.

2. In connection with the reunion of the differing branches of the Presbyterian Church in 1870 importance was attached to the establishment of harmonious relations between the several Presbyterian theological seminaries and the General Assembly of the reunited church. This was in no wise an essential element in the reunion, but was an incident of the general plan. In aid of this desired end and especially in the interest of the seminaries under the ecclesiastic supervision of the so-called "Old School" Assembly, whose professors were appointed directly by the Assembly and not by their Boards of Directors, and who desired relief from this embarrassing control, it was proposed that the General Assembly should confer on those seminaries over which it

had proprietorship and control, the power of electing their own professors, the appointments to be reported to the Assembly, and no appointment "to be considered as a complete election if disapproved by a majority vote of the Assembly."

The Union Theological Seminary, by a minute of the Board of Directors passed May 9, 1870, after reciting that it had been formed before the disruption of the Presbyterian Church, and belonged to neither of its branches, and was administered upon its own independent charter, and also that its Board of Directors was "desirous of doing all in their power to establish confidence and harmony throughout the whole church in respect to the education of its ministry," and that the appointment of professors in any seminary directly by the General Assembly was, in their judgment, objectionable, resolved to memorialize the General Assembly to adopt the plan above referred to in the exercise of their proprietorship and control over the several theological seminaries, and agreed in case of its adoption to conform to the same.

The General Assembly complied with the request and recommended that all seminaries controlled by the Assembly should conform to the plan as proposed by the Union Theological Seminary (General Assembly's minutes, 1870, pp. 62–64).

3. It is evident that by this action the Union Theological Seminary acquired nothing. It received no benefit or advantage from the plan adopted, except in the sense of having promoted the particular interests of kindred institutions and the general well being of the church. It retained, unimpaired, the power of appointment of its professors as an inherent part of its corporate franchise, but it conferred on the General Assembly, by way of gratuitous concession and grant, the power to disapprove by a majority vote of any such appointment. This action was apparently taken without any consideration of the question whether the surrender or delegation of corporate power which it involved was within the scope of the authority of the Board of Directors under the charter of the seminary. Assuming for the present that it was within the power of the board, the transaction as finally made constituted a compact between the seminary and the General Assembly, by which the latter was empowered to veto the appointment and election of a professor. The source of this power was the delegation of it by the seminary to the Assembly, and as it was purely

voluntary, it did not involve the transfer of any corporate right, and necessarily stood as to its execution upon the good faith and continuing co-operation of the respective parties to it, without any power on the part of either to compel its continued performance upon any basis of acquired right recognizable by the law.

4. In the practical operation of the arrangement, the annual reports of the seminary presented to the Assembly since 1870, have included all matters of administration and among these the appointments and elections of professors and no instance has occurred of any disapproval of an appointment or election.

5. The concession made by the seminary to the Assembly of the veto power under the circumstances above stated was so far in derogation of its own absolute powers that it cannot be held to grant any privilege beyond its precise terms and these must be strictly pursued by the Assembly and cannot be enlarged by any implication.

The seminary has maintained and has acted upon the view that the power of disapproval given by it to the General Assembly did not apply to or in any wise affect the right of the Board of Directors of the seminary to regulate the duties of the professors whose election having once become complete by the failure of the Assembly to disapprove of their election, constituted them thereafter a part of the faculty of the seminary to perform such duties of instruction as might be designated by the Board of Directors; the assignment of new duties to any professor, or the transfer of a professor from one chair to another chair, or to a new chair, being all matters of corporate administration not subject to any review or control by the Assembly and in no way coming within the terms of the compact.

6. The Assembly which recently convened at Detroit appears from the published reports of its proceedings to have adopted a different view of the subject, and to have given an interpretation to the compact of 1870, which extends the veto power so as to make it applicable not only to appointments and elections of professors as declared by its terms, but also to the case of the transfer of a professor duly elected, and not disapproved by the Assembly, from one chair in the seminary to another chair. Acting upon its own interpretation and construction, the Assembly, by a majority vote, has assumed to disapprove of the transfer of Dr. Briggs from the chair of Hebrew and Cognate Languages to the chair of Biblical Theology, thus asserting a like power in respect to the action of the Board

of Directors in making such a transfer as in the case of an original appointment and election of a professor.

7. Without discussing at present the question of the validity of this action of the Assembly, it is enough to say that it is the act of one party to an agreement upon its own *ex-parte* interpretation and construction of it, without the consent of the other party and in violation of what the other party claims to be its true interpretation and construction. It is simply the case of an assertion and an attempted exercise of a power claimed under an agreement by one party and denied by the other party. The seminary is not bound to accept the construction put upon the contract by the Assembly and the Assembly is powerless to enforce its action by any proceeding or process affecting the right of the seminary to continue Dr. Briggs as its professor of Biblical Theology or the right of Dr. Briggs to retain the professorship. Holding the view that the action of the Assembly is not within the scope of its power and, therefore, *ultra vires*, the Board of Directors of the seminary must regard it as ineffectual for any purpose relating to the seminary or to Dr. Briggs.

9. As between the seminary and Dr. Briggs the case is different and the relation is one of contract founded on a valid consideration and enforceable at law. Having been elected a professor and his election not having been disapproved by the General Assembly and having entered on the discharge of the new duties devolved upon him, as a professor by the Board of Directors, he is entitled, subject to the terms of his employment, to the enjoyment of his office under his agreement with the seminary, any breach of which would be the violation of a contract obligation. And so long as the seminary and Dr. Briggs are in accord on this point, no third party can intervene to annul or impair the existing relation between them.

No present action, therefore, seems to be required on the part of the Board of Directors either in reference to the General Assembly or to Dr. Briggs, unless the board should think proper to re-affirm by resolution, its adherence to the interpretation of the arrangement with the General Assembly which it has heretofore maintained and upon which it acted in its transfer of Dr. Briggs from the chair formerly filled by him to that of which he is now the imcumbent.

Yours truly,

(Signed) WILLIAM ALLEN BUTLER.

D.

In giving Mr. Carter's opinion it is proper to give also the following report of the Executive Committee, presented to the Board of Directors on October 13, 1892, recommending and submitting that opinion:

At a meeting on the 9th of June last, the Executive Committee having heard the report of Mr. E. M. Kingsley concerning his special mission to Portland, carefully deliberated as to the course to be pursued under the circumstances. The unanimous conviction of the committee was that some reply to the action of the Assembly should be prepared for submission to the Board of Directors. As our minutes show, a Sub-Committee was appointed for this purpose with the understanding that informally Dr. Prentiss should be consulted in the preparation of the paper. After free discussion, it was agreed that while we have hitherto wisely abstained from seeking a legal opinion on the questions involved in our case, the time has come when it is imperative that we should know whether the character of this institution is imperilled, as has been intimated, by the existing agreement with the General Assembly. While the Executive Committee does not feel itself authorized officially to seek an opinion, the unanimous though informal conclusion was that it would be very desirable that the Sub-Committee should secure such an opinion from some lawyer of the very highest standing. In the informal conference upon this matter, several names of conspicuous and able lawyers were mentioned, but the desire was to select some man who is in no way, personally or ecclesiastically, related to members of this Board or to the Presbyterian Church. The name of James C. Carter, Esquire, answered all these conditions, and it was felt that his independent position and his very high standing in his profession would make his opinion conclusive with all reasonable or unprejudiced minds. The Sub-Committee therefore secured from Mr. Carter his opinion upon the questions involved in the present relation of this institution to the General Assembly, which opinion was presented to the Executive Committee on Tuesday the 27th inst., with the request that it be submitted to the board.

The Executive Committee also presents herewith the official copy of the action of the General Assembly in reply to our memorial and would call attention to the character of the language used. In our memorial we did not ask the Assembly to "break" a compact, but only "to concur with us in annulling the arrangement of 1870."

Notwithstanding the character of the Assembly's reply, it was deemed best that our response thereto should be kept free from every sign of irritation, and should calmly and clearly state our deliberate conclusion. This paper, unanimously adopted by the Executive Committee, is now respectfully submitted to the board for its consideration.

Here is the opinion of Mr. Carter:

OPINION OF JAMES C. CARTER, ESQ.

The Union Theological Seminary in the City of New York was incorporated by Act of the Legislature of the State of New York, passed March 27th, 1839. It constituted Thomas McCauley and other persons who were declared by the first section of the act to be the present directors, and their successors, a body corporate by the name of the Union Theological Seminary in the City of New York.

It is declared by the second section of the charter as follows:—

The government of the seminary shall at all times be vested in a Board of Directors, which shall consist of twenty-eight members, one-half of whom shall be clergymen and the other half laymen.

Subsequent to the incorporation of the Seminary a constitution and by-laws were adopted by the Board of Directors. Sections 3 and 4 of Article 1 of the Constitution are as follows:—

Sec. 3. In order to carry out the powers vested in them by the act of incorporation, the Board of Directors shall have authority to make their own by-laws; hold, manage and disburse the funds of the seminary; appoint all officers, professors and teachers; fix their salaries, determine their duties; make laws for the regulation and government of the institution; and, in general, to adopt all such measures, not inconsistent with the provisions of the said act (the charter) and this constitution, as the interests of the seminary may require.

Sec. 4. The board shall watch over the fidelity of all who may be employed in giving instruction; shall judge of their competency, doctrines, morals; and shall have power to remove any officer, professor or teacher from office. The board shall also exercise a general supervision over the whole seminary, including the discipline of students by the faculty.

The first section of the Second Article of the Constitution is as follows:—

Sec. 1. The faculty shall consist of a President and professors, all of whom shall be ordained ministers of the Gospel, and all of whom shall be appointed by the Board of Directors.

These are the only provisions of the charter concerning the body in which the power of government is lodged.

On the 16th day of May, 1870, the Board of Directors adopted resolutions designed to be a Memorial to the General Assembly of the Presbyterian Church of the United States, which were as follows:—

Resolved, That the Board of Directors of the Union Theological Seminary, being all ministers and elders of the Presbyterian Church, do hereby memorialize the General Assembly to the following effect:—

That so far as the election of professors is concerned, the Assembly will commit the same to their respective Boards of Directors on the following conditions, viz.:—

1st. The Board of Directors of each Seminary shall be authorized to appoint all professors for the same.

2nd. That all such appointments shall be reported to the General Assembly, and no such appointment shall be considered a complete election if disapproved by a majority vote of the General Assembly.

Be it further *Resolved,* That if this plan is adopted by the General Assembly they will agree to conform to the same, the Union Theological Seminary being in this respect on the same ground with other theological seminaries of the Presbyterian Church.

The General Assembly adopted a resolution accepting the offer of the seminary contained in the foregoing memorial of the latter body.

On the 8th day of May, 1876, Charles A. Briggs was elected as professor to fill the Davenport Chair of Hebrew and Cognate Languages. His election was not disapproved by the General Assembly, and he was continued as such professor until the 11th day of November, 1890, when he was transferred to the Edward Robinson Chair of Biblical Theology by the following resolutions, passed by the Board of Directors of the seminary:

Resolved, That Charles A. Briggs, D. D., be transferred from the Davenport Professorship of Hebrew and Cognate Languages to the Edward Robinson Chair of Biblical Theology.

In the By-laws relating to the action of the Board of Directors, it is provided as follows:

Sec. 5. In the appointment of any member of the faculty, a nomination shall be made at least four weeks before the election.

No such notice was deemed necessary to the transfer of Dr. Briggs from the Davenport to the Edward Robinson chair, and none was given.

Dr. Briggs was inaugurated on the 20th of January, 1891, when he delivered an inaugural address.

No new duties were assigned to him on the transfer from the one chair to the other.

The General Assembly of the Presbyterian church is not an incorporated body, but is a representative body of over six hundred members chosen annually by the different Presbyteries. The Assembly meets annually, and continues in session about fifteen days.

There are twenty-eight Directors of the Board of the Union Theological Seminary. Only nine of the present directors were members of the board in 1870; and only six of that nine were present at the meeting of May 16, 1870.

Upon the foregoing case my opinion is requested on the following points:

First: Had the General Assembly capacity to make the agreement referred to in 1870?

Second: Had the Board of Directors of the Union Theological Seminary power to delegate to the General Assembly the absolute authority to thereafter veto the appointment for election of a professor made by the Board of Directors of the Union Theological Seminary?

Third: If not, was the action of the Board illegal and void?

Fourth: Is the present Board of Directors legally or morally bound by the said action of the Board in 1870?

Fifth: If such action of the Board in 1870 was illegal or void, what action should be taken by the present Board in relation to it?

OPINION.

If the offer of May 16, 1870, contained in the Memorial of the Union Theological Seminary to the General Assembly of the Presbyterian church, and accepted by the General Assembly, creates an obligation binding upon those bodies, or either of them, it must be because that offer and its acceptance constitute a contract between those bodies.

Aside from the question of the power of the seminary to enter into any contract of such a nature, there would be very serious obstacles in the way of any conclusion that this offer and its acceptance created any contract at all. It would not be easy to make out that the General Assembly has that corporate and perpetual existence which would make it a person in the eye of the law competent to become a party to such a contract; and it certainly was not the intention to bind the individuals composing any particular General Assembly in their capacity as natural persons.

Nor would it be easy to show what valid consideration there was to sustain the supposed contract, or that it was really intended by the parties to impose any legal obligation upon each other. The offer and acceptance appear to me to be designed rather to express a present acquiescence in a line of policy, and a willingness to follow it until some change in opinions should take place, than as an intent to create a perpetual obligation which would forever bind the parties even though one of them should at some time believe that a further continuance of it would be unwise.

But I put these difficulties aside, in view of the presence of another which seems to me to be absolutely insuperable. Assuming that the offer and acceptance were intended to create and were quite sufficient to create, a binding contract, if the seminary had the legal power to make it, every one must agree that, in the absence of any such power, the attempt to make such a contract would be wholly ineffectual.

Did, therefore, the directors of the seminary have the power to confer upon the General Assembly the authority of vetoing any appointment which they might make to a professorship; that is to say, the power to transfer a most important part of the power of governing the seminary to the General Assembly, and, to that extent, to divest themselves both of that power, and of the duty attached to it?

It is, as it seems to me, too plain for argument that they never possessed any such authority. Who are to exercise the powers of a corporate body is a matter which the Legislature alone can determine; and upon looking into the charter of the seminary we find the following provision, which is quite decisive:

Sec. 2. The government of the seminary shall at all times be vested in a Board of Directors, which shall consist of twenty-eight members; one-half of whom shall be clergymen and the other half laymen.

There would be no insuperable difficulty in permitting this board to devolve its functions, in whole or in part, upon others; but a necessary requisite in an authority so extraordinary would be an act of the Legislature conferring it in the most clear and unequivocal language. There is no pretense that such an authority has been conferred by the charter, or by any other legislative act.

Undoubtedly the Board of Directors in the discharge of any of their duties may seek and obtain the advice and assistance of others. But they can not abdicate any of their official duties, in whole or in part. The determination of the fitness of any candidate for the office of professor is a part of the government of the seminary; and if it be competent to the Board of Directors to clothe the General Assembly with the power of defeating an appointment made by the board, by the expression of disapproval, it is competent to that body to transfer to the General Assembly the whole power of appointment, and indeed the whole power of governing the seminary.

Should the General Assembly veto an appointment to a professorship made by the Board of Directors, and the members of the latter body should be, nevertheless, of the opinion that the best interest of the seminary demanded that the place should be filled by the candidate thus rejected, it is very clear that they should not, consistently with their official duty, acquiesce in the rejection.

It may be that it would be a wise arrangement to make the seminary in some manner subordinate to the general authority of the Presbyterian church; but that is not the arrangement made by its present charter.

If these views are well founded, it follows that the attempt to make the alleged contract was not only ineffectual, as being beyond any power conferred upon the Board of Directors by the charter, but was illegal and contrary to the duty of the members of the board, because it was an attempted surrender of a duty the performance of which they had taken upon themselves by their acceptance of the office of director. And inasmuch as the charters of all corporations are given upon the condition that the powers conferred by them shall be exercised in the manner prescribed, this attempted making of an illegal contract, and all subsequent acquiescence in it would be a breach of the condition, and subject the seminary to the hazard of a forfeiture by judicial decree of its corporate existence.

I answer the particular questions submitted to me as follows:

1. I am inclined to the opinion that the General Assembly had no legal capacity to make the contract referred to, assuming that it was its intention to make a binding contract; but I am not prepared to announce a definite conclusion upon this point for the reason that I cannot arrive at one without a fuller statement of the facts relative to the constitution, purpose and authority of that body than is contained in the case submitted to me.

2. I am clearly of the opinion that the Board of Directors of the Union Theological Seminary had no power to delegate to the General Assembly an authority to veto the appointment or election of professors made by such board; and that any such appointment or election could not be in any manner deprived of its efficacy by any action of such General Assembly.

3. I am clearly of the opinion that the action of the Board of Directors of the seminary in attempting to make a binding contract relative to the appointment of professors, assuming as before, that such was the intent of the offer contained in the Memorial to the General Assembly, was illegal and void.

4. I am clearly of the opinion that the present Board of Directors of the seminary is not legally bound by the action referred to of the board in 1870.

I do not profess to be competent to advise others upon moral questions in general, but I think I may safely declare in this instance that the present members of the Board of Directors cannot be morally bound by an act of its predecessors which was in violation of the duty they had taken upon themselves by accepting the office of director.

5. It is, in my opinion, the duty of the present Board of Directors to disavow any intent to abdicate their functions, or to delegate them to others; and, to that end, to rescind and annul, by a formal vote, the apparent offer contained in the Memorial of 1870, to the General Assembly, and to advise the latter body of such action.

Signed, JAMES C. CARTER.

June 23, 1892.

E.

OPINION OF JUDGE NOAH DAVIS

AS TO THE POSITION OF UNION THEOLOGICAL SEMINARY TOWARD THE GENERAL ASSEMBLY.

Upon a careful examination of the Act of the Legislature of the State of New York incorporating the Union Theological Seminary in the city of New York, and of the several acts amendatory thereto, and of the constitution and by-laws of said corporation, in connection with the Memorial presented by the directors of said seminary to the General Assembly of the Presbyterian Church of the United States, in May, 1870, and the action of such General Assembly thereupon, together with the memorandum and argument of John J. McCook, Esq., presented to the late General Assembly, I have reached the following conclusions of law:

1. That by the Act of incorporation of said seminary, commonly called its charter, all power of government and control of said seminary is wholly vested in its Board of Directors. The second section of the Act is in these words:

Section 2. The government of the seminary shall at all times be vested in a Board of Directors, which shall consist of twenty-eight members, one-half of whom shall be clergymen and the other half laymen. This grant of power is broad, exhaustive, and exclusive. It neither recognizes nor permits any superior governmental power, that can dictate, control, or limit the action of the Board of Directors in the exercise of what is called by the "Act" "the government of the Seminary." The directors cannot abdicate this power of government in favor of any other body or person. They can, of course, appoint and act through agents and servants whom they may select, and to whom they may give the *subordinate* functions necessary to carry into execution their own powers of government, because that course is simply a mode of efficiently executing their own authority.

The third section of Article One of the Constitution (as it is called) correctly defines the power of the Directors in these words: "Sec. 3. In order to carry out the powers vested in them by the Act of Incorporation, the Board of Directors shall have authority to make their own by-laws; hold, manage, and disburse the funds of the Seminary; appoint all officers, professors, and teachers; fix their salaries; determine their duties" . . . .; and the fourth section declares that "The board shall watch over the fidelity of all who may be employed in giving instruction, shall judge of their competency, doctrine, and morals, and shall have power to remove an officer, professor, or teacher from office" . . . .

The first section of Article Two provides that the Faculty shall consist of a President and professors, all of whom shall be ordained ministers of the Gospel, and all of whom shall be appointed by the Board of Directors. And section five of the by-laws prescribes the deliberation with which the appointment of any member of the Faculty shall be approached and conducted; and section eleven defines the mode in which the by-laws may be changed.

All these provisions of the Constitution and by-laws define and accentuate the powers of the Directors under the charter and *exclude* their exercise by any other body, with or without the consent of the board. It cannot be doubted that the power of appointing the Faculty and its several members, stands in the front rank of all the authority conferred by the charter upon the board who are to act and speak as, and for the corporation. The *Faculty* are the essential elements of the corporate vitality and usefulness. Whoever can appoint *them*, holds in his or their hands the effective utility of the body corporate; every act or attempt of the directors to divest themselves of *that* power and confer it upon another body, or subordinate it to the will or judgment of another, or make its effective use so conditional upon such will or judgment of others, that its exercise by the corporate board is dependent upon the "veto" or *sic volo* of such other, is *utterly void* and not only *ultra vires*, which may be simply an excess of power, but is incurably *void* for its utter lack of authority, and its unwarranted conflict with a plain statute.

In my opinion, therefore, the resolution of the Board which handed over to the General Assembly the vital and principal function, without the exercise of which the objects and purposes of the corporation could not be made or kept alive and effective, as the act of the Legislature clearly intended, was void *ad initio*, and has continued to be void during the whole of its existence. The Legislature has not created a corporation for religious instruction, whose Faculty, that is to say, whose instructors, shall be appointed or controlled, or their appointment prevented or forbidden, by some other religious body, however wise and noble it may be, *other* than that which the Act itself brings into corporate existence. It is true the directors may *consult* and take advice in respect to their appointees with whomsoever they like, and may act upon such advice in making or *refusing* to make any appointment, but the *ultimate and creative act* must be their own, and they can confer no power upon another corporation or person to veto and thereby prevent the operation of their own appointment.

It is asserted and elaborately urged that some sort of contractual relation sprang up between the corporation and the General Assembly and other like corporations, by means of which the Seminary is bound *in perpetuam* to this surrender of its most vital function to the General Assembly. There is no principal of law upon which such an idea can stand. First, there is no *contract*, from the utter lack of power to make one; all parties knew, or, what is the same thing, were bound to know, that there could be no such contract. Second, the abdication of a vital corporate function by one corporate body to another, is not the subject of contract, where the nature of the power is such, that without its exercise by its legislative grantee, the function cannot be used as the Legislature has prescribed. No corporation can contract with another that the latter may *veto*, and thereby prevent the choice of its effective officers, when chosen by the board or body to whom a charter has given the sole power or right of choice. To admit the idea that a *longer* or shorter submission to such an attempt *binds* the submitting corporation by perpetual contract, introduces an unheard of element, worse than that of putting corporate functions into a trust held by one corporation for the benefit of many.

The government that grants the power in such a case cannot be stopped by such an abuse of its use, and no contract of the parties can be asserted in answer to an action to annul the charter.

The parties to such a contract are in *pari delicto*, and neither can allege the contract as a defense against the State.

Past acts in violation of corporate powers may sometimes be condoned, as between *parties* to them, where equities arise from valuable considerations paid, or conditions are changed so that great prejudice may arise from the avoidance of such acts, but in no case can any corporation for public uses compel another to continue to violate the plain requirements of a statute, because it has wrongfully or ignorantly violated them in the past; and least of all will the law imply a contract to compel one Board of Directors, as in this case to violate a statute in performing a corporate duty, because some former boards have done so. The repudiation in this case of any sort of action of former boards which abdicated their absolute and exclusive power to appoint the Faculty of the Seminary, is simply a return to an obedience of the law of their being.

I cannot, therefore, bring my mind to doubt that the appointment of Professor Briggs, over which the question has arisen, was and is lawful and effective, notwithstanding the action of the General Assembly.

NOAH DAVIS.

NEW YORK, October 28, 1891.

INDEX.

A.

B.

C.

H.

J.

S.

T.

U.

V.

W.

Y.